Community Policing in Indigenous Communities

Community Policing in Indigenous Communities

Edited by
Mahesh K. Nalla and
Graeme R. Newman

CRC Press
Taylor & Francis Group
Boca Raton London New York

CRC Press is an imprint of the
Taylor & Francis Group, an **informa** business

Cover image credits: Unidentified aboriginal man, Courtesy of Regien Paassen /Shutterstock.com. Unidentified Amerindians, Courtesy of Faraways/ Shutterstock.com.

CRC Press
Taylor & Francis Group
6000 Broken Sound Parkway NW, Suite 300
Boca Raton, FL 33487-2742

Library of Congress Cataloging-in-Publication Data

Community policing in indigenous communities / editors, Mahesh K. Nalla, Graeme R. Newman.
       p. cm.
   Includes bibliographical references and index.
   ISBN 978-1-4398-8894-0 (hardcover : alk. paper)
   1. Community policing--Case studies. I. Nalla, Mahesh. II. Newman, Graeme R.

HV7936.C83C692 2013
363.2'3--dc23   2012037827

Visit the Taylor & Francis Web site at
http://www.taylorandfrancis.com

and the CRC Press Web site at
http://www.crcpress.com

Contents

Foreword

The group of words, *police, polity, politics, politic, political, politician* is a good example of delicate distinctions.

Maitland 1885: 105

This important book traces, and makes explicit, much of the variety of policing that takes place today under the sign of "community policing" across the globe. By doing so, it provides a very useful counterweight to the wealth of research and writing that has taken place within Anglo-American societies, where the term "community policing" originated. While "community policing" has been used in a variety of ways within this Anglo-American context, perhaps the most central meaning has been that it refers to policing that takes place with the active support of citizens. This idea of what is often termed "consensual policing" fits closely with the second of the nine principles of good policing that have been ascribed to Sir Robert Peel—the Secretary of State at the time the London Metropolitan Police were established in 1829. This principle, as Reith (1948) reports it, is as follows:

> To recognize always that the power of the police to fulfil their functions and duties is dependent on public approval of their existence, actions, and behavior, and on their ability to secure and maintain public respect.

Reith 1948: 64

What the chapters in this volume make clear is that this idea is one that has had widespread appeal and is one that has been practiced in many different ways in many different places long before it was associated with "community policing." What has "traveled" (Karstedt 2002), and traveled widely, is not the idea but the sign that is increasingly being used to refer to it in many diverse contexts. This idea, as Graham Ellison notes in this volume, was nicely brought to the fore by the Independent Commission of Policing in Northern Ireland (1999) via their phrase "policing with the community." In the Commission's report, which sets out a blueprint for reimagining policing in Northern Ireland, it became apparent that the term "community policing" is, as often as not, used to inspire police to practice forms of policing that are "inclusive" rather than "extractive" (Acemonglu and Robinson 2012). As the Northern Ireland example makes clear, this is very often the case in situations of conflict where established forms of policing have been used to enforce orders that are associated with domination. In these contexts, as several of the chapters in this volume make clear, established policing arrangements have often been about imposing an order that is not supported by many, and often most, of those being policed.

In broadening the focus of inquiry into "community policing" as widely as the chapters of this book do, Mahesh K. Nalla and Graeme R. Newman have assembled a book that is not only important, but also courageous. It is courageous because, in encouraging thought about what "community policing" is, and might be, in societies that have not been consensually ordered, it steps outside of established conceptual frameworks. This book seeks to move "community policing" beyond what Ericson et al. (1993) termed a "hurrah" word, which carries with it warm connotative meanings that have been employed to paper over denotative difficulties.* In doing so, Nalla and Newman have sought to open up a new genre of research and thinking on "community policing" that recognizes that the term itself, along with the policing it is used to promote, is often enmeshed in political and analytic quagmires that deserve to be identified and explored.

I write these words soon after the Marikana miners massacre in South Africa (Herskovitz 2012), where police are members of a police organization explicitly committed, as Minnaar notes in his chapter, to a philosophy of "community policing" but who, in this instance, acted in ways that display little evidence of consensual ordering. What these events, and similar ones that can be found across the globe on a daily basis, remind us is that community policing, where it exists, is very often practiced within a context of significant conflicts and contested and "negotiated orders" (Henry and McAra 2012). And again, as many of the essays in this volume make clear, these conflicts are often very much what the advocates of community policing seek to manage by drawing communities into the business of policing.

By being willing to delve deeply into these contested spaces, both the editors and chapter authors, take us on a journey that goes a long way toward moving us beyond the "hurrah" connotations that have so often enveloped analyses of community policing.

The lens Nalla and Newman have chosen to enable us to access policing within societies where orders are contested are societies in which indigenous communities live alongside others—often others who have been their colonizers. This is a difficult territory to traverse. It is the editors' and authors' willingness to explore the idea of community policing within contested contexts that makes this book both important and courageous.

What the chapters of this book repeatedly recognize is that indigenous communities are typically communities that challenge and contest the orders and laws of the nation states of which they have become, often very reluctantly, a part. Through the case studies that comprise the chapters, this book explores community policing, its meanings and practices, as a feature of the policing of what are often very deeply divided societies.

In the case studies that are the foci of the chapters to follow, community policing is revealed as a strategy, not simply for policing with consent but for policing in contexts within which there is often little, if any, consent. This shifts the discussion of "community policing" from Ericson et al.'s "hurrah" status to one that reveals the complexities of policing within the complex and contested settings that characterize our contemporary world. In this world, consent is something that cannot be taken for granted, and, whenever it exists, it is always a hard-won accomplishment. It is these accomplishments of cooperation and consent that constitute the subject matter of many of the chapters. This is a book about whether, and how, more inclusive forms of policing might be practiced.

In this book, community policing is revealed as an aspirational practice that, it is hoped, will enable police and communities, within contested contexts, to cooperate in a variety of ways that will recognize that, even within deeply contested spaces, there are often many win–win gains to be made that will enable communities to live within spaces in which they can live, work, and play in relative safety. In a contested world of conflict and compromise, community policing is revealed as a set of normative aspirations that

---

* It is worth citing Ericson et al.'s (1993: 47) words here: "Community policing offers boosterism, a feel-good politics in the vein of quality-of-life advertising. It does so by associating 'community' with other hurrah words such as 'progress' and 'democracy'... "

sometimes can find concrete expression. Implicit throughout these chapters is an ongoing analysis of the conditions under which the hope of community policing might be realized.

What this analysis reveals is that community policing, in the real world of contested orders, is much more than the simple idea that policing with consent suggests. Community policing is revealed as a strategy for realizing small but significant accommodations within a context of often-fundamental disagreement. In doing so, the chapters of this book say something about the nature of day-to-day conflicts within the context of contested orders and the nuanced patterns of agreements that established boundaries within which life can sometimes be lived in relative, albeit fragile, safety. In the chapters to follow, we find discussions of the variety of ways in which the tensions that contesting of orders generates are recognized and negotiated in ways that sometimes give rise to possibilities of peace—albeit "peaces" (Maitland 1885) that may well be limited in both space and time. In doing so, these analyses recognize the complex and nuanced role that police can, and do, play in these contexts.

In these chapters, one often finds that what community policing arrangements make possible is often not police "policing with communities" but rather "policing by communities," in contexts of negotiated orders and disagreements about orders, that sometimes involves the police. What these chapters reveal, in the variety of settings on which they report, is a complex field of nodal policing characterized by shifting policing assemblages. Sometimes these processes and the assemblages that they constitute bring state police and the institutions of policing within communities closer together, but this is not always the case. Often, nodal policing arrangements established boundaries between policing agencies and policing assemblages. These boundaries often prove to be important for creating spaces of peace, even though they often also create tensions between agencies that may or may not be well managed. The boundaries, the crossing of these boundaries, the creation of policing assemblages, and so on constitute the features of nodal policing, features that these chapters reveal. An example— one among many—of this is provided by the chapter on Peru, where the authors consider how indigenous forms of policing coexist with state policing. In this analysis, we find a challenge to what Johnston and I have recently termed the "fallacy of nodal-network equivalence" (Shearing and Johnston 2010), namely, a challenge to the notion, often associated with ideas of community policing, that community policing involves the creation of integrated policing networks. While this is sometimes the case when state policing is undertaken "with communities," it is often not the case, especially when policing is undertaken "by communities."

In its "hurrah" form, conceptions of community policing have tended to assume that different sources of policing—different auspices and providers—can be made to align nicely with each other in ways that enable policing to be cooperative and networked. What the chapters in this book make clear is that, while this is sometimes the case, it is often not the case. Community policing understood as "policing by communities" often involves the emergence of sets of policing nodes that operate together, and sometimes even cooperate, not because collaboration dominates but because nodes find ways of managing tensions that arise from very different conceptions of order and the methods to be used in maintaining them. Within these nodal arrangements, auspices and providers of policing sometimes cooperate; at other times, they are indifferent to each other, and sometimes they contest each other, at times very vigorously. From the vantage point of this lens, community policing becomes a sign that covers a wide variety of policing engagements within nodal fields in which the state is recognized as one node among many. The comparative perspective that this book affords readers is one that compels us to recognize the enormous diversity of practices that are, and can be, arranged under the sign "community policing." In opening up the exploration of "community policing" in this way, the authors in this book compel us to "bracket" taken-for-granted assumptions about what community policing is and require us to use the lens of contested policing to explore a wide variety of ways in which communities can, and do, engage in policing.

In doing so, these chapters remind us of Robert Reiner's (2010: 32–36) insistence that policing is, by definition, fundamentally political. This is so, as he makes clear, because order is fundamentally political. What Reiner argues, and what this book demonstrates, is that policing, our hopes and aspirations for it notwithstanding, does not exist above politics but rather as part of, and because of, politics. It is precisely this insight that is so clearly understood by many of the authors of this volume. Policing, and the struggles that surround it, is an inevitable feature of ordering and the various inequalities that orders maintain.

To suggest, as I have done, that as policing scholars, we need to leave behind the normative veils that so often limit our ability to empirically scrutinize the worlds we study does not mean that we should not empirically explore the normative stances that shape policing. Values and ideals are a crucial feature of policing precisely because policing is so thoroughly political. This means that to understand the "politics of policing," it is essential to examine the normative layering that shapes policing activities by both those who seek to legitimize it and those who would discredit it.

As researchers, analysts, and theorists, we not only study the worlds in which we, and others, live, we also shape these worlds through our understandings and the analyses that promote them. As actors who constitute, as well as study, worlds, it is incumbent upon us not only to study politics but also to take political stances.

What the chapters in this book, each in different ways, do is to ask how the ideals that have informed community policing might be best used to promote policing, in the context of contests over order, which are the rule, not the exception, across the world.

Clifford Shearing

References

Acemonglu, D., and Robinson, J.A. (2012). *Why Nations Fail: The Origins of Power, Prosperity and Poverty*. London: Profile Books.

Ericson, R.V., Haggerty, K.D., and Carriere, K.D. (1993). "Community Policing as Communications Policing." D. Dolling and T. Feltes (Eds.), *Community Policing: Comparative Aspects of Community Oriented Police Work, (Band 5)*. Holzkirchen, Germany: Felix Verlag. p. 47.

Henry, A., and McAra, L. (2012). "Negotiated Orders: Implications for Theory and Practice." *Criminology and Criminal Justice*. Vol. 12, no. 4: 341–345.

Herskovitz, J. (2012). "Mine "Bloodbath" Shocks Post-Apartheid South Africa." Available online at http://www.reuters.com/article/2012/08/17/us-safrica-lonmin-idUSBRE87G04K20120817 (accessed October 4, 2012).

Independent Commission on Policing for Northern Ireland, 1999. *A New Beginning: Policing in Northern Ireland*. Belfast, United Kingdom: Independent Commission on Policing in Northern Ireland, Northern Ireland Office. Available online at http://www.nio.gov.uk/a_new_beginning_in_policing_in_northern_ireland.pdf (accessed October 18, 2012).

Karstedt, S. (2002). "Durkheim Tarde and Beyond: The Global Travel of Crime Polities." *Criminology and Criminal Justice*. Vol. 2, no. 2: 111–123.

Maitland, F.W. (1885). *Justice and Police*. London: Macmillan and Co.

Reiner, R. (2010). *The Politics of Police*. 4th edition. Oxford: Oxford University Press.

Reith, C. (1948). *A Short History of the British Police*. London: Oxford University Press.

Shearing, C., and Johnston, L. (2010). "Nodal Wars and Network Fallacies: A Genealogical Analysis of Global Insecurities." *Theoretical Criminology*. Vol. 14, no. 4: 495–514.

Contributors

James Olabisi Ayodele lectures at the Obafemi Awolowo University, Ile-Ife, Nigeria, in the Department of Sociology and Anthropology. He is a native of Ikere-Ekiti, Ekiti State, Nigeria, and has received his BSc and MSc degrees from Ondo State University (now Ekiti State University) in sociology/criminology. His research interests include police–community relations, intergroup relations and global insecurity, aging and victimization and mask and criminality, e-matchmaking, and so forth, and he has been published in the *Nigerian Sociological Review* (Lagos, NISOS), *African Sociological Review* (Kenya, CODESRIA), *Indian Journal of Gerontology*, and *Journal of Applied Security Research* (USA, Taylor & Francis).

Elaine Barclay is a Senior Lecturer in Criminology at the University of New England in the School of Behavioral, Cognitive and Social Sciences. She is a native of Armidale, New South Wales, Australia, and received her PhD in criminology from the University of New England. She has 17 years' experience in rural social research working with colleagues in Australia, the United States, and the United Kingdom, specializing in the area of rural crime. She has authored numerous papers and reports on rural crime and has published two books, *Crime in Rural Australia* (Federation Press, 2007) and *The Problem of Pleasure, Leisure and Crime* (Routledge, 2011).

Ester Blay is a lecturer on Criminology at the Universitat Pompeu Fabra (Barcelona) in the Department of Law. She is a native of Barcelona, Spain, and has received her law degree from the Universitat de Barcelona and her doctorate in law from the Universitat Autònoma de Barcelona. Her research interests include community penalties, sentencing and judicial decision making, as well as policing, and she has published on these topics in the *European Journal of Probation* and the *Journal of Probation*, as well as in numerous Spanish reviews.

Kaan Boke is police commander at the Turkish National Police in the Department of Training. He is a native of Ankara, Turkey. He received his PhD degree in criminal justice from Michigan State University. His research interests include organizational change, organizational culture, policing, and so forth, and he has published in several books and numerous articles about the aforementioned topics.

Krunoslav Borovec is an advisor to the Croatian Minister of the Interior. He is native of Zagreb, Croatia, and he has received his social pedagogies degree from the University of Zagreb. Borovec is completing his PhD in prevention science at the Faculty of Special Education and Rehabilitation, University of Zagreb. During his 20-year-long police career, he obtained many different leading positions within the police system. In 2009, Borovec won the Communicator of the Year Award by the Croatian Public Relations Association. His research interests include the areas of crime prevention, urban prevention, public perception of police, public relations, and internal communication. He is the author of numerous articles in the field of policing and "The Public Relations Strategy of the Ministry of the Interior of the Republic of Croatia." He is also the author of the book *The Situational Approach to Crime Prevention: From Theory to the Evidence Based Practice* (AKD, 2011).

Stefano Caneppele is an assistant professor at the Università Cattolica del Sacro Cuore in the Faculty of Political and Social Sciences and a member of Transcrime (Joint Research Centre on Transnational Crime). He is a native of Rovereto, Italy, and has received his PhD in criminology from the University of Trento. His research interests include crime prevention and policy evaluation, and he has published in the *Journal of Money Laundering Control*, in *Transcrime Reports*, and with Wolf Legal Publishers. He is also the managing editor of the *European Journal on Criminal Policy and Research* published by Springer.

Don Clairmont is the director of the Atlantic Institute of Criminology in the Sociology and Social Anthropology Department, Dalhousie University, Halifax, Nova Scotia, Canada. He is a native of Hamilton, Ontario, Canada, and received his PhD in sociology from Washington University at St. Louis Missouri. Research interests include aboriginal justice, policing, the criminal justice system, restorative justice, and race relations. He has published in Canadian, American, and British Journals, and his books include *Africville: the Life and Death of a Canadian Black Community* (McCelland and Stewart/Canadian Scholars Press, 1999) and *To the Forefront: Community-Based Policing* (Canadian Police College Press, 1990).

Sutham Cobkit is a professor of criminal justice at Kennesaw State University in the Department of Sociology and Criminal Justice. He is a native of Bangkok, Thailand, and has received his PhD degree in criminal justice from Sam Houston State University. His research interests include community policing and comparative criminal justice, and he has published in the *Journal of Criminal Justice*, *Police Quarterly*, and *The New Criminal Law Review*.

Vaughn J. Crichlow is a PhD candidate in criminal justice at Michigan State University. He is a native of Trinidad and Tobago and an alumnus of Rowan University and the University of the West Indies. He also received a law degree from the University of London, and his research interests include immigrants, ethnicity and justice, comparative policing, and private security.

Graham Ellison teaches at Queen's University Belfast, Northern Ireland, in the School of Law. He was born in Northern Ireland and received his undergraduate and graduate degrees in political science and sociology from Queen's University and the University of Ulster (Northern Ireland). His research interests include an analysis of policing in divided societies and the relationship between police reform and political change, and he has published widely in these areas. He (with Nathan W. Pino) is the author of *Globalization, Police Reform and Development: Doing it the Western Way* (Palgrave-Macmillan, 2012) and *Policing in an Age of Austerity: A Postcolonial Perspective* (with Mike Brogden, Routledge, 2012).

Thomas Feltes has been, since 2002, a chair and professor at the Ruhr-University Bochum (Germany) in the Department of Criminology and Police Science, Law Faculty. From 1992 until 2002, he was the director of the police university in Baden-Wuerttemberg. He has received his PhD in law and his MA in social sciences from the University of Bielefeld (Germany) and habilitation in law from the University of Tübingen (Germany). His research interests include juvenile crime, sentencing, policing, and police reform in countries in transition, and he has published more than 150 articles and 12 books (see http// www.thomasfeltes.de).

Roy Fenoff is a research associate with the Anti-Counterfeiting and Product Protection Program (A-CAPPP) at Michigan State University in the School of Criminal Justice. He received his Bachelor of Science degree from the University of Georgia in 2004 and a Master of Science degree from the University of Wyoming in 2007. He is also a forensic document examiner and an expert in forgery detection. He provides expert scientific advice and conducts forensic document examinations for individuals, businesses, law enforcement agencies, and law firms throughout the United States and overseas. His research interests include counterfeiting, forgery, science in the courts, crime prevention, and crime in Mexico.

Evgheni Constantin Florea was born in Chisinau, the capital of the Republic of Moldova. He studied at the Moldova State University Law Department and obtained a JD diploma, Summa cum Laude. Upon completion of his studies, he received an offer to start a professor's career at the University as an assistant lecturer, which he accepted. In 2000, he completed an LLM program in criminal law and criminology at his *alma mater*. After that, he was promoted to university lecturer. In the same year, he became a PhD student at M.V. Lomonosov Moscow State University, from which he successfully graduated in 2003. His dissertation topic was "Criminal Personality: Criminal Law and Criminological Research." In 2005, he was promoted to assistant professor. In the same year, he won a Fulbright grant and was a research scholar at the University of Memphis School of Law (Fall 2005 to Spring 2006). In 2008, he was promoted to associate professor. Evgheni Florea is the author of 30 academic publications in the field of criminal law and criminology, including a monograph, "Fundamentals of Criminal Personology," for which he was awarded the Moldovan Criminologist of the Year Prize (2008). In 2009, he was named dean-interim, and in 2011, dean of the Foreign Languages Department of the University of European Studies of Moldova. In 2010, he obtained a bar license, and he currently is combining professor's work with legal practice.

Susan Gade is a crime analyst with the Milwaukee Police Department. She is a native of the United States and received her bachelor's and master's degrees in criminal justice from Michigan State University, where she previously served as a research coordinator for a public–private partnership program. Her current research interests include intelligence-led policing, community policing, and social capital.

Karina Garcia is an independent researcher who has conducted research in Mexico and the United States aimed at exploring the interrelation of behavior and cultural practices. She has worked in the public and private sectors and has received training in engineering and social work. The convergence of these disciplinary fields has developed her interest in investigating the causal attributions for social problems, including crime, from both a scientific and a social approach. Garcia is a native of Mexico City, Mexico, where she completed her degree in industrial and systems engineering at the Instituto Tecnológico y de Estudios Superiores de Monterrey; she received her master's in social work at the University of Wyoming in 2006. Her work has been published in the *Hispanic Health Care International Journal*.

John S. Gitlitz is an associate professor at the Purchase College, State University of New York, in the Departments of Political Science and Latin American Studies. He is a native of Binghamton, New York, and received his doctoral degree in political science from the University of North Carolina–Chapel Hill. Since the 1980s, his major research interest has focused on peasant organizations in Peru, particularly the rondas campesinas of Cajamarca, and the informal administration of justice by peasant communities. He has been published in the *Journal of Latin American Studies* and edited volumes. His articles in Peru have appeared in *Estudios Andinos, Apuntes*, the *Boletin del Instituto Riva Aguero*, and *Ius et Veritas*, as well as at the *Instituto de Defensa Legal*. He is also a member of the Instituto de Justicia Intercultural of the Superior Court of Cajamarca, Peru.

Meredith L. Gore is an assistant professor at Michigan State University in the Department of Fisheries and Wildlife and School of Criminal Justice. She is a native of Westborough, MA, and has received her BS in environmental studies from Brandies University, her MA in environment and resource policy from George Washington University, and her PhD in natural resource policy and management from Cornell University. Meredith's research interests focus on public perceptions of environmental risk; community-based natural resource management; conservation criminology; and gender, justice, and environment. She has published in *Conservation Biology, The British Journal of Criminology, PLoSONE, Journal of Wildlife Management*, and *Human Dimensions of Wildlife*.

M. Enamul Huq was born in Godagari, Rajshahi, Bangladesh. He obtained a master's degree in history from Rajshahi University (Rajshani, Bangladesh) and his LLB from Dhaka University (Dhaka, Bangladesh). After retirement, he earned his PhD in public administration from the University of New Orleans, LA.

He joined the Police Service of Pakistan in 1964 (before Bangladesh, formerly known as East Pakistan which seceded from Pakistan in 1971), was trained at the National Police Academy, Sardah, and the International Police Academy, Georgetown, Washington, DC. He served in both wings of the then-Pakistan in various capacities. A freedom fighter, he actually participated in the Liberation War in 1971. Later on, he held many important positions in the president's and prime minister's secretariat. He was made principal of the police academy and served as commissioner of the Dhaka Metropolitan Police. He held the post of additional inspector general, Police HQ, CID, and worked as director general of the Department of Narcotics Control before he was appointed as inspector general of police, Government of the Peoples Republic of Bangladesh.

A regular contributor in local dailies and periodicals, he was the chief editor of the Detective–Police journal. He has authored a good number of publications and presented many a paper in different seminars and workshops, both at home and abroad, relating to the administration of the criminal justice system and allied subjects. He has been associated with the United Nations Development Programme, United Nations International Drug Control Program, United Nations Children's Fund (as a consultant), JICA (advisor), ACPF (president), and the Advisory Board of the United Nations Crime Prevention Forum at Vienna (member).

Being elected as member of the Executive Committee of Interpol, he took an active part and was twice made chairperson of finance and drug sessions of the Interpol General Assembly in Lyons and Ottawa. A widely traveled person, he has endeavored hard to promote international understanding and cooperation and was the recipient of the Interpol Medal. Besides being an active Rotarian for his contribution in social upliftment, he is an ambassador with the 3H Program. He is honored to be a visiting professor at the United Nations Asia and Far East Institute, Japan. A renowned writer, his interests are spread over a wide range of learning and awareness.

Lanre Olusegun Ikuteyijo is a lecturer at the Obafemi Awolowo University, Ile-Ife, Nigeria, in the Department of Sociology and Anthropology. He is a native of Ikare Akoko, Ondo State, in southwestern Nigeria, and he obtained his BSc and MSc degrees in sociology and anthropology, specializing in the areas of criminology and social research methods, from Obafemi Awolowo University, Ile-Ife. His research interests include policing, migration, urbanization, and qualitative research methods. He has been published in reputable journals like the *International Journal of Police Science and Management* (Vathek Publications, United Kingdom) and *Journal of Social Work* (Sage Publications). He has also contributed to a number of books and written a number of encyclopedia entries published by Sage and Blackwell Publishers. He has written a number of backgrounders on migration published on the African Portal, managed by the Center for International Governance Innovation (CIGI), Waterloo, Canada. He has also consulted for a number of international organizations like the European Union, United Nations Children's Fund, and the Bill and Melinda Gates Foundation.

Lisbet Ilkjaer is the senior legal and strategic adviser to the DIHR program in West Africa. She is Danish and has received her LLM in public international law from King's College, London. Her work experience includes working as public prosecutor and teaching public international law at Copenhagen University. Since 2002, she has managed and advised on human rights projects with police and other state actors in China, the Balkans, and West Africa (Burkina Faso and Niger). She has a special interest in working with police, human rights, and reform.

Zvonimir Ivanović, LLD, is an assistant professor at the Academy of Criminalistic and Police Studies in Belgrade in the Department of Criminalistics. He is a native of Belgrade, Serbia, and has received his LLD in the field of criminal procedure and criminal law, criminalistics, from the University of Kragujevac. His research interests include criminal procedure and criminal law, criminology, and criminalistics, and he has been published in various journals in Serbia and Southeastern Europe, including *Policing in Central and Eastern Europe—Social Control of Unconventional Deviance, Security, Science Security Policing, International Politics, International Law Life, Law Life,* and in two books: *Crimes of Cybercrime* and *The Sword in the WWW—Challenges of Cybercrime.*

Sanja Kutnjak Ivković is a professor at the School of Criminal Justice, Michigan State University. She holds a doctorate in criminology (PhD, University of Delaware) and a doctorate in law (SJD, Harvard University). Her research focuses on comparative and international criminology, criminal justice, and law. Professor Kutnjak Ivković's most recent book,

Reclaiming Justice: The International Tribunal for the Former Yugoslavia and Local Courts (Oxford University Press, 2011), coauthored with John Hagan, was just published by the Oxford University Press. Professor Kutnjak Ivković is the author of *The Fallen Blue Knights: Controlling Police Corruption* (Oxford University Press, 2005) and *Lay Participation in Criminal Trials* (1999). Professor Kutnjak Ivković is a coauthor along with Carl Klockars and Maria R. Haberfeld of *Enhancing Police Integrity* (Springer, 2006) and a coeditor along with Carl Klockars and Maria Haberfeld of *Contours of Police integrity* (Sage, 2004), which received American Society of Criminology International Division honorable mention. Professor Kutnjak Ivković's work has appeared in leading academic and law journals, such as the *Law and Society Review; Journal of Criminal Law and Criminology; Criminology and Public Policy; Law and Policy; Stanford Journal of International Law; Cornell International Law Journal; Policing and Society;* and *Policing: An International Journal of Police Strategies and Management.*

Maja Jere is a junior research fellow and a PhD student at the Faculty of Criminal Justice and Security, University of Maribor, Slovenia. She is a native of Slovenia. Her research interests include crime prevention and provision of safety and security in local communities. She has been published in the *European Journal of Criminology, Journal of Criminal Justice and Security,* and *Journal of Criminal Investigation and Criminology.*

Shanhe Jiang is a professor of criminal justice at the University of Toledo in the Department of Criminal Justice and Social Work. He is a native of Hubei, China, and has received a PhD from the University at Albany, State University of New York, in sociology. His recent research focuses on comparative criminal justice and criminology and methodology. Comparative studies include the views of formal and informal crime control, death penalty, community policing, and community corrections. He has been working on two projects in methodology. One is on the effects of collinearity in hierarchical linear modeling. The other is about joint modeling for categorical and continuous dependent variables.

Pa Musa Jobarteh is originally from Gambia, where he once served as the deputy director of Immigration. He holds a bachelor's degree in police studies from John Jay College of Criminal Justice of the City University of New York and a master's degree in international criminal justice from Michigan State University. He has an interest in international police field operations and management systems. He was a chapter contributor in *Crime and Punishment in Africa and the Middle East (Vol. 1)* edited by Mahesh K. Nalla (ABC CLIO, 2010).

Wook Kang is an assistant professor at the University of Central Oklahoma in the School of Criminal Justice. He is a native of Seoul, South Korea, and has received his PhD in criminal justice from Michigan State University. His research focuses on various aspects of police organizations, operations, and behavior. This includes studies of organizational change, officer decision making, and officer perceptions. He has been published in *Policing: An International Journal of Police Strategies and Management* and *Asian Journal of Criminology.*

Mary Fran T. Malone is an associate professor at the University of New Hampshire in the Department of Political Science. She is a native of Philadelphia, PA, and has received her PhD in political science, with a concentration in Latin American studies, from the

University of Pittsburgh. Her research centers on the rule of law in Latin America, examining the impact of the current crime epidemic on citizens' evaluations of their justice systems and support for the rule of law. Professor Malone's recent publications have appeared in *The Latin Americanist, Journal of Politics in Latin America*, and *Latin American Politics and Society*. Her book monograph, *The Rule of Law in Central America: Citizens' Reactions to Crime and Punishment*, was published in 2012 (Continuum Press).

Juanjo Medina is a senior lecturer in criminology at the University of Manchester in the School of Law. He is a native of Seville, Spain, and has received his PhD in criminal justice from Rutgers University. His research interests include youth gangs, violence against women, and crime control policy, and he has been published in, among others, *Violence Against Women, Punishment and Society, Children and Society*, and *Homicide Studies*.

Gorazd Meško is a professor of criminology at the Faculty of Criminal Justice and Security, University of Maribor, Slovenia. He is a native of Slovenia. He obtained his PhD degree from the University of Ljubljana, Slovenia. He has been a visiting scholar at the University of Cambridge and University of Oxford, United Kingdom. His research interests are related to a variety of criminological, penological, and victimological topics. He recently was a guest editor of *Policing—An International Journal of Police Strategies and Management* and *The Prison Journal*.

Anthony de Villiers Minnaar has since January 2009 served as the program head of security management for the merged Department of Criminology and Security Science in the School of Criminal Justice, College of Law, at the University of South Africa.

In the early 1990s, he published largely on issues of political violence and conflict inter alia migrant labor hostel violence, warlordism, massacres, and the proliferation of firearms and self-defense units. In the mid-1990s, his research interests turned to other forms of violence such as land disputes, informal settlements, illegal squatting, and evictions; minibus-taxi industry conflicts; violence around witchcraft accusations; xenophobia and undocumented migrants; and vigilantism. In more recent times, he has researched border controls; illegal motor vehicle importations; migrants' rights; motor vehicle hijackings; use of force by police; the murder of police officers; informers and witness protection programs; and most recently, the struggle to legislate for stricter gun controls; the declarations of persons to be unfit to possess a firearm; and security measures at ports of entry. His research interests currently are in the broad field of criminal justice, dealing with the specific issues of corruption prevention, border controls and undocumented migrants, xenophobia, and refugees; use of firearms in violent crime, civilian oversight of public and private policing, and private security industry issues (specifically crime prevention and private policing as well as community policing and community safety initiatives); regulating and monitoring the Private Security Industry in South Africa; security at ports of entry; information security and cybercrime; and the use of closed-circuit television surveillance systems for security and neighborhood safety/crime prevention.

Doel Mukerjee, PhD in 1999 from Jawaharlal Nehru University, New Delhi, India, has worked in Afghanistan and developed the concept of "police e mardumi" for the United Nations Development Programme in Afghanistan between 2009 and 2010. Over the last 17 years, she has worked on justice sector reforms with specialized work in human rights, judicial reforms, informal justice sector, police reforms, and gender justice with grassroots organizations and international development agencies. She has worked for the United Nations Development Programme in Bangladesh on access to justice and human rights, steering legal reforms and legal aid in the country. Currently, she heads the Justice and Human Rights in Afghanistan Project, working closely with the Ministry of Justice.

Mahesh K. Nalla, PhD in 1988 from the State University of New York at Albany, New York, is a professor and interim director of the School of Criminal Justice at Michigan State University in East Lansing, United States. His research interests include police organizational and work cultures in the developed, emerging, and new democracies; trust and legitimacy of police in the new democracies; and private security in the emerging markets. His research appeared in *Justice Quarterly, Journal of Research and Crime and Delinquency, European Journal of Criminology,* and *Journal of Criminal Justice,* among others. One of his major United Nations projects resulted in forming the cornerstone of the draft (United Nations Economic and Social Council) *International Protocol Against the Illicit Manufacturing of and Trafficking in Firearms, Ammunition and Other Related Materials,* as a supplement to the United Nations Convention Against Transnational Organized Crime. He is the editor in chief of the *International Journal of Comparative and Applied Criminal Justice.*

Raymund E. Narag is an assistant professor from the Department of Criminology and Criminal Justice at Southern Illinois University-Carbondale. He is a native of the Philippines and a PhD candidate from Michigan State University. His research interest centers on the structural, organizational, and cultural constructions of communities and how these impact the delinquent and criminal behaviors of residents. Narag is also interested in crosscultural and comparative administration of justice. His previous articles were published in the *Prison Journal* and *Criminal Justice and Behaviors.* He has also written a book on the conditions of prisons in the Philippines.

Greg Newbold is a professor of sociology at the University of Canterbury, New Zealand. He was born and educated in Auckland, New Zealand, and has an MA in anthropology (1978) and a PhD in sociology (1987) from the University of Auckland. His MA, on the social organization of a maximum security prison, was completed while serving a 7.5-year prison sentence for selling drugs in the 1970s. Since his release in 1980, he has published seven books and more than 70 articles and book chapters on crime, criminal justice, policing, and corrections. Currently recognized as one of New Zealand's leading criminologists, Newbold frequently acts as a consultant and policy advisor to the New Zealand government on matters pertaining to law and order.

Graeme R. Newman is a distinguished teaching professor at the School of Criminal Justice, University at Albany, and an associate director of the Center for Problem-Oriented Policing. He has advised the United Nations on crime and justice issues over many years and, in 1990, established the United Nations Crime and Justice Information Network. His major works include *Super Highway Robbery* with Ronald V. Clarke (Willan 2003), *Outsmarting the Terrorists* with Ronald V. Clarke (PSI International 2006*), Crime and Immigration* with Joshua Freilich (Ashgate 2006), *Designing Out Crime from Products and Systems* with Ronald V. Clarke (Willan 2006), *Policing Terrorism: An Executive's Guide* with Ronald V. Clarke (US Department of Justice 2008), a new translation of Cesare Beccaria's *On Crimes* *and Punishments* with Pietro Marongiu (Transaction Press 2009) and *Reducing Terrorism through Situational Crime Prevention* with Joshua Freilich (Criminal Justice Press 2010), and *Crime and Punishment around the World* in four volumes (ABC-CLIO 2010).

Izabela Nowicka is a professor of law and dean of the Internal Security Department at the Police Academy in Szczytno, Poland. She is a native of Szczytno, Poland, and received her professor of law degree from the University of Bialystok, Poland, in May 2012. Her research interests include criminology, minor crimes issues in the context of police, law on misdemeanor, and penal law, and she has been published in several different journals, both internal and international, such as the *Journal of Environmental Studies*, *Police Use of Force*, *Global Perspective*, *Internal Affairs and Justice in the Process of the European Integration and Globalization*, *EuroCriminology*, *Organized Crime and Terrorism*, *Reasons—Manifestations—Counteractions*, and many more. She has also conducted research on the issues related to the police reaction to misdemeanor.

Nabil Ouassini is a PhD student at Indiana University, Bloomington in the Department of Criminal Justice. He is a native of Las Vegas, NV, and has received his master's in criminal justice from the University of Nevada, Las Vegas. His research interests include comparative criminology/criminal justice, with a special interest in the Arab world. He has published in the *Journal of Youth and Adolescence* and his chapters on *Counterterrorism: From the Cold War to the War on Terror* (Praeger, 2012) and "Policing Minorities in Egypt, Lebanon, and Saudi Arabia" in *In Policing Muslim Minorities* (Springer, 2012) appeared in an edited volume on comparative issues of policing in various Muslim communities.

Emil W. Plywaczewski is a full professor of criminal law and criminology of the Faculty of Law at the University of Bialystok (Poland), director of the Chair of Criminal Law, and head of the Department of Substantive Penal Law and Criminology. Since May 2012 he has been a dean elect of the Faculty of Law. He is a native of Jeziorany (Poland) and has received his first (PhD) and second (Dr hab) degrees in field of law (criminal law/criminology) from Nicolaus Copernicus University in Torun. His research interests include organized crime, money laundering, criminal policy, and public security issues. His literary output comprises more than 340 publications (more than 20 of them are monographs) in the field of criminal law, criminology, criminal policy, organized crime, terrorism, and money laundering issues, published in Poland and abroad (65 publications). He was the first author in Poland to publish monographs on organized crime (Warsaw 1992) and on money laundering (Toruń 1993).

Most of the 65 publications abroad (articles and chapters) were published in peer-reviewed international journals and books. He is an editor and coauthor of the only book series in Europe in which are combined two disciplines (penal law and criminology) and two languages (English, most important for criminology, and English, most important for penal law), with participation of the many international distinguished scholars from both fields. The fifth volume of this series, *Current Problems of the Penal Law and Criminology* (with participation of some 50 scholars representing all continents) was published in Polish in June 2012 by Wolters Kluwer.

He won the Distinguished International Scholar Award of the International Division, American Society of Criminology (San Diego, 1997). Many times, he was a guest lecturer or visiting professor at 54 universities in Australia, Austria, Belgium, Brazil, the Czech Republic, Germany, Lithuania, France, Greece, India, Japan, China, the Netherlands, New Zealand, Italy, South Korea, the United States, Switzerland, and Finland. He also gave lectures in institutions linked to law enforcement and administration of justice in Germany, the Netherlands, Greece, India, and the United States. Since 1994, he has been a representative of Poland in the International Examination Board of the Central European Police Academy. Since 2001, he has been serving as a United Nations consultant. Since 2005, he has been a chief coordinator of the Polish Platform for Homeland Security (PPHS)—a unique initiative in Europe, whose activities are aimed at creating integrated computer tools to support the broadly defined efforts to improve public security.

Mushtaq Rahim, an Afghan, is an expert in the area of crisis prevention and recovery. He has worked in the area of rule of law for more than 4 years focusing on peace building, disarmament, reintegration, police development, and police reforms. Rahim is currently working for the United Nations Development Programme in Afghanistan as head of Crisis Prevention and Recovery.

Lala Jean Rakotoniaina is a Malagasy. He received his bachelor degree in sociology at the University of Antananarivo. He was a high school teacher for 20 years and traveled across Madagascar's most remote areas. He then decided to work for Durrell Wildlife Conservation Trust–Madagascar Programme as its community conservation coordinator. He was the pioneer of community conservation in Madagascar. He was the first to initiate the famous approach called SCOFA (sensibilization, conscientization, organization, formalization, and action), in which the local community can successfully manage their biodiversity. He created hundreds of villager associations and taught good governance throughout Madagascar. He coauthored the chapter "How Do Cultural Anthropologists and Conservationists Help Each Other to Save Endangered Species" in *Greening the Red Island* (Africa Institute of South Africa, 2010) edited by Jeff Kauffman. He was always solicited by the director of forests and environment within the Ministry of Environment and Forests to organize workshops for wetlands in general and Ramsar in particular. His good work was widely recognized around the world. Therefore, he was designated as the Disney Hero in 2007 for saving world species from extinction.

Jonah Ratsimbazafy is a native of Madagascar. He received his PhD in physical anthropology from the State University of New York at Stony Brook. He is the training and conservation coordinator of the Durrell Wildlife Conservation Trust in Madagascar. He is also an adjunct professor in the Department of Paleontology and Anthropology and the Department of Veterinary Medicine at the University of Antananarivo. His research interests include primate behavior and ecology. He has studied behavioral ecology of lemurs in Madagascar. He coauthored the second and third editions of the *Field Guide Series: Lemurs of Madagascar* (Conservation International, 2010). From 2006 to 2008, he was the vice president of the International Primatological Society for Conservation. He is the secretary general of a Malagasy Primate Group (Groupe d'Etude et de Recherche sur les Primates de Madagascar). He is a member of the IUCN/SSC Specialist Group in Madagascar.

John Scott is professor at the University of New England (Australia) in the School of Behavioural, Cognitive and Social Science. He is a native of Newcastle, Australia, and has received his PhD in sociology from the University of Newcastle. His research interests include rural sociology and the sociology of crime and deviance. Scott has published more than 50 books, book chapters, and journal articles, and he is currently working on major grant-funded projects on masculinity and violence in rural areas, indigenous community policing, and the male sex industry.

Andrej Sotlar is an assistant professor at the University of Maribor in the Faculty of Criminal Justice and Security. He is a native of Slovenia and has received his PhD in defense studies from the University of Ljubljana. His research interests include national security, security systems, plural policing, and private security, and he has been published in, among others, *Policing: An International Journal of Police Strategies and Management*, *Kriminalistik*, *Journal of Police Studies*, *Journal of Criminal Justice and Security*.

Staci Strobl is an associate professor in the Department of Law, Police Science and Criminal Justice Administration, at John Jay College of Criminal Justice and the 2009 winner of the British Journal of Criminology's Radzinowicz Memorial Prize for her work on the criminalization of domestic workers in Bahrain. Her area of specialization is gender, race, and ethnicity as they relate to policing in the Middle East and Eastern Europe. Earlier in her career, she worked as a US probation officer and a crime journalist. Dr. Strobl completed her doctorate in criminal justice at the City University of New York's Graduate Center, received her MA in criminal justice at John Jay, and her BA in Near Eastern studies at Cornell University.

Anthony Thomson is a professor at Acadia University, Canada, in the Department of Sociology. He is a native of Halifax, Canada, and received his PhD in social and political science from the University of Cambridge. His research interests include social theory, restorative justice, and community policing, and he has been published in the *Canadian Journal of Political and Social Theory*, *Labour/Le Travail*, and the *Canadian Journal of Sociology,* and by Oxford University Press.

Sergej Uljanov, LLM, is research fellow at the Institute for Comparative Law in Belgrade. He was born and raised in Belgrade, the Republic of Serbia, and has received his LLM degree in criminal procedure and criminalistics from the Faculty of Law at the University of Belgrade. He has been focusing his research on criminal procedure, criminal law, criminalistics, criminology, penology, environmental protection, game theory, and futurology.

So far, he has been published in numerous journals in the Republic of Serbia and Western Balkans: *Security, International Politics, Science Security Policing—The Journal for Criminalistics and Law, European Legislation, Law Life, International Law Life, Securitas—The Journal for Theory and Praxis on Security, Gdansk Talks on Terrorism 2005*, and *Review for Criminology and Criminal Law.*

As a perspective student, he visited the University of Illinois at Chicago and Chicago Police Department in July 1994 and published an article considering the relation between the phenomena of juvenile delinquency and civil war. Between April and May 2003, he visited Washington DC, Austin, Albuquerque, Seattle, and New York regarding the "Security Issues" program for law enforcement officers.

He is working on his LLD on the importance of the relation between phenomena of modus operandi and detection of crime.

Mark Ungar is a professor of political science and criminal justice at the Graduate Center and Brooklyn College of the City University of New York. He received a PhD in political science from Columbia University. His research and work focus on police and judicial reform, and publications include the books *Policing Democracy: Overcoming Obstacles to Citizen Security Reform in Latin America* (Johns Hopkins, 2011) and *Elusive Reform: Democracy and the Rule of Law in Latin America* (Lynne Rienner, 2002). He is on the General Assembly of the Inter-American Institute of Human Rights and is an advisor to the United Nations, Inter-American Development Bank, and governmental agencies in Latin America.

Arie van Sluis received his PhD in 2002 in Social Sciences from Erasmus University in Rotterdam, the Netherlands where he works as an assistant professor. His main areas of research include the study of police organization and the relations of the police with democratic institutions and public safety policy. His current research is a study on the impact of performance steering within the police on relations with local stakeholders.

Sirpa Virta is a professor at the University of Tampere, Finland, in the School of Management. She is a native of Finland and has received her PhD in political science from the University of Tampere. Her research interests include police management, community policing, and security strategies, and she has published several books and research reports in Finnish as well as articles in *Policing: An International Journal of Police Strategies and Management, American Behavioral Scientist*, and *Theoretical Criminology*. Professor Virta is also a head of the European Society of Criminology Working Group on Crime, Science and Politics.

Tom Winfree is affiliated with Arizona State University in the School of Criminology and Criminal Justice. He is a native of Wytheville, VA. He received a doctor of philosophy degree in sociology, with an emphasis in criminology and deviant behavior, from the University of Montana. His research interests include police professionalization, restorative policing, community policing, youth gangs and law enforcement, and deaths in police custody. He has coauthored 14 textbooks and readers, including *Expert Witnesses: Criminologists in the Courtroom* (State University of New York, Albany Press, 1987); *Crime and Justice: An Introduction* (Nelson-Hall, 1992); *Understanding Crime* (3rd edition, Wadsworth, 2010); *Essentials of Corrections* (5th edition, Wiley-Blackwell, in press); *Juvenile Justice* (3rd edition, Wolters Kluwer, CCH, 2012); and *Social Learning Theories of Crime* (Ashgate Press, 2012). He has authored or coauthored nearly 100 refereed journal articles published in *Justice Quarterly, Criminology, Journal of Drug Issues, Policing, Journal of Criminal Justice, American Journal of Police, Journal of Police Science and Administration, International Journal of the Addictions, Rural Sociology, Youth and Society, Sociological Spectrum, Journal of Security Administration, Policy Studies Review, Juvenile and Family Court Journal, Victims and Violence, The Justice System Journal, Journal of Quantitative Criminology, Journal of Contemporary Criminal Justice, The Prison Journal, Journal of Crime and Justice, Justice Research and Policy, Crime and Delinquency, Police Quarterly*, and *Youth Violence and Juvenile Justice*.

Lena Y. Zhong is an associate professor at the City University of Hong Kong in the Department of Applied Social Studies. She is a native of Hunan, China, and has received her PhD from the University of Hong Kong in criminology. Her research interests include Chinese policing, crime prevention, and drug abuse, and she has published articles in journals such as *International Journal of Offender Therapy and Comparative Criminology*; *Crime, Law and Social Change*; and *Police Practice and Research*. She has also published reports to the Hong Kong Special Administrative Region government on cocaine abuse and offender rehabilitation and a book, *Communities, Crime and Social Capital in Contemporary China* (Willan/Routledge, 2009).

Introduction

Although in proposing this book to our publisher, we used the standard definition of community policing developed by the Office of Community Oriented Policing Services of the United States (COPS), that community policing has three components: community partnerships, organizational transformation, and problem solving, we did not present this definition to our authors because we thought it too narrow. That's right. Too narrow. We wanted, in contrast to the critics of community policing who consider it to be a term that is so broad as to be meaningless, to demonstrate that its breadth is actually its depth. Looked at globally, community policing does not always or even often follow the COPS prescription; rather, it has emerged as a product of the physical environments and cultures in many different locations around the world. This book shows that community policing is far from meaningless. The diversity of description and analysis of community policing in the array of cultures presented here demonstrates the opposite: community policing is full to overflowing with meaning.

The idea of community policing—and it is an idea—is most difficult to grasp because it means different things to different people. We understood this from the start, so when we approached potential contributors to the book, we prepared a brief list of topics we wanted them to cover: the origin of community policing in the indigenous community, how does community policing work there, what community police actually do, the relationship of community policing to the criminal justice system, and finally, the effectiveness of community policing. Many of our contributors more or less complied with this list, but many did not. Being experienced editors, we anticipated this. The intent of our list was not so much to force authors to organize their chapter in a particular way (though it would have been nice) but to create a particular viewpoint that we hoped the author would adopt: the idea that the roots of community policing might be found in indigenous communities.

What we did not anticipate, however, was that the term "indigenous communities" would be more difficult for authors than the term "community policing." We were initially disappointed when quite a few chapters came in that did not appear to address the indigenous community aspect of community policing at all. Then we realized that in some cultures with more than a thousand years of recorded history, it was a matter of conjecture at what point in history one could clearly identify the indigenous community. Were the people that lived in Germany, for example, prior to occupation by the ancient Romans the true indigenous communities, and anything after that an imposition? Is the complexion of German policing today indigenous—a reflection of the imposition of ancient Roman rule? That is, at what point in history are indigenous cultures the reflection of the imposition of a policing style by an occupier?

Colonial imposition of policing styles and organization are the preoccupation of many of the chapters on Africa and Asia, given the comparatively recent history of colonial rule by the British, French, Dutch, Portuguese, and Spanish. The authors of some of these chapters are usually at pains to point out that community policing—or something like it, a kind of romantic notion of informal justice at the village level—preceded the typical militaristic model of policing used by colonial powers to impose law and order in their colonies. In some countries, this colonial model has overwhelmed the former informal justice system of indigenous communities to the extent that those forms of justice have all but disappeared. This is so in cases where the colonial powers, particularly the British, co-opted or transformed the existing informal policing structures into their own centralized militaristic and bureaucratic styles of policing and justice. A number of the African chapters demonstrate this process clearly.

It is popular these days to view this colonial imposition as all bad, that something valuable was lost when the colonial powers imposed their systems of justice on indigenous communities. It is certainly true that the past is the only resource we humans have in order to understand ourselves as people. So to lose any of the past is an awful loss. This is why great cultures and civilizations keep extensive records of their histories. It is also why it is a tragedy when a culture is lost completely or reduced to a small glimmer of what it once was, for whatever reason: colonialism, globalization, economic development, and so forth. The remnants of such cultures these days are referred to as "minorities." These minorities may remain in place in the face of cultural destruction, or they may try to take their cultures with them when they migrate to a more attractive place and become immigrant communities. Either way, they present a challenge to policing, and it is of considerable interest that a number of our chapters address this issue: community policing is used as a vehicle to connect with minorities, to exploit or enhance the partially lost informal justice systems in minority communities. This role of community policing is well demonstrated in the chapters on Canada and Australia.

Other countries, in contrast, have embraced the colonial style of policing once they achieved independence, recognizing that it was the most efficient way to structure a community fractured by social change and rapid economic development. The chapter on Bahrain is such an example. At issue is the problem of maintaining an efficient economic system in a global economy, which requires a centralized governmental structure. The emergence of nation-states toward the end of the nineteenth century demands a centralized government in order to deal with the global demands of trade and economic development. The chapter on India exemplifies this incompatibility, perhaps even a paradox. India, a young and independent nation-state that is rapidly emerging as a world power, has struggled mightily to cope with indigenous policing in its vast rural and tribal areas. There have been attempts to impose or even replace indigenous informal policing structures in rural India with a more formal style, but these often failed and ended up reverting to the indigenous structures. In other tribal areas, attempts have been made to "modernize" the indigenous policing through education and other kinds of outreach but to leave the actual structure of the informal justice system in place. India stands out as a vast laboratory for experimenting with a diverse range of indigenous community policing styles because of its huge rural population and naturally decentralized mechanisms of control that were mostly left in place by the British, if not exploited by them.

Similarly, there a number of chapters where community policing has been used in an effort to return policing to the people, to attempt to maintain a centralized command structure but to designate local police offices and stations as those that should connect with the local community. In fact, at least from the chapters in this volume, this role of community policing is probably the most dominant one: a vehicle for softening the militarized or bureaucratically centralized administration of policing in many countries, especially those that either are economically well developed or are countries recently emerged from non-democratic rule. In other words, community policing is seen as synonymous to "reform." What exactly, though, does reform mean when community policing is used as its vehicle?

The popular answer to this question is to point to the "top-down"–"bottom-up" paradox of policing reform. Can community policing be imposed from above, or must it emerge from the bottom up, that is, involve from the very beginning local (indigenous?) communities. Herein lies the very crux of policing in modern society. The ideal would be (and it is the romantic image of indigenous societies) that small communities can police themselves, that there would be no need for police as we think of them, uniformed, patrolling, ordering. There have been many real-life experiments in this regard, some of which are well described in this volume. The most difficult experiment, still ongoing, has been that of policing in Northern Ireland, with its history of self-policing during times of political conflict. Parallel justice systems emerged—complete with police patrols and punishment of offenders—often violent. Similar "vigilante" policing occurred in Mexico, Peru, and Argentina over a period of years preceding eventual democratic rule.

The civilized version of parallel justice in "respectable" community policing is, of course, neighborhood watch. Even here, though, the line between watching and punishing is thin indeed. In most assessments of community policing in chapters on developed countries, neighborhood involvement of some kind is seen as an essential element of community policing. Yet in almost all chapters that describe this reform process, there is an element, sometimes identified, sometimes hidden, of suspicion from both sides: the old policing guard views citizens as potential offenders, so any collaboration with them is seen as weakness, which is certainly a mistaken view. And even the reform advocates insist on strict rules and training of citizens who will join neighborhood watch in order to avoid neighborhood watch becoming too much like police—that is, usurping their prerogative to use violence. So it must be said that in no instances where community policing was used as a reform vehicle did its style emerge from the bottom up. In every case, it was a top-down reform.

Of course, the ideal of community policing is for citizens and police to work together—for there to be a bottom-up and top-down approach working in partnership. But how can this occur, for example, in communities full of gang or tribal violence, demoralized by poverty or scarce resources? One doubts that this ideal can ever be reached for the simple reason that, as the author of the Northern Ireland chapter observed, community policing works best where it is least needed, that is to say, in communities where there is mutual trust between citizen and citizen and between police and citizen. In other words, communities that hardly need policing at all. Sounds wonderful, until one realizes that it was exactly this style that was used by Mafia organizations in Chicago and New York in the early part of the twentieth century and long before in southern Italy. That is to say, protection of citizens is a racket. One must pay a price for protection. The only issue is to whom?

To think of modern police as a kind of protection racket is, of course, outrageous, though it does help explain the chronic disease of corruption that seems to attack many police forces around the world. At issue here is the question of how crime is viewed in modern society compared to indigenous (local) communities. Nation-states in which all modern policing operates demand that the state itself is the victim of crime and that the immediate or actual victim is secondary, or even the excuse for the state to exert its force on the offender. Viewed in this light, community policing appears to be quite a threat to the nation-state, for it shifts emphasis considerably onto the immediate or potential victims of crimes and, in some versions of community policing, works hard to help citizens to avoid becoming victims. Perhaps this is why community policing has been difficult to introduce as a reform measure in nations that are used to the state playing a large direct role in prosecution, investigation, and punishment of offenders both operationally and legally, such as, for example, many of the east European states and South Africa where, the author tells us, community policing was tried and eventually abandoned.

If our foregoing discussion seems rather too cerebral, there is a reason for it. Why not address the practical question: does community policing work or not? Very few authors were able to cite empirical research that showed convincingly that community policing "worked" in their particular communities. Apart from the problem of specifying what the criteria for success would be in evaluating the effectiveness of community policing, even when the objectives of any project were specified, there was little empirical research to show that they were achieved. Yet, in almost every case, authors concluded that community policing would be continued and that its objectives were laudable and desirable, even if their effectiveness could not be verified. We take this as evidence that community policing in the communities covered in this book is accepted on faith, and that it is an idea with intrinsic merit. One could hardly get more cerebral than that.

Mahesh K. Nalla
Graeme R. Newman

Africa and the Middle East

I

Bahrain

STACI STROBL

1

Contents

Community policing is a broad strategy that has been adopted by many police forces around the world. Rather than merely responding to crimes after they occur, the strategy involves taking a proactive approach to the problems police encounter in their day-to-day duties while also strengthening the ties between the citizen and the police. After a police professional movement that had isolated officers in a detached, patrol-car-dominated modus operandi, community policing emerged in the 1980s in the United States as a means of grounding policing in local communities. It necessitated the devolution of some police discretion to local precincts and neighborhoods, increased police transparency and accountability, focused on public relations, reinstated foot patrols, and facilitated police–community meetings, among other activities. Because of the globalization of police professional networks in the 1990s, with the Internet and the proliferation of international police conferences, many forces around the world developed or adopted their own community policing strategies, creating nothing less than a global community policing movement.

Bahrain, a small country located on a desert archipelago off the eastern coast of Saudi Arabia in the Persian Gulf, boasts being the first Arab country to adopt the community policing strategy in its daily police operations in 2005. It was considered to be a means by which the community could be more involved in the coproduction of public safety in the context of a developing state. Modern state-dominated policing in Bahrain did not have its advent until the 1920s, and many indigenous community-based criminal justice practices were not phased out until decades after that. However, the new community policing movement is almost entirely a product from Western societies, ignoring the kinds of indigenous practices such as mediation by trusted tribal or village elders. An additional irony has surfaced since the beginning of the Bahrain Spring in early 2011. Since then, the government has been actively using the police to suppress political opposition through the use of heavy-handed riot forces to put down demonstrations and night raids on the homes of political opposition figures to arrest them for antigovernment activity. Paramilitary police techniques have resulted in the deaths of 35 people (13 from fired tear gas canisters) and injuries to approximately 3000 (*New York Times* 2012). Despite this police-related violence, the community policing unit continues to act as a representative of a police force that touts cooperation with Bahraini communities.

This historical account of community-based and community-oriented policing in Bahrain emphasizes the ironic rise of community policing at the same time that a parallel trend of paramilitary policing has occurred. It suggests that indigenous practices that could help bind the national police and the community are being forgotten in favor of Western-style approaches to community–police relations, which struggle for legitimacy in light of the paramilitary policing of the Bahrain Spring. Postcolonial spaces like Bahrain are often hybrid in nature, featuring both imperially imposed institutional transplants and demised, but not dead, local practices (Abu-Lughod 1998; Said 1993; Spivak 1999). Looking for indigenous policing in Bahrain, then, is to focus on the limited use of traditional forms of mediation to resolve disputes reported to police, a practice that is increasingly atypical and not placed under the umbrella of community policing. As such, the police have not correctly identified their most grassroots and community-based practice as community policing, engaging in a kind of institutional forgetting of what community has traditionally meant in favor of a state-based and Western-transplanted notion of community-oriented policing.

Colonial Legacy of Policing in Bahrain

Bahrain is a small Muslim country, which is home to a population of approximately 1.2 million people (Central Intelligence Agency 2012). It is a constitutional monarchy under King Hamad bin Isa Al-Khalifah, a Sunni Muslim monarch in a majority Shi'a Muslim state.* Much of the country's wealth during the twentieth century was derived from exploiting oil and natural gas deposits, as well as refining oil, although this industry is now in decline due to resource depletion. Bahrain's police force consists of approximately 3000 primarily Sunni officers, many of whom are foreign born. Approximately 5% of the forces are policewomen (Strobl 2011). Contemporary policing in the country is the product of the modernization efforts of the British during the colonial period of the early twentieth century, during which Bahrain had protectorate status within the larger empire.

The British usurped control from precolonial means of maintaining order in society based on tribal and kinship networks in favor of a more centralized consolidation of police functions in the colonial state. Treaties between the British and the Al-Khalifah tribe were signed in 1861, 1880, and 1882. Political agents dispatched from London, along with the long-standing British political advisor to the monarchy, Sir Charles Belgrave, institutionalized a uniformed police force, loosely based on the Royal Irish Constabulary, while slowly edging out indigenous forms of policing. From the mid-1920s until 1955, Belgrave served as the commandant of the newly created State Police. Although his memoir indicates that he hoped to employ indigenous people in the police, most of the police personnel during

---

* In the seventh century, Islam split into two major sects after a dispute over who should follow the Prophet Muhammad in leadership of the Muslim people. Those who would become Sunnis supported Abu Bakr, a trusted advisor to the prophet, while those who became Shi'a felt that 'Ali, his son-in-law, was the correct ruler (Esposito 1988). In Bahrain, sectarianism has been a force that has split the nation socially, politically, and economically. Shi'a, many of whom are of Persian origin, have lived on the island for centuries. Meanwhile, Sunnis, who form the ruling elite, are the product of Sunni presence on the island since the eighteenth century. Shi'a are more likely to be unemployed, and overall have less wealth, than the Sunnis. Shi'a are the majority of the country's inhabitants but are disenfranchised from the political process (Strobl 2011).

Belgrave's tenure were foreign born and often manumitted slaves, from around the British Empire (Belgrave 1960). As with many colonial forces around the world, the police acted as a local military, used to defend the colonial state from external threats, in addition to providing local law and order. As such, London instructed the Bahraini police in the activities of intelligence gathering, security, and training. By the 1960s, many officers in the top ranks of the police were British nationals who were shoring up the force for eventual departure at the time of decolonization (Sinclair and Williams 2007).

In precolonial Bahrain, tribes were united by honor and loyalty to a patriarchal and hereditary social structure (Lienhardt 2001). The prevalence of tribal structure persisted for some time through the colonial period, particularly in rural communities. As the historian J. E. Peterson (1991) explains:

> ...the tribe was central to the individual's existence: in many ways it formed something of a self-contained entity, politically, economically, and certainly socially. Allegiance to a larger state structure was ephemeral, produced either by force or transitory self-interest. (p. 1437)

Disputes within tribes were handled by an all-male council (*majlis*) of tribal leaders (*shaykhs*) who would hear the grievances of people wronged and rule as to the tribal response. Sanctions and solutions to wrongdoing were enforced by the council as the chief protectors of the safety of their people. Routine consultation on decision making with other adult males in the tribe maintained the legitimacy of the *shaykhs* within the *majlis* (Khuri 1980). Conflicts related to Muslim law (*shari'ah*) were handled in consultation with the local *qadi* (customary judge) and his circle of *ulema*, or learned elite (Onley and Khalaf 2007). Self-appointed third-party mediators also often emerged to solve conflicts before they were brought to the *majlis* and *ulema* (Lienhardt 2001).

Traditional conflict resolution practices in the Gulf are connected to larger Arab and Muslim notions of "sensitive symbolics" (Yassine 1999, p. 7). Quranic injunctions instruct Muslims to keep the peace among themselves, hence the need for *hal wassat* (solution as middle way). Because of the Arab cultural primacy of honor (*sharaf*) to one's reputation, and the interconnectedness of the individual's reputation with the larger family, clan, or tribe, face-saving techniques are preferred to overt conflict. Helping the parties in "saving face" (*dakhilah*)* is a major part of the role of an Arab mediator. Traditionally, Arab mediation (*wisatah*) is face-to-face and personal and eschews putting anything in writing. It is distinct from other forms of traditional dispute resolution involving religious authorities: mediation as *takhim* (arbitration), which has occurred around conflicts of religious succession, or *qadi* justice, which is dispute resolution by a Muslim judge or scholar (Yassine 1999). However, in the Gulf context, it appears that *wisatah* is not as distinct an activity and involves any dispute resolution engaged in by *shaykhs*, *qadis*, or *ulema*. The use of *takhim* is not reported in accounts of Gulf dispute resolution related to crime and deviance, but rather, it is used in commercial disputes.

According to Arabian Gulf ethnographer Peter Lienhardt (2001), who immersed himself in the remaining traditional clans in the region in the 1950s, the cultural preference is for nonviolent solutions to wrongdoing, including crimes of an intertribal nature. He found that most frequently occurring intertribal crimes were sea piracy, Bedouin raids,

---

* *Dakhilah* is more literally translated as "inner self," but Arab mediators translate it functionally as "saving face" (Yassine 1999).

and the evasion of tolls owed to local *shaykhs*. In the cases of intertribal murder, traditional Bahrainis followed the rule of *damna was damhum wahid, daynna wa daynhum wahid* (our blood is their blood, our debt is their debt), meaning that a system of blood money (*diyah*) was followed. This system, however, occasionally failed to satisfy the kin of the victim, and blood feuds developed.

State Building and the Suppression of Indigenous Practices

After independence in 1971, the police force was renamed Bahrain Public Security under the Ministry of the Interior. Some vestiges of precolonial order maintenance remained within the more recently formed state-controlled police force. For example, individual police officers sometimes used traditional mediation practices to solve crime-related disputes, and police report that the payment of *diyah* (blood money) occasionally occurred after the colonial period, though this practice is technically illegal (Strobl 2007). Although tribal leaders no longer routinely inserted themselves directly into matters of criminal justice, they remained important as political leaders in their communities as part of a state of postcolonial hybridity in which they embraced state-based modernization while also holding on to traditional sociocultural markers (Seikaly 1994).

Modern policing in Bahrain is a creature of the colonial experience and, as a result, an institution beholden to the modern nation-state. The centralization of the "...chief concentrated means of violence" forms the basis of sociologist's Charles Tilly's (1985, p. 170) notion of the modern state. He theorizes that the nation-state emerges only after it has wrestled control over those internal groups who have previously held the authority for legitimate violence. Taming tribal or clan-based dispute resolution and violence is the necessary precursor to modern policing so that local communities become subordinate to the government rather than to their traditional patrons. Bahrain's early twentieth century colonial police history reflects a similar consolidating effect even in a relatively small nation as it is. Colonial officials, such as Sir Charles Belgrave and the imperial British agents of the time, set up a modern policing and court system, which eventually delegitimized and replaced the kinship and tribal forms of justice. Rather than invite in the *qadi*s and other community leaders to participate in justice and security, the locus of control shifted to the state, where it has remained, tempered only by more recent globalization forces such as the rise of multinational corporations and international laws and treaties around human rights standards.

Promise of Community Policing in Bahrain

In 2003, Bahraini police officials began to explore a community policing strategy, which hypothetically could represent a mild decentralization of the state's monopoly on justice and security. The Bahraini police became interested in the community coproduction of safety and security reportedly after being exposed to other police forces' experiences with community policing through global police professional conferences, associations, and networks. That year, the Bahraini government hosted an International Police Executive Forum conference entitled "Community and the Police" as a means of bringing in experts from around the world (Strobl 2011). According to one newspaper account, police participants from Australia and Japan particularly impressed the Bahraini police officials with their ideas about how a more public relations-oriented approach to policing could help them overcome perceived problems of legitimacy and ensure human rights, transparency, and accountability (Fakhri 2005), particularly since they are a primarily Sunni police force serving a majority *Shi'a* population. In other media coverage, police cited Singapore and the United Kingdom as having the ideal community policing strategies, while a conference participant interviewed told this researcher that the Bahraini police primarily looked to Finland, Japan, and the United States for community policing advice and consultation. Regardless of who most inspired the Bahrainis, after the conference, the Ministry of the Interior subsequently sent officers to the United Kingdom to train in community policing techniques and philosophies. Afterward, those officers went on to offer a course on the subject to their colleagues and new recruits at the Royal Police Academy in Jaw, Bahrain (Strobl 2011).

In 2005, the first community police officers were sworn in as a special unit of 190 officers, 20 of whom were policewomen, and began foot patrols in local marketplaces (*suqs*). Their duties were said to also include taking on intractable conflicts that lead to repeated police cases, educating the community about crime and safety, and helping local police stations be more service oriented. According to a police colonel, one of the goals of the community policing unit is to increase the number of *Shi'a* in the Sunni-dominated forces (Strobl 2011), of which at least half of the 20 community policewomen were so identified (Strobl 2007). Unlike the other units of the police who wear military-style khaki uniforms, community police officers are issued new blue uniforms, reportedly to distinguish themselves as agents of change. The Minister of the Interior, Shaikh Rashid bin Abdullah Al-Khalifa, explained to the press that community policing is intended to help policing enter "a modernization phase to ensure better services" (Hamada 2005, p. 3). Further, a police major indicated that wearing blue softens the police image and assists them in reaching out to community members to help them with any problems they have or perceive (Strobl 2011).

Strange Coupling of Community Policing and Paramilitarism

Since their advent, the community policing unit has grown even as the use of riot control police and Gulf Cooperation Council (GCC) Peninsula Shield forces to quell citizen demonstrations has also been on the rise. Since the beginning of the so-called Bahrain Spring in 2011, the opposition movement, dominated by the majority *Shi'a* underclass, has called on the Bahrain government to further democratize the country, better include *Shi'a* in political and economic decision making, and ensure human rights for all citizens, including in the criminal justice context.

Despite a very contested political climate, on January 12, 2012, the Ministry of the Interior announced its intention of hiring an additional 500 community police officers. According to the head of Bahrain Public Security, "[They] will be our conduit with the community as well... There must be soft policing as well as hard policing" (Toumi 2012). Reportedly, community police officers will be deployed to the municipalities in which they live and assist in implementing the police reforms called for in the Bahrain Independent Commission for Inquiry (BICI) report (Toumi 2012). The commission, empanelled in 2011 and chaired by Egyptian war crimes expert Mahmoud Cherif Bassiouni, investigated the government's crackdown on the opposition movement, including the declaration of martial law from March 15, 2001, to June 1, 2011; the deployment of GCC forces to squash demonstrators; and allegations of police torture during indefinite detainments. Among the findings of the commission's report was the forensic documentation of 60 individuals tortured by police and five more who were the victims of excessive use of police force during demonstrations (Bahrain Independent Commission of Inquiry 2011).*

Despite the BICI report and promises from the King to implement reforms, tactics such as the use of tear gas and water cannons continue to be used against protestors and opposition. On the first anniversary of the Bahrain Spring uprising, armored police vehicles patrolled Manama, and police fired tear gas at dozens of protestors near the site of the now-destroyed Pearl Monument, symbol of the opposition movement.† Meanwhile, the Minister of the Interior has hired two police consultants to help them manage the alleged police reform, former Miami Police Chief John Timoney and former British Metropolitan Police Assistant Commissioner John Yates. Interestingly, Yates quit his position with the Metropolitan Police after questions surfaced as to his involvement in the famous phone-hacking scandal (Jones 2011). And Timoney has long been criticized for his heavy-handed antidemonstration tactics during free-trade protests in 2003 in Miami (National Public Radio 2012).

A similar simultaneous rise of both community policing and paramilitary police approaches has often gone ignored by police scholars in the American context. Whereas numerous academic papers and police conferences have documented the promises and challenges of community policing, the proliferation of special weapons and tactics (SWAT) teams has gotten much less attention (Kraska and Paulsen 1997). The American approach to policing shifted in the 1990s from being a tool of the last resort to a necessary part of policing diverse situations, from demonstrations to drug raids (Kraska 1996). Recent police-related events in Bahrain seem to suggest a similar coupling of community policing and paramilitary policing. But such a coupling is inherently ironic. Whatever closeness to the community that may be developed in the first strategy can easily be undone by the second. A more cynical view suggests that the community policing strategy with its public overtures to dialogue and cooperation and its friendly foot patrols in town centers is merely used as perception management to counter the public outrage about more militaristic police techniques.

Can Bahraini Police Mediation Be Considered Indigenous Community Policing?

During 2005 and 2006, the author conducted an ethnographic study of Bahraini policewomen (see Strobl 2008). The fieldwork provided a glimpse into the newly formed

---

* Police have also cracked down on speech the government considers threatening. A Bahraini poet, Ayat al-Ghermezi, was arrested for incitement after reciting an original poem publicly. The poem includes the lines "We are the people who will kill humiliation and assassinate misery/We are the people who will destroy the foundation of injustice/Don't you hear their cries, don't you hear their screams?": She reportedly addressed it to King Hamad bin Isa Al-Khalifah and the Prime Minister, Prince Khalifa bin Salman Al-Khalifah (Blomfield 2011). In addition, blogger Mahmood Al-Yousif, a Sunni who advocates political nonsectarianism, was arrested on March 30, 2011, for writing about the Shi'a opposition in a way perceived by the government as sympathetic to them (Vila 2011).

† On March 18, 2011, the government demolished the monument, site of the largest Bahrain Spring protests in the month preceding. It then closed the roundabout around the monument site and renamed it from the "Pearl Roundabout" to "Al-Farouq Junction" (Hammond 2012).

community policing unit during which an additional irony was palpable. Contemporary police use of traditional mediation methods, which were grounded in indigenous and long-standing community-oriented approaches to crime, was not included under the umbrella of the new community policing strategy. Rather, they were hidden in the everyday and hardly notable routine of local police stations. It is notable that mediation is not officially classified as part of the community policing strategy even if it is probably the most indigenous and community-based practice that the contemporary police force offers.

In contrast, in the United States, the turn toward community policing has been one factor in creating "...a more supportive context for police to consider mediation" (Volpe and Phillips 2003, p. 263). Its benefits include helping police departments gain the respect and cooperation of the communities they police (Cooper 2000) and solving ongoing problems before they escalate (Halstead et al. 2000), and it has been shown to reduce crime rates because community cooperation surfaces more witnesses and information about crimes (Webb and Katz 1997). In Native American communities, a return to traditional dispute resolution and peacemaking practices has been undertaken in the last couple of decades as a means of legitimizing contemporary justice processes through a return to older, precolonial American practices. Aside from these programs, sidelined on American reservations and seemingly most developed in the Navajo communities of the Southwest (Meyer et al. 2009), most contemporary American calls for police use of mediation are not a return to past practices but rather a means of solving the problem of the perception of police as disinterested and alienated from the community in a general sense. Police mediation in the United States is often sold as an effective means of working within specific cultural and subcultural contexts, as well as across cultures in a diverse society, but not because the methods are perceived as rooted in a particular indigenous culture or history (Syeed-Miller 2006).

Police mediation in Bahrain, though performed by a police officer as an agent of the contemporary nation-state, is grounded in a general sense of indigenous tradition. According to Bahraini police procedure, if a case does not meet the legal requirements of *junhah* or *junaiyah*,* it can be deemed *shukiah idariah* (an administrative case). In these cases, police decide whether to refer the course directly to court or to engage in mediation between victims and complainants first. Interestingly, there is no formal training in mediation, although verbal de-escalation and negotiation techniques are a part of the regular police curriculum for new recruits. Rather, officers appoint themselves as mediators, often relying on mediation credibility gained in nongovernmental, tribal, or community-based social contexts in which they participate off-hours. As one police mediator explained, there is no "technique" per se; rather, mediation is based on traditional and local norms. He commented, "Arabs are private people. If they can resolve a case among themselves before making a formal prosecution, they will." He further explained that his own local legitimacy as a police mediator came from his family's long-standing presence in the community and that prior generations had served as mediators in a nonpolice capacity, suggesting a hereditary element to being considered a worthy mediator in the Bahraini context.

On the other hand, it must be noted that police mediators as state agents have sworn to uphold the laws of the state above all other considerations. As mediators, their latitude

---

* *Junhah* and *junaiyah* are roughly equivalent to felonies and misdemeanors in the American system. *Junhah* are less serious crimes, punishable by less than 3 years in prison, while *junaiyah* are serious offenses punishable by more than 3 years' imprisonment (Strobl 2007).

for facilitating problem solving may be constrained by ultimately having to uphold the law, both procedurally and substantively (Rowe 1985). Another problem rests with the police powers around the use of force, which violate core principles of mediation such as self-determination and voluntariness (Volpe and Phillips 2003). These problems have been discussed in the literature on dispute relation with differing opinions of whether the imperfectness of police as mediators means they should not engage in such activity (Rowe 1985; Cooper 2000). Similarly, Bahraini police mediators are also imperfect for the above reasons. By virtue of being police, they are not the traditional community-oriented Bahraini mediators of the past who could exercise the mediation ideals of third-party neutrality, voluntariness, and self-determination.

In Bahrain, if police mediation occurs and a resolution to the case is found, parties can sign a form of good manner and character (*ta-ahud husin al-sirah wa al-saluk*) or a peace report (*mahdar salih*) or draft an individualized agreement. If there is no resolution of the case, the police officer can forward the case to prosecution. One police mediator, in a municipality in the northeast of Bahrain, described two cases he successfully mediated in 2006. One involved theft in which a woman stole several expensive dresses from a retail store and resold them from her home. Through mediation, the perpetrator consented in an individualized agreement to pay back the retailer in monthly installments. Another case centered on nonpayment for automechanic services and was similarly solved. Both cases are officially recorded in the police stations as *tanazul*, meaning "concession" and equivalent to "case dropped."

This author observed a police mediator facilitate the mediation of a case in 2006 in a municipality in the northeast of Bahrain. The case involved a female US naval employee who was allegedly recklessly driving and may have been drinking. The Bahraini male complainant became concerned that the American driver could end up hurting someone, so he followed to her destination (her house), where the two argued. The complainant filed a police report about the incident the next day. The mediation occurred in a seated circle in a private room of the police station. The participants were the complainant, the female navy officer, two community liaison officers from the U.S. Navy (one American, one Bahraini), and the police mediator. The mediation occurred in English and Arabic—all participants could use both languages except the naval employee, who relied on one of the navy community liaison officers for translations from Arabic to English and vice versa.

The complainant indicated that he did not know the identity of the reckless driver until the argument ensued. Subsequently, he became upset that an American—a guest in his country—would put his family and Bahraini people in general at risk on the roads. The complainant, though agreeing to the mediation, desired to take the case to the public prosecutor. The American naval employee seemed silent, distraught, and seemingly unapologetic during most of the mediation. The naval liaison officers explained that the employee was indeed apologetic, under stress, and in need of counseling (which was to be provided). One officer said, "The Navy takes this seriously and is very concerned about the message her behavior sends to the community."*

The police mediator hoped to convince the complainant to solve this informally without prosecution. He indicated that the traffic police should have been called from the road in order to intervene and that the complainant, though morally justified in his concern,

* Author's translation.

took matters into his own hands by following the American driver home and arguing with her. Further, because the traffic police were not called on the spot, the allegation that the American may have been under the influence of alcohol could not be confirmed. The mediator pressed the female naval employee to apologize. He reprimanded her for her reckless driving, which showed disrespect to the local people. She ultimately apologized, seemingly reluctantly and with coaching from the community liaison officers. Ultimately, the outcome of the case was filed as *tanazul*, and a *mahdar salih* (peace report) was signed by both parties.

In observing the mediation session, it was apparent that the police mediator's credibility was known and respected by the complainant. This was instrumental in convincing the complainant to agree not to take the case to court. It also was instrumental in providing a safe space for the complainant to air his concerns to the American naval employee directly. As a local community member, the mediator understood the importance of sending the message to the American that respecting local people mattered. Underlying the incident was a more generalized critique on the part of the complainant that American service people deployed to Bahrain often did not show respect for local people in general when they engaged in certain behavior, including being inebriated, which, though legal, according to Bahraini laws and customs, should not be publicly displayed and certainly not endanger others. Although this mediation session was a prime example of the modern legacy of a long history of Bahraini dispute resolution practices being used to confront community wrongdoing, it was never considered a part of the new community policing program, nor are police mediators necessarily community police officers. Instead, this practice exists in local police stations where credible police mediators have emerged and where the local police leadership approves of such practices as a means of potentially diverting cases from public prosecution. The practice, though diminished from colonial and precolonial times, has managed to hold on in a diminished form. Interestingly, it is a practice that often remains unnoticed by outsiders who consult with the Bahrain government about mediation. At least one mediation effort in Bahrain has been imposed by Westerners under the assumption that similar processes were not already extant in Bahrain, a joint initiative by the American Bar Association and the Bahraini Ministry of Justice as part of its Rule of Law program. The program, undertaken in 2007, involved law clerks in family mediation techniques (American Bar Association 2007)—techniques from the American system that were developed by mediators only in the last few decades. Absent from any consideration in this program were any indigenous strategies for mediation that were being practiced contemporaneously, such as in the local police stations, that may have cultural antecedents in Bahrain. Although not lost, Bahraini mediation efforts seem to be forgotten as something that deserves institutional respect and official development. A similar program to develop commercial arbitration by a Bahraini law firm heavily staffed by Western expatriates also failed to acknowledge any local practices of commercial dispute resolution when, in fact, the now-defunct pearl-diving industry had extensive commercial dispute resolution customs firmly rooted in the local norms (Belgrave 1960).

What Is Modern Is Better: Downplaying Indigenous Practices

For the Bahrain government, what is modern is generally preferred. The aspiration to be considered a fully modern state by outsiders has led to such recent events as the building of an impressive, skyscraping world trade center and the hosting of yearly Formula One car races. Under this logic, if community policing is a new strategy learned from the West, it must matter only in so much as it is considered modern and trendy. Given the newness of the state itself, this might not be surprising. Historically speaking, the ruling family, and the Sunni citizens they have since attracted, are late arrivals to the Bahrain archipelago and are less indigenous than the *Shi'a* population. Though both sects had similar cultural practices around dispute resolution in the context of tribal and village small-scale societies, the Sunni, in being shored up by British colonial powers, threw their lot in with modernization. In doing so, their legitimacy over the preceding two centuries has largely been derived not from local buy-in, but, rather, through careful alignment with the British during colonial times and the Americans after independence. The government's inclination to look outward for external legitimation, rather than inward, means that it will continually favor external, global, Western trends in policing over any return to or revival of indigenous practices.

The need for external legitimacy makes Bahrain, like many postcolonial states, susceptible to cultural transplants like community policing, adopting them in a way that makes more sense in the Western contexts from whence they came. Indeed, the persistence of community-based mediation, though suppressed, in local police stations would have been a natural foundation to develop a Bahrain-specific community policing program. Legal scholar Robert B. Porter, in discussing the Seneca tribal context in the northeast United States, has explained that the Anglo-American criminal justice system adopted by the Seneca has helped them to assimilate into the larger American national culture. They adopted the American system of justice as

> ...structured aggression in which the parties, assisted by lawyers, engage in a self-interested pursuit of justice... [and through court proceedings] render a decision as to who is the ultimate "winner," a result that is enforced by the state. (Porter 1996–1997)

This was in direct contrast to Seneca values of justice for the benefit of the community, rather than individuals. It was also counter to the principles of finding mutually beneficial solutions through a mediator who is known to the disputing parties, draws on oral rather than written tradition, and has legitimacy through organic social and kinship networks. Although the widespread suppression of indigenous dispute resolution happened a century earlier in New York State than in Bahrain, a similar fissure is at work in a broad sense, as local community dispute resolvers (whether *shaykh*s, *qadi*s, or *ulema*) were stripped of their authority with the onset of modern policing and court systems. As theorist Gayatri Chakravorty Spivak (1999) has argued, such imperial encounters cannot easily be undone if at all. Further, the hybridity created by colonial disruptions spurns delicate power balances after independence, involving precarious national governments more empowered by their connections to the West than by forms of local legitimacy. Indeed, community-oriented police strategies are highly politicized and, in contested spaces, are directly related to much larger issues of national sovereignty.

In Bahrain, embracing a truer form of community policing grounded in traditional mediation practices would be to give legitimacy to the practices of the very communities that are currently demonstrating against the state. In shoring up the nation-state in Bahrain, external pressure for democratization of policing through community policing cannot go deep into the community without giving power to local forces that threaten the legitimacy of the nation-state itself. Community policing in Bahrain, therefore, is likely to continue to be an ironic parallel to the rise of paramilitary policing and be used primarily for managing public relations—a key power maintenance strategy for police in a state undergoing a profound crisis in political legitimacy.

References

Abu-Lughod, L. (1998). Feminist longings and post-colonial conditions. In L. Abu-Lughod, *Remaking Women: Feminism and Modernity in the Middle East* (pp. 3–31). Princeton, NJ: Princeton University Press.

American Bar Association. (2007, August 20). *Bahraini Legal Clerks Receive Family Mediation Training.* Retrieved March 26, 2012, from http://www.americanbar.org/advocacy/rule_of_law/where_we_work/middle_east/bahrain/news/news_bahrain_practical_skills_trainings_0310.html.

Bahrain Independent Commission of Inquiry. (2011, November 23). *Report of the Bahrain Independent Commission of Inquiry.* Retrieved 26 March, 2012, from http://www.bici.org.bh/BICIreportEN.pdf.

Belgrave, C. (1960). *Personal Column.* London: Hutchinson & Co.

Blomfield, A. (2011, June 2). *Female Poet Brought Before Bahrain Military Tribunal.* Retrieved March 26, 2012, from http://www.telegraph.co.uk/news/worldnews/middleeast/bahrain/8552429/Female-poet-brought-before-Bahrain-military-tribunal.html.

Central Intelligence Agency. (2012, February 15). *Bahrain.* Retrieved March 23, 2012, from https://www.cia.gov/library/publications/the-world-factbook/geos/ba.html.

Cooper, C. (2000). Training police officers to mediate disputes. *Law Enforcement Bulletin, 69,* 7–10.

Esposito, J. (1988). *Islam: The Straight Path.* Oxford: Oxford University Press.

Fakhri, A. (2005, April 13). New unit will be "model for the nation." *Gulf Daily News,* p. 1.

Halstead, A., Bromley, M., & Cochran, J. (2000). The effects of work orientations on job satisfaction among sheriff's deputies practicing community-oriented policing. *Policing: An International Journal of Police Strategies and Management, 23,* 82–104.

Hamada, S. (2005, September 22). First batch of 190 community police personnel graduates. *Bahrain Tribune,* p. 3.

Hammond, A. (2012, February 15). *Bahraini Police Disperse Protests on First Anniversary of Uprising: Shi'ites Are Growing Increasingly Angry at Poor Treatment by Sunni Monority.* Retrieved February 27, 2012, from http:www.ottawacitizen.com.

Jones, C. (2011, December 2). *Former Metropolitan Police Chief John Yates Hired by Bahrain to Reform Force.* Retrieved March 26, 2012, from http://www.guardian.co.uk/uk/2011/dec/03/john-yates-bahrain-police-force.

Khuri, F. (1980). *Tribe and State in Bahrain.* Chicago: University of Chicago.

Kraska, P. (1996). Enjoying militarism: Political/personal dilemmas in studying U.S. police pramilitary units. *Justice Quarterly, 13(3),* 405–429.

Kraska, P., & Paulsen, D. (1997). Grounded research into U.S. paramilitary policing: Forging the iron fist inside the velvet glove. *Policing and Society, 7(4),* 253–270.

Lienhardt, P. (2001). *Shaikhdoms of Eastern Arabia.* New York: Palgrave.

Meyer, J., Paul, R., & Grant, D. (2009). Peacekeepers turned peacemakers: Police as mediators. *Contemporary Justice Review, 12(3),* 331–344.

National Public Radio. (2012, January 18). *Timoney Discusses New Job Training Bahraini Police.* Retrieved March 26, 2012, from http://www.npr.org/2012/01/18/145413376/timoney-discusses-bahraini-police-force.

New York Times. (2012, March 9). *Bahrain—The Profest.* Retrieved March 24, 2012, from http://topics.nytimes.com/top/news/international/countriesandterritories/bahrain/index.html.

Onley, J., & Khalaf, S. (2007). Shaikhly authority in the pre-oil Gulf: An historical–anthropological study. *History and Anthropology, 17(3),* 189–208.

Peterson, J. (1991). The Arabian peninsula in modern times: A historigraphical survey. *The American Historical Review, 96(5)*, 1435–1449.

Porter, R. (1996–1997). Strengthening tribal sovereignty through peacemaking: How the Anglo-American legal tradition destroys indigenous societies. *Columbia Human Rights Law Review, 28*, 235–305.

Rowe, K. (1985). The limits of the neighborhood justice center: Why domestic violence cases should not be mediated. *Emory Law Journal*, 855–910.

Said, E. (1993). *Culture and Imperialism*. London: Vintage.

Seikaly, M. (1994). Women and social change in Bahrain. *International Journal of Middle Eastern Studies, 26(3)*, 415–426.

Sinclair, G., & Williams, C. (2007). "Home and away": The cross-fertilization between "colonial" and "British" policing. *Journal of Imperial and Commonwealth History, 35(2)*, 221–238.

Spivak, G. (1999). *A Critique of Postcolonial Reason: Toward a History of the Vanishing Present*. Cambridge, MA: Harvard University Press.

Strobl, S. (2007). Women and policing in Bahrain. Unpublished dissertation, City University of New York Graduate Center, NY.

Strobl, S. (2008). The Women's Police Directorate in Bahrain: An ethnographic exploration of gender segregation and the likelihood of future integration. *International Criminal Justice Review, 18*, 39–58.

Strobl, S. (2011). From colonial policing to community policing in Bahrain: The historical persistence of sectarianism. *International Journal of Comparative and Applied Criminal Justice, 35(1)*, 19–37.

Syeed-Miller, N. (2006). Developing appropriate dispute resolution systems for law enforcement and community relations: The Pasadena case study. *Ohio State Journal on Dispute Resolution, 22(1)*, 83–103.

Tilly, C. (1985). War making and state making as organized crime. In P. Evans, D. Rueschmeyer, & T. Skocpol, *Bringing the State Back In* (pp. 169–187). Cambridge, MA: Cambridge University Press.

Toumi, H. (2012, January 9). *Bahrain to Recruit 500 Policemen from Both Communities in Fresh Start*. Retrieved March 24, 2012, from http://gulfnews.com/news/gulf/bahrain/bahrain-to-recruit-500-policemen-from-both-communities-in-fresh-start-1.959734.

Vila, S. (2011, March 30). *Bahrain's Most Popular Blogger Arrested*. Retrieved March 26, 2012, from http://www.movements.org/blog/entry/bahrains-most-popular-blogger-arrested/.

Volpe, M., & Phillips, N. (2003). Police use of mediation. *Conflict Resolution Quarterly, 21(2)*, 263–267.

Webb, V., & Katz, C. (1997). Citizen ratings on the importance of community policing activities. *Policing: An International Journal of Police Strategy and Management, 20(1)*, 7–23.

Yassine, N. (1999). Arab political dispute resolution. Doctoral dissertation, Wayne State University, Detroit, MI. UMI/Pro-Quest. http://wwwlib.umi.com/dissertations/fullcit/9954227.

Gambia

2

PA MUSA JOBARTEH

Contents

Background

The Gambia is a former colony of Britain located on the West Coast of Africa. It gained independence from Britain in 1965 and became a Republic in 1970, with an elected president as head of state. It has a land size of about 11,000 km^2 (approximately 4100 mi.^{2}) with an estimated population of 1.7 million people (CIA 2011). A river runs through its entire length emptying into the Atlantic Ocean. It is a country surrounded by Senegal on all parts except for the outlet into the Atlantic Ocean, which is why some describe it as the "tongue in Senegal's mouth."

The Gambia inherited most of its modern system of democratic governance from the British. Most of the institutions of the government such as the police continue to operate in some modified version of the British system. The Gambia Police Force (GPF), as it is called, is a centralized organization with its headquarters in the capital city of Banjul. The Constitution established a Police Council that advises the President on policy matters relating to national internal security (The Republic of The Gambia 1997 Constitution) and any such matter relating to policing. The chief of police officers of Gambia, known as the inspector general of police (IGP) and deputy inspector general (DIG), are appointed by the president in consultation with a National Police Council. There is no evidence to suggest that the National Police Council is active; however the National Security Council that brings all the security chiefs and key security stakeholders together meets regularly under the chairmanship of the vice president. As prescribed in the 1997 Constitution, s.178 (3), "No person or authority shall raise any other police force or service except by or under the authority of an Act of the National Assembly."

The Gambia is divided into five regions comprising of eight local government area councils. The regions are headed by a governor appointed by the president, with the area councils headed by a mayor or chairman. Each of the councils is further divided into districts headed by a local chief known as a *Seyfo*, appointed by the president, and villages headed by an *Alkalo* who is appointed by the minister of local government (The Gambia Local Government Act 2002). The Alkalos are generally the first point of call for settling local crime and disputes. In Gambia, there is a general expectation of the public to exercise the right to police their own communities because the police are not readily available everywhere.

About 50% of Gambians live in the rural villages (CIA 2011) engaged mainly in agricultural activities such as farming and cattle rearing. There are eight main ethnic groups, comprising the Mandingo (42%), Fula (18%), Wolof (16%), Jola (10%), Serahule (9%), and others (4%) (CIA 2011).

Gambia is a secular society, and its people pride themselves on the level of religious tolerance and interfaith mixing; however, religion still dictates the way of life of the majority. About 90% of the population are Muslims, with 8% Christians and 1% other faiths, including traditional practices (CIA 2011). There is abundant evidence in Islam that supports the existence of policing and religion as a means to social control, and morality is still a key consideration for many in Gambian society, particularly in the rural areas. However, the influence of religion on policing has its limits as the overall matter of policing is reserved to the state.

For policing purposes, the GPF is divided into nine police administrative boroughs strategically located in the following key towns and city, which sort of mirror the administrative capitals of the various local government area councils: Banjul Police HQ, Serekeunda (being the biggest city in the country and not necessarily the seat of a council), Brikama, Basse, Mansakonko Janjanburay, Kerewan, Kuntaur, and Kanifing Police, the latter hosting the Police Intervention Unit (PIU), which is a paramilitary armed unit (Gambia Police Force Five Years Strategic Development Plan 2002–2007). The 5-year plan is not a publicly available document, but it is an authoritative document that is relied upon to inform the annual ministerial budget speeches; see for example the 2004 Budget Speech, which is accessible online and mentions the government's commitment to community policing.

Origin of Community Policing

Community policing exists in Gambia. The question is whether the method in practice meets the theoretical description of the modern concept of the idea. Community policing as a new concept of modern policing is relatively new to the Gambia police but a highly acclaimed idea, which unfortunately is mostly misapplied or muddled up in practice. Gambia, as mentioned above, has inherited its policing model from the British, which remains mostly the case to date. In essence, community policing and policing strategies in Gambia in general are mainly a version of what has been adopted from the Western systems plus bits of what has been informally reserved or devolved to local communities as a result of custom, tradition, and religious influences. The informal devolving or relegation of certain police function to communities in Gambia would be a stark contrast to what in the Western sense would otherwise be considered a key police responsibility. However, this is perhaps the best example of what can be understood in the Gambian context as community policing in practice.

In 2005, through a Canadian International Development Agency grant, community policing was trialed under a project named Community-Based Policing and Restorative Justice in Gambia, by Dr. Stephen Perrott (2009).

According to Perrott (2009), supported by some of his comments in other magazine and online reviews, the project was premised on the notion that future prosperity in Gambia depends on its people feeling safe and perceiving that they have a stake and voice in the activities of a fair and competent police force. And perhaps in anticipation, Perrott said: "Because the police are only part of the equation in community policing, the project will assist with initiatives to encourage the public at large to become a partner in crime prevention and the larger service mandate now being fulfilled by Western forces." Some of the project activities involved providing practical training for front-line officers, a certificate program in community policing, and restorative justice that was to be developed and offered jointly by the GPF and Gambia College. The project focused on working with officers and community members in the capital city of Banjul and two rural towns.

Perrott shared his experience that, in Gambia, many criminal matters never come to the attention of the police but are settled by a council of elders under the leadership of Alkalos or regional chiefs, which in itself is a factual statement attesting to the existence of community policing in some form in Gambia. Before Perrott's study, which was a 5-year longitudinal study, there has never been any such focused examination of community policing in Gambia, except for the occasional mention of some elements of community policing in the media and other research works. However, it is this author's view that Perrott's disappointment in achieving his project objectives has been one of the best indicators of the existence of community policing in Gambia.

As stated above, community policing does exist in Gambia, and it would be wrong to think that the concept was imposed or imported. Gambian tradition, culture, and religious inclination by default have some of the concepts of community policing already embedded in them. In Gambia, although the police are stationed throughout all the regions, not all areas are easily accessible due in part to lack of police resources and poor road infrastructure. Therefore, in most of rural Gambia where there is no police presence, community members are the first responders to all sorts of crimes, and the village Alkalo is the first-tier adjudicator.

It is, however, obvious that, in Gambia, the concept of community policing, though very much diluted by the several indigenous structures, customs, religion, and traditions, does play an important and recognized role in the overall criminal justice system.

Policing in Gambia, as in most developing countries, is a highly centralized and politically controlled organization. This is supported by Perrott's (2009) observation, which gave the picture of a militaristic-style GPF with "a cultural orientation that shapes social interactions in many parts of the developing world characterized by rigid hierarchies and strict adherence to the power of the status and rank," which according to Perrott are "at odds with [his] intended [project goals] and impede progress." The role of communities as partners in policing in Gambia is a concept applied in a very different manner. Though the informal community policing methods in practice are not enshrined in the formal policing strategies, they are widely accepted but balanced by a degree of self-censorship.

How Does Community Policing Work?

Community policing as defined by the U.S. Department of Justice (2012) is a philosophy that promotes organizational strategies, which support the systematic use of partnerships and problem-solving techniques, to proactively address the immediate conditions that give rise to public safety issues such as crime, social disorder, and fear of crime. Notably, other common key words associated with the concept of community policing include decentralization, foot patrol, and crime prevention.

Based on the above definition and with the key words in mind, this section will attempt to share an understanding of how community policing is manifested in Gambian society by looking at how some of its different elements and concepts are played out in the local society.

Community Policing as a Philosophy

This suggests some form of citizen input and partnership in policing communities. Due in part to its custom and tradition, communities in Gambia do exercise some rights to self-police. Such rights are recognized and generally accepted by society at large, including the key player in the criminal justice system. Regardless of the recognition of this right of communities to self-police, just like in any partnership, communities are very clear of their unwritten share of the policing pie. The GPF without doubt puts a lot of effort to introduce several methods of what is understood locally by officer and communities alike as community policing. The police take any opportunity including initiatives undertaken by Perrott and his group to attract media headlines in promoting the concept of community policing.

There is no formal recruitment of volunteers for community policing purposes, but the very nature of rural communities and their involvement in dealing with local issues are known to be narrated and understood by many as community policing at an informal level.

Community Policing as Crime Prevention

Although police are stationed throughout the country, because of the lack of resources such as vehicles and because poor roads in most rural areas in Gambia are hard to access, when a crime occurs in most parts of the country, local communities are understood to be the first to respond and, where necessary, do a citizen's arrest and involve the police at their discretion depending on the nature and extent of the offense. In Gambia, it is accepted within the general criminal justice system that the police can reasonably deal with some but not all community problems, such that even in the urban areas, several minor crimes that may require police intervention are relegated to the community to deal with.

Decentralization of Police Powers

This suggests community empowerment by giving up some police powers to communities and devolving power internally to the rank and file, such that junior officers on the beat and the communities they work with can lead on dealing with minor local issues without management interference. If one were to ask the GPF whether power is decentralized within the understood concept of community policing, the answer would be a resounding yes. Is it decentralized enough? Perhaps not, but given the complex construct nature of Gambian society with its culture, tradition, and widely dispersed rural nature of communities, a lot of police powers are decentralized. An ordinary police officer in the rural areas is a highly respected person of authority and power. Such an officer knows how to share and exercise power. Communities are always at the core of how police exercise their power. How these power relationships are put into play is a unique partnership of its own.

Another interesting look at community policing in Gambia by Davidheiser (2005) shares that in his "two-year study of mediation among rural villagers in Gambia, [he] found stark contrasts to popular American beliefs regarding disputing and peacemaking.... Gambians frequently focused more on reconciliation than on bargaining or working out the issues." Furthermore, this strongly reflects Gambian society's expectation of how communities have a key role in avoiding engagement of the criminal justice system.

Foot Patrol

Foot patrol has always been recognized as one of the basic signs of community policing in practice, and by foot patrol, there is the suggestion of police presence and visibility at the local level. If foot patrol is one of the best examples of community policing, then Gambia qualifies. A regular police officer is not armed, and due in part to scarce police resources such as motor vehicles, the life of the police officer in Gambia is doomed to foot patrol. Access to a police car is limited to a few senior officers or assigned to specific police stations or units. It is firsthand knowledge to this author as a former senior member of the immigration police that officers are regularly deployed to different sectors of the community, maintaining high visibility in the urban areas and strategic locations including hospitals. More than 90% of officers on the beat are on foot patrol in the communities, particularly in the busy market areas and major shopping districts. Police are highly visible in major towns where they are stationed, and it is common to come across police checkpoints or find an officer hanging out with a neighborhood crowd or sitting at a shop chatting with business people. Whether the motive of the officers on patrol is to engage in the desired effects of community policing through foot patrol is a matter that is highly questionable, but their mere presence in communities, engaging, familiarizing with, and building relationships, does in fact satisfy the need for the police to know their local community, maintain a presence, and perhaps, questionable as it may be, win their trust and confidence. However, the high visibility of officers of the GPF may not be a strategy designed to meet the requirements of the modern concept of community policing, but the mere existence of the practice does qualify it as some form of community policing.

Responding to Calls for Service

Generally, the police in Gambia are limited by access to a vehicle, but they would normally respond to calls for service where the issue involves a serious criminal matter; in their absence, one can always count on the local community member to take up their local community police duty. Unfortunately, the motive for police response to calls for service is mostly influenced by external factors not related to policing strategies. Some of these factors would include the nature and extent of the crime and how well connected the victim is.

Effectiveness of Community Policing

Crime in Gambia is at a very low level compared to most African countries, and this more so in the rural parts of the country. Gambia prides itself on being one of the most peaceful countries in the world, and this can be attributed mostly to the level of tolerance in how society, through its tradition, religion, and customs, is allowed in some form to control local crime and disorder. Communities and community leaders play a key role in the monitoring and controlling of local crime-related problems and disorder, and in doing so, they exercise lots of discretion as to when to engage the formal criminal justice process. Local communities in essence are allowed lots of leverage in dealing with community-based low-level crime. They exercise several informal means of intervention, which contribute to reducing the number of crimes that end up in trial, thus saving the courts and the state cost and reducing caseloads.

Both Perrott (2009) and Davidheiser (2005) gave us some indication of community policing in Gambia. But to fully appreciate the context in which community policing is understood, one would require a historical review of the local press with its several examples of media stories that have been dubbed under the front-page headlines "community policing." Most of these media stories reflect the very understanding of the concept by the police, which, if to be described accurately, are nothing more than crime-fighting stories. The police are also in the habit of making public statements to the media about some policing operation or initiative undertaken, which may not necessarily qualify in full as community policing..

Conclusions

Community policing in Gambia does not manifest itself in the same manner as it is known in the Western context. Based on the understanding that community policing comprises elements already existing in Gambia, it can be best described as a process that continues to exist in parallel with the formal policing system, with the latter accepting the informal system as something tolerable so long as it does not infringe on the formal law enforcement process.

One of the most common definitions of community policing includes an understanding that it is a philosophy with practical strategies that complement each other to produce a desired policing system and suit a given community. Some of the common strategies include citizen empowerment, partnership working, police visibility in communities through foot patrol, and the decentralization of police powers. No matter how well understood the concept is around the world, it cannot escape a very simple definition coined by the father of modern policing: according to Sir Robert Peel (1829), "the police are the people and the people are the police," and for this reason, community policing will always have some presence anywhere in rural-based communities.

As mentioned above, community policing or aspects of it have always existed as a form of the informal law enforcement and criminal justice management system of Gambia. It is not something fully embedded as part of the formal policing service, and with some credit to the GPF, there are some elements of the modern model of community policing in practice that can be encouraged. The question is whether the methods in practice within the formal process conform to the main objectives of modern community policing, and the answer would be yes but to a very minimum.

In essence, in Gambia, community policing will survive not as a project, but as one that should adapt to what already exists and promote those elements that are already in practice, and gradually, the results can be sustained and measurable.

References

CIA. 2011. *The World Factbook*. https://www.cia.gov/library/publications/the-world-factbook/geos/ga.html (accessed February 2012).

Davidheiser, M. 2005. Mediation and multiculturalism: Domestic and international challenges. *Beyond Intractability*, eds. G. Burgess and H. Burgess. Conflict Research Consortium, University of Colorado, Boulder. http://www.beyondintractability.org/bi-essay/mediation_multiculturalism (accessed December 2011).

The Gambia Local Government Act 2002.

Perrott, S.B. 2009. Vertical collectivism as an obstacle to democratic policing and restorative justice in the Gambia: Africa Peace and Conflict Network, Occasional Paper No. 3. http://www.africapeace.org/home/content/o/l/u/oluwakorede/html/images/file/FINAL%20Perrott%20Occ%20Paper%20Formatted&ready_(1).pdf (accessed January 2012).

Saliu, Y.S. 2009. Crime Watch: Community policing in crime prevention: Another effective way of controlling and preventing crime in our community is through community based policing. *The Daily Observer*. 30th July.

The Point Newspaper Online. 2010. Settling conflict at community level. 9th Dec. http://thepoint.gm/africa/gambia/article/settling-disputes-at-community-level.

The Republic of The Gambia 1997 Constitution.

U.S. Department of Justice. 2012. Community Oriented Policing Services. http://www.cops.usdoj.gov/default.asp?item=36 (accessed January 2012).

Lebanon
Community Policing in Nahr al Bared Refugee Camp

3

NABIL OUASSINI

Contents

Introduction

Located between the crossroads of the Mediterranean Sea, and the countries of Israel and Syria, Lebanon is a strategically situated country in the Middle East that is a product of multiple civilizations and cultures. As the Arab world's most religiously diverse country, Lebanon has 18 officially recognized sects. The largest of these sects consist of Shiite and Sunni Muslims, Maronites, and Greek Orthodox Christians, as well as other religious sects including the Druze, Baha'is, Buddhists, Hindus, and Jews. Lebanon is also home to a mixture of indigenous ethnicities that include Arabs, Armenians, Assyrians, Greeks, Kurds, and Turks. Palestinian refugees constitute the largest minority group in Lebanon, migrating after the Nakba (the Palestinian Catastrophe) in 1948 and the Six-Day War in 1967. In recent years, many migrant workers from around the world have also settled in Lebanon to make a living.

Historically, Lebanon was ruled by the Ottoman Empire from the sixteenth century to the end of World War I. The Lebanese first adopted a police system during the reign of Emir Fakhredine II in the early seventeenth century and established its first modern police force in 1861 with the creation of the Lebanese Gendarmerie (Internal Security Forces 2005). After Turkey's defeat in World War I, Lebanon was mandated to the French, and the police forces were reorganized and based on the French system. The French mandate lasted until 1943, when Lebanon achieved independence.

Upon attaining independence, the Lebanese established a confessional democracy by distributing political and administrative functions based on the proportion of its religious communities. The unwritten agreement known as the National Pact required that the president be a Maronite Christian, the prime minister a Sunni, and the president of the National Assembly a Shiite. The agreement also included a confessional formula that divided the seats in parliament between Christians and Muslims by a ratio of six to five. The confessional system eventually spread to other institutions including the police and the gendarmerie, which later integrated to form the Internal Security Forces (ISF). The ISF recruited a fixed portion from Lebanon's religious groups and assigned officers to work in communities that included members of their own religion. Through the first two decades after independence, both the ISF and the Lebanese Armed Forces (LAF) arbitrated between the various political parties, and the LAF's internal security services, the Second Bureau or *Deuxie`me Bureau*, were in charge of security in the numerous Palestinian refugee camps set up in different parts of the country. In the aftermath of the Six-Day War, Palestinian resistance groups assembled in Lebanon, and the LAF signed the Cairo Agreement in 1969 agreeing to withdraw from Palestinian refugee camps completely while permitting the Palestinian Liberation Organization (PLO) to provide internal security. The growth of Palestinian activity in Lebanon was seen by some religious groups as an opportunity, while others sensitive to the country's gradual change in demographics perceived the growth as a threat. These issues along with numerous other political and economic factors led to the Lebanese Civil War in 1975 where both the LAF and ISF weakened and were no longer viable institutions. The LAF was perceived as an apparatus for the Maronite president, while most ISF officers defected to sectarian militias.

At the end of the Lebanese Civil War, members from Lebanon's parliamentarians, political parties, militias, and leaders reached a new compromise known as the Taif Agreement. The agreement addressed the structure of the political system, the disparities between confessions, and the overall sovereignty of the country after the intervention of foreign states in Lebanon's internal affairs. The LAF and the ISF continued to consist of a multisectarian force that recruited members according to the new confessional ratio of one to one between Christians and Muslims. The expulsion of the PLO leadership from Lebanon to Tunisia during the civil war and the Lebanese government's decision to withdraw from the Cairo Agreement gave the LAF and ISF complete jurisdiction over Palestinian refugee camps. Yet, the LAF and ISF continued to refrain from exercising authority over the camps, allowing Palestinian popular committees to control the camp politically while Palestinian security committees policed the camps. In 2005, the Council of Ministers and former Prime Minister Fouad Siniora established the Lebanese–Palestinian Dialogue Committee (LPDC) and permitted the PLO to reopen an office in Beirut the following year as a means of improving relations between the Lebanese and Palestinian governments.

Many challenges continue to exist for both the LAF and ISF. The confessional system that was set up as a temporary arrangement between religious sects after independence continues to dominate both Lebanese politics and security. One of the greatest challenges to policing in Lebanon is linked to the influence and involvement of foreign countries on Lebanese internal affairs. The Cedar Revolution, the conflict between Hezbollah and Israel in 2006, and the 2008 Doha Agreement are recent examples of how the divisions in Lebanon can lead to further violence at any time. Although these events continue to shape policing in Lebanon, it was the conflict between Islamic extremists and the LAF in the Nahr al Bared Palestinian refugee camp that introduced Lebanese police forces to the concept of community policing.

Although Lebanon is a diverse nation of different religions and ethnic groups, the concept of community policing was introduced into Lebanon only after the conflict in the Nahr al Bared refugee camp (NBC). The NBC is a Palestinian refugee camp in Northern Lebanon that was established in 1949 and is home to nearly 30,000 residents. The tension began when Fatah al Islam, an armed Islamic extremist group with an ideological link to al-Qaeda, overran the NBC.

According to Rougier (2008), the group wanted to establish their own interpretation of Islamic law and institute a military training program for global jihad under the guise of Palestinian nationalism (as cited in Hanafi 2010). The residents of the NBC struggled to drive members of Fatah al Islam out of their camp and even engaged in armed skirmishes with the militants in an attempt to take back control (Abboud 2009). However, the NBC's popular and security committees did not have the adequate training or the organizational capacity to handle the incursion. The security void that existed in the NBC was attributed to the absence of the rule of law, the nonexistence of a unified Palestinian leadership, and the lack of control of arms into the camps (United Nations Relief and Works Agency [UNRWA] 2008). Rougier (2008) describes how the NBC solicited the Lebanese government to intercede, but it refused to get involved in what it described as an internal Palestinian power struggle in spite of the fact that members of Fatah al Islam were predominantly composed of non-Palestinians (as cited in Hanafi 2010). The Lebanese government's indifference toward the crisis forced the head of the NBC's popular committee to resign in protest (Hanafi 2010).

The conflict between the Lebanese government and Fatah al Islam occurred after militants killed 13 Lebanese soldiers at a military checkpoint in retaliation for a prior raid by the LAF on an apartment building belonging to members of the extremist group. For the next 3 months, in the first instance of police force used against a Palestinian camp in decades, the LAF launched heavy artillery attacks on the NBC in an effort to force members of Fatah al Islam out of hiding. In the aftermath, more than 50 civilians from the camp, 179 Lebanese soldiers, and 226 members of Fatah al Islam were killed, and 215 were captured. The conflict had an immense economic and social impact on the 33,000 refugees who fled from the fighting as they witnessed and experienced over $300 million worth of damage to their homes and the NBC (UNRWA 2008).

After the near-complete destruction of the NBC, the LAF took complete control of the camp and prohibited residents from returning to their homes. The NBC turned into a military zone, and all movements in and out of the camp were controlled by the LAF. The Lebanese military has been involved in all aspects of the camp's reconstruction and civil affairs. International organizations led by the UNRWA have also been involved in the process of reconstruction and created the Nahr al Bared Reconstruction Commission for Civil Action and Studies (NBRC) with a focus on aid rather than security in a grassroots partnership with community-based committees in the NBC (UNRWA 2008). In a partnership with UNRWA and the PLO, the Lebanese government designed, negotiated, and approved a reconstruction proposal of the NBC for an international donor's conference planned in Vienna sponsored by the Arab League, the European Union, UNRWA, and the Austrian and Lebanese governments.

Establishment of Community Policing

At the donor conference held in June of 2008, the Lebanese government presented their proposal for the NBC in what was informally called the Vienna document and emphasized security as the main theme guiding the reconstruction of the NBC so that any previous factors that facilitated the takeover by Fatah al Islam would be eliminated forever. The Lebanese government in collaboration with the LPDC and in agreement with the PLO proposed to institute community policing as the main method of reestablishing Lebanese sovereignty over the camps. According to the UNRWA document (2008, p. 51), community policing would build trust, "promote community engagement, partnership and proactive problem solving," and train officers in "problem solving, conflict resolution, and communications skills." The new community police forces within the ISF would be trained on Palestinian cultural, social, and political history and would be sensitive to the needs and views of the refugees given the turbulent relationship between Palestinians and the Lebanese government. All parties in the conference agreed to the document, and $5 million was budgeted for the ISF to train officers in community policing (UNRWA 2008).

In the last few years, the United States has been the training headquarters for the ISF's community policing program in the NBC. After the conference in Vienna, a delegation of senior officers from the ISF toured the United States in a program sponsored by the US Department of State's Bureau of Narcotics and Law Enforcement (Smith 2010). Since 2007, the United States has spent more than $100 million assisting the ISF in training and equipment (Addis 2011). The Department of State's Bureau of International Narcotics and Law Enforcement Affairs (INL) has been actively training the ISF in various community policing strategies and has helped the ISF construct a police station near the camp (Addis 2011). An example of such a program includes a month-long training course at the University of Louisville's Southern Police Institute. In the course, academics and police officers teach courses on crime prevention, democratic policing, ethics, and problem solving that included ride-alongs and field exercises (UofL 2009).

The Vienna document's proposal for the concept of community policing is supported by the Lebanese government and the overall organization of the ISF. The program has generated millions of dollars from the international community in aid, equipment, and training for the ISF. More important, the use of community policing in the NBC addresses all of the Lebanese government's security strategies and goals. Community policing contributes to the plans that the Lebanese government has for reconstruction and security in the camps while improving its image and relations with the residents of the NBC. The security model used in the NBC is an opportunity for the Lebanese government to experiment and transform the way Palestinian refugee camps are run in Lebanon. The Lebanese pilot experiment with community policing has far-reaching implications as the success in the security model designed for the NBC would be replicated in all 12 Palestinian camps in Lebanon.

Despite the international support for the Vienna document, Palestinian refugees contend that the document does not reflect the interests of their community. Through his fieldwork with the NBC refugees, Sari Hanafi (2010), a sociologist from the American University of Beirut, presents numerous reasons why the Palestinians feel that the community policing program developed through the Vienna document serves only the interests of the Lebanese government. In drafting the document, the Lebanese government ignored the popular and security committees, the groups in charge of security and other affairs in the NBC, and consulted only with the PLO. The PLO approved the use of community policing in the Vienna document without conferring with the popular and security committees or anyone from the NBC community. Many members of the NBC had been quite critical of the PLO and did not believe that it represented their views, especially since Mahmoud Abbas, the chairman of the PLO, had openly supported the Lebanese government's excessive use of force against the NBC during the conflict with Fatah al Islam. The NBC community felt that the implementation of the program was being forced on them without their consent. Additionally, the Vienna document gave other external international agencies and nongovernmental organizations a formal role in the reconstruction of the NBC while completely overlooking the role of the popular and security committees.

Thus, the popular and security committees' abilities to repress and prosecute crime had been reduced to a symbolic role devoid of any contribution to the community policing program (Hanafi 2010; Hanafi and Long 2010; Hanafi and Hassan 2009). As Hanafi and Hassan (2010, p. 41) explain, "The document uses the attractive term 'community policing,' with its connotations of community empowerment and citizenship action, but the policing it describes is performed exclusively by the ISF."

The tension and mistrust between the Lebanese government and the NBC community have increased since the Vienna document and are undermining the community policing program at the NBC. Partnerships with leaders and groups in the NBC have remained generally weak. Some members of the PLO and the LPDC have been working in coordination with the ISF while being mistrusted by the NBC community. There have been no official discussions on how the Lebanese attitude to security and reconstruction is causing enmity amongst the refugees or how the Lebanese unnecessarily obliterated the whole camp during the conflict. The interaction between the NBC community and both the LAF and ISF has also been quite negative as many refugees believe that the Lebanese's narrow approach to the destruction and reconstruction of the camp and its circumvention of the popular and security committees during the conflict was a political conspiracy to occupy their camp (Hanafi 2010). Many residents are still apprehensive toward the Lebanese and are wondering why the army is still present in the camp along with the ISF. Both the LAF and ISF patrol the streets of the NBC to keep order by controlling all movement in and out of the camps and by checking whether residents have permission to be in the camp. The description of the interaction between the Lebanese and the refugees is reminiscent of when the Second Bureau or the *Deuxie`me Bureau* ran the security of the refugee camps before the Cairo Agreement. For the residents of the NBC, the approach used by the LAF toward security is an unremitting allegation that they were complicit with the war declared by Fatah al Islam on the LAF.

Furthermore, community members are recruited by the LAF and ISF based on a system of surveillance and intelligence gathering rather than solidarity with members of the community. The ISF has created an environment of suspicion and fear reminiscent of military rule rather than community policing. Informants are recruited by the ISF to report suspicious behaviors and get rewarded with special perks and other benefits for their information including phone cards and special access in and out of the camps (Smith 2010). The LAF and ISF still use popular and security committee members when they are needed as informants or to carry out orders but continue to be marginalized by undercutting their resources or assistance to complete any jobs on their own (Hanafi 2010).

Tensions are further fueled by the fact that access to the NBC is authorized only with permits granted by the LAF at the entrances to the camp. Residents of the NBC have complained that their mistreatment in the LAF checkpoints has caused tremendous rifts and mistrust between them and the LAF (Hanafi and Long 2010). Academics, foreigners, journalists, and activists are especially subject to being denied entry to the camps by the LAF. Human Rights Watch has documented several cases of activists being harassed by LAF officers, including the arrest of a volunteer at the entrance of the NBC only because he published an article criticizing the Lebanese authorities' management of the NBC in the *As-Safir* newspaper (Human Rights Watch [HRW] 2010b). Other well-known cases involve the arrest and interrogations of Ghassan Abdallah and Hatem Meqdadi from the Palestinian Human Rights Organization (PHRO), who were forced to close down their office in the NBC due to the LAF's harassment (HRW 2010a).

Effectiveness of Community Policing

Most research on community policing focuses more on the favorable examples than on the lessons that can be learned from unsuccessful attempts (Lyons 1999). Although further empirical research is needed to measure the effectiveness of this recent program in Lebanon, the initial signs do point to a mere facade to the standards set in the community policing literature. The current initiative by the Lebanese government seems to be a rather forceful form of saturation policing in an area that both the LAF and the ISF have long been absent from. As Barnett and Call (1999) have suggested, the transplanting of a particular model without seriously considering the surrounding conditions can be quite precarious.

The largest impediment to achieving conciliation between the Lebanese authorities and the refugees from the NBC is the suspicion that each community has toward the other. The circumstances before, during, and after the NBC conflict gave plenty of reasons for the residents of the NBC to feel apprehensive toward the Lebanese government's security plans. The manner in which the LAF carried out the campaign against Fatah al Islam was preventable, excessive, and unreservedly disorganized, especially in the indiscriminate bombing of the camp. The NBC's popular and security committee could have helped the LAF in their campaign against Fatah al Islam either through military tactics, since they knew their way around the refugee camp, or by negotiating the terrorists' surrender. In a matter of a few months, everything the NBC refugees built in three generations was razed. The NBC and its refugees experienced what Ramadan (2009, p. 153) describes as "urbicide in a space of exception." NBC refugees felt victimized and persecuted by the same LAF that did not even defend itself against an Israeli offensive only a year prior to the NBC conflict. The unilateral approach to security after the conflict only made matters worse for the NBC refugees. The community policing program assumes that residents of the NBC want close contact with Lebanese authorities when previous research on community policing in minority communities has shown that residents in these communities wanting to work with the police were typically unverified (Skogan and Hartnett 1997). The NBC community is concerned about the potential for abuse by the Lebanese authorities as they continue to be free from accountability since neither the LAF nor the ISF is subject to the scrutiny of the Palestinians or any of their representatives. The LAF and ISF's exclusion of the popular and security committees increases the chances for corruption in the Lebanese forces. Many NBC refugees recount how their houses had been looted and ransacked during the conflict by the same officers who they were now supposed to work with in community policing programs. The popular and security committees were perceived as legitimate in the NBC community because they are both from the same community of people. The committees had an easier time formulating community bonds, and the community experienced fewer cases of police abuse.

Future of Community Policing

The Lebanese mistrust of the NBC refugees stems from its blaming the Palestinians for the cause of its multifaceted civil war and its 22-year occupation by Israel. The Lebanese feel that they have paid more than their share of dues to the Palestinian cause compared to other nations in the Arab world. The antagonism transcends all groups in Lebanon as the suggestion of *towteen* or the permanent settling of the Palestinian refugees in Lebanon continues to be a political issue that all of Lebanon's different confessions can unite behind (Nasrallah 1997). The Lebanese perceptions that the Palestinian refugees threaten their sovereignty and interfere with the nation's confessional system are the reasons why the Lebanese continue to handle the reconstruction of the NBC only through the position of security. This lack of trust will continue to undermine any efforts in community policing that will be made by the ISF toward the NBC. The ISF must be able to engage all groups in the community and expand its interaction with a variety of community leaders in order for it to be perceived as a professional police force by the NBC community (Shusta et al. 2002). Under these conditions, the United States can ensure that the ISF implement its training by serving the NBC's needs rather than its own short-term interests by featuring an evaluation conducted by Palestinian groups on the Lebanese efforts in community policing. By overlooking the NBC community in the formulation of the Vienna document and the reconstruction of their camp, the Lebanese government has already launched their community policing program on the wrong track.

Any dialogue on community policing in the NBC must address the issue of Palestinian rights and must be realistic enough to know that in this context, the social and political inequalities that exist among Palestinian refugees in Lebanon will lead to the program's failure. The NBC community must have a say in all of its affairs and should not have to submit docilely to whatever the Lebanese choose for it. Without negating their right to negotiate with Israel for a future state, the NBC refugees should be entitled to more than just aid from international organizations and security from the Lebanese. Similar to Skogan and Hartnett's (1997) study in Chicago, the mending of relations in this case needs more than just community policing. Community policing programs cannot address all the other fundamental problems that Palestinian refugees face, including discrimination, poverty, and unemployment. Human rights reports constantly describe how even after 60 years of living in Lebanon, Palestinian refugees are still kept from the right to work certain professions, face discrimination in the labor market, and are denied the rights to adequate housing, healthcare, or a proper education for many Palestinian children, as well as a list of many other grievances (Amnesty International 2007; HRW 2011).

Finally, the Lebanese must consider a much more holistic socioecological approach to the recovery of the NBC community. This approach was suggested by the PHRO's (2011) latest report on the NBC. The report describes the deteriorating condition of the refugees and advocates for an emphasis on human security rather than state security. Human security in the report consisted of economic, food, health, environmental, community, personal, and political security (PHRO 2011).

References

Abboud, S. (2009). The siege of Nahr al-Bared and the Palestinian refugees in Lebanon. *Arab Studies Quarterly,* 31: 31–48.

Addis, C.L. *U.S. Security Assistance to Lebanon.* CRS Report for Congress, Congressional Research Service, January 19, 2011. Retrieved from http://knxasl.hsdl.org/?view&doc = 137765&coll = limited.

Amnesty International. (2007). *Lebanon—Exiled and Suffering: Palestinian Refugees in Lebanon.* October 17, 2007, MDE 18/010/2007. Retrieved from http://www.amnesty.org/en/library/info/MDE18/010/2007.

Barnett, M., & Call, C.T. (1999). Looking for a few good cops: Peacekeeping, peacebuilding and UN Civilian Police. *International Peace Keeping,* 6(4): 43–68.

Hanafi, S. (2010). Reconstructing and governing Nahr el-Bared camp: Bridge or barrier to inclusion? *ArteEast Quarterly*. Retrieved from http://www.arteeast.org/pages/artenews/extra-territoriality/272/.

Hanafi, S., & Hassan, S. (2009). Constructing and governing Nahr el-Bared camp. An "ideal" model of exclusion. *Majallat al-Dirasat al-Falastiniyya (Journal of Palestine Studies)*, 78: 39–52. (Arabic).

Hanafi, S., & Long, T. (2010). Governance, governmentalities, and the state of exception in the Palestinian refugee camps of Lebanon. *Oxford Refugee Studies*, 34–60.

Human Rights Watch. (2010a). *Lebanon: Cease Harassment of Human Rights Activists for Documenting Torture*. New York: Human Rights Watch. August 4, 2011. Retrieved from http://www.hrw.org/news/2011/08/04/lebanon-cease-harassment-human-rights-activist-documenting-torture.

Human Rights Watch. (2010b). *Lebanon: Critic of Nahr al-Bared Reconstruction Efforts Detained*. New York: Human Rights Watch. August 20, 2010. Retrieved from http://www.hrw.org/news/2010/08/20/lebanon-critic-nahr-al-bared-reconstruction-efforts-detained.

Human Rights Watch. (2011). *World Report 2011: Lebanon*. New York: Human Rights Watch, Inc. Retrieved from http://www.hrw.org/world-report-2011/lebanon.

Internal Security Forces. (2005). November 2, 2011. Retrieved from http://www.isf.gov.lb/English/LeftMenu/General%20Info/History/Pages/History.aspx.

Lyons, W. (1999). *The Politics of Community Policing: Rearranging the Power to Punish*. Ann Arbor, MI: University of Michigan Press.

Nasrallah, F. 1997. Lebanese perceptions of Palestinians in Lebanon. *Journal of Refugee Studies*, 10: 349–359.

Palestinian Human Rights Organization. (2011). *Camp in Fear, Camp in Want Human Security Assessment for Nahr El-Bared Camp*. Beirut: Palestinian Human Rights Organization. March 2011. Retrieved from http://www.palhumanrights.org/rep/ENG/Camp%20in%20Fear-Camp%20in%20Want_Final-A4.pdf.

Ramadan, A. (2009). Destroying Nahr el-Bared: Sovereignty and urbicide in the space of exception [Abstract]. *Political Geography*, 28: 153–163.

Rougier, B. (2008). 'Fatah al-Islam: Un re´seau jihadiste au coeur des contradictions libanaises', in Rougier, B. (ed.) Qu'est-ce le salafisme. Paris: Presses Universitaires de France.

Shusta, R., Levine, D., Harris, D., & Wong, H. (2002). *Multi-cultural Law Enforcement: Strategies for Peacekeeping in a Diverse Society* (2nd ed.). Upper Saddle River, NJ: Prentice Hall.

Skogan, W.G., & Hartnett, S.M. (1997). *Community Policing, Chicago Style*. New York: Oxford University Press.

Smith, R. (2010). *Lebanon Tightens Control over Palestinian Refugee Camps*. Inter Press Service. January 19, 2010. Retrieved from http://electronicintifada.net/content/lebanon-tightens-control-over-palestinian-refugee-camps/8632.

United Nations Relief and Works Agency. (2008). *A Common Challenge. A Shared Responsibility*. New York: United Nations Relief and Works Agency. June 23, 2008. Retrieved from http://www.unrwa.org/userfiles/201001193369.pdf.

UofL Today. (2009, December 4). Lebanese police to apply skills learned at UofL to refugee camps. Retrieved from http://louisville.edu/uofltoday/campus-news/lebanese-police-to-apply-skills-learned-atuofl-to-refugee-camps.

Madagascar

JONAH RATSIMBAZAFY
MEREDITH L. GORE
LALA JEAN RAKOTONIAINA

4

Contents

Background

Madagascar is the fourth-largest island and the largest oceanic island in the world. It is about the size of the state of Texas, covering roughly 225,000 mi.^{2}. Although it is located only 250 mi. off the eastern coast of Africa, Madagascar has been isolated from other land-masses for more than 80 million years, meaning that most of the plant and animal species found there evolved apart from the rest of the world and are unique to the island (Jamal and de Wit 2002; de Wit 2003). It ranks as one of the world's top biodiversity hotspots— geographic regions that harbor the highest concentration of Earth's plant and animals and are at great risk of extinction (Conservation International 2000; Ganzhorn et al. 2000; Meyers et al. 2000; Mittermeier et al. 2010; Raxworthy et al. 2008). Madagascar has huge reserves of natural resources such as gemstones and other minerals. This ecological context has attracted the attention of the international conservation and development communities (Ratsimbazafy 2003).

The Malagasy people are of mixed Asian and African origin, and are thought to have inhabited the island for only 2000 years. Among approximately 20 different Malagasy ethnic groups, Asian features are predominant in the Central Highlands people (e.g., Merina and related Betsileo), while the coastal dwellers (e.g., Sakalava) have African features (Flacourt 1648; Grandidier 1942). The Malagasy language has Polynesian roots, but French and English are also official languages (Tyson 2005). Today, approximately 52% of the population is animist (i.e., has indigenous religious beliefs), 41% is Christian, and 7% Muslim. Madagascar has a high population growth rate (e.g., 3%), an estimated population of 20 million people, a per capita GDP at US$421 in 2010, and an infant mortality rate of 43/1000 births (World Bank 2012).

Formerly an independent kingdom, Madagascar became a French colony in 1886 and regained independence in 1960. During Madagascar's precolonial period, Merina monarchs established hegemony with British assistance. Since reindependence, the Republic of Madagascar has held many presidential elections but has still witnessed multiple political crises. Most recently, in 2009, Madagascar entered into a political crisis termed a coup d'état by the international community. As a large country with poor infrastructure, Madagascar currently has a weak, decentralized government with little effective control in remote areas.

Madagascar's geological, ecological, cultural, and political characteristics create a unique context for community policing. Herein, we discuss key and unique attributes of community policing in Madagascar, including background about state-level police organizations, the characteristics and activities of community-level policing, and the efficacy and limitations of community-level policing. We devote special attention to the role of community policing in conservation because Madagascar's unique natural resources, and the living things that depend on them, face multiple threats. For example, dozens of Malagasy endemic reptiles, birds, and mammals are currently on the verge of extinction due mainly to habitat loss and illegal poaching. The role of community police in conservation and reducing these threats is both unique and essential.

National Police

We begin our discussion by identifying the missions and objectives of the National Police (Police Nationale Malagasy, http://www.policenational.gov.mg), because it collaborates with the CP, and these missions and objectives affect the nature of policing at a community level in Madagascar.

Missions

The missions of the state police are to (1) assure the hierarchical and functional administrative control of the National Police, taking care to conform activities to all relevant laws, regulations, and government decrees; (2) provide support to the federal government in political, social, cultural and economic, national, and international fields; (3) execute the administrative, judicial, and economic police missions, especially with regards to anti-corruption and financial delinquency activities; (4) protect Malagasy territories and borders from illegal immigration and emigration as well as the transnational circulation of people and prohibited or controlled goods; (5) regulate weapons, heavy engines, and other substances that could constitute a threat to national security; (6) assure the security of private organizations and people affected by private enterprise activities; (7) participate in the fight against international crime in any form; and (8) collaborate with other ministerial departments, organizations, and publics to foster respect for and awareness about laws and regulations, prevent delinquency, protect the environment, and protect civilians.

Objectives

The objectives of the National Police are to (1) abide by the constitution and protect the institution of the republic; (2) guarantee the free exercise of collective and individual constitutional liberties; (3) respect the application of laws and regulations; (4) safeguard national sovereignty and the integrity of Malagasy territories; (5) protect people and goods; (6) protect national interests; (7) engage in international efforts against transnational crime; and (8) protect common rights in any form.

Community Police

Community policing in Madagascar must be interpreted within the context of the *fokonolona* (i.e., a group of people living within the same village or Malagasy indigenous community [IC]) (Wright 2010). All members of the *fokonolona* are born and live in the same communal territory. Migrants who establish themselves in that territory, enter in by marriage, or have their descendants born into the community are considered part of the *fokonolona*. Migrants and newcomers to a *fokonolona* integrate easily because the statutes of different communities, one of origin and the other of receipt, are similar. The *fokontany* is the administrative zone harboring all social entities that compose the *fokonolona*.

Three invariable attributes define a *fokonolona* IC, including (1) being the unique, identical, social, and environmental basis of the indigenous multiethnic and multicultural community; (2) maintaining the same model and structure throughout the political history of Madagascar, regardless of geographic region; and (3) having a coherent social unit sufficiently dynamic to accommodate changes in local and environmental development. Aside from these characteristics, the *fokonolona* has three orientations. First, the *fokonolona* possesses unbiased power for territory governance and can distribute resources to members according to traditional rights used for all entities ("COBAs" or community of base roots, segments of lineages, sociocultural associations, socioprofessional groups). Second, within its geographic territory, the *fokonolona* is the only unbiased actor for authorizing development strategies. All environmental and economic initiatives and all benefactor activities must be approved and concretized by the *fokonolona*. Third, the *fokonolona* is the supervisor of all natural resource management zones (e.g., humid, forest, savannah, economic, social, cultural) within its geographic areas. Further, the *fokonolona* has the power to recognize new or different zones within its territory that are beholden to the traditional and legal norms of the *fokonolona*.

The characteristics, structure, and sociocultural role of the *fokonolona* that persisted through the precolonial period were severely threatened by French colonization, so much so that *fokonolona* evolved to guard against French invasion. Able village men were tasked with assuring the day-to-day security of their *fokonolona*; the obligation to participate in this Malagasy form of CP is *andry masom-pokonolona*. This obligation persists today and has been further evolved to address the current security and safety needs of the community (Table 4.1).

Table 4.1   Community-Level Policing Obligations Fulfilled by *Fokonolona* throughout Malagasy History

Historical Period		Malagasy Term for Community Police Role and Responsibility within the *Fokonolona*	English Translation for Community Police Role and Responsibility within Community
Clan era		Mpanara-maso	Control agent
Monarchic era		Mpiköka	Alert agent
		Mpiamby kijo	Territory guardian
Colonial era		Mpiambina	Guardian
		Antily	Guardian of all risks
Present era	Traditional	Andrimasom-pokonolona	Committee of vigilance
		Mpanara-dia omby	Followers of zebu tracks
	Administrative	Ben'ny Ala	Forestry chief
		Vaomieran'Ny Ala	Forest committee
		Komity Miady am-Doro Tanety	Committee against bush fires
		Kartie Mobile	Village policy
	Environmental	Komitin'Ala sy Tontolo Iainana	Forest and environment committee
		Mpanara-maso ny Ala Ifotony	Contrôle forestier Local (local forest patrollers/monitors)
		Polisin'ny Ala	Forest police
		Polisin'ny Rano	Water/fishing police

Community Policing in Practice

The practice of community policing within *fokonolona* in Madagascar involves multiple dimensions including, for example, recruitment, partnerships, reward and penalty schemes, patrols, embeddedness within the community, community relationships, intelligence, and responses. In the following, we describe how community policing functions within the *fokonolona*.

Recruitment

The common method for recruiting members of the CP within the *fokonolona* or IC is as follows: (1) candidates are proposed by each social entity composing the IC; (2) a discussion ensues about the behaviors and personal capacities of these candidates, and the advice of the *sojabe* (i.e., IC notables) is considered; (3) *fokontany* members debate the choices levied by the General Assembly of the IC; (4) the *fokontany* chief approbates candidates chosen by the General Assembly of the IC; (5) candidates are vetted by the relevant division authorities (e.g., communes for the Kartie Mobile, Madagascar National Parks [MNP] for the villager guardians of the biological and cultural heritage sites of the National Parks); (6) candidates are nominated by the chief of district or the DREF (regional director of the environment and the forest); (7) candidates engage in technical training from the brigade commander of the state police/gendarme or the commissioner/sheriff of police of urban communes; (8) candidates sign a contract with their responsible authority and the organism of support in logistics, material/equipment and uniforms, and finances; (9) candidates engage in a public ritualization on the ethics of the CP position within the IC; and (10) candidates take an oath.

Partnerships among *Fokonolona* Leaders or Groups

The success of collaborations among *fokonolona* leaders hinges on the degree of agreement regarding missions that need to be conducted under the supervision of the IC chief or representative and within the traditional administrative jurisdiction. The CP is indebted in front of the IC (i.e., *sojabe*, chief of *fokontany*, and *fokontany* General Assembly) or the local technical or administrative authorities with which they are connected. CPs have the ability to seek advice from IC individuals or the IC group and cross-check information destined for crime reports. CPs are obligated to complete duplicate written reports that must be reviewed by the chief of *fokontany* before being transmitted to the CP chief.

Reward and Penalty Schemes

CPs can be both rewarded and penalized in diverse ways; however, decisions are levied by a pair of referees: an administrative referee and a financial referee. Rewards may be moral in nature, for example, letters of acknowledgment, recognition of the accomplished services, or devotion in the achievement of the perilous tasks. Rewards can be organizational in the form of promotion in the function or affectation in a service of confidence; they can also be material in the form of pecuniary bonuses, salary increases due to exceptional advancement, decoration, or recognition grants funded by external benefactors. CPs may be sanctioned. For example, CPs may be verbally warned, receive written warnings, be temporally expelled, be judged by an IC disciplinary committee, be declassified, be fined according to the collective convention of the IC, be demoted, be expelled, be transferred to a different division depending on the offense, and be taken to court according to the nature of the criminal act. Administrative referees levee rewards and sanctions are based on a CP's wages as well as the mechanisms discussed above.

Functions and Duties of CP Officers

CP officers are tasked with conducting investigations of criminal acts after they learn about an infraction or delegating the responsibility to one of their subordinate agents. CPs may use organized or sudden controls of the individuals or groups of individuals that are under investigation. They are able to conduct investigations by themselves so as to avoid bias associated with working with other CPs, or they can conduct investigations with other CPs to avoid superficial and harmful judgments. CP officers must supervise both field and office agents depending on their mission. Importantly, CP officers have a duty to assure the follow-up and the assessment of their agents and to correct/strengthen their weaknesses to improve their agents' capacity and operational efficiency. The quality of a CP is not innate; expertise must be acquired and learned. Thus, CP officers routinely provide training for their agents to build agent capacity.

Embeddedness within Communities

CP agents may be formally or informally integrated into the communities within which they work. Formally, CP agents, once recruited, have responsibilities not carried out by non-CP villages. CPs have the responsibility to enforce the laws of their community. However, CPs, after their official ritualization, return/rejoin with their community by a domestic ceremony. They must ask for the blessing of their *sojabe* for this reinstatement. Other times, CPs must be informally embedded within a community, especially when they engage in behaviors that are socially unacceptable (e.g., drunk and disorderly behavior, insubordination) and betray their profession. In these instances, CPs must be attentive, respectful, and cooperative toward the *fokonolona*. Repenting in this way will help restore their status within their IC. If they fail to repent, they will be considered foreigners and marginalized.

Training

Any villager can become a CP with extensive training. With repeated training, the capacity of individuals to become effective CPs can be enhanced—specifically, CPs can be trained in the roles, functions, and styles of policing relevant to their IC. Once individuals have been trained to become a CP, they are given a probationary period during which they gain experience to complement their expertise. With expertise and experience, any villager can become a very effective agent and even reach an officer's level.

Intelligence

CPs are tasked with collecting information about illegal activities within their community. In order to collect useful and valid information, CPs must have a clear understanding about the community culture, politics, and reality. With this understanding, they may collect data about illegal behaviors through interviews, observation, cross-checking secondary data, or data analysis with a team. Once a CP has collected and analyzed data, the data must be communicated to CP officers or superiors in order to vulgarize the concerned party.

Sanctions

CPs employ multiple intelligence tools in order to determine the details of a crime. Before they sanction an offender, CPs must have the sanction approved by a superior. In practice, the *fokontany* chief (CF) reviews a sanction to make sure that the CP is within his or her jurisdiction, the chief of service confirms a CP jurisdiction, and a judicial police officer (JPO) confirms the veracity of all necessary details. The JPO then sends a sanction report to the agents of pursuit (APs) to determine the appropriate penalties associated with the sanction. Sometimes, the JPO enlists the assistance of the court system in determining the details of sanctions.

Responses to Crime

CPs have diverse responsibilities in responding to different types of crime; they are charged with patrolling the neighborhoods of their own *fokonolona*, but there are times when CPs may be engaged in patrols of other villages or districts. In these latter instances, CPs must have an order of mission. With approval, a CP may serve as either a leader or a team member in a neighboring community. The CP is responsible for ensuring that the periphery of the *fokonolona* is secure; if a nearby *fokonolona* is experiencing delinquencies, the CP may engage in activities to prevent the delinquencies from transferring into his or her own *fokonolona*. CPs also deal with domestic disturbances, direct and control traffic, monitor and enforce drug laws, and ensure airport security.

Criminal Justice

In Madagascar, the implementation of the *dina* (i.e., agreements on common rules and regulations) has greatly helped ICs establish security and maintain good intravillage and intervillage relationships. *Dina* still exists in countryside throughout Madagascar despite some justice officials' vocal concerns about its use. It persists in part because of corruption occurring within the justice system that makes people lose trust in justice officials. Indeed, bringing disputed affairs to the justice official is often the last option for people living in the countryside. *Dina* offers mechanisms for solving problems at a village (or individual, family, or group) level in lieu of engaging the justice system. For example, in some rural areas of southern Madagascar, *dina* involves "Fitsarana ambany kily," or the judgment of a delinquent occurring under the shade of a big tamarind tree where all villagers can assist.

CP and Conservation

CPs play an essential role in Malagasy conservation. For example, the growing illegal trade in reptiles for pets is of concern to the Malagasy authorities (Raxworthy and Nussbaum 2000). Because the pet trade traffic involves international networks, different police groups must be involved at multiple levels of conservation, from the grassroots community level to the National Police level. CPs must work together in investigating, tracking, and prosecuting traffickers. Unfortunately, during periods of political turmoil, when limited government control shrinks drastically or functionally vanishes, illegal trade activities increase in regions where unique and rare species exist. CPs are often the first and only line of defense in such instances. For example, in the mid-2000s, four foreign tourists were arrested by MNP agents in Masoala National Park for illegally collecting chameleons, geckos, and other small endemic reptiles. CPs played an integral role in detecting and detaining the tourists; they also collaborated with other police divisions, the local forest chief, and justice officials during the prosecution and sentencing of the tourists (Jonah Ratsimbazafy, pers. comm., 2012). Because the majority of biodiversity violations occur at the IC level, CPs are often in the best position to capture and transmit intelligence about illegal conservation activities. Recognizing the invaluable role that CPs may play in conservation, several conservation nongovernmental organizations (NGOs) and civil society groups have worked to empower CPs to help stop illegal exploitation (e.g., of rosewood trees, ploughshare tortoises). For example, the Durrell Wildlife Conservation Trust provides training and support to local community associations that engage CPs in conservation. And, the Malagasy civil society group Alliance Voary Gasy was formed after the 2009 political crisis to help reduce biodiversity exploitation through training government authorities in good governance activities. These two groups, and others, have engaged CPs because other community-based conservation approaches have proven effective in helping to conserve biodiversity, especially in isolated rural regions of the country where state control is weak, enforcement agents have limited resources, and endangered species persist (Sommerville et al. 2010). One challenge to this approach, however, is that too many NGOs can become active in a particular region or for a particular species. NGO crowding may lead to a lack of cohesion and police efficacy.

Madagascar is a signatory to international nonbinding conventions such as the Convention on International Trade in Endangered Species of Wild Fauna and Flora (CITES) and is a member of the International Union for the Conservation of Nature (IUCN). Membership is operationalized at a national level as laws and regulations that classify infringements and crimes against species (i.e., poaching or collecting IUCN- and CITES-listed species within protected zones). CPs in ICs, during their regular patrols, have the opportunity to monitor critical biological sites (often protected areas) and enforce these laws. CPs can also collaborate with a group of police from various jurisdictions (e.g., rural commune, district, regional levels) called the Mixed Brigade of Controls (BMC) to monitor protected areas, collect data about and monitor infringements (e.g., species poaching, arson), conduct investigations, and provide supporting information to judicial agents as needed. CPs are in contact with port and airport police regarding the import and export of live species, animal parts, or animal products, per CITES requirements.

Challenges Associated with Community Policing in Madagascar

CPs play an essential role in the criminal justice system within Madagascar. However, community policing and police in Madagascar suffer from a number of challenges, some internal to the *fokonolona* system and others external. First, in general, there is a low level of educational attainment for CPs; in many ways, CPs are considered simple agents of rule and law execution. Low educational and associated motivational levels can result in CPs that lack the motivation to systematically synthesize criminal situations, especially those that are complicated, for example, crimes associated with conservation. Because CPs are integrated into the *fokonolona*, they are often overly influenced by the *fokonolona* and its members to the point that some crimes go undetected and some laws go unenforced. Further, responsibilities can become mundane; service may become routine for CPs, especially those that do not have strong supervision or opportunities for training and advancement. Second, CPs may become corrupt. For example, they may be inclined to take bribes because they typically have a low salary and heavy social responsibility. The temptation to take a bribe may be increased when CPs are interacting, often alone, with criminals who profit from delinquency; CPs may think that taking a bribe may go unnoticed by others in the community. Personal aspiration may also motivate a CP to become corrupt—some CPs may be attracted to the authority associated with the professional position of a CP but abuse their power to exploit others. Such corruption may be the result of bad influence of colleagues or the pressure of influential people both internal and external to the *fokonolona*. Third, the influence of family on a CP cannot be understated. Interfamilial and intrafamilial relationships that are historical, personal, or social in nature may make a CP hesitant to apply sanctions because there could be family-level repercussions (e.g., threats).

Conclusion

Community policing in Madagascar has existed since before the island was colonized; the system has endured through many social, political, administrative, and economic changes.

Today, community policing is especially important in the countryside, where *dinas* continue to be used with *fokonolona* to ensure security at the IC level. Madagascar's community policing system faces what arguably could be its biggest challenge—the protection and conservation of the island's unique biodiversity in the face of poverty, weak governance, and corruption. How effective and efficient will the community policing system prove to be in the face of this challenge? How can community policing be prioritized in remote regions with no effective government? How can an effective criminal justice system be supported, especially in the face of international pressures? Answers to these, and other questions, will only be born out over time.

References

Conservation International. (2000). Megadiversity countries. http://www.conservation.org/web/ fieldact:megadiv/maps.htm. Accessed April 27, 2012.

De Wit M.J. (2003). Madagascar: Heads it's a continent, tails it's an island. *Annual Review of Earth and Planetary Sciences* 31: 213–248.

Flacourt E. (1658). Histoire de la Grande île de Madagascar: Collection des ouvrages anciens concernant Madagascar t. VII. Paris, France.

Ganzhorn J.U., Goodman S.M., Ramananjato J.-B., Rakotondravony D., Rakotosamimanana B. & Vallan D. (2000). Vertebrate species in fragmented littoral forests of Madagascar, pp. 155–164. In: *Diversity and Endemism in Madagascar*. W.R. Lourenço, Goodman S.M. (eds). *Mémoires de la Société de* Biogéographie. Muséum Histoire Naturelle, Paris, France.

Grandidier A. (1942). Histoire politique et coloniale t. I: De la découverte de Madagascar à la fin du règne Ranavalona Ière (1861). Brodard, Paris, France. HarperCollins Publishers, New York. 375 pp.

Jamal D. & de Wit M.J. (2002). Containing Gondwana links between northern Mozambique, India, and Madagascar using geochronology and aeromagnetics. *Gondwana 11: Correlations and Connections, Program Abstract, University of Canterbury, New Zealand*.

Meyers N., Mittermeier R.A., Mittermeier C.G., Fonseca G.A.B. & Kent J. (2000). Biodiversity hotspots for conservation priorities. *Nature* 403: 853–858.

Mittermeier R.A., Richardson M., Louis E.E., Hawkins F., Schwitzer C., Langrand O. et al. (2010). *Lemurs of Madagascar*. 3rd edition. *Tropical Field Guide Series*, Conservation International, Washington, DC. 731 pp.

Police Nationale Malagasy. (2012). http://www.policenational.gov.mg. Accessed April 27, 2012.

Raxworthy C.J. & Nussbaum R.A. (2000). Extinction and extinction vulnerability of amphibians and reptiles in Madagascar. *Amphibian and Reptile Conservation* 2(1): 15–23.

Ratsimbazafy J.H. (2003). Lemurs as the most appropriate and best current didactic tool for teaching. *Lemur News* 8: 19–21.

Raxworthy C.J., Pearson R.G., Rabibisoa N., Rakotondrazafy A.M., Ramanamanjato J.B., Raselimanana A.P. et al. (2008). Extinction vulnerability of tropical montane endemism from warming and upslope displacement: A preliminary appraisal for the highest massif in Madagascar. *Global Change Biology* 14(8): 1703–1720.

Sommerville M., Jones J.P.G., Rahajaharison M. & Milner-Gulland, E.J. (2010). The role of fairness and benefit distribution in community-based Payment for Environmental Services interventions: A case study from Menabe, Madagascar. *Ecological Economics* 69(6): 1262–1271.

Tyson P. (2005). *The Eighth Continent: Life, Death, and Discovery in the Lost World of Madagascar*.

World Bank. (2012). Madagascar country profile. http://www.worldbank.org. Accessed April 27, 2012.

Wright P.C. (2010). Madagascar: The forest of our ancestors. du Vivant, R. (ed). Castelau-le-Lez, France. 235 pp.

Niger

LISBET ILKJAER

5

Contents

Background

Niger is a republic in West Africa covering 1,267,000 km^2, and 75% of the land is desert. The country has been independent from France since 1960. Niger is one of the driest and hottest countries in the world; it is completely landlocked and borders Benin, Burkina Faso, Mali, Algeria, Libya, Chad, and Nigeria. Agriculture, which the economy primarily relies upon, is affected by the tough climate and the old-fashioned production techniques. Niger is often facing serious drought and hunger catastrophes. Niger was, in 2011, ranked 186th out of 187th on the United Nations Human Development Index.

Niger has approximately 16 million inhabitants, with more than 95% being Muslim. The population is composed of many different ethnic groups: Haoussa, Zarma-Sonraï, Touareg, Kanouri, Peulh, Toubou, Arabe, Gourmanché, and Bodouma. The life expectancy is 54.7 years. The official language is French; however, more than 70% of the inhabitants are illiterate, two of three inhabitants live under the poverty level, and more than 80% live in rural areas.

Following the independence of the country, a military regime was installed. The regime decided at the end of the 1970s to create a national police institution. The Direction for National Security, was a repressive instrument for the military regime. However, since the transition period into democracy at the beginning of the 1990s, the police in Niger have gone through a successful transformation from being repressive to considering itself as a service to the public.

In Niger, there are three different institutions with a policing mandate: the National Police, the National Guard and the Gendarmerie. The Police and the Guard are under the authority of the Ministry of Interior, Public Security and Decentralization, whereas the Gendarmerie is under the Ministry of Defense. While the respective mandates are different, the activities of the three institutions are complementary. This chapter will focus on the community policing work carried out by the National Police. However, it is important to mention that community policing activities also take place in the work of the Gendarmerie and the National Guard. Key missions of the National Police are maintenance of law and order, public safety, and public health (including judicial policing tasks, intelligence, immigration, emigration, and the protection of persons and their belongings). The National Police works primarily in urban areas, while the Gendarmerie's missions focus on rural areas.

There are eight regions in Niger: Niamey, Zinder, Maradi, Tahoua, Dosso, Tillabery, Diffa, and Agadez.

The examples in this chapter mainly come from the region of Tahoua, which boarders both Nigeria and Mali.

Coauthor Mahaman Abdoussalam, who was a regional commissioner in the Tahoua area at the time of the research for this article, provided information on community policing in the region. The area of the region is 113,371 km², and there is a population of 2,500,000 inhabitants. Tahoua is under the authority of a governor nominated by a decree. The nomads in the region are organized in tribes, and the nonnomads are living in villages. As in the whole of Niger, the society builds on the system of traditional chiefs elected for a lifetime on the basis of family heritage. This system is recognized and coexists with the formal administrative system, and the traditional chiefs also play certain roles in the formal administration. Only approximately 350 police officers cover the whole region.

Origin of Community Policing in Niger

Currently, there is no formal legal basis for community policing in Niger. The community policing approach stems from a policy decision taken by the director of the police that the police should strive at getting closer to the population to become more efficient. In many parts of Niger, community policing already exists but not as a result of a formal system.

Community policing in Niger is inspired by Western models but has been simplified and adapted to the local context of the country. External actors have not imposed the system of community policing since before the more modern version of community policing, a system of informal community policing was already used in the different villages and tribes in Niger where the Guard of the traditional chiefs was taking care of security in the villages. This informal system exists today alongside the more modern methods of community policing. The informal system reinforces the formal system.

In the annual reports from the National Police, it is possible to find some information on community policing. In the part that relates to "working methods," it is briefly explained that the actions employed by the police are based on a policy of community policing. It emphasizes the importance of proximity of the police in relation to the field and the population. Furthermore, elements such as visibility in relation to the population as well as the importance of responsiveness to issues that the population perceives as threats to their security are key factors in successful policing.

Functioning of Community Policing in Niger

As mentioned above, there is no formal integrated system of community policing in Niger. It is more a new orientation for the police in Niger on how to interact with the population, a change of working methods that involves the population to a greater extent than before.

The region of Tahoua was the first to take the initiative in relation to community policing with the full support of the director of the police. Representatives from the population primarily carry out community policing in Tahoua. Community policing primarily relies on the traditional village chief system and the guard of the traditional chief. Before colonization, this guard was in charge of providing security for the village. The political, economic, and social powers were all invested in the traditional chief position. Also, today, the traditional chiefs have some formal influence in relation to public administration as well as on community policing in form of their guards.

The guard consists of young voluntaries that are concerned with their community and its security. The voluntary members from the local communities are recruited based on their moral integrity recognized by the community. The list of young volunteers is sent officially to the police. Then the police analyzes the list and checks the identity of each volunteer and that they have no criminal history. Following the approval, the volunteers receive training by the police, which essentially underlines the importance of the presence of the group in the community and that their contributions should focus on *securing security of persons and materials within the respect of law and human rights*. The training is followed up in the form of briefing and debriefing sessions.

In Tahoua, the National Police has carried out a substantial campaign in relation to the population, the traditional chiefs, religious leaders, opinion setters, unions' representatives, as well as the locally elected authorities. The objective of the campaign has been to involve all these key actors in the issues of daily security protection of the villages and tribes. The interested members organize themselves in groups patrolling in the villages—a kind of citizens' watch.

The religious leaders play a crucial role in social life in Niger, and they are, therefore, essential actors in relation to policing. Especially, in order to ensure preventive police work, religious leaders play an active role in addressing youth in relation to religious values and so forth. Also, the mayors in the region are very much involved in daily community policing. The mayors contribute to paying the voluntaries from the guard for carrying out patrols, and they also pay for the different kinds of training conducted by the police. There is not enough money on the overall national police budget for this type of activity.

The anchorage in the community is of both a formal and an informal character. However, due to the increased involvement of key societal leaders, the concept of community policing is getting more and more formalized. For example, there is a clear tendency that the mayors now include community policing in the yearly budgets, which previously was not the case.

The population not only contributes with members for the groups patrolling the villages. It also contributes to the identification of existing security problems. Furthermore, the community takes part in suggesting solutions that most efficient for keeping crime down.

When the National Police in Niger gathers information, it is crucial that information is sought from different poles of the society. As mentioned in the beginning, there are many ethnic groups in Niger with many different traditions, and therefore, the police strive to get information from all groups. Due to the importance of religion in Niger, it is crucial that the police maintain a close relationship with the religious leaders, both in order to identify problems and, maybe more importantly, because of the influence of religious leaders on the population. Therefore, the police hold regular meetings with them.

The police supervise the community policing patrols. Groups of volunteers are formed, and the patrolling area is divided into zones. Patrolling takes place at nights, and a police officer is in charge of each group.

Dialogue between key actors is one of the most important ways to reinforce local security protection. One of the roles of the National Police is to direct the actors towards the relevant persons and services in case of problems in the community. Sometimes, the National Police also directly facilitates contact between relevant actors in order to keep down certain social tensions. This means that in some instances, the National Police has a very active role in solving problems.

One example in the region of Tahoua was the problem with the *Kabous Kabous* or taxi motorbikes that were not formally organized. This led to an increase in accidents where taxi motorbikes were involved and where the perpetrators fled from the crime scene because the vehicles could not be identified. This unorganized situation of motorbikes also led to an increase in the theft of these. The various and increasing crimes involving motorbikes pushed the National Police to engage in having the taxi motorbikes organized, and that the young drivers were sensitized on what this job really meant. Under the influence of the police, a union for the Kabous Kabous was created, and the police played an active role building bridges between the driving schools and license permit authorities.

Today, the union has headquarters in Tahoua, which works closely with the police and is also part of the national union, which held its congress in Tahoua in 2011. The union accompanies the police on patrols ensuring discipline of motorbikes in traffic. As a consequence of this cooperation, road crimes involving motorbikes have decreased more than 60% in the region. Since becoming a motorbike driver is a popular occupation, another crucial effect of the organization of the motorbike drivers into a well-functioning union is that it has now become even more popular to be a motorbike driver, which is part of reducing youth unemployment and emigration to neighboring countries.

The same cooperative approach has been used in relation to sex workers in Tahoua. The police have worked on sensitizing sex workers on the importance of being better organized, and that it is in their interest to carry out regular medical visits. In the city of Konni bordering Nigeria, the police have encouraged women sex workers to organize themselves in an association. The association has an office, which registers the problems of sex workers and discusses them with the police. There is a very efficient cooperation in relation to combating illegal prostitution and sexual exploitation of minors.

A very interesting aspect of community policing in Tahoua is the importance of markets and market days. This is the day in the week where the local community can meet and mingle with people from other parts of the region. The market is not only a forum for commercial transaction; it is just as much an opportunity to get the latest news about family members, the rain, the status of the harvest, and so forth. Very important, the weekly market day is a possibility for the nomads, who usual come from very isolated and distant areas, to catch up with new rules.

Finally, an important factor is that since 2002, the Danish Institute for Human Rights (an independent state institution), a national human rights institution, has had a partnership with the National Police in Niger. The partnership has, among other things, consisted of the development of human rights training material for the police and the integration of human rights in initial and in-service training. Lately, the partnership has concentrated on the development of performance indicators for the police as well as discussions on police reform and democratic policing. It is clear that the respect for human rights is a crucial aspect of community policing since this is the base for creating trust and respect. Ten years ago, a study was carried out on the perception of the police and human rights. Abas and Garba (2012) began a new study in order to see whether there have been any impactful changes from all the work done on human rights by the police.

Relationship to Criminal Justice System

Community policing in Niger is closely connected to the criminal justice system. The police have the possibility of using conflict resolution in certain minor crime matters, and most of these mediations take place in front of the traditional chiefs. The traditional chiefs play a crucial role in settling many disputes because of both their general positive influence on the population as well as their spiritual leader role.

The traditional chiefs play a crucial role in helping the police. Very often, the conflict settlement takes place at the house of the traditional chief and not at the premises of the police. It is much easier for a community member that the first contact is the traditional chief and not a formal police service. The involvement of the traditional chiefs facilitates the dialogue between parties, and the solutions achieved as part of a chief conciliation also contribute to the fact that the community as such accepts these solutions more easily.

Traditional chiefs will often be the first to receive information about a crime, and then, based on the gravity of the crimes, victims are directed towards the police or the prosecutor. However, most conflicts mediated through traditional chiefs are divorces, marriages, neighbor conflicts, and problems with minors. Traditional chiefs have the power to rule on compensation in favor of the victim.

Effectiveness of Community Policing

Even though there are very few data available, the National Police sees the concept of community policing as a success due to the results obtained so far. In developing countries such as Niger, community policing allows immediate and efficient response to quite a number of crimes and thereby also guarantees citizens a security without which development would not happen.

In Tahoua, there have been several successes working with community policing, and this approach has resulted in a decrease in crime, the prevention of public order problems, regular sensitization of the communities on new rules in force, and assisting the population in getting certain crucial documents such as a driving license.

As previously addressed, the success with community policing is based on all the partnerships built up by the National Police: the truck drivers' union, the taxi drivers' union, and so forth. This has resulted in direct dialogues between the relevant actors and the police, which is the basis for peaceful prevention of crime as well as conflict settlement. The police in Tahoua have also established a close cooperation with the media, which takes part in the work of community policing by communication and information.

The police in Tahoua state that some of the most important results from taking these community policing initiatives are:

- Better protection of people and property
- More stable payment of taxes
- Creation of driving schools, enabling people to get driving licenses
- More effective fight against juvenile crimes and sexual exploitation of young girls
- Respect of traffic rules

One of the challenges when working with policing in one of the poorest countries in the world covering a vast desert area is of course to ensure police presence all over the country. There are many areas where the police remain unknown and where the population does not understand its role at all.

In Tahoua, there are communities where police services have only been established since 2010. By emphasizing the good reception of people by police services, active listening of citizens, and regular communication, the police has now made the population better understand its role.

The population has far more trust in the police than ever before. Community members now spontaneously offer to assist the police by giving the names of crime perpetrators and their accomplices. In some cases, local notabilities have visited police services to thank them for their good cooperation and the improvement of security protection.

The police in Niger are moving towards the concept of democratic policing. It has for a long period worked to detach itself from former repressive images and is now moving towards a reality where the police are perceived as a service for the public, accessible to all.

The results so far are very encouraging, and the population has started to get a new image of the police as a service that exists for the population and not to preserve current authorities' power through repression. In some instances, the population has more confidence in the police than in other official authorities, including the elected ones.

Some of the best practices in order to obtain professional and efficient community policing have been identified:

- Ensure good communication externally.
- Reach towards the population and create the conditions for good dialogue.
- Prioritize active listening.
- Improve the reception of people when they come to the police stations.
- Make the population understand that the police are there as a public service and that they are accessible to all and can be contacted at any time.
- The police must show interest in participating in social activities, for example, marriages, births, and funerals.
- Ban all provocative behavior.
- Always remain open and accessible.

All these best practices contribute to create an atmosphere of trust between the police and the population. To ensure security, the police need to be efficient, but in order to be efficient, the police must absolutely enjoy the trust of the population.

One of the challenges is how to integrate community policing more formally in the work of the National Police in Niger. Some of the elements in such a model could be:

1. The establishment of a **communication focal point**: a sort of spokesman/woman for the police, who would be responsible for informing the population on events and rules, thus avoiding the spreading of false rumor within the population. Media (local radios especially) are essential in order to make such a focal point efficient, but this will also require that the police allow media to have access to information that they have had no access to previously.

2. A **formal forum** between the security sector and key society actors should be established in the different communities. Those actors are, for example, local politicians, business people, drivers, opinion leaders, teachers, religious leaders, and so forth. The regions in Niger are very different; therefore, it is important to be very aware of the specific local contexts of each region. This will also be an element when prioritizing the most important partnerships in exactly that specific region. It is important to work based on the premise that "one size does not fit all." Such a formal forum will enable both the police to gather important information from the population and be an important factor in order to make the actors interested in security in their local area. Such a forum is also a crucial part of an improved communication strategy from the National Police as described in the above-mentioned point.
3. A formal introduction of community policing will also require that **more commissariats** are created all over the country so that the police can have more presence and be more visible than they are today.

Finally, it is clear that the community policing approach in Niger would benefit from putting more effort into the preventive part of community policing: setting up more formal partnerships with schools, sports clubs, and so forth in order to address the youth before they come into trouble. In this context, it would also be very useful if the police could provide the traditional chiefs, religious leaders, and union leaders with tools on how to work with youths to prevent them falling into crime.

Conclusion

The National Police in Niger are determined to introduce community policing as a key working method for the whole service. However, community policing does not exist in a vacuum of its own; introducing community policing will be more efficient if it is part of an overall reform of the police in Niger.

The partnership between the National Police and the Danish Institute for Human Rights will now move into activities in the reform area. The key objectives for the next 2 years will be to continue the work on training police officers in human rights, to develop an internal and external communication strategy, and finally, to initiate reform discussions and indicator development (Ilkjaer and Boureima 2010).

When working with police reform, it is crucial that local context is respected and that the local police (and not international experts) manages the reform. This is not to say that technical input and experiences are not important, but the National Police must remain in the driver's seat. However, it is crucial that the police in Niger find partners to finance a proper and thorough police reform, since the second-least-developed country in the world needs financial support to ensure that the police can work under acceptable conditions.

There is an increased interest from the international society in policing in Niger due to the current threats from AQMI (al-Qaida in Maghreb Islamique) and kidnappings that have taken place in the north of the country, having a disastrous impact on security, movement, and trade in that part of the country. The European Union has drafted a strategy on how to improve security in the Sahel, including Niger. The action plans are currently in the process of being developed. But it is already known that one of the strategy's recommendations is to support police reform in the region. In the neighboring country Burkina Faso, where the threats from AQMI also exist, there have been many positive experiences with community policing in the sense that close cooperation between the police and its population can prevent external actors such as al-Qaida from establishing themselves among the population.

Notes

The material was synthesized from various conversations held with the following during the spring of 2012.

1. Issoufou Yacouba, directeur genereale de la police nationale, Niger (French title) (director of the National Police in Niger, equivalent to an English police commissioner—the person responsible for the whole National Police).
2. Commisaire Mahaman Abdoussalam, directeur régional de la police nationale de Tahoua, Niger (French title) (probably regional commissioner).
3. Paul Zagré, director of community policing, Burkina Faso.

References

Abas, M., Garba, M.L. (2012). Etude d'impact de l'enseignement des droits de l'Homme dans la Police Nationale au Niger. DIHR, Niamey, Niger (July).
Ilkjaer, L., Boureima, S.S. (2010). A model for developing performance indicators in Niger. *International Journal of Police Science and Management, 12(2).*

Nigeria

6

IKUTEYIJO OLUSEGUN LANRE
AYODELE JAMES OLABISI

Contents

Background

Nigeria, the most populous black nation in the world, has an official population of 150 million (National Population Commission 2006) and a projected population of 167 million as of October 2011. The country is located on the gulf of the Guinea in West Africa and shares borders with Niger, Cameroon, and the Chad Republic in the north; the Republic of Benin in the west; and the Gulf of Guinea and the Atlantic Ocean in the south. The climatic condition of the country is diverse and ranges from arid to humid equatorial, with predominantly two seasons: rainy and dry. Despite its vast arable lands, the economy of Nigeria changed from agriculture driven to petroleum driven in the 1970s, when massive oil exportation began following the increase in world oil price. Although crude oil was discovered in 1956 by Shell–BP, production and exportation began only in 1958. Nigeria is also naturally endowed with mineral resources such as tin, columbite, limestone, gold, coals, bitumen, and kaolin, among others.

The process culminating in the emergence of Nigeria as a nation commenced with the Lord Frederick Lugard's amalgamation of the Northern and Southern Protectorates in 1914 and climaxed with independence from Britain on October 1, 1960. About 250 hitherto-independent ethnic nationalities and cultures were brought together by fiat under a British colonial government between 1900 and 1960. Nonetheless, different parts of the present-day Nigeria have varying experiences under the 60-year British administration, hence the disparity in their socioeconomic development. In fact, the colonial rule was characterized by frequent reclassifying of different parts for administrative convenience. Nigeria was structured in three political regions (North, East, and West) in 1951 with both the East and West granted self-government in 1957 and the North in 1959. Nigeria became a republic in 1963, experienced first military rule in 1966, and fought a civil war cum secession attempt by the Eastern Region from 1967 to 1970, which led to the creation of 12 states. At present, the country has 36 states and a Federal Capital Territory in Abuja. British English language was adopted as Nigeria's lingua franca at independence, while Yoruba, Ibo, and Hausa are the major indigenous languages. Interethnic and interreligion relations have remained two major threats to security in postindependent Nigeria (Ayodele and Onu 2006).

In Nigeria, a state-organized police force was part of the colonial project, which began in 1861, particularly under Governor McCosky with the establishment of the 30-man Consul Guard based in Lagos. Essentially, colonial police machinery functioned solely to protect colonial interest and safeguard the colonialists (Crowder 1978; Alemika 1988). Put differently, the paramilitary colonial police was formed "to ward off attackers from the trading depots of British merchants" (Tamuno 1975, p. 5) and to coerce "recalcitrant" traditional rulers (Ahire 1991, p. 38) to submission. Lending credence, Mbaku and Kimenyi (1995, p. 298) intimated that the colonial police force was "never intended to be a crime fighter in the traditional sense. Its main duty was to conquer and subjugate the people … and provide British merchants the wherewithal to monopolize the regions commercial activities." That colonial police was named the Hausa Constabulary (consisting of officers from the linguistically and culturally distinct ethnic group from the North of the country) after 2 years of establishment. Subsequently in 1879, the Hausa Constabulary was regularized by a colonial ordinance. It was renamed Lagos Police Force in January 1896. Other notable police formations in colonial Nigeria include the Royal Charter Constabulary established in 1888 (it was split into the Northern Nigeria Police Force [NNPF] and the Northern Nigeria Regiment [NNR] in 1900) and the Oil River Protectorate, which had a separate armed constabulary in 1891 (renamed the Niger Coast Constabulary in 1893 and, later, Southern Nigeria Police Force [SNPF]). By 1906, four major formal police machinery gained prominence in colonial Nigeria, namely, the NNPF, the NNR, the SNPF, and the Southern Nigeria Regiment (SNR). Together, these formations were responsible for dealing with internal disturbances and external aggressions in addition to normal police duties. However, all colonial police machineries were merged in April 1930 to form the Nigeria Police Force (NPF) with headquarters in Lagos and commanded by an inspector general of police (IGP). Meanwhile, Native Authorities Police were allowed during the country's first democratic experiment in all regions for political expediency (Rotimi 1993).

Due to sustained public outcry against inefficiency and brutality of the NPF, successive governments in Nigeria (and in Africa generally) have made only feeble attempts to reform and reorient the national police to be people-sensitive (Alemika 2007). Over the years, the NPF has been described with adjectives such as underfunded, ill equipped, understaffed, ill trained, uncivil, partisan, reactive, repressive, and irresponsive (Ebo 1993; Alemika 1999; Alemika and Chukwuma 2000; Agabi 2003; Aboribo and Oghene 2002; Human Rights Watch 2005). At present, the NPF has its Force Headquarters in Abuja (the Federal Capital Territory) headed by the IGP, 12 zonal commands each headed by an assistant inspector general (AIG), and 36 state commands under a commissioner. The FCT Command is also headed by a commissioner of police.

Origins of Community Policing in Nigeria

Community policing is a philosophy that promotes community partnership and a problem-solving approach to public safety. Put differently, it is a strategy in Western democracies anchored on the unilateral action of the police to promote community self-rule (Wisler and Onwudiwe 2007). It is a formal policing strategy aimed at reorienting police personnel toward a collaborative partnership with host communities with a view to solving crime problems before they occur. Unlike community policing, however, community-based policing is an informal approach to public safety using civilians or members of communities.

Thus, community-based policing is indigenous to Nigerian people, whereas community policing strategy is alien. In these rural communities, vigilante groups often act as the core grassroots security body protecting lives and property (Williams 2011). Community-based policing has very deep cultural and historical roots, as the art of policing was not alien to precolonial communities comprising contemporary Nigeria. In fact, scholars agreed that prior to colonialization, indigenous African communities were characterized by "self-policing" because of the existence of social control forces other than the "police" maintained by the rewards and punishment, built into every relationship (Banton 1964). Indeed, European scholars and explorers such as Ibn Battuta (1975), Blyden (1908), and Banton (1964) do not share the Eurocentric notion that precolonial African societies were "lawless and disorderly" prior to their contact with Europeans.

During a visit to Mali in 1352–1353, Ibn Battuta recalled seeing "good qualities" such as zero tolerance to injustice, prevalence of peace, and relative absence of vices such that travelers were "not afraid in it nor is he who lives there in fear of the thief or of the robber by violence" (Crowder 1977, p. 33). This nonprejudicial stance hinges on the overwhelming evidence about the existence of "informal" but effective law enforcement mechanisms before the advent of the colonialists in Nigeria (Rotimi 1993; Danbazau 1994). Similarly, Achebe (1984) documented that security of lives and property in precolonial communities was basically a joint responsibility of both the living and the dead. Writing on the criminal justice system (CJS) in the eastern part, Achebe (1984) noted that the "ancestors partook in almost all affairs" because "the land of the living was not far removed from the domain of the ancestors" (p. 85). Thus, the strategy involved in maintaining order and security in precolonial Nigeria was community-based policing. It goes without saying that indigenous Nigerian communities could conveniently dispense with the services of any formal police machinery introduced by either the Arabs or Europeans using certain indigenous restraints (e.g., sanctions of gossip, ostracism, and moral pressure) to curb antisocial behavior (Oluyede 2002). The efficacy of the informal precolonial police machinery indeed triggered the recent introduction of the community policing strategy in Nigeria.

Following the surge in crime and the lackluster performance of the NPF (the only statutory police body), ethnic-based groups such as the Oodua Peoples Congress (OPC), the Bakassi Boys (BB), the Egbesu Boys (EB), and the Arewa Peoples Congress (APC) emerged to perform security-related duties in the South–West, South–South, South–East, and North, respectively (Adebayo 2005). Apart from these groups, vigilante groups (Neighborhood Watch) were formed in many Nigerian communities to complement the efforts of the NPF. Each of these groups enjoyed the support of the communities in which they operated even though many lacked governmental or legal supports.

Similarly, the Nigeria Security and Civil Defence Corps (NSCDC), which was community based initially, has been integrated into the conventional security system and charged with the responsibility of safeguarding governmental installations (e.g., petroleum pipelines). However, all unconventional security outfits are now to legally and technically operate under the Vigilante Group of Nigeria (VGN).

Techniques of Community Policing in Nigeria

Informal policing involved virtually all members of society, largely on part-time and nonsalaried basis (this technique contrasts formal full-time policing by a few members on salary). Notably, some identifiable techniques include communality, collaboration between the living and the dead members, collective shaming, and royal supervision.

One major ingredient of community-oriented policing is what Blyden (1994) tagged the "we and not I" philosophy. According to him,

> The tribes have laws regulating every function of human life and the laws are known to all the members of the tribe, and justice is administered by the tribal chiefs in the presence of the whole people in the village or town, where any violation of tribal law may have taken place. There is no need for Standing Armies. The *whole people of the villages or town are jointly and severally guidance and preservers of peace.* (Blyden 1908; emphasis added)

Thus with "no standing armies," we-ness did not only permit "communal property and cooperative effort;" it also prevented stealing/theft because "everybody has his rights and has enough" (Blyden 1908; cited in Lynch 1971, pp. 163–164). One major technique guaranteeing security of lives and property in community-based policing is 24-h patrol or coverage.

Under community-based policing, enforcement of "laws" was done with heavy dependence on the supernatural forces and juju, heads of various family, age grades (especially among the Yorubas, Igbo, and Edo), skilled hunters cum warriors, and *dogarai* or *yan-doka* (among the Hausas). These indigenous police machineries were later reorganized in the First Republic into Native Authority Police for regional security. Except for communities in the northern part of Nigeria where the *dogarai* or *yan-doka* was directly and functionally controlled by the Emirs (Blench et al. 2006; Alemika 2010), the influence of traditional rulers in other parts of Nigeria allowed indigenous police machinery greater independent operations.

In contemporary Nigerian communities, however, informal police machinery functions to complement (and not substitute for) the Nigeria Police, hence the variations in their strategies. Since only the Nigeria Police has the statutory power to prosecute crime suspects (the judiciary to trial/punish and the prison to treat/rehabilitate), indigenous police outfits are required only to facilitate the process. Thus, informal outfits are expected to invite the police to arrest or to hand over to the police whoever is suspected for unlawful behavior. However, the strategies involved in security maintenance include surveillance, foot patrol, arrest, prototrial, and punishment. Surveillance is carried out effectively because members of these informal outfits are recruited from their respective host communities (potential recruits are recommended by traditional rulers). Informal police outfits arrest suspects occasionally because the Nigeria Police frequently expose many of them to paramilitary trainings. At times, community-based informal police machineries conduct mini-trials for people caught for petty offences and apportion whatever punishment is considered appropriate.

To ensure probity, members of informal police machinery are made to swear to an indigenous oath, after which they are usually empowered to function. Empowerment of members requires the invocation of ancestral or supernatural power to protect them from criminally minded persons and make them accountable to the community. Describing the aftermath of empowerment, Adebayo (2009, p. 7) states that many members of informal community-based security groups usually "decorate their bodies with all manner of charms" in a bid to fortify themselves. But since membership is voluntary, recruits are usually not forced to partake in the oath-taking cum empowerment process even though they are constantly reminded that refusal makes them vulnerable to attacks from criminals. We need to stress here that the empowerment is an ongoing thing subject to periodic renewals (this is akin to practices in formal policing where officials are exposed to in-service training and promotion examinations).

In terms of operations, both the OPC and VGN have a four-tier system (national, state, council, and community). However, VGN has more national spread than the other groups (OPC, BB, APC, and EB) even though the latter is more feared in its respective domain of operation in Nigeria. In addition, while the VGN relies on near-formal arrangement, the OPC (or BB, APC, EB) favors strictly nonformal arrangement. However, one thing common to the VGN and other groups is the heavy involvement of traditional rulers in the recruitment of members. To ascertain the identity of members, each is recruited based on very strong recommendation from his or her traditional rulers or village heads (nowadays, a duly signed and stamped attestation letter is requested).

Relationship of Community Policing to CJS

As earlier observed, community-oriented policing has become an integral part of the CJS in contemporary Nigeria in spite of the constitutional provision recognizing only the NPF. Despite this arrangement, security exigencies have necessitated that communities be encouraged to participate in security provision. In recent times, rather than abandoning the security business to the few salaried police personnel, security is seen "as everybody's business." Thus, informal community-based police machineries are to perform the primary function (not exclusively though) of surveillance, investigation, arrest, and sorting. Officially, community policing became popular and adopted by the NPF during the era of Tafa Balogun as the IGP, and it was launched on April 27, 2004, by former President Olusegun Obasanjo (Anucha 2007). This was seen as one of the numerous reforms embarked upon by past IGPs. The "new" policing style was sponsored by both local and international agencies, most prominent of which was the British Council through the Network of Police Research in Nigeria (NOPRIN). Consequently, a number of trainings were embarked upon for selected members of the police force within and outside the country. Expectedly, those who went abroad for their training were sent to Britain, being not just the colonial masters but also the progenitor and promoter of the idea of community policing to the NPF. However, the idea of community policing as practiced in Britain needs to be implemented in the Nigerian context, given the nature of antecedents of the Nigeria Police (Ikuteyijo 2009).

Until 2004, when the community policing strategy was officially adopted in the country, the NPF have viewed informal community-based vigilante groups, especially the OPC, as adversaries (the federal government under President Olusegun Obasanjo once placed the shoot-at-sight order on OPC members). Consequently, many members of the self-appointed anticrime vigilante group became victims of police brutality, including extra-judicial killings, torture and detention without trial (Human Rights Watch 2005).

Since crime is seen as offense against the state, only the formal police agency discharges the business of prosecuting crime suspects. Nonetheless, other agencies, such as the Economic and Financial Crime Commission (EFCC), National Drug Law Enforcement Agency (NDLEA), National Agency for the Prohibition of Traffic in Persons (NAPTIP), and National Agency for Food and Drug Administration and Control (NAFDAC), to mention a few, are occasionally directly involved in prosecuting suspected offenders in courts. This is due to the enabling laws/acts establishing these agencies. In the case of community-based police groups such as the VGN and OPC, they rely heavily on the police to prosecute whoever is arrested on the suspicion of unlawful activities.

Most importantly, informal community-based security outfits depend on formal police agencies for requisite hands-on trainings. According to the commandant general of the VGN, members of the group are usually trained by Nigeria Police "and sensitized on ways of complementing the efforts of the security agencies towards combating crimes and ensuring the security of lives and property on Nigerians" (Williams 2011, p. 1). Specific training is given on how to gather information on crime and other social vices, which is passed on to the police, and how to protect property of both government and citizens. This collaboration between formal and informal police agencies is crucial to the enhancement of security of lives and property. With adequate training, informal community-based security groups would be well positioned to combat crimes at the grassroots level.

Effectiveness of Community-Based Policing

The effectiveness of community-oriented policing has been documented by several authors (Akinyele 2001; Babawale 2001; Ikuteyijo and Rotimi 2010). To write off informal community-based police machinery because of observed inefficiencies and/or excesses will amount to a great disservice. In spite of their documented nuances, informal policing groups have succeeded in strengthening the psychological wellbeing of people in Nigeria because citizens feel safer and perceive their respective communities as safer (Alemika and Chukwuma 2003). The documented successes of informal security across Nigerian communities attest to their increasing relevance in contemporary times. In the Gwagwalada Area of the Federal Capital Territory, a vigilante group at Dagiri arrested three burglars at around 2:12 am in November 2011 and handed them over to the police (Isah 2011).

In June 2001, the former governor of Lagos State, southwestern Nigeria, Bola Ahmed Tinubu, publicly announced his willingness to invite the OPC to assist the state to combat criminals who seemed to have overwhelmed the police in Lagos State (Babawale 2001; Ikuteyijo and Rotimi 2010). Furthermore, in the southeastern part of the country, some state governments legitimized the Bakassi outfit; an example was in Anambra State, where the State House of Assembly enacted the Anambra Vigilance Services Act in 2001, which recognized the outfit and changed their name from Bakassi Boys to Anambra Vigilante Services (AVS). Another example was in the Niger Delta, (South–South Nigeria), where the EB and Movement for the Emancipation of the Niger Delta (MEND) were, at various points in time, engaged by the state governments to assist in the security of lives and property in the area.

However, due to improper or absence of supervision, community-based policing has resorted to jungle justice and persecution of perceived opponents alike. In fact, US-based Human Rights Watch (2003) and Maldar (2005) once bemoaned the spate of violence by ethnic militias and vigilante groups across Nigeria. Describing them as a threat to security. The report adds that ethnic militias, especially the OPC had killed many people without giving them the opportunity to be tried in a normal judicial process or at least give them fair hearing. Apart from improper supervision, inadequate funding (and, by extension, inadequate crime-fighting equipment) is another great obstacle facing informal community-based police outfits (Williams 2011). Similarly, unhealthy rivalry, suspicions, and contests for relevance among informal community-based security groups are a bane to their effectiveness.

Conclusion

There is no gain in saying the fact that effective community policing has a positive impact on crime in the neighborhood, helping to reduce fear of crime and enhancing the quality of life in the community. Since neither the police nor the CJS can bear the responsibility of ensuring a safe and secure community alone (Skolnick and Bayley 1988; Ikuteyijo and Rotimi 2010), members of the community have to play an active role in ensuring public safety. The implementation and monitoring of community-based policing strategies will deliver the needed peace and safety of communities and ensure healthy relationships among various stakeholders in the business of safety and security. To this end, the following best practices are suggested for implementing community policing in indigenous Nigerian communities:

- The NPF should provide a well-thought-out framework to coordinate informal community-oriented crime-fighting groups to utilize/maximize them effectively with a view to curtailing their excesses.
- The rivalry among informal security groups in the country and hostility between them and the NPF should be ironed out to forestall the recurring breakdown of law and order in the country.
- Political interference in security matters should be minimized as most politicians are reportedly hijacking the affairs of the VGN and other ethnic militias, using them to harass political opponents. These have led to most of the security problems witnessed in different parts of the country, with the most recent being the Boko Haram crisis.
- The NPF should have regular meetings with stakeholders like civil society organizations, students' unions, workers' unions, market women, and the academia, among others. This will serve as a form of appraisal, and issues emanating from the operations of the police and other informal police structures will be regularly monitored and corrections made where necessary.
- The NPF should also partner with research-based organizations, especially the academia, to have feedback from members of the community on the effectiveness of policing in the community.
- The multiethnic nature of the country should also be considered in the implementation of security-related policies. This is because various communities are likely to be confronted with different crime problems; hence, the responses of these communities to crime will vary according to cultural differences.
- The local government, being the closest to the community, should create synergy among various informal security groups and supervise the activities of these groups at the grassroots level as well as ensure their registration with the Divisional Police Headquarters.
- In the long term, the constitution should be amended to allow for the establishment of state police for effective supervision of these informal community-based security groups.

References

Aboribo, I. R. and Oghene, J. (2002). "The Police and the Problems of Law and Order: A Daunting Task in Public Administration." In Jike, V. T. (ed.): *Ethnic Militia and Youth Rebelliousness in Contemporary Nigeria. A Book of Readings*. Lagos, Nigeria: NISS Publications.

Achebe, C. (1984, orig. 1958). *Things Fall Apart*. Lagos: Academy Press Ltd.

Adebayo, F. (2005). "Ethnic Militias versus the Federal Government." *The Guardian Newspaper*, Sunday, November 6, pp. 60–64. Lagos, Nigeria.

Adebayo, B. (2009). "OPC, Vigilante Groups, Threat to Nation's Security." *Vanguard Newspapers Online*, October 18. Available at http://www.vanguardngr.com/.

Agabi, K. (2003). "Towards Effective Policing in Nigeria." In Alemika, E. E. O. and Chukwuma, I. C. (eds.): *Civilian Oversight and Accountability of Police in Nigeria*. Lagos, Nigeria: Mbeyi and Associates Ltd for CLEEN and Police Service Commission.

Ahire, P. T. (1991). *Imperial Policing: The Emergence and Role of the Police in Colonial Nigeria, 1860–1960*. Milton Keynes, England: Open University Press.

Akinyele, R. T. (2001). "Ethnic Militias and National Stability in Nigeria: History as Tool for Managing the Problems of Cultural Pluralism." In Eruvbetine, A. E. (ed.): *The Humanistic Management of Pluralism*. Lagos, Nigeria: Faculty of Arts, University of Lagos.

Alemika, E. E. O. (1988). "Policing and Perceptions of Police in NIGERIA." *Police Studies*, 11(4): 161–176.

Alemika, E. E. O. (1999). Police–Community Relations in Nigeria: What Went Wrong? Presentation at the seminar on *Role and Function of the Police in a post-Military Era*, organized by the Centre for Law Enforcement Education in Nigeria, CLEEN, and the National Human Rights Commission, March 8–10, Abuja, Nigeria.

Alemika, E. E. O. (2007). Police Reform in Africa: Issues and Challenges. Presentation at the *Police Reform in Post-Conflict African Countries Conference*, March 12–15, Pretoria, South Africa.

Alemika, E. E. O. (2010). History, Context and Crises of the Police in Nigeria. Presentation at the Biennial Retreat of the Police Service Commission on *Repositioning the Nigeria Police to Meet the Challenges of the Policing a Democratic Society in the 21st Century and Beyond*, November 1–4, Le Meridian Hotel, Uyo, Akwa Ibom State, Nigeria.

Alemika, E. E. O. and Chukwuma, I. C. (2000). *Police–Community Violence in Nigeria*. Lagos, Nigeria: CLEEN and the National Human Rights Commission.

Alemika, E. E. O. and Chukwuma, I. C. (2003). *The Poor and Informal Policing in Nigeria: A Report on Poor People's Perceptions and Priorities on Safety, Security and Informal Policing in A2J Focal States in Nigeria*. Lagos, Nigeria: CLEEN.

Anucha, C. (2007). "Community Policing Gets Boost: 53 Cops Given Special Training." *Daily Sun Newspapers Online*, Thursday, March 15. Available at http://sunnewsonline.com.

Ayodele, J. O. and Onu, F. O. (2006). "Democracy and Ethnic Conflicts in Contemporary Nigeria." In Akinwumi, O.; Okpe, O. O. & Je'adayide, G. D. (eds.): *Inter-group Relations in Nigeria during the Nineteenth and Twentieth Centuries*. Proceedings of the 1st National Conference of History Department, Nasarawa State University, Keffi, June 8–11, 2005. Makurdi, Nigeria: Aboki Publishers, pp. 641–655.

Babawale, T. (2001). "The Rise of Ethnic Militias, De-Legitimisation of the State, and the Threat to Nigerian Federalism." *West Africa Review*, 3: 1.

Banton, M. (1964). *The Policeman in the Community*. London, England: Basic Books.

Blench, R.; Longtau, S.; Hassan, U. & Welsh, M. (2006). *The Role of Traditional Rulers in Conflict Prevention and Mediation in Nigeria*. Lagos, Nigeria: DFID.

Blyden, E. W. (1908). African Life and Custom. Cited in Lynch, H. R. (ed.). 1971. *Black Spokesman: Selected Published Writings of Edward Wilmot Blyden*, London, England: Frank Cass & Co. Ltd.

Crowder, M. (1978). *Colonial West Africa: Collected Essays*. London: Frank Cass & Company Limited.

Danbazau, A. B. (1994). *Law and Criminality in Nigeria*. Ibadan, Nigeria: University Press Plc.

Ebo, P. E. (1993). "Human Resources Management and Policing." In Tamuno, T. N.; Bashir, I. L.; Alemika, E. E. O. & Akano, A. O. (eds.): *Policing Nigeria: Past, Present and Future*. Lagos, Nigeria: Malthouse Press Ltd.

Human Rights Watch (2003). "The O'odua Peoples Congress: Fighting Violence with Violence." Vol. 15. No. 4 (A), pp. 1–61. Washington, DC: Human Rights Watch.

Ibn Battuta (1975, orig. 1355). *Tuhfat al-nuzzar fi ghara'ib al-amsar wa-ajaib al-asafar* (English translation of Accounts of East and West African Travels by Said Hamdun and Noel King—Ibn Battuta in Africa). London, England: Rex Collins.

Ikuteyijo, L. (2009). "The Challenges of Community Policing in Nigeria." *International Journal of Police Science and Management*, 11(3), 285–293.

Ikuteyijo, L. and Rotimi, K. (2010). Community Partnership in Policing: The Nigerian Experience. Presentation at the *International Workshop on Policing and the Policed in the Post-Colonial State*, April 29–30, Institute of Commonwealth Studies, London, England.

Isah, A. S. (2011). "Vigilante Group Arrested Suspected Burglars at Dagiri." *Daily Trust Newspaper Online*, Friday, November 11. Available at http://dailytrust.com.ng.

Maldar, S. (2005). "Rest in Pieces: Police Torture and Deaths in Custody in Nigeria." Vol. 17. No. 11 (A), pp. 1–61. Washington DC.

Mbaku, M. J. and Kimenyi, M. S. (1995). "Rent Seeking and Policing in Colonial Africa." *The Indian Journal of Social Science*, 8(3): 277–306.

National Population Commission (2006). Nigerian Population and Housing Census. National Population Commission, Abuja, Nigeria.

Oluyede, P. A. (2002). *Nigerian Administrative Law*. Ibadan, Nigeria: University Press Plc.

Rotimi, K. (1993). "Local Police in Western Nigeria: End of an Era." In Tamuno, T. N.; Bashir, I. L.; Alemika, E. E. O. & Akano, A. O. (eds.): *Policing Nigeria: Past, Present and Future*. Lagos, Nigeria: Malthouse Press Ltd.

Skolnick, J. H. and Bayley, D. H. (1988). "Theme and Variation in Community Policing." *Crime and Justice*, 10: 1–37.

Tamuno, T. N. (1970). *The Police in Modern Nigeria*. Ibadan, Nigeria: University Press Plc.

Williams, S. (2011). "Nigeria: Vigilante Group Wants Funding for Community Policing." *Daily Trust Newspaper Online*, Saturday, November 10. Available at http://dailytrust.com.ng.

Wisler, D. and Onwudiwe, I. D. (2007). Community Policing: A Comparative View. Presentation at the *International Police Executive Symposium*, Working Paper No. 6, May. Available at http://www.ipes.info/WPS/WPS%20No%206.pdf.

South Africa

ANTHONY MINNAAR

7

Contents

Introduction

The geographical area of the southern tip of Africa, now the country of South Africa, started its colonial history of European settlement with the landing of the Dutch administrator, Jan van Riebeek, on April 16, 1652. He proceeded to establish a Dutch colony at the southernmost tip in the area now where the city of Cape Town is situated. In the early 1700s, independent farmers/settlers from Europe moved into the interior. The fledgling colony of the Cape of Good Hope changed hands to British control in 1795 with formal annexation by Great Britain in 1806. Thereafter, the British encouraged settlement by British settlers (first wave arriving in 1820). The expansion in the nineteenth century of this colony led to a number of so-called Frontier Wars with the clash between settler farmers and indigenous African inhabitants. However, the efforts by the British colonial authorities to Anglicize the administration of the colony alienated the previous settlers of Dutch, German, and French extract who were forging their own new African identity, making up the group termed Afrikaners (Boers) with their own language (Afrikaans), traditions, and culture. This alienation was further exacerbated with the emancipation of slaves in 1834. As a result, sections of this group broke away from the Cape of Good Hope Colony and moved into the interior, initially into the eastern area now known as KwaZulu-Natal, where they attempted to set up an independent republic. In the process, they fought a war against the Zulu Kingdom, defeating them at the Battle of Blood River. The British authorities followed the Afrikaner settlers (so-called Trekkers) and, after a brief war with them annexed, the KwaZulu-Natal area (excluding the so-called Zululand area north of the Tugela River), establishing the colony of Natal. The Afrikaner Trekkers moved away and further into the interior, eventually setting up the two independent republics of the Orange Free State (in 1854) and the Zuid-Afrikaansche Republiek or ZAR, also known as the Transvaal (in 1856). This process of colonization by both British and Afrikaners followed a pattern of arbitrarily annexing areas inhabited by local indigenous tribal Africans. In the process, numerous "wars" were fought with various tribal groupings. In some areas, the indigenous Bantu speakers maintained their independence, most notably in the northern Natal territories, which were still unmistakably the kingdom of the Zulu. Almost all were eventually to lose the struggle against white overlordship—British or Boer.

In 1872, the Cape Colony was granted self-government (only white males could vote for the representative legislature set up in 1853). However, in the late 1890s, British colonial expansion into the interior was driven by their desire to control not only land area (in the era of African colonization by the various European powers) but also the mineral wealth (discovery of diamonds in 1860s and large deposits of gold in the 1870s). The British colonial expansion in southern Africa led to them fighting two wars with the independent Afrikaner (Boer) republics. After the defeat of the latter in the so-called Second Anglo–Boer War (1899–1901), the British annexed these two republics. But the Afrikaners regained political control of them, and in 1910, the Union of South Africa came into being, consisting of the four British colonies, which became the four provinces of Cape, Natal, Orange Free State, and Transvaal covering the area of present-day South Africa. This political union was dominated by the white Afrikaner grouping and excluded all black indigenous African people (blacks were barred from becoming members of parliament). This exclusion led to the establishment on January 8, 1912 of the African National Congress, which in later years led the liberation struggle culminating in their assumption of political power in April 1994, when the first ever democratic elections were held in South Africa. However, prior to 1994, the Afrikaner political party, the National Party, particularly after 1948 when they took power, instituted the legislated racially discriminatory and exclusionary (of black African people) policy of Apartheid. As part of this policy, the National Party established so-called Tribal Homelands or nominally "independent" Bantustans (the former were the Kwa-Zulu, Lebowa, QwaQwa, KwaNdebele, KaNgwane, and Gazankulu areas; the latter were Transkei, Bophuthatswana, Venda, and Ciskei states). This policy had driven much of the social, cultural, economic, and political development of South Africa until its dismantling post-1994.

Currently, the country South Africa, situated at the southern tip of the African continent, is a multiparty democracy with a three-tier centralized form of government, at a national, provincial, and local (municipal/district) level. While English is the main language of government administration and education, there are 10 other official languages, namely, Afrikaans, Ndebele, Northern Sotho, Sotho, Swazi, Tsonga, Tswana, Venda, Xhosa, and Zulu. In 1994, the four provinces (Cape, Natal, Orange Free State, and Transvaal) and the 10 Bantustans were amalgamated into nine administrative provinces, namely, the Eastern Cape, Freestate, Gauteng, KwaZulu-Natal, Limpopo, Mpumalanga, Northern Cape, North West, and the Western Cape. South Africa itself is bordered by the countries of Namibia, Botswana, Zimbabwe, Mozambique, and Swaziland, while encircling the independent country of Lesotho. The 2011 population estimates put the total population of South Africa at 49.5 million people.

Historical Policing of South Africa

With unification of the four colonies in 1910, plans for a unified police force were made, and the South African Police (SAP) came into being in 1913 with the passing of the South African Police Act and delegated the duty and responsibility for upholding the law and maintaining law and order. With the start of the political protests in the late 1950s and early 1960s (e.g., ANC Defiance Campaigns against Pass Laws and agitation for political freedoms), there was a subtle shift in the way the black population, and in particular, political activists, were policed. In the 1970s, the most active branch had been the Criminal Investigation Division, but with the rise in civil unrest and public disorder in the 1980s, the Security Branch and the Riot Police Unit became far more active with the policing of protest marches and boycott campaigns and the arrest and detention and placing under covert surveillance of political activists. As a result, the SAP was increasingly being used as a political tool of repression and oppression by the Apartheid regime.

The Need for Community-Oriented Policing

Within this context, the negotiations in the early 1990s for a peaceful transfer of political power to the black majority, the negotiators were well aware of the need to transform the SAP. First, there had to be a change in the way that the South African public was policed (away from the previous apartheid repressive and authoritarian policing style). Second, previously underpoliced (in pure policing terms) communities (largely the black townships that had approximately only 20% of existing police resources allocated to them, with the rest allocated to the more affluent, largely white-populated residential urban neighborhoods) had to be better policed with regard to service delivery and the allocation of resources. Third, this policing should strive to follow a more democratic and human rights–oriented form of policing. To fulfill this new "vision for policing" in South Africa, the policy makers decided to make so-called community policing the core of this transformed policing approach in South Africa.

While it can be said that South Africa had no real tradition of any form of formal community policing, in the days of political repression, there were various forms of community self-policing that did occur. Here we think of the activities in the black townships of the "anticrime street committees" and the "people's courts" that euphemistically self-administered "popular justice" in the townships in the late 1970s and 1980s—whose largely politicized struggle activities were all but put an end to by 1988 with the then-government's use of the Emergency Regulations powers to suppress all political dissent and public protest. However, a number continued to perpetrate anticrime vigilante acts in trying to self-police their neighborhoods in a covert manner (see Minnaar 2002). The subsequent massive increase in violent political protest all but halted formal policing in many areas (that were being made ungovernable by ANC political protest activities), with the exception where shows of massive force were implemented—but all in an effort to bring down the political violence rather than crime control initiatives.

As a consequence, it was politically expedient for the new ANC-led government post-1994 to be seen to be making efforts to restore the legitimacy and credibility of the old SAP and restore trust and confidence in policing activities by all members of the community. One of the first measures in this was the renaming of the old SAP to the South African Police Service (SAPS) and changing the military-style rank structure to more acceptable civilian labels (e.g., general to commissioner, brigadier–director, etc.).

To give structure and form to this envisaged new form of policing in South Africa, various study trips overseas were made to look at various forms of community policing (notably the Community-Oriented Policing [COPS] style from the United States and the Belgian model).

One of the results of this was the formulation and insertion into the interim (The [Interim] Constitution of South Africa 1993) of the concept of Community Police Forums (CPFs), which in the South African context were designed to be the link between communities and the new SAPS, in order to oversee the implementation of the new model of community policing.

As early as the end of 1994 and building on the Interim Constitution, a Green Paper on Safety and Security was issued as a policy guide for policing in the "new democratic" South Africa. This outlined principles such as community policing, democratic control, and accountability, as well as introducing a new style of policing that required a demilitarized approach whereby civilian values would inform every aspect of the new policing services.

Furthermore, an immediate start was made in drafting a new piece of legislation to restructure the amalgamated policing agencies (the old SAP and the 10 policing agencies of the former Bantustan/Homelands structures of the former apartheid South Africa). This new piece of legislation, the SAPS Act No. 68 of 1995, was passed in early 1995. The Act provided for an accountable, impartial, transparent, community-oriented, and cost-effective police service. Other changes looked at such aspects as training, which was adapted to reflect a nonmilitary style of policing, different policing styles or approaches such as community policing, and even a brief flirtation with "zero tolerance."

There was a quick recognition by top management of the new SAPS and the National Police Secretariat that an urgent look at policies, legislation, and guidelines for a new way of policing in South Africa was needed. Work began in 1995 on the *National Crime Prevention Strategy* (NCPS) (approved by Cabinet in May 1996). Although the NCPS was of necessity a wide-ranging document covering the whole criminal justice system, many of the issues raised in this document focused more on the role of the police in operationalizing these needs in fighting crime than on operational aspects of community policing.

The Green Paper (Department of Safety and Security 1994), the SAPS Act of 1995 (South African Police Service), and the NCPS (Department of Safety and Security 1996), in advocating a new approach to police practices, made an important policy or paradigm shift by strongly advocating that policing be made more community oriented. To ensure that these principles were implemented in actual policing and building on the impetus given by the policy acceptance of the NCPS and the Green Paper, the Minister of Safety and Security approved the development of a White Paper in June 1997.

Prior to the actual release of the White Paper in 1998, the Department for Safety and Security had released a detailed document titled *Policy Framework and Guidelines for Community Policing* in April 1997. As a consequence, the White Paper made little operational reference to community policing per se other than to mention that the SAPS policing approach continued to be "underpinned by the philosophy of community policing" and that this focus was "directly in line with international trends in policing which demonstrate that the participation of communities and community policing form the bedrock of effective law enforcement" (Department of Safety and Security 1998, pp. 3 and 10).

Implementation of Community Policing in South Africa

What then of the accepted philosophy of community policing by the SAPS? As part of the policy changes (Green Paper, Police Act, NCPS, and the latter White Paper) in formulating a new way of policing, the SAPS had officially adopted community policing as the way to go. *The Community Policing Policy Framework and Guidelines* (CPPFG), released in April 1997, was intended to serve as guidelines for implementing this official policing style in South Africa.

The Community Policing Model as outlined in the policy framework was largely an adaptation of traditional Western European and American principles, inter alia the emphasis on establishing police–community partnerships within a problem-solving approach responsive to the needs of the community (South African Police Service 1997). The CPPFG further accepted the following broad concepts of (1) service orientation (community being the client and SAPS the service provider); (2) partnerships (cooperative effort to facilitate a process of problem solving); (3) problem solving (joint identification and analysis of the actual and potential causes of crime within communities); (4) empowerment (creation of sense of joint responsibility—joint capacity for addressing crime and service delivery); and (5) accountability (mechanisms for making police answerable for addressing needs and concerns of communities) (South African Police Service 1997).

The policy document itself gave detailed guidelines for the establishment of CPFs in every policing precinct—every police station commissioner was instructed to be "responsible for the establishment of Community Police Forums in their respective areas" (South African Police Service 1997, p. 5). Furthermore, they were delegated to undertake "the identification and mobilization, through consultation, of community resources and organizations that may assist in combating and preventing crime and the constant development of this capacity" (South African Police Service 1997, p. 4). Moreover, all police members were tasked (in the policy guidelines) "to develop new skills through training which incorporates problem solving, networking, mediation, facilitation, conflict resolution and community involvement" (South African Police Service 1997, p. 4). This in itself was a tall order for the SAPS—undertrained, underskilled, poorly resourced, and almost overwhelmed by a high workload and persistent high levels of crime as they were, without even mentioning the other socioeconomic problems facing an emerging democratic and developing country like South Africa.

Subsequently, various endeavors were embarked upon to institutionalize community policing in South Africa. As from the beginning of 1998, a comprehensive program was launched within the SAPS to train all members in the philosophy, values, and principles of community policing. It must be remembered that the old SAP certainly did not have the ethos or culture of following such a type of "softer" policing (as opposed to the more "hard" militaristic and forceful style of the past). In the South African context, this policing style was based on the premise that a community and its police service are equal partners with shared responsibilities in ensuring safety and security.

The community policing document also focused on the establishment of CPFs and CPF Area Boards as official structures to coordinate partnership policing initiatives at community level, while the White Paper provided for a supplementary role for local government in CPF activities by directing the CPFs toward a more cooperative relationship with municipalities and metropolitan councils in what was termed "social crime prevention." Thus, the CPFs' community role shifted to one of community mobilization in order to address priority crimes in each community by maximizing civil participation in crime-prevention initiatives (Smit and Schnetler 2004, p. 14).

From the SAPS and the government side, in this rollout of CPFs and community policing, the most important thing in this situation was for the authorities to formalize the whole system of "informal vigilante" justice by channeling these anticrime activities into a more formal structure, that is, the new CPF/street committees in liaison with the local police structures. However, with the implementation of CPFs (as the foundation of the new community policing), there very quickly arose disputes between forum members and local police station members, particularly over the operational independence of the SAPS themselves; clashes erupted over CPF community crime priorities and the official SAPS priorities—which were set at national level (Shaw 2002).

In fact, it took only a little more than 5 years after the initial community police policy document for the new community policing style to largely become abandoned (or at best simply ignored or disregarded in terms of operational planning) in all but name throughout the SAPS. This "abandonment" (with SAPS personnel strongly believing it to be "too soft" for the tough crime conditions in South African townships) was also due in part to a number of inherent constraints, one of these being that at the time of its inception, the personnel of the SAPS were still largely undertrained and underskilled, with estimates that almost 25% of its 128,000 members considered to be functionally illiterate (Pelser 1999).

Even more members had never received formal training in the actual methodology of community policing. Initially, the SAPS members had also tended to ignore the local CPFs or alternately took the initiative in setting up (in other words, co-opting) members from the community onto the CPFs, which were in any case administered (had their meetings at and resourced from local police stations) by the local police station commissioner. CPFs doing their critical monitoring role and advising police on priority crimes in their areas or even what crime prevention programs should be implemented (theoretically in partnership with communities) were few and far between. Moreover, in the more affluent, predominantly white areas, the tendency was for the local CPF to turn itself into a Section 21 Company (not for profit) and then to contribute money toward the purchase of equipment and vehicles for the use of the police station in their area so as to ensure that the type of quality policing previously received (in the apartheid era) from a well-resourced police station would continue to be received by its residents (Pelser 1999).

This was a very deliberate response to what was perceived as the siphoning off of resources to the previously (pre-1994) underresourced and poorly policed areas in the black townships. So inequalities in levels of policing continued—albeit unintended—to be perpetuated since CPFs in poorer areas could not afford to equip their local police station at all. The whole effectiveness of CPFs was being questioned, particularly since they ended up being unelected, that is, co-opted by the local police station commissioner (community elections were tried but became a waste of time since very few community members turned up for voting at community meetings; particular interest groups such as minibus taxi associations got their members voted onto a local CPF, thereby dominating proceedings with their narrow crime concerns; or even criminals infiltrated and became privy to policing activities in their areas of operation) or consisted of local individuals who had a specific interest in improving police performance. Within the SAPS itself, they were treated with disdain and regarded "as a necessary evil" required by law to bring members of the public into contact with the police. CPFs ended up having little impact or say on the day-to-day conduct of the police. In addition, this situation led to disputes arising between CPF members and the SAPS as to the latter's operational independence, and eventually, those CPFs (other than the ones who merely funded additional equipment and vehicles) were sidelined and ignored (Shaw 2001).

In a study conducted by Pelser, Schnetler, and Louw in 2002, it was found that essentially, community policing and CPFs appeared to have been subtly downgraded (operationally as well as a guiding policing philosophy) by the Ministry and the SAPS as far as policies, regulations, and funding were concerned, while communities had also (through apathy and disinterest) abrogated any involvement in community policing viewing crime prevention, reduction, and control as solely "police business" (Pelser et al. 2002).

Community policing in South Africa, originally intended as an alternative policing model to assist the police to prevent crime in communities, soon came to be subsumed into other forms of policing. Although not initially apparent, while still paying lip service to a community-oriented approach (using all the appropriate terminology), the SAPS, as early as the launch of the Community Safety Plan in 1995, had already demonstrated—if one carefully reads between the lines and observes the special operations launched as part of this plan—"their intention to revert to more traditional methods to combat crime" (Burger 2007, p. 136). In addition, all pretense to community policing was in fact abandoned with the more formal Policing Priorities and Objectives (otherwise known as the Police Plan) of 1996/1997 and the implementation of special high-density area concentrated special operations such as Operation Sword and Shield with its "return to basics" policing approach.

So, in essence, in South Africa, community policing per se faded into the background, and other forms of policing (such as visible and sector policing) were pushed forward by the SAPS, ostensibly in support of community policing. However, these were all designed more to improve the SAPS operational effectiveness in fighting crime than to deal directly with community sensitivities, and the need to be policed in a more considerate, sympathetic, compassionate, and sensitive manner.

Visible Policing

The 1998 White Paper had emphasized the implementation of more of what was termed "visible policing," linked to better service delivery to victims, as well as coordinating an integrated criminal justice system. The White Paper advocated a dual approach to safety and security—effective and efficient law enforcement and the provision of crime prevention programs to reduce the occurrence of crime, inter alia by implementing targeted (active) visible policing. Visible policing was designed to fill the gap between operational crime-combating activities and community policing by "providing a proactive and responsive policing service that will prevent the priority crimes rate from increasing" (South African Police Service 2007, p. 31). The emphasis was, however, on specialized crime prevention operations.

Core to the visible policing approach was the implementation of the following three phases: (1) preventative patrolling, that is, a constant police presence in, for instance, an identified "hot spot" crime area; (2) directed patrol, that is, police officers assigned for a limited period for a particular purpose; and (3) sector policing (Department of Safety and Security 1998).

Of the three forms of visible policing as outlined in the White Paper, sector policing became the most important of the new initiatives with reference to the implementation of community policing. But this required an unprecedented change not only in training but also in the thinking of ordinary policemen and women on the ground. The overloading of police officers and detectives within the context of the continued high crime levels made it virtually impossible to implement meaningful training programs across the board. Members could simply not be spared to go off on training courses for weeks on end.

So while the policy changes seemed to be on the right track in practical terms, policing in South Africa still continued to suffer from ineffectiveness and delays or lack of full implementation. Ultimately, this failure led to no significant and meaningful reductions in reported crime levels, especially from the perspective and perceptions of the public as reflected in the official crime statistics.

By the turn of the 21st century, 6 years after democratization, there still remained huge structural and operational problems facing a transforming SAPS. With the realization that much of the intended changes were simply not being properly or adequately operationalized, the new Minister of Safety and Security, Steve Tshwete, initiated a review of the NCPS, and a Strategic Implementation Plan was approved by the Cabinet in September 1999. In addition, a Justice, Crime Prevention and Security Cluster (JCPS) was established in order to focus on addressing the incidence of crime and public disorder while improving the efficiency of the criminal justice system (Minister of Safety and Security 2007). The JCPS developed a National Security Policy (NSP) aimed at integrating crime prevention and crime-combating activities with socioeconomic upliftment (Smit and Schnetler 2004).

As part of implementing the priorities of the JCPS cluster, the SAPS developed its own National Crime Combating Strategy (NCCS), launched on April 1, 2000 (as outlined in the SAPS Strategic Plan: 2002–2005) (Smit and Schnetler 2004; South African Police Service 2000).

Sector Policing

As part of the NCCS, the SAPS also launched (as envisaged in the White Paper of 1998) an intensive policing and patrol strategy officially termed "sector policing." This approach basically meant that each police station area (precinct) was divided into smaller, more manageable areas. Police resources were then directed to those specific high-crime identified areas within the precinct in order to increase police visibility, improve community involvement by inter alia building trust and getting the public to report all crime and any suspicious activities in their neighborhood, and try to address the causes of crime and the fear of crime (Smit and Schnetler 2004, p. 17). Better visible and sector policing was based on the premise that if crime levels could be brought down, communities would feel safer, trust the police more, and as a consequence, better report crime to the police. Hence, operational improvements and increased policing effectiveness would then indirectly support and grow community policing.

Sector policing, as one of the prioritized focus areas in the SAPS Strategic Plan (2002–2005), was officially launched only in 2001 with a pilot project in the Johannesburg area. It was seen as the final practical manifestation of community policing. The official SAPS view then being that the concept of community policing as "focusing on building partnerships at a broader level in specific areas" was now strongly coupled to a planned national rollout of sector policing whereby the SAPS was to work on mobilizing and organizing "communities at microlevel (for example within the boundaries of neighborhoods, or sectors) to bring police closer to the communities" (South African Police Service 2010, p. 39). In other words, sector policing was to be a tool for the full implementation of community policing.

The basic concept of sector policing as exhibited in the South African context consisted of at least one police official being allocated on a full-time basis to a sector (i.e., geographically manageable area within a police precinct) for which he or she is responsible to enhance safety and security.

Crucial to the successful implementation of this concept is the involvement of all role players in identifying the policing needs in that particular sector and in addressing the root causes of crime as well as the enabling and contributing factors. The responsibilities of the sector police official also included determining policing needs on a continuous basis, in cooperation with nonpolice role players, and identifying crime problems, tendencies, crime, "hot spots," criminals, and so forth. In addition, their role included initiating and cocoordinating of policing projects, for example, special patrols, and other safety and security initiatives. They would also be responsible for overseeing the activation of other role players (e.g., municipalities, government departments, and nongovernmental organizations). Underlying these actions would be first establishing direct communication with community members, often via CPFs—if there was one functioning in the area. Alternately, sector police officers would usually start off with a public awareness campaign sometimes involving "knock-and-drop-off" of information sheets and pamphlets actions and the holding of monthly crime discussion meetings with community members. Essentially, the "new" sector policing initiative looked at addressing local crime problems and, where possible, the root causes of crime.

At the end of 2003, the SAPS had sent out a directive to police stations across the country to start implementing sector policing on the basis of the positive results from the Johannesburg pilot project. (But many precincts delayed and dragged their feet on this implementation citing a lack of resources, operational vehicles, and manpower in preventing them in setting up sector units dedicated to each neighborhood [sector] in their precincts.) Ironically, it was only with the approaching Soccer World Cup held in South Africa from June to July 2010 that a National Directive for the national rollout of sector policing was sent out at the end of 2009 and that such dedicated sector policing units were established in policing precincts countrywide (see Bezuidenhout 2010).

In essence, sector policing is an amalgam of past policing initiatives drawing on elements of CPF structures, community policing, visible policing, special operations, crime analysis, and intelligence-led policing. It also creates a perfect platform for the involvement and integration and coordination of policing activities of certain sectors of the private security industry. Within all these policy changes, there were persistent calls by the private security industry to be allowed to play a larger role in assisting the police to combat and prevent crime, or at least to outsource certain services still being provided by the SAPS that could very easily be outsourced without compromising any strictly policing functions of the SAPS.

Conclusion

By the end of 2007, while the policy framework made provision for the wider implementation of community policing through such initiatives as social crime prevention and CPFs and supported by the activities of visible and sector policing, it had been accepted only as a wider philosophical guideline without real community implementation and participation in its envisaged form. Since its official acceptance in 1994, it was largely accepted only through other, largely police operational structures, with the communities having limited say in the evolvement of an adapted South African model.

Currently, real community policing is occurring in South Africa at neighborhood level via the new Community Safety Initiative policy but not the strictly policy-driven and operational form as envisaged by the government. The SAPS, while instituting sector policing in most policing precincts (that have been allocated additional resources, particularly patrol vehicles) countrywide, particularly urban residential areas, still implements an operational traditional reactive type of policing, that is, where the police will still react as quickly as possible (response times have improved with the regular sector policing neighborhood patrols), but again mostly a reaction based on reported crimes in progress.

Actual community policing South African style is largely dependent upon active CPFs and their local sector subcommittees and private neighborhood watch members who commonly have set up their own voluntary community safety initiatives reliant on voluntary neighborhood patrols often backed up with partnership contractual agreements with private security companies for the provision of proactive preventative private policing activities.

From mid-2009 onward, the institution of so-called Community Safety Initiatives in neighborhood after neighborhood grew apace as resuscitated or existing CPFs set about, with renewed vigor, setting up formal links and relations with local police station precinct sector commanders. Security and crime prevention strategies, coordinated with the sector policing activities (visible patrols, reporting of suspicious activities and crimes in progress, sharing incident report information, etc.), were launched in many communities (albeit starting in the more affluent urban neighborhoods in the major cities) where residents in neighborhoods/sectors became more involved in "looking after their own safety and security needs" in the fight against crime. Generally, the safety and security of residents in each sector were based on such initiatives as negotiating with a dominant private security company for the institution of a 24/7 proactive patrol vehicle. Such a contracted private security company patrol vehicle would typically have only one unarmed security officer dedicated to patrol only in one sector as a visible crime deterrence presence in what was being termed in company jargon as "localized security services" (LSS). Such service was to be based on a written service-level agreement (SLA) outlining its functions and patrol activities. Such an LSS patrol vehicle would not only be connected to the contracted security company's radio control room but also link into the specific neighborhood sector's—and oftentimes adjacent sectors'—local two-way radio network and cell phone SMS systems.

Other community policing activities involved residents of a sector (neighborhood) organizing their own patrols (day and nighttime); setting up a two-way radio network (sometimes on a repeater sending station); having a "roll-call" check-in via the radio network every evening; linking all residents (or those willing to participate) in an SMS cell phone service whereby any suspicious activities, crime incidents, or other information could be rapidly spread on via cell phone to the sector's residents; as well as alerting the local sector police commander to such incidents for possible police response.

Sector committees are also increasingly doing their own fundraising to purchase such security surveillance equipment as closed-circuit television (CCTV) cameras placed on high masts at the street entrances to their sectors/neighborhoods. As these Community Safety Initiatives became better organized, reductions in crime from their sectors began to be reported. The security systems (see Minnaar 2011 for more detail on these) as outlined above also lead to a number of successes where community patrol members observed crimes and immediately alerted the local police, continued to follow the suspects until the police arrived, and gave chase apprehending the perpetrators. Such overlapping levels of security have infinitely improved the safety levels within such organized sectors. Currently, this form of community policing in conjunction with the sector policing roll-outs (in 2010) has led to many neighborhoods becoming more confident that they can deal more effectively with existing crime levels in their areas and go a long way toward reducing existing crime. But like all past community policing initiatives, the levels of effectiveness and success are largely dependent upon the buy-in, commitment, and participation of each resident in a sector, even if only to be the "eyes and ears" for one's neighbor or the houses in the street in which one lives. Unfortunately, even at this early stage of the rollout of sector policing, there are signs that, after the initial burst of cooperative enthusiasm and involvement, interest has tended to fall away and participation dwindle, once again leaving a small core of between 10% and 15% of sector residents actively involved in various ways. It therefore remains to be seen how sustainable and ongoing this form of South African community policing will be in the near future.

References

Bezuidenhout, C. (2010). Sector policing: Case closed—or not? Paper presented to the 17th Annual International Police Executive Symposium: *Tourism, Strategic Locations and Major Events—Policing in an Age of Mobility, Mass Movement and Migration*. Valletta, Malta. 14–19 March 2010.

Burger, J. (2007). *Strategic Perspectives on Crime and Policing in South Africa*. Pretoria, South Africa: Van Schaik Publishers.

Department of Safety and Security. (1994). *Green Paper on Safety and Security*. Pretoria, South Africa: Department of Safety and Security.

Department of Safety and Security. (1996). *National Crime Prevention Strategy*. Pretoria, South Africa: Department of Safety and Security.

Department of Safety and Security. (1998). *White Paper on Safety and Security: In Service of Safety—1999–2004*. Pretoria, South Africa: Department of Safety and Security.

The (Interim) Constitution of South Africa. (1993). Act No. 200 of 1993. *Government Gazette*, 27 April 1994.

Ministry of Safety and Security. (2007). *Justice Crime Prevention and Security (JCPS) Cluster Media Briefing: 1st Cycle of 2007*. Pretoria, South Africa. 10 May.

Minnaar, A. (2002). The "new" vigilantism in post-April 1994 South Africa: Searching for explanations. In D. Feenan (ed.), *Informal Criminal Justice*: 117–134. Advances in Criminology series. Aldershot, England: Dartmouth/Ashgate Publishing.

Minnaar, A. (2011). Private security companies, neighbourhood watches and the use of CCTV surveillance in residential neighbourhoods: Case studies from Pretoria-East, Tshwane. Paper presented to the Criminological and Victimological Society (CRIMSA) Bi-ennial Conference: *Criminal Justice and Criminology—A Futuristic Perspective on Crime Trends and New Crimes*. University of KwaZulu-Natal, Durban, South Africa. 27–30 September 2011.

Pelser, E. (1999). *The Challenges of Community Policing in South Africa*. Occasional Paper No. 42. September. Pretoria, South Africa: Institute for Security Studies.

Pelser, E., J. Schnetler, and A. Louw. (2002). *Not Everybody's Business: Community Policing in the SAPS' Priority Areas*. ISS Monograph No. 71. Pretoria, South Africa: Institute for Security Studies.

Shaw, M. (2001). *Marching to a Different Tune: Political change and Police Transformation in South Africa and Northern Ireland*. Johannesburg, South Africa: South African Institute of International Affairs.

Shaw, M. (2002). *Crime and Policing in Post-Apartheid South Africa: Transforming under Fire.* Bloomington, IN: Indiana University Press.

Smit, J. and Schnetler, J. (2004). Policies guiding the police and policing. In J. Smit, A. Minnaar, and J. Schnetler (eds.), *Smart Policing for Law-Enforcement Official:* 10–24. Claremont, CA: New Africa Education.

South African Police Service. (1995). Act No. 68 of 1995. *Government Gazette,* 15 October 1995.

South African Police Service. (1997). *The Community Policing Policy Framework and Guidelines.* Pretoria, South Africa: Government Printer/SAPS.

South African Police Service. (2000). *Strategic Plan for the South African Police Service: 2002–2005.* Pretoria, South Africa: Strategic Management, SAPS HQ.

South African Police Service. (2000–2010). *Annual Report of the South African Police Service.* Pretoria: Government Printer/SAPS (all reports are available on the SAPS website at http://www.saps.org.za).

The Americas

II

Argentina

8

MARK UNGAR

Contents

Introduction: Community-Oriented Policing as Foundation of Reform

The combination of federalism and political transformation has put Argentina at the forefront of community-oriented policing (COP) in Latin America. Its 23 autonomous and diverse provinces have together established a diverse range of COP programs that are diverse in design but all rooted in principles, such as human rights and institutional transparency, whose importance grew after wrenching changes such as the 1983 transition from a brutal dictatorship and the 2001 economic collapse.

As centralized and repressive forms of policing gave way to citizen-based approaches, they also led to other reforms needed to sustain COP but often neglected in policy and analysis. If the social service and criminal justice systems do not adequately address the causes and consequences of crime, in particular, COP will struggle to gain popular and political traction. Many reforms, discussed below, have been adopted by most provinces to strengthen that larger approach. One is institutional restructuring to make policing more efficient by establishing civilian-led Ministry of Justice and Security, dividing provincial police agencies to correspond to judicial districts, and forming separate preventative, investigative, transport, and prison units. A second area of reform has been judicial, mainly through new penal process codes to transfer investigative power from the police to the prosecutors, replace written with oral trials, and create new courts. Another common trait among provincial reforms was opening up policing to public scrutiny, such as establishment of internal affairs units, disciplinary bodies, ombudsmen, and divisions for underserved areas in Santa Fe, Mendoza, Neuquén, Córdoba, San Luis, and Buenos Aires provinces. Education was also overhauled. Many provincial academies adopted new curricula and entrance requirements, and provinces like Buenos Aires, San Luis, and Mendoza created entirely new civilian-run academies.

COP Approaches and Programs

All these changes provide a foundation for COP, which, rather than being another reform, constitutes a fundamental change in the nature of policing by placing citizens at the forefront of crime fighting, tailoring policies to local conditions, and focusing on prevention rather than response. Along with the Autonomous City of Buenos Aires (hereafter Federal Capital), 17 provinces have adopted specific COP programs that range from specialized police units to neighborhood councils. In provinces like Formosa, community policing divisions help guide the larger force toward more flexible and localized actions. Most provinces that are largely rural and sparsely populated—such as Chaco, Corrientes, Río Negro, and Catamarca—do not have special community policing programs but are improving preventative coordination among state agencies or infusing their police with COP approaches. La Pampa Province's Special Prevention Group and Rapid Patrol, for example, are trained for preventing and handling quickly escalating conditions of criminal violence. As discussed in the next section, most of these programs have faced political, institutional, and societal opposition. But as this section discusses, Argentina's wide extent of COP programs and principles has helped it overcome these inevitable obstacles to become the kind of fundamental change that it is intended to be.

Citizen and Community Empowerment

Although the community has been COP's biggest catalyst, its role in actual COP programs is often limited by a continued dominance of police agendas and reliance on traditional approaches. In Argentina, the provinces of Buenos Aires, Chaco, Chubut, Córdoba, Entre Ríos, La Pampa, La Rioja, Mendoza, Río Negro, Santa Fe, and San Luis centered COP on channels of community input. Those channels were most effective, though, when centered on citizen fora with substantial authorities and support networks. The Federal Capital's Citizen Security Program, for example, is backed by over 50 Crime and Violence Prevention Councils composed of residents, business owners, nongovernmental organizations (NGOs), and social agencies to help residents draw up crime maps, improve police relations, and help at-risk groups. Supporting these bodies is a Community Police Office, formed by the Federal Police (PFA: *Policía Federal Argentina*), as well as Neighborhood Auxiliaries that direct crime victims to appropriate services and channel citizen requests to city agencies. Taking advantage of their wide leeway to develop and publicize creative solutions to insecurity, these agencies have substantially reduced the percentage of residents with negative views of the police.[*] The Federal Security Ministry, which oversees the city's policing, has also promoted COP. Its 2011 Plan of Urban Security aims to base patrol assignments more on citizen demands and crime maps, and the National Plan of Participación Comunitaria aims to help citizen forums monitor and support each police district (*comisarías*).[†]

---

[*] Author interview, Claudio Súarez, Chief, Federal Capital Security Program, May 27, 2004. See also DNPC/Ministerio de Justicia de la Nación, *Encuesta de victimización de la ciudad de Buenos Aires*, 1997–2000.

[†] "Argentina: La ministra lanzó el programa de participación comunitaria para la prevención del delito," *La Nación*, April 5, 2011.

In Buenos Aires province, Law 12.154 of 1998 boosted citizen power beyond almost every other COP program through formation of strong fora at the neighborhood, municipal, and departmental levels that have fully taken advantage of the law's citizen "rights" to participate in the "elaboration, implementation and control of public security politics," (This quote is from Article 11 of Law 12.154) in at least four areas of action. The first is identification of crime's causes through reports, meetings, and mapping. Concurrent with police districts, in particular, neighborhood fora are designed to encourage participation, channel complaints, and formulate preventative action. Those powers are boosted by the second area of activity, which is monitoring of policing by developing performance criteria and writing officer evaluations that are part of the Professional Certification Unit's annual review. Municipal fora, focusing on policy and authorities such as electing *Defensor Municipal de Seguridad,* also help design integral plans of municipal security. A third area of fora action, reflecting the Security Ministry's focus on vulnerable sectors,* is developing programs on socioeconomic issues like school safety, public space, and family violence. Most fora, finally, have improved criminal justice with aims like simplifying crime report filing. A range of state programs supports these efforts. The Security Ministry's Multiple Response Program helps develop prevention strategies in low-income areas, for example, and schools of community participation in security offer courses in security policy for community groups.

Beyond their policy roles, the fora's appeal comes from their promotion as depoliticized ways to maximize community power and minimize social differences through creative and coordinated responses.† After one study revealed that a majority of detained youth had not completed elementary school, for example, one group developed new education programs. The citizens' forum also placed notebooks at different locations on officers' routes for them to sign, helping make sure they stick to their patrols. In a virtual cycle that boosts COP, the approach has also made people more willing to call the police. For example, car robbery and dismantling—one of the province's most persistent crimes—has been reduced through raids based on resident calls. COP fora enjoy similar responses in other provinces. In La Rioja, for example, 80% of respondents in a survey attribute what they regard as improving police–citizen relations to COP's prioritization of cooperative preventative projects. As in Buenos Aires, such support corresponds to crime reductions. Over two-thirds of the La Rioja survey respondents also said that COP has reduced violent, property, and drug crimes.‡

Institutional Change

COP cannot work in Argentina without efforts to make its militarized and centralized police structures more localized, flexible, and preventative. One step toward that goal is reducing the militarized hierarchies, which provinces like Santa Fe have begun by eliminating the division between official and subofficial ranks. Mendoza province's reform focused on personnel support for officers, such as a program to secure bank loans at favorable rates

---

* Author interview, Martha María Arriola, Subsecretaría de Participación Comunitaria, Ministerio de Seguridad, Provincia de Buenos Aires, July 19, 2007.
† Author interviews, Lomas de Zamora, July 19, 2007; Néstor Borri, Secretario Ejectivo de Nueva Tierra, Escuelas de Ciudadanía; July 18, 2007; e-mail correspondence, Norma Landolfo, forum coordinator, 2011.
‡ This survey was funded by the CUNY Collaborative Project on COP of the City University of New York (CUNY).

and training for prison officials to relieve police officers of that responsibility, and making aptitude trump seniority in promotion (Binder et al. 2005). More broadly, Mendoza's 1998 security overhaul included a clearer penal code, a stronger *Fiscalía*, a civilian-led Ministry of Justice and Security, and a police decentralization into District Police corresponding to the province's four judicial districts (del Valle Barrera 1998). Also established were judicial, scientific, transport, and other specialized units. A General Inspector of Security (IGS: *Inspección General de Seguridad*) was created to investigate police abuses, in part by placing trained mediators in police stations, and supported by a Disciplinary Board to prosecute them. The reform regeared police education with a new academy, the University Institute of Public Security (IUSP), a joint effort of the government and the National University, along with seven satellite academies.

The country's most sweeping transformation was in Buenos Aires province—which long had one of Latin America's most corrupt, powerful, and abusive police forces. But public support for its tough policing amid high crime in the 1990s diminished as it failed to slow crime down, eventually leading to overhauls like establishment of a civilian-led Justice and Security Secretariat and the split-up of the preventative 35,000-officer Security Police into the province's 18 judicial departments. After police resistance and the 1999 election of an antireform governor halted these changes, in 2003, a new government introduced a "new paradigm" that nearly amounted to "the abandonment by the State in the formulation of security policies."[*] The official and subofficial hierarchies were fused, the number of ranks nearly halved, and operative control transferred to 32 department headquarters. A Communal Police was established for cities with populations under 70,000, Security Police for those of over 70,000, and the Buenos Aires 2 police for the high-crime *conurbano*, the industrial belt surrounding the Federal Capital. Civilians were incorporated into the hierarchy, and an emergency line to the Subsecretariat of Community Participation was set up. Education was strengthened through the Center for Advanced Studies in Police Specialties (CAEEP: *Centro de Altos Estudios en Especialidades Policiales*), and accountability was strengthened with a General Auditor of Internal Affairs.

Coordination and Local Control

One of the main reasons for social services' ineffectiveness is the poor coordination among them. Agencies on education, health, culture, and other areas often work at cross purposes without the benefit of holistic responses to crime's causes. Many COP projects, therefore, are centered on better social services. In Misiones Province, the Office of Community Policing is based on an interdisciplinary team that offers preventative course in areas such as Juvenile Violence Prevention to Inter-Personal Sensitivity. Jujuy Province centers COP on its community mediators trained by the government and Justice Ministry's Secretaría de Protección a la Comunidad. Integrated into the police and its daily activities, the mediators offer mediation technique to a range of civil society organizations with key strategies such as "Active Listening" and "Opening up Dialogue" in order to allow citizens to resolve conflicts amicably.

---

[*] Author interview, León Arslanián, Buenos Aires Security Chief, Lima, Perú, April 1, 2007, and Buenos Aires, July 26, 2007.

La Rioja province's 2003 Strategic Plan of the Police, one of the country's most ambitious COP overhauls, was led by four social service consortiums: a Strategic Government Coordination Committee, Intersectional Operational and Coordination Councils (COCI: *Consejos Operativos de Coordinación Intersectional Zonal*), a COP Planning and Implementation Team, and Neighborhood COP Councils. These four entities focused on tailoring policies to each neighborhood by bringing together security officials with social services and central actors like schools and churches.* The police were integral to that change with initiatives such as home visits, uncivil behavior registries, seminars on issues like domestic violence, and a restructuring of two capital city *comisarías* based on foot patrols. Mendoza also girded COP with social service initiatives such as an antifamily violence project, local health centers, and a School for Fathers to build parental self-esteem. It established a Coordinator of Security to coordinate police–society relations; Department Security Councils of municipal officials, police, and citizens; and neighborhood forums to implemented COP projects like *alarmas comunitarias* to alert all the homes of a community to a crime. Its *Policía a Mano* and *Policía Puerta a Puerta* policies placed officers into teams of block-by-block prevention.

Such coordination has been particularly effective when mayors and city councils marshal their political and social structures in support of it. The police chiefs of smaller cities in Buenos Aires province are chosen through local elections, for example, while many of the province's larger cities have devoted more resources to prevention. Morón, La Plata, and Ituzaingo have begun programs such as youth centers, free telephone lines, and placement of law student interns in police stations.[†] Ituzaingo's Municipal Center for Victims of Insecurity provides medical and legal services, while Morón allows city buildings to double as venues for after-school youth programs and rights seminars. In Mendoza, the low-income municipality of Las Heras enacted a set of wide-ranging programs, based on citizen-supplied dates, to target youth truancy, alcohol consumption, and bus stops (Guzmán et al. 2002).[‡]

Focus on Vulnerable Sectors

Much of that coordination is geared toward society's most vulnerable sectors. Chubut province began COP in 1997 with pilot projects in three cities under the rubric of "strategies and instruments for intersectorial work" centered on foot patrols who use training in psychology, sociology, human relations, addiction, and quality of life to develop interneighbor mediation and guide crime victims through the criminal justice system. A primary focus of Argentine COP is youth, whose rates as both crime victims and perpetrators are far higher than any other sector. La Rioja's first reform was the 2003 formation of the police's Community Prevention Brigade to work with young people at risk, draw up a map of gang territories, and educate people on services available. The *Programa Integrar* gives work stipends to youth, while the "Ecological Brigade" trains them in sectors with high

---

* Author interviews, Jorge Viñas, Security Secretary, La Rioja Province, July 25, 2005; Ángal Maza, Governor, La Rioja Province, La Rioja, July 26, 2005; Alberto Paredes Urquiza, Government Minister, La Rioja Province, La Rioja July 2005, and New York, November 2006.
† Author interview, police officials and youth, Morón, Ituzaingo, and La Plata, June 2004, February 2005, and July 2007.
‡ Author interview, Rubén Miranda, Mayor of Las Heras, June 4, 2004.

job placement such as water maintenance.* There is also an Education Center for former gang members and COCI-facilitated programs on school reintegration, support for parents, and antidrug projects such as You Choose. The *Mesa Coordinadora Provincial de la Problemática Juvenil* (Provincial Coordinating Council of the Juvenile Problem), in addition, coordinates agencies to carry out intervention based on individuals' level of risk. To limit the preset responses likely when one agency is in charge, many programs were led by a Matrix Team composed of police, youth agencies, and representatives of ministries ranging from education and employment to health and sports. One of the team's most significant initiatives was the Education and Work program that placed a thousand youths into schools or jobs. Officials estimate that this range of programs reaches up to 90% of at-risk youths. In program areas, residents report diminishing insecurity, and police report the unprecedented fact of parents reaching out to them for support with their kids.

Challenges and Obstacles

Public Opinion and Socioeconomic Divisions

Public fear of crime, which leads to support for traditional policing, is a constant threat to COP throughout Argentina. As the number of crimes and youth gangs increased after Mendoza's reform, the police continued traditional modes such as detaining youths to check their identification, with judges choosing prison over alternative sentencing.[†] Even when they endure, many COP programs split apart on class lines. In well-off Federal Capital areas like Palermo, COP was fortified by preexisting networks experienced in making collective claims. Councils in areas without such advantages, in contrast, say that police do not support efforts to address insecurity. In the industrial zones of the Constitución area, for example, kiosk owners trying to organize to reduce robberies said that the local station had not been responsive. In La Rioja, the marginalized sectors rebuffed the Community Prevention Brigade because they felt deceived by its undercover work. Although Quilmes formed Buenos Aries Province's first School of Community Participation in Security, residents complained of violence by Buenos Aires 2 agents. Throughout the country, relations are tensest in the *villas* (urban shantytowns), where gaps between community needs and police presence are widest. Police tend to focus on particular suspects or incidents, though, or explain why their presence is limited. Officers at the Constitución station responded that their hands were tied by headquarters, for example, and officers in the nearby Zona Zabatela say that poor illumination makes patrols hazardous and a constant influx of poor newcomers makes community relations too difficult.[‡]

Underlying Conditions and Limited Coordination

Even with a concerted focus on the causes of crime, many of them are simply beyond the capacity of COP and interagency coordination. One of the most pernicious of those causes is *paco*, a doctored and smokeable form of cocaine sold for about a dollar a hit. Though

---

* Author interview, Nito Brizuela, staff member, and youth participants, July 27, 2005.
† Author interview, Aida Kemelmajer de Carlucci, Justice, Mendoza Supreme Court, 1 June 1, 2004.
‡ Author interview, Comisaría 32, June 23, 2004.

addiction rates among young people and consequent levels of property crime have shot up, policy responses have been slow. Residents often step into that vacuum with actions from physically expelling dealers to referring addicts to social services.* In Ciudad Oculta, a group of women called the Amazons gather and loudly clap in front of homes known for domestic violence. But without social service or police support, such efforts are limited. Youth unemployment and delinquency continue to be huge burdens for both society and the criminal justice system, seen for example in a 92% rise of Minor Court cases in Buenos Aires province between 1992 and 2002. Another example from Buenos Aires was the greater attention brought by citizens to chronic insecurity in the commuter train system, which defies easy responses because it is run by private companies through a patchwork of municipal agreements. A manifestation of socioeconomic division particularly challenging to COP is security privatization, which leads many areas to opt out of it. Demonstrating the boom in this field throughout the country, Buenos Aires province has nearly 900 registered private security agencies and up to 70,000 officers (Clarin 2006). Because of salaries as low as $200 per month, many of them are moonlighting public police officers.

Institutional Resistance and Interstate Relations

Much of the obstruction to COP comes from agencies responsible for implementing it. Mendoza's reform triggered "ferocious resistance"[†] by a police force that saw it as an attack on its interests. Along with ongoing crime increases, the governor at the time, said resistance made it "impossible" to implement change.[‡] In Buenos Aires and Mendoza in 1999, as well as other provinces, ambitious reforms are left on the wayside when the opposition party captures the governorship. Police officers in San Luis province say that because "Congress does not consult" with them, "there is no" long-term citizen security plan to deal with problems such as an influx of "immigrants" from other provinces (a common object of blame for crime).[§]

Relations between the city and state governments, particularly when headed by different parties, compound these problems. In the Federal Capital, the PFA halted its 500-officer Community Police in 2009 because of the large debt owed to it by the city government. Two years later, the city government rejected the PFA's Community Police. Such politicization is aggravated by claims that political parties use COP projects for partisan activities such as monitoring opponents. In response to such conditions, the president's June 2011 *Plan Unidad Cinturón Sur* sent 2500 officers from the Nacional Gendarmes and the Navy to the high-crime southern zone of the city and reassigned 1000 PFA agents to surrounding areas. But the effect has been limited by inadequate operative coordination among these agencies and the exclusion of the city's mayor, a political rival of the president. Other efforts are obstructed by local politics. Residents in Almirante Browne who developed a disarmament program, for example, say they are blocked by local officials "tied in" with

---

* Author meetings with neighborhood groups in Ciudad Oculta, Buenos Aires city, May 2004 and July 2007.
† Author interview, Alejandro Salomón, Secretary of Security, August 15, 2002.
‡ Author interview, Arturo Lafalla, Governor of Mendoza Province 1995–1999, Mendoza, June 3, 2004.
§ Author interview, Manuel Objeta, Comisario General, and Carlos Machiavelli, Comisario Mayor, San Luis, August 5, 2002.

resistant police officials.* Major nongovernmental agencies such as the Church and Bar Association are understandably wary of being pulled into such disputes, worsening the politicization. Of the 20 organizations that residents in the La Rioja survey cited as active in COP, only three were small NGOs.

Discussions in *comisarías* clearly indicate far more support for COP among the lower ranks than the upper ranks, but even reforms supported by *comisarios* often do not survive them. When La Rioja's two pro-COP *comisarios* left their positions, the new chiefs were simply "not convinced" of the need for it. In every province, COP-area residents complain of poor continuity, resources, and government commitment, which can lead COP to be "completely sidelined."† In La Rioja, one *comisaría* has just one vehicle to patrol dozens of neighborhoods, and small police modules failed when there were no personnel to fill them.

Criminal Policy: Confusion and Contradiction

Changes and uncertainties in criminal policy have aggravated COP, with politicians adopting the facile position that COP is incompatible with tough policing. Since its reform, for example, Mendoza officials have proposed laws to permit searches and seizures without a warrant, and one congressman advised Mendoza to follow the tough policing of New York, where, he said, "People were not allowed to walk on the main avenues after 5:00 in the afternoon."(Diario Uno 2002). Such policy changes are accelerated by many provinces' succession of security ministers, such as the five who served under Cobos during his 2003 to 2007 administration. It is also worsened by the creation of additional forces. In 2000, Mendoza formed an Auxiliary Police, whose poor training led to worse policing, while the capital city's 2003 to 2007 promano dura administration created and then disbanded an abusive community police.

Training and Promotion

As in other countries, police preparation and police work need to be better integrated to implement COP. Mendoza's IUSP is weak on practical training for preventive and other COP-centered approaches, IUSP's director acknowledges, while police chiefs did not send many of their officers to community policing courses. Of the 42 courses in the La Rioja police curricula, just one is on human rights and just one on social relations. Despite formal adoption of COP courses, in addition, COP courses are often tacked on to regular training with little incorporation into practice.‡ Many chiefs justify this approach by saying that professionalism requires officers to separate themselves from the community, not become closer to it. Patrols and promotion often underscore such approaches. In many provinces, street officers are simply assigned to a corner "to look but not to see," in the words of one officer. Many lack the instructions, autonomy, and even radios needed for basic, much less community-oriented, policing. Promotion in many provinces, in addition,

---

* Author interviews, Margarita Gandolfo, President, Foro Vecinal de Seguridad, Almirante Brown, July 24, 2007; Roberto Castronuovo, Jefe Distrital de Lomas de Zamora, July 27, 2007.
† E-mail correspondence, Óscar Ibáñez, Director, Brigada de Prevención Comunitaria, June 4, 2008.
‡ Author interviews, Hugo Alberto López, Sub-Comisario, Policía de Mendoza, August 15, 2002; Hugo Duch, IUSP Director, May 31, 2004.

is from areas of high citizen contact to administrative work—depriving COP of needed expertise and status.

Weakness in Enforcement and the Judiciary

Such problems limit the police from providing what citizens most want out of COP: better law enforcement. Excessive alcohol consumption, for example, is a major cause of insecurity in low-income areas but is weakly policed. La Rioja police officials, for example, say that they enforce the province's Law of Prevention of Alcohol Consumption through a combination of fines, registration of lawbreakers, and follow-up with juvenile offenders. But residents counter that the law is openly flaunted through bribes by "whiskerías," residential stock houses, and large purchases right before the after-midnight prohibition of alcohol sales.

Criminal investigation, the core of police work, is also weak in Argentina. Efforts to improve coordination between street and Judicial Police lag, while resource-deprived crime labs resolve few crimes through scientific investigation. Fewer than half of crimes are reported in Argentina, and statistics on those that are collected are insufficiently studied and distributed. Compounded by *comisarías'* lack of autonomy to use the information they do have, these limits make it difficult for police to track crimes' location, time, manner, and other information that makes COP worthwhile to residents. In the courts, penal process codes are stalled by financial restrictions, low institutional capacity, resistance by veteran judges, and the uncertainty of changing roles for police and prosecutors.* In provinces like La Rioja, the same judge oversees investigation and sentencing, adding to backlogs and confusion. Lack of follow-up and information sharing by the courts is a perennial complaint among the police, and particularly contentious disputes have been between the police and the Minor Courts over handling youth cases. Insufficient collaboration has also meant that COP programs like registries of uncivil behavior have not led to the judicial action they require for long-term impact.

References

Guzmán, Mauricio, Patricia Gorri, and Gustavo Lucero. (2002). *Plan estratégico municipal de seguridad ciudadana para el departamento de Las Heras*. Mendoza, Argentina: Municipalidad de Las Heras.

Binder, Alberto, Marcelo Sain, Alejandro Poquet, and Mariano Ciafardini. (2005). *Lineamientos para un sistema de seguridad pública democrática y eficiente para la Provincia de Mendoza*. Mendoza, Argentina: Instituto latinoamericano de seguriad y democracia.

Barrera, María del Valle. (1998). *La crisis policial de octubre en Mendoza*.

Clarín. (2006). *En la Provincia de Buenos Aires, solo los agentes de seguridad privada podrán custodiar boliches y bares*.

Diario Uno. (2002). *Más sobre delitos juveniles*. Mendoza, p. 21.

* Author interviews, Jorge Nanclares, President, Mendoza Supreme Court, June 1, 2004; Daniel Correllio, Juez de Instrucción, June 1, 2004.

Canada
Aboriginal

9

DON CLAIRMONT

Contents

Introduction

Until the 1960s, virtually all of the hundreds of Aboriginal communities in Canada—currently 644 with a total on-reserve population of roughly 450,000, a mean size of 642, and a range from at least 12,000 to fewer than 100 residents—were policed by the Royal Canadian Mounted Police (RCMP), the federal police organization that also provided, by contract, provincial policing in all provinces and territories except the two most populous, namely, Ontario and Quebec. As the contracted provincial police, the RCMP was responsible for all policing outside cities and towns and in select urban areas by special supplemental contract. The few reserves within municipal boundaries were everywhere usually, policed by the extant municipal police services. As the 1960s evolved, major changes in the police organization and approach in Aboriginal societies began to occur, leading ultimately to the First Nations Policing Policy (FNPP) in 1991 and the subsequent FNP Program in 1992. The FNPP required greater Aboriginal involvement and partnership in policing in First Nation (FN) communities and also encouraged the growth of self-administered, independent FN police services. It mandated a "community-based policing plus (CBP+)" strategy of policing, parallel to the "citizenship plus" conception of Aboriginal rights in Canada, as rooted in treaties and protected in the Constitution Act of 1982. The FNPP, with its central features, especially the mandated tripartite partnerships among federal and provincial governments and the FNs, made Canada the only country that had developed a comprehensive national policing approach for its Aboriginal people (Lithopoulus 2008). The FNPP remains in force today and continues to evolve (Public Safety Canada 2011) at the program level.

Outside of Ontario and Quebec, provinces where there is no direct community level policing by the RCMP, the vast majority of the Aboriginal communities continue to be policed by this service. In this brief overview of policing developments in Aboriginal Canada, RCMP policing in the community of Elsipogtog, New Brunswick, is highlighted since it represents a "best practices" example of how a CBP+ approach to policing has led to significant social change and resulted in an effective combination of professional-based and community-based policing strategies. Elsipogtog, a Mi'kmaq community of 3000 residents, roughly 90 km from Moncton, the geographical hub of Canada's Maritime Provinces, has had and continues to have a very high level of social problems, including high underemployment, high levels of single-parent households, and rates of serious violent crime and of substance abuse far greater than neighboring mainstream towns and cities. For example, at least one of every seven adults in Elsipogtog between the ages of 18 and 33 either is authorized by provincial health authorities to receive regular methadone treatment or regularly and illegally consumes addictive drugs (mostly prescription drugs), a rate 50 times greater than in metropolitan Halifax, deemed by many as the drug capital of Atlantic Canada. At the same time, the community has an extensive Health and Social Services capacity, leads the province in its progressive justice programming, and has national renown for its Eastern Door program (focusing on the prevention, diagnosis, and treatment of FASD). As will be discussed below, the RCMP's CBP+ policing strategy in Elsipogtog has become a positive transformative force largely because of its emphasis on problem solving and in-depth cultivation of community partnerships in conjunction with its continued commitment to professional-based policing.

Aboriginal Policing Context

From the formation of the Canadian Confederation (1867) and the Indian Act (1876) until the 1960s, all policing in Aboriginal communities was federal and involved a broad policing mandate wherein officers carried out a wide range of tasks additional to conventional law enforcement (such as census gathering and linking people to social services), and Aboriginal persons engaged with the policing service were helpers and clients rather than colleagues or partners (e.g., "band scouts" were engaged to assist with language interpretation and observation). The style of policing was community sensitive in a colonialist, paternalistic context, where the RCMP officers worked closely with the Anglican and Roman Catholic churches, operating schools and hospitals, the Hudson Bay traders, and the appointed Indian Agents. Beginning after World War II, but picking up steam in the 1960s, the old order was transformed as Aboriginals received the right to vote in federal elections, government bureaucrats assumed the dominant leadership role in providing services in Aboriginal communities, and the Indian Agent position was gradually abolished in favor of the empowered band council. The traditional, broader police role had some CBP features, but it was thoroughly enmeshed in the assimilation policies of the federal government in that colonialist context and did not employ Aboriginal members nor acknowledge accountability to Aboriginals. It also did not generate significant trust among Aboriginal people; for example, few Aboriginals reported any abuse in the Indian Residential School system to the RCMP, an abuse that in retrospect has been shown in both personal accounts and court materials to have been quite widespread (LeBeuf 2009). The RCMPs, along with the federal government and the churches leaders, have profusely apologized in recent years for their complicity in this approach to Aboriginal people and communities.

The three central events in shaping Aboriginal policing in the modern era have been (1) the withdrawal of the RCMP from regular policing in FNs in Ontario and Quebec announced in the 1960s, coupled with a contraction of its policing mandate in the face of expanding federal government bureaucracy, as without an explicit CBP philosophy to fall back on, the RCMP approach became exclusively professional enforcement; (2) Department of Indian Affairs and Northern Development (DIAND) 1971 Circular 55 policy on policing Aboriginal communities, which identified principles that should guide such policing, such as greater consultation and "ownership" by Aboriginals, and allowed for special Aboriginal constables who would not be restricted to policing band bylaws; and (3) the FNPP in 1991. In a nutshell, the RCMP's withdrawal from FN policing in Ontario and Quebec resulted in diverse styles and arrangements in Aboriginal policing and ultimately in a context where self-administered FN policing could be meaningfully experienced and assessed. DIAND's Circular 55 articulated for the first time the federal government's objectives and principles of Aboriginal policing and facilitated the growth of the band constable services as well as greater Aboriginal participation as advisors and colleagues in reserve policing carried out by the RCMP or the Ontario or Quebec provincial police services. The FNPP advanced significantly upon the objectives and principles of Circular 55 and also launched new organizational structures (e.g., the Aboriginal Policing Directorate under the Solicitor General Canada), new funding arrangements, and the tripartite agreement format—the aegis of the federal government, the provincial government, and the designated FN—for the development of either self-administered, fully authorized FN police services (SAs) or community tripartite agreements (CTAs) where the RCMP (linkages with other police services are possible though rare) provided the policing services under specified contractual terms.

The policing of Aboriginal people steadily if slowly became appreciative of cultural sensitivity and local priorities and the need for collaboration and partnership with Aboriginal people. The band constable system began in the mid-1960s and grew significantly over the next 20 years. Here, typically, the officers were local residents hired and paid for by the bands, modestly trained, appointed under RCMP warrant, and in effect, village constables under the guidance of the RCMP or provincial police to whom they turned over any cases involving the criminal code or offenses under other federal or provincial legislation. In the mid-1970s, special Indian constables began to be hired directly by the RCMP (and the provincial police in Ontario and Quebec) to complement the work of the credentialized, regular members. And, increasingly in the 1980s, some Aboriginal people were recruited as full-time regular members into these services. Generally, this evolution in policing was assessed positively by Aboriginal leaders who rated the successive steps as valuable enhancements. Nevertheless, evaluation studies also showed that they always wanted more, essentially an accountable, community-based policing service if not their own fully credentialized, self-administered service. Each advancement was also subsequently found wanting by Indian Affairs, which focused on the continuing major public safety issues in FN communities, by a slew of independent inquiries and commissions focused on policing shortcomings in specific cases, and by the mainstream police leaders themselves in their assessments of their effectiveness and lack of meaningful partnership with Aboriginal people; most strikingly, RCMP assistant commissioner Head concluded his 1987 in-depth, countrywide assessment of policing in Aboriginal communities with the warning, "The RCMP will have to dramatically change the way it polices Aboriginal communities or it will soon find itself out of business there" (p. 20, Clairmont 2006).

Since 1991, the FNPP has provided the framework for policing Aboriginal communities. Clearly the result of significant federal policy development in response to the above critical forces, its major principles and imperatives harkened back to the 1971 Circular 55 policy of Indian Affairs but incorporated as well contemporary approaches to policing such as community-based policing and current government acknowledgment of the constitutional and treaty rights of Aboriginal people to exercise as much self-government as is feasible in their communities. The three chief FNPP objectives are listed as follows: (1) enhance the personal security and safety of FN communities; (2) provide access to policing that is professional, effective, and culturally appropriate; and (3) increase the level of police accountability to FN communities. The two principal tripartite policing models for possible selection in FNs are the CTA (basically RCMP policing) and the SA (self-administered FN policing). Upon selection of one or the other, the band constable system in the FN, if there was one, would be disbanded.

Currently, there are 46 SA police services in Canada policing 190 Aboriginal communities. Thirty-eight of the 46 are located in Ontario or Quebec, where both the provincial government and its police service strongly support and appear to prefer the self-administered FN policing arrangement. The small number of SA police services elsewhere has declined in recent years, and the FN communities involved have switched to CTAs with the RCMP. With few exceptions (the handful of SAs, several municipal quadripartite agreements, and a score of band constable police services continuing primarily in Manitoba), all Aboriginal communities outside Ontario and Quebec are policed by the RCMP whether in a CTA model or a legacy model predating the FNPP. The RCMP as an organization has committed to assisting SAs in the areas where it is the provincial/territorial contracted policing, but it has also emphasized its historic role in policing Aboriginal communities, has officially declared such policing to be one of its four priorities as a police organization, and, to underline that prioritization, in recent years has made a number of senior appointments (e.g., chief superintendent for Aboriginal Policing) and recruited heavily among Aboriginals (fully 8% of the roughly 20,000 RCMP officers are now self-declared Aboriginal, about three times the percentage of Aboriginals among the RCMP's policed clientele at the community level).

Policing in Canada's Aboriginal communities faces much challenge, due to the combination of colonialist legacy (e.g., racism, dependency), scant economic opportunities in conjunction with the decline of traditional activities in the often off-the-beaten-path locations, and a high level of need for and local expectation of the policing service. Violent and property crime levels have been very high, and the 24/7 local demand for policing has usually far exceeded the police resources available. Police officers, whether in SAs or the RCMP, in national surveys have consistently and increasingly identified "unsolvable social problems" as the major issue negatively impacting on their policing. The SA police services have been especially vulnerable because they are underresourced and their officers discouraged by local political pressures, the small scale of their police organization, and the lack of job opportunity it provides. The few larger SAs, regional services policing a number of different FNs, in addition must confront centrifugal forces as each FN protects and advances its interest as a "First Nation." The vulnerability of the SAs is experienced most intensely where the RCMP is the contracted provincial police since it is usually willing to take over the policing responsibility when FN leaders opt to disband their SA. RCMP policing of FNs also faces specific challenges such as the regular reassignment of officers limiting their stay to a few years, the status of "outsider," and common perception of inadequate accountability to the FNs policed. Both types of police services emphasize professional enforcement, but the SAs complement that with a strong local service approach, while the RCMP complements theirs with more formal community programs. Despite these differences, national surveys have found that the two types of police service have roughly equal approval ratings among community residents.

Challenge of FN Community Policing: Elsipogtog Case

Elsipogtog is one of the roughly 260 Aboriginal communities policed by the RCMP. The classic reserve problems of high levels of violence and substance abuse have characterized this FN for many years and have shown little sign of diminishing despite many other positive community developments, strong testimony perhaps to the deep roots of the underlying causal factors. The RCMP assumed full control of Elsipogtog policing in late 2002 and since then has gradually evolved a policing approach that combines strong professional enforcement with extensive community crime prevention programming. Most importantly and more uncommonly, the local RCMP leadership has emphasized collaborative problem solving with and accountability to Elsipogtog political leaders and community justice program staffers. An explicit strategy has been to effectively contain if not diminish the offending, responding swiftly and professionally to improve public safety while emphasizing crime prevention and participating fully in community efforts to get at the deep roots.

Between 2004 and 2005, the RCMP reported that Elsipogtog had the highest crime rate among all RCMP detachment units in Canada. The subdetachment, headed by a corporal, had a complement of five or six officers, and it was basically absorbed in dealing with the offenses (plus making many arrests under the Mental Health Act). The everyday approach to policing, by necessity rather than choice from the police perspective, was the conventional, professional-based policing approach. The evolution in Elsipogtog policing since that time has seen more police officers (eight in 2006 and 13 in 2012); more Aboriginal officers (from two to seven in 2012); an organizational change to a more independent, Elsipogtog-focused detachment status; and a staff sergeant in charge with much experience policing in Aboriginal communities who espoused the importance of communication, partnership, and problem solving. These changes were in significant part the result of strong community pressure on the senior RCMP management by the Elsipogtog police advisory committee. Its claims that public safety considerations and the need to get at the roots of the offending required these specific changes were accepted (e.g., 13 officers meant a police-to-population ratio of 1 to 240, a ratio much higher than elsewhere in Atlantic Canada).

In the early 2000s, before the RCMP subdetachment was well entrenched in the community, there was a fair consensus among Elsipogtog leaders and activists in the justice field that, "When we talk about justice, we need to step back and ask ourselves, what values do we promote? What are the beliefs that influence our vision of justice?" In general terms, the direction they advanced was to promote the values and practices of restorative justice (RJ) and healing. Like residents in the poor urban areas of America, two decades earlier, when the community-based policing movement became popular, they wanted to reduce crime and enhance public safety by getting at the roots of the inappropriate behavior, not solely by prosecuting and jailing "our people." There was also a widespread view that while the replacement of the band constable system by the RCMP was a positive step, "the community has no power over the RCMP" and that effective action on root problems required close collaboration between police and community.

Even prior to the evolution in policing, there was a holistic approach to problems and solutions adopted in Elsipogtog, clearly evident in that all justice programming had been—and continues to be—embedded in the Health Center and managed by its directors. The evolution in the policing approach made for a good fit with this holistic approach; indeed, it accelerated further kindred developments, especially a more extensive use of RJ and sentencing circles (the latter beginning in 2009 and 2010). In recent years, the Elsipogtog justice program has handled far more RJ cases than the other 14 New Brunswick FNs combined, and roughly the same number as in all the province's RCMP detachments combined. It is the only FN regularly involved with sentencing circles. A major accomplishment this year has been the successful implementation of the first problem-solving court (a Healing to Wellness court similar to drug treatment or mental health courts) to be located in an Aboriginal community, or any mainstream community of such small population size, in Canada.

RCMP policing in Elsipogtog has the usual features found in many RCMP detachments' policing in Aboriginal communities, such as a police advisory committee, a service delivery plan (the CTA agreement) including an annual performance plan, school programs such as Drug Abuse Resistance Education and Aboriginal Shield delivered by a designated officer or in collaboration with local civilians, Neighborhood Watch, participation in varied community committees (e.g., Violence and Abuse), and close collaboration with a band-funded crime prevention worker across a large variety of activities. One difference has been that the detachment commander has put major effort into making these features effective through personal and other members' attendance and record keeping, and indeed going beyond the usual expectations. For example, in addition to the commander's own meeting regularly with chief and council, all Elsipogtog officers have been assigned a band councilor to meet with on a monthly basis to discuss any concerns, and such monthly contacts are documented on a detachment file. The staff sergeant has also been quick to bring to Elsipogtog innovative programs that further communications and understanding between the police and the community (e.g., the Aboriginal Perceptions program). Most importantly, the local RCMP has been an active mobilizer for RJ and the Healing to Wellness court and other programs that can hopefully get at root problems through collaborative effort and healing. The staff sergeant summed up his approach as follows:

> Community based policing is very important to me. I believe it is important to be involved with community events, building partnerships with Elders, service providers, community and band council. From day one it was my focus to be transparent and ensure that the members working in Elsipogtog be involved in the community, collaborating with key people in the community to identify problems of crime and disorder and to search for solutions to these problems. My focus is partnerships between the RCMP and the community. It is very important to respect people in the community and gain their trust. (Craig Yorke, per. comm., January 18, 2012)

The impact of real community-based policing in Elsipogtog is still a work in progress. The crime rate remains sky-high, especially interpersonal violence, and drug and alcohol abuse is widespread. The RCMP does report less property crime, fewer assaults against the police officers, and a much-improved relationship with youths, but the hard data are not unambiguously supportive of these claims. It is contended that significant trust has been achieved and that there is less underreporting of assaults, especially domestic violence and sexual assaults, but the victims who do come forward still usually stop short of following through on the initial complaints to the police. Familism, a classic response to colonialism, generates much bias and rivalries, which augment the other deep-rooted problems of lifestyle and socioeconomic disadvantage. There appears little doubt, however, that Elsipogtog and the RCMP detachment have forged a partnership and are on the right track to getting at the deep roots of the crime and enhancing public safety. The aspect of the colonialist legacy that causes people to protect or shield their own versus the outside justice system is increasingly incongruent with the current realities based on greatly enhanced band council authority and administrative responsibility; the significant, if modest, economic and political developments especially over the past decade; and the policing approach that has developed.

Conclusion

Aboriginal communities in Canada often have much higher crime rates and far more serious public safety and related social problem concerns than their mainstream counterparts. And these issues remain very significant even though over the past several decades, both federal and provincial governments have adopted more progressive policies and significantly increased FN funding. Aboriginal people continue to be vastly overrepresented in prisons despite ostensibly dramatic changes in sentencing and other policies designed to eradicate this differential. The Grand Chief of the Assembly of First Nations in 2004, in addressing the National Aboriginal Policing Forum, emphasized the need for safer FNs and better police efforts in that regard and commented, "The root cause of our difficulties—the problems in education, physical and emotional health, and economic and social development—must be examined as part of community relations, community policing and strengthening a sometimes rocky relationship between the law enforcement agencies and Canada's Aboriginal peoples." In Elsipogtog, there is evidence that such an examination has been happening, that approaches that emphasize a strengthening relationship have been implemented, and, further, that outputs have included strategies to get at the "roots of the difficulties" in a healing fashion, which are being pursued without sacrifice to public safety concerns. It remains to be seen how effective this collaborative problem solving fueled by a community-based policing philosophy will be and how institutionalized it will become.

References

Clairmont, Don, Aboriginal Policing in Canada: An Overview of Developments in First Nations. Toronto, ON: Ipperwash Inquiry, Ontario Department of Justice, 2006.

Gill, Rick and Don Clairmont, Socio-Demographic Survey of Police Officers Serving in Aboriginal Communities. Ottawa, ON: Public Safety Canada, 2008.

Hamilton, Alvin and Sinclair, Murray, The Justice System and Aboriginal People: Report of the Aboriginal Justice Inquiry Manitoba. Winnipeg, MA: Queen's Printer.

Head, Robert, Policing for Aboriginal Canadians: The RCMP Role. Ottawa, ON: RCMP, 1989.

LeBeuf, Marcel-Eugene, The Role of the Royal Canadian Mounted Police during the Indian Residential School System. Ottawa, ON: RCMP, 2009.

Lithopoulus, Savvas, International Comparison of Indigenous Policing Models. Ottawa, ON: Public Safety Canada, 2008.

Public Safety Canada, 2009–2010 Evaluation of the First Nations Policing Program. Ottawa, ON: Public Safety Canada, 2011.

Canada
The Annapolis Valley

10

ANTHONY THOMSON
DON CLAIRMONT

Contents

This chapter examines small-town and rural policing in the Annapolis Valley region of Nova Scotia during the Community-Based Policing era against the background of modernization and regionalization. The Annapolis Valley is a geographical and social region dominated topographically by the North and South Mountains. The valley floor is primarily agricultural, with generally small farms interspersed with villages. Historically specializing in fruit tree production, principally apples, Valley farmers have diversified into mixed farming. The major industrial employer is Michelin Tire, established in rural Nova Scotia because of an available and compliant work force. Nova Scotia is relatively homogenous ethnically and linguistically. Approximately 95% of its population of nearly 1 million is Caucasian. The Valley region is even less diverse, with two small First Nations reserves, a very small black community, and few Francophones.

The focus of this chapter is the evolution of the independent town police services through professionalization and the Community-Based Policing movement, in the context of macro-contextual factors such as regionalization. Town policing in Nova Scotia is either carried out by an independent, municipal police service or is contracted by the town to the Royal Canadian Mounted Police (RCMP), the national police service, which is also contracted provincially for rural and some urban policing in most Canadian provinces and territories.

For most of the last century, the majority of cities and small towns in Nova Scotia were policed by local, municipally controlled and financed police departments, which were small in size, had simple structures, and emphasized the use of informal methods (Murphy 1986). In rural Nova Scotia beginning in the 1960s, police interest groups demanded a more professional and "modern" style of policing. Although professional policing did impact positively on the quality of small-town policing (STP), that did not translate into a safe and secure niche for independent small-town police services. The apparent stability achieved in the 1980s by small municipal police services was precarious and frequently short lived.

Many small-town police departments throughout the Western World have been eliminated and the policing assumed by larger police services. The same is true of Nova Scotia, which has had decades of slow economic and population growth leading to steady out-migration and depopulating many of the small towns and rural counties outside the metropolitan capital district. Over the last two decades, the number of municipal police departments in Nova Scotia has declined from 28 to 11, roughly half being absorbed into two urban regional police services, which emerged in the mid-1990s as part of a general regionalization of municipal government services, collapsing a total of eight small-town police departments. The largest of the urban police services is the Halifax Regional Police, which serves a population of 400,000 in collaboration with the RCMP (a unique model of two police services policing different areas of the municipality). The second largest, Cape Breton Regional Police, serves a population of 100,000. As of 2012, nine additional municipal police departments in Nova Scotia have been left standing. They represent the classic small-town police service model, providing policing to long-established towns with a median population of 4000 residents.

The comparative research on which this chapter is based began in 1989 and continued informally into the early 2000s. The study compared municipal police departments in the Annapolis Valley with rural RCMP policing and involved five small towns that initially financed independent, municipal police services: Hantsport, Wolfville, Kentville, Berwick, and Middleton (see Thomson et al. 2003). By 2001, four of these municipal departments opted for RCMP contracts. Only the towns of Kentville (population 5200) and Annapolis Royal (population 500) have retained independent police services. Kentville likely represents the best model of a small-town, community police service in the province.

Small-Town Community Policing

STP in Nova Scotia has a long and often controversial history. Until the 1960s, local police departments in the Valley generally consisted of little more than a chief and a night patrolman. Policing followed a watchman style (Wilson 1970) and was closely integrated into the demands of elite stakeholders and local politicians. Policing was a "department" of the town often located symbolically in the basement of Town Hall. Being hired and fired at will by Town Council, chiefs and members of the police department were potentially in the pockets of the politically influential. In this context, STP was characterized by a three-tiered discretionary system: favoritism toward the local elites, maintenance of minor matters of public order affecting the majority, and repression with respect to members of minority groups and the underclass whose deviance was public and troublesome. In contrast, the RCMP modeled an alternative, enforcement-oriented, equitable, and "legalistic" policing style (Wilson 1970), which was largely autonomous from local political control.

As rural Nova Scotia was transformed socially and economically in the 1950s and 1960s, the inefficient and inequitable policing style in the small towns came into conflict with citizens' demands for higher standards, fairness, and equitable enforcement. Police chiefs sought to have the political independence of policing enacted in legislation, and patrol officers turned to unionization to better their interests. Pressure from all these stakeholders culminated in a movement to enhance the professionalism of STP, from recruitment and training to equipment and organizational structure. The gap between the more parochial town police and the professional RCMP narrowed.

Professional-based policing (PBP) was a positive response to citizens' calls for equitable, effective, enforcement-oriented policing to combat perceived and real problems of crime and disorder, as well as the long-standing inequities of STP. At the same time, PBP models created major contradictions for traditional STP, creating a disjunction between ideal policing and the realities of policing a small town. The professionalization of policing, to an extent, removed officers from routine, daily contact with citizens and changed the expectations of police officers, reinforcing images of their work as "crime fighters" that were largely unrealizable in small towns. The contemporary Community-Based Policing movement was introduced, in part, as a counterpoint to these deficiencies.

Origin of Community-Based Policing

The "movement" for Community-Based Policing (CPB) was modeled after reforms arising in urban policing from internal organizational pressure as well as from reform movements seeking to provide an alternative to the revealed shortcomings of big-city policing (Clairmont 1991). In Canada, Community-Based Policing originated largely as a national, "top-down" movement, which was given ideological and entrepreneurial support through the federal Department of the Solicitor General. In small-town milieus and in the case of Aboriginal communities, there were some significant pressures on the police services (municipal departments and the RCMP) to incorporate CBP, coming from the federal and provincial governments, the Auditor General, academics, and native leaders. In its institutionalization, CBP can be seen as embedded at the ideological level but with modest implementation and impact at the operational level.

Ideologically, CBP harkened back to a supposedly earlier and simpler model of policing, which had developed spontaneously in small communities. According to this perspective, CBP was neither new nor innovative; it was simply traditional STP writ large. This connection between CBP and STP is made explicit in the perceptions of small-town and rural police officers (Weisheit et al. 1994). The image of rural policing/STP emphasized peacekeeping within a consensual, watchman style, an essentially social, nonintrusive, community-influenced, conciliatory policing based on shared values, as opposed to legalistic policing where the style was reactive and the goal was crime fighting. In the modern Community-Based Policing movement, the police are the visible symbols of local values, and rooted members of their close-knit communities.

The CBP philosophy was positive for STP in the Valley, effecting a more community-sensitive policing, which was more inclusive and service oriented, and compatible with fair and equitable policing. Both the movement for professionalism and that for community policing have contributed to the modern, effective, and community-engaged police services in municipal police- and RCMP-serviced towns in Nova Scotia.

Impact of CBP on the Key Dimensions of STP

Community policing generally has several elements, including changes in the organization of policing and in the delivery of policing services; close police–community relations; reiteration of the foot-patrol function to maintain personal connections between officers and citizens; a wide mandate for responding to citizen complaints; a proactive, problem-solving mandate including crime prevention initiatives; and the creation of a more expansive constable generalist role for uniformed officers (see Murphy 1988). In discussing the impact of these elements of CBP, we focus especially on the independent Kentville Police Service with some comparative references to RCMP policing in the Annapolis Valley.

CBP celebrated some of the classic strengths of STP such as the constable generalist, local knowledge, personal relations, local control, and a conception of the police role that goes well beyond dealing with serious crimes and even modest criminal code infractions. Unlike its urban counterpart, the development of an explicit CBP philosophy or strategy of policing did not entail much organizational change. Town police services, especially independents such as the Kentville Police Service, continued to be, as Murphy (1986) depicted them, small in size, simple in organization, and with minimal bureaucratic hierarchy. The heart of community policing, traditionally and in CBP, remains the development of a close relationship between the police and the community.

Police–Community Relationships

Policing in a small town is more intimate than would be the case in either a rural setting, where the police are spread thinly over a large area, or in a city, where the population is large and more anonymous. Close connections with the community benefited the police by encouraging integration and cooperation with the citizens. CBP in Kentville involves getting input into policing from local leaders and from the general public through formal research surveys. Organizationally, the police have developed closer ties with other emergency responders, such as fire, ambulance, search and rescue, and emergency measures.

Close connections lead to relatively rich knowledge about the community and the policed population. Complaints involving offenses such as vandalism are frequently settled by talking to local residents and neighborhood children. The reverse side is public knowledge of the police. Living a private life in a small town is difficult for a police officer. People sometimes call officers during off-duty hours to make a complaint or ask for information. Small-town police are particularly conscious of being under scrutiny, both on and off duty, by taxpaying residents who claim to pay their salaries.

The needs of the independent municipal police forces are shaped by the vagaries of local politics and fought over annually in budget allocations. Demands from the police service for a share of town revenue elicit the reciprocal demand from Council for accountability and quantifiable evidence of police productivity. This means that policing necessarily becomes more legalistic, emphasizing close monitoring of complaints and the management of public order. Town Police Commissioners scrutinize not only police expenditures but also the statistics on criminal activities and calls for service. Typically, they demand more foot patrol, more enforcement of town bylaws, and greater police visibility, and through their control over the budget, they have some mechanisms to realize these desires. Small-town leaders are willing to invest in these police practices, but, while they might appreciate other CBP programming, they do not invest much public money in them as compared to the more "watchman" police activities.

Patrols

One manifestation of the proactive bent of the Kentville police is the emphasis of foot patrol and germane, self-generated duties in the central, downtown core of the towns.

Foot patrol is sometimes unpopular among the officers, but it is required by the chief and demanded by business leaders and other influential stakeholders. Such patrol is primarily for visibility, but it also facilitates police–citizen contacts. Traffic complaints about speeding cars, squealing tires, and improper parking make up a considerable number of citizen-initiated police contacts. The police response tends to be expedient; for example, running radar in particular spots tends to slow traffic temporarily. Traffic enforcement in small towns has to be carefully handled because it often brings ordinary citizens into negative contact with the police.

More significant, in terms of patrol, are the focused business and property checks, which are often systematic and not self-generated. Officers check specific downtown properties on foot and also perform "outer checks," driving to a business, getting out, "rattling the doors," and looking for broken windows. These checks are sometimes denigrated by the officers as "mere security work," but this tangible watchman service is popular among citizens who believe that their property is receiving special police protection. Overall, the actual effectiveness of patrol may be in question, but the department's commitment to highly visible, service-oriented policing is well received by citizens, local business owners, and political interests.

Order Maintenance and Calls for Service

There is a general if implicit agreement among the town elite (small business owners and professionals) as well as the majority of stable and established residents that a primary responsibility of the police is to maintain public order. The targets of public order maintenance are frequently youth, particularly but not exclusively disadvantaged youth. Much of the disorder in the towns, however, is generated by persons from surrounding areas. This is inevitable given the administrative, retail, and service roles the towns play for the surrounding rural communities. The policed population, therefore, is greater than the population of the town.

Order maintenance activities are usually centered on the public bars in the downtown area or in specific neighborhoods or even houses. In the case of the Kentville, there was a perception among residents that public-order disturbances were less frequent after the reiteration of Community-Based Policing in the 1980s. Under the direction of town businesses, the municipal police try to prevent youth from congregating downtown using mostly informal means (including loudspeakers playing classical music) but also sometimes laying charges. More problematic is the observation that domestic disputes were frequently handled informally, despite the provincial directive to the police to lay charges in situations where they believe the evidence warranted a prosecution.

In small towns, police exercise a much wider service mandate and operate a more generalist policing style, more out of necessity than design (Weisheit et al. 1994). CBP entails more emphasis on minor and often nonlaw enforcement problems. This is one major factor that distinguishes the practice of independent small-town police services from both metropolitan forces and the RCMP. Our research showed clearly that a wide variety of calls for service were handled by the independent STP, including lost animals, barking dogs, funeral escorts, and minor, unsolvable thefts. Small-town citizens requested and the police accepted a wide mandate for police service. Taking all calls for service often entails informal dispute resolution, with arrest as a last resort, common in independent STP; for example, small check frauds may be resolved without the laying of charges. In contrast, police in small towns with RCMP contracts and city police respond less quickly to minor matters and give little attention to small thefts.

Crime Prevention

The key terms of community policing in Kentville are crime prevention, problem solving, and community development. In most cases, the police service takes the initiative in efforts to coordinate preventive services. Under CBP, organized strategies designed to reduce the incidence of crime in communities were initially based on urban life experience. Block Parents, Neighborhood Watch, street proofing, and fingerprinting children, for example, emerged from the urban experience of substantial anonymity, fear, and social dislocation. Arguably, the experience of residents in small towns and rural areas has been different. The practices that such prevention programs were designed to replicate occurred informally in close-knit communities as a matter of course. Grassroots involvement in policing in the small towns is primarily informal, through contacts with the police through mutual organizations, such as service clubs and sports activities, or through complaints passed directly to officers rather than formally to the chief or the Police Commission.

Where there is at least a full-time crime prevention officer, as in the Kentville Police Service and Kings Detachment of the RCMP, considerable effort has gone into mobilizing community resources and heightening awareness of the need for crime prevention. Programs have been developed for rural areas that respond to the perceived needs of the citizens. Rural Watch, for example, protects private property and helps to control public access on foot or on motorized vehicles to private land. Coastal watch, while centrally instituted, has involved some citizens in a strategy that has been linked to some of the major drug seizures in the province.

In the small towns, CBP programs target bicycle safety, stopping shoplifting, safe driving, property identification, in-school liaison, and child find. Officers have given public talks and antibullying workshops in schools and have hosted displays. In Kentville, the police service is at the forefront of attempts to solve community problems by integrating service delivery with other social agencies, adopting a problem-solving approach. In recent years, the chief of police has initiated a movement to coordinate intervention into prescription drug abuse in the town, a concern identified at the root of a number of social problems, including overdose deaths and property crime. The police have convinced some physicians to reduce their prescriptions of the narcotic Dilaudid. In addition, as serious frauds target seniors, some banks have agreed to give a police-produced pamphlet on fraud prevention and elder abuse to senior citizens who unexpectedly withdraw large amounts of cash.

In the rural Valley area, the RCMP Citizen's Patrol initiative has involved dozens of citizens consciously working as the eyes of the police. In addition, a Victim's Support initiative was undertaken, under detachment control but with civilian co-coordinators and volunteers. In the 1990s, detachments initiated a restorative justice program centered on what the RCMP referred to as "community justice forums" (CJFs) as problem-solving initiatives, blurring the gulf between the enforcement and service functions of policing. Very few conferences or CJFs have taken place over the last 6 or 7 years, however, partly because of resource scarcity and because, in Nova Scotia, an extensive restorative justice program is in place, coordinated and funded by the provincial government but delivered by local non-profit agencies. Independent STP services are usually, though not always, the chief source of referrals to these agencies, and Kentville PS in particular has been a strong supporter of the restorative justice initiative. In practice, little success was achieved through the formal, consultative, or intervention mechanisms, and their functions devolved largely into citizen involvement in crime-prevention and fund-raising initiatives.

The RCMP is well-placed to offer a wider variety and greater number of programs designated under Community-Based Policing than the local town police services. This difference is largely a question of resources, but it also reflects the official adoption by the RCMP of the CBP philosophy. Currently, however, RCMP crime-prevention and service programs are increasingly add-ons to standard, legalistic policing, rather than reflecting an effort to transform police–community interactions. They serve public relations purposes more clearly and directly than actual crime prevention. This form of CBP, then, is entirely consistent with and thrives within bureaucratic, legalistic policing.

Effectiveness

The effectiveness of various programs is difficult to measure. The clearest indication of the effectiveness of CBP is that community initiatives make the public feel safer and enhance the popularity of the police force. Crime prevention is notoriously difficult to document, a problem frequently raised by enforcement-oriented officers. In addition, the appropriate role for the community to play in determining policy and supervising policing is controversial. The RCMP is largely independent of local control, but for town police, the chief's job and even the existence of the town police services are on the line. Within the limits of this formidable, ongoing constraint imposed by the powerful stakeholders one often finds in such milieus, STP chiefs face the challenges of guarding their autonomy from the interference of elected officials, local elites, and other citizenry, as well as dealing with the ever-present threat of being absorbed into a regional police service or being replaced by the RCMP.

People want both close community connections, including public accountability, and fair, equitable enforcement. These goals present the police with a difficult balancing act. A close community relationship is one of the benefits of municipal policing in a small town that has both negative and positive aspects. Community policing tries to strike a balance between being close to the community and doing the job equitably, which requires some distance; close public ties present aspects of a "double-edged sword." Often expressed in police conversation was the claim that CBP tipped the balance away from police enforcement and overemphasized community service. As a result, officers are more comfortable providing, and many citizens accept, a "watch" style of policing interspersed with quick response to all complaints.

Conclusion

Community policing in Kentville and, in general, in the small-town milieu, is subject to profound challenges and powerful, external threats to survival such as the move to regionalization. The dominant themes over the past two decades in the Valley have been, on the one hand, the considerable improvement in the quality of the independent small-town service because of the PBP and CBP movements, and on the other, the decline of the independent STP model and the incorporation of town police into the RCMP. Nevertheless, CBP resonates with the small-town municipal police services, and for those that have continued to exist, including Kentville, the institutionalization of CBP as a component of the modern, professional model is an important element of their survival strategy.

Provincial and regional police services have adopted formal CBP (advisory groups, special programs, etc.), drawing upon their greater capacity. STP has difficulty challenging them on formal CBP criteria, and many CBP features are not an arena where STP can prevail. The larger and more formalized organizations, such as city policing and the RCMP, can offer many of the elements of service that are close to the demands voiced by community residents and elites alike. Consequently, their claim to be doing community policing gains considerable currency. The RCMP, for example, brings to the small town greater access to resources, more training, greater independence for the service, and much less "fishbowl" effect for small-town officers.

One area where there is a large continuing difference in STP versus other organizational forms of policing is the significant impact of local leaders, since the very existence of the small-town police services in Nova Scotia is dependent on the Town Council not opting to contract out the services to the RCMP. Policing style is not just a question of community size, however; organizational structures also shape policing practices. Organizational priorities substantially limit the informal side of community policing in RCMP-controlled towns. Legalistic policing sacrifices foot patrol and the watchman activities but also the in-depth personal relationships, responsiveness to community concerns, and local accountability. In the small towns with municipal police services, a formal CBP philosophy is grafted onto more traditional community policing practices associated with small size, such as close contact with the policed population, intense community involvement, and quick response to all calls for service. As small-town police services face an uncertain future, community policing, in its traditional and CBP forms, is a strategic key to their survival, although in the long run, it may not be enough to save the independent small-town police service in the Valley or elsewhere in Canada.

References

Clairmont, D. (1991). "Community based policing: implementation and impact." Halifax: Atlantic Institute of Criminology, Occasional Paper Series.

Murphy, C. (1986). "Social and formal organization of small town policing; comparative analysis of R.C.M.P. and municipal police." Toronto: University of Toronto, Ph.D. Dissertation.

Murphy, C. (1988). "The development, impact and implications of community policing in Canada." In J. Green and S. Mastrofski (Eds.) *Community Based Policing: Rhetoric or Reality?* New York: Praeger, 177–191.

Thomson, A., D. Clairmont, and L. Clairmont. (2003). "Policing the valley: Small town and rural policing in Nova Scotia." Halifax: Atlantic Institute of Criminology, Occasional Paper Series. http://www.acadiau.ca/~thomson/policingvalley/title&contents.htm.

Weisheit, R., L. Wells, and D. Falcone. (1994). "Community Policing in Small Town and Rural America." *Crime and Delinquency*, Vol. 40, No. 4 (October): 549–567.

Wilson, J. Q. (1970). *Varieties of Police Behavior*. New York: Athenaeum.

Chile

11

MARY FRAN T. MALONE

Contents

For much of its history, Chile has enjoyed a reputation of exceptionalism, sidestepping many of the problems plaguing other Latin American countries. Prior to a right-wing military coup in 1973, Chile had long boasted a strong, democratic tradition that was the envy of many of its neighbors. In keeping with this democratic tradition, Chile upheld the rule of law, particularly through well-trained and professional public servants like the national police force, the Carabineros of Chile. Under Chilean democracy, disputing parties resolved their differences through political channels, and widespread protection of civil liberties and political rights created political space for competing interests and visions. The 1973 military coup interrupted this democratic tradition for 16 years, replacing democracy and the rule of law with repression, arbitrary detention, torture, and murder. Military rule also tarnished the reputation of the Carabineros, as the national police supported the military's repression (Dammert 2006).

In 1989, democratic elections put an end to military rule and ushered in a new era for Chilean democracy. While the restoration of democracy faced several hurdles, in many respects, Chile returned to its exceptional roots. Chile's early embrace of the neoliberal economic model has promoted strong economic growth, and with an average income of US $17,400, Chile ranks among the world's middle-income countries. Still, like its Latin American neighbors, income inequality is high—the richest 10% of the population control 42.5% of the country's wealth. Chile's population of approximately 17 million is also overwhelmingly urban, as 90% of Chileans live in cities. With the exception of a very small indigenous community (approximately 5% of the population), the vast majority of Chileans are of European descent, and 70% are Roman Catholic. The influence of Catholicism has reinforced a conservative political culture; for example, Chile legalized divorce only recently in 2004.

Chilean exceptionalism extends to other parts of political and daily life. Despite some problems, legal reform in Chile has rehabilitated the judiciary and strengthened the rule of law. In a region wracked by high crime rates, Chile registers rates of violent crime on par with those of European countries. Crime rates in Chile did rise with the return to democracy, but much of this increase is due to a rise in property crimes. Chile is widely considered to be the safest country in Latin America, although public fear of crime is high. Chileans have not been assuaged with comparisons to Chile's more violent neighbors; rather, they have registered alarm that crime rates within Chile have risen under democracy (Dammert 2009; Dammert and Malone 2003).

Chile also differs markedly in its policing practices. The country has two national police forces, the Carabineros of Chile (established in 1927) and the Investigative Police (instated in 1933). The Carabineros are responsible for patrolling the streets and maintaining public order, and the Investigative Police are relegated more narrowly to the investigation of crimes and border control. With more than 41,000 members, the Carabineros are far more numerous and work more closely with the public (Frühling 2009). Historically, the public has held the Carabineros in high regard, registering strong approval for a police force that is professional, educated, and well-trained (Frühling 2009). This good reputation has persisted to the present day. Despite the Carabineros' complicity with the military regime and initial tensions with the newly elected civilian government in the early 1990s, the Carabineros managed to rehabilitate their image and reestablish positive relationships with Chilean society (Dammert 2006). In public opinion surveys, Chileans consistently have registered significantly higher levels of trust in the police than in all other countries in the western hemisphere—even higher than in the United States and Canada (Ahmad et al. 2011). Chileans also report far lower rates of police misconduct than all other Latin American countries. According to the Latin American Public Opinion Project, in a 2010 survey, Chileans reported the lowest incidents of bribery in the region—less than 2% of Chileans stated that police had solicited a bribe in the past 12 months (Orces 2008).

Chilean policing has also emphasized community participation in formulating crime control policy. Throughout the 1990s, when the Carabineros were rebuilding their ties to Chilean society, a series of initiatives sought to incorporate the community into policing strategies. Rather than responding to crime increases with knee-jerk *mano dura* (iron fist) decrees, Chilean policy makers sought to address crime increases and public insecurity with a series of municipal and national policies that emphasized community involvement.

Origin of Community Policing

Community policing initiatives were part of a broader movement of justice reform. After the Cold War, the international community promoted rule of law reform as a panacea for democratic governance and economic growth. In the context of Latin America, international consultants and donors stressed the importance of reforming legal codes, modernizing institutions like the courts and police, and replacing written proceedings with oral ones. Many domestic actors reacted favorably to such international initiatives, recognizing the need for widespread reform of justice systems throughout the region. While international and domestic actors have frequently not agreed on the types of reforms needed, or on the way in which reforms should be implemented, there has been consensus on the need for reform.

In the specific case of community policing initiatives, most programs have emerged at the behest of domestic political officials; in some cases, even after their implementation, citizens themselves were not aware of community policing initiatives in their own neighborhoods. In addition to the initiatives of elected and appointed leaders, some domestic nongovernmental organizations have also been important actors in addressing issues of public security more broadly. Perhaps most prominently, the Fundación Paz Ciudadana (Citizen Peace Foundation) has emerged as a major policy institute concerned with the issue of public safety and has collaborated with government agencies to design policies that promote citizen engagement with public security policies (Dammert 2006).

These domestic actors addressed policing practices during Chile's transition to democracy. As Chile discarded authoritarian practices and institutions in favor of democratic ones throughout the 1990s, reformers targeted the justice system as a crucial part of their efforts (Pásara 2009). Still, the constellation of actors in the postauthoritarian environment, and their institutional setting, slowed down the reform process (Weeks 2003). Former authoritarian officials wielded a substantial amount of power in the early years of Chile's return to democracy, and Chilean political institutions were designed to preserve this power. Although right-wing parties and leaders garnered the support of only a third of Chilean citizens, institutions inherited from authoritarian rule magnified their power and allowed them to block or dilute reform efforts they did not support (Oppenheim 2007). For the police, this meant that the reform process would be gradual. The Carabineros retained their highly centralized, hierarchical, military structure. The return of democracy did not completely sever the Carabineros' tie with the military. Resisting reformers' calls that the Carabineros report to the Ministry of the Interior, the national police remained under the jurisdiction of the Ministry of Defense, guaranteeing the Carabineros a great deal of institutional autonomy (Dammert 2006; Fuentes 2002).

Despite some doubts, this process of gradual reform has served the Carabineros well. The Carabineros have rebuilt their ties to Chilean society and are typically commended for their professionalism and ability to maintain public order. This acclaim is not universal, however, as social groups at the bottom of the socioeconomic ladder register significantly less favorable evaluations of police performance and report far more personal experiences with police misconduct (Frühling 2009). Still, it is notable that the police enjoy such a positive reputation given that crime rates themselves are rising.

The gradual reform of the Carabineros opened the door to community policing initiatives. To distance the Carabineros from the legacy of authoritarian rule, reformers introduced a series of changes to bring the police closer to the public. Reformers stressed the Carabineros' preventative role in maintaining public security and the critical role the community can play in supporting police activities. In the late 1990s, reforms altered the internal structure of the Carabineros, increasing the number of officers engaged in operational activities. These officers were then redeployed under new programs designed to integrate the police into the neighborhoods they served. For example, in 1994, the Programa Puertas Abiertas (Open-Door Program) aimed to make the police more visible in the public eye. Under this program, Carabineros initiated a series of dialogues with neighborhood organizations and leaders, aiming to learn about local concerns and disseminate basic information such as emergency telephone numbers (Dammert 2006). The Programa Seguridad Compartida (Program for Shared Security) followed close on its heels and also strived to publicize the importance of public collaboration with the police to confront crime, as well as train Carabineros to work with community organizations (Dammert 2006). In 1998, mobile police stations emerged to increase police presence at the local level and establish liaisons with communities.

In 1999, the official rhetoric extolling community involvement in crime control policy became more concrete with the implementation of Plan Cuadrante (the Quadrant Plan). Plan Cuadrante aimed to increase the street presence of police by dividing the national territory into zones (or cuadrantes) and assigning a police station to each zone, along with the necessary vehicle and personnel resources (Frühling 2009). Appointed personnel have been responsible for thoroughly personalizing themselves with the communities in their zone. To facilitate this personalization, each zone also has a community relations division to work with residents and civic organizations, as well as designated officials responsible for dialoguing with residents to identify security concerns and solve community problems. Each cuadrante official carries a cell phone to receive calls from members of the community, facilitating direct communication between citizens and their local police officers (Candira 2006). The Carabineros describe this program as one of "preventive patrolling practices in coordination with the community" (Candina 2006, p. 91).

Community Policing in Practice

Plan Cuadrante initiated a series of activities that engaged the community in the policing strategies of their neighborhoods. For example, the Carabineros held public hearings to explain their policing practices to neighborhood leaders and solicited feedback from the corresponding communities. When the Ministry of Finance commissioned an evaluation of Plan Cuadrante, however, it found that the plan was effective in terms of managing financial and personnel resources but did not adequately incorporate the community in identifying and prioritizing security concerns (Frühling 2009). Policy makers sought to address these concerns and, throughout the early and mid-2000s, developed a series of initiatives to strengthen community involvement in security policies, with varying degrees of success.

Plan Cuadrante sought to strengthen the Carabineros' ties to local communities; subsequent plans have striven to build upon these ties to deepen communities' involvement in policing practices. Two programs in particular sought to build upon police–community relationships to formulate public safety policies: Comuna Segura Compromiso 100 (Safer Cities Program) and Barrios Vulnerables (At-Risk Neighborhoods). Comuna Segura Compromiso 100 came to fruition in the mid-2000s due to the collaboration between the Interior Ministry and the Citizen Peace Foundation. This program encourages community groups to diagnose crime-related problems in their neighborhoods and develop a local agenda to prioritize the most pressing issues. Once the community prioritizes its security needs, it designs crime-fighting initiatives and requests government financing of its security program (Dammert 2006). Initial successes have encouraged the growth of Comuna Segura Compromiso 100, which has completed four phases of implementation and now includes over 56 communities, comprising more than half of the national population.

Barrios Vulnerables emerged in roughly the same time period, targeting high-crime neighborhoods with drug trafficking problems in metropolitan Santiago. It aimed to address the many facets of crime plaguing at-risk neighborhoods. Barrios Vulnerables invested in social programs, particularly those benefiting the communities' youth. It also encouraged communities to work with the police to provide intelligence to disrupt the networks of the drug trade. While Chile's geography has isolated it from the major international drug trading routes, and it has not experienced as sharp an increase in internal drug consumption as other Latin American countries, drug use has increasingly become a problem and caused crime to increase in some neighborhoods. Barrios Vulnerables sought to combine an investment in social programs with community collaboration with the police to increase public security in at-risk neighborhoods. Evaluation mechanisms for the program are still in development, but hopes remain high for a program that combines investment in social welfare with police disruption of drug trafficking (Dammert 2006).

Not all of these community policing programs have been successful, however, as measured by their longevity. For example, in 1998, the national government encouraged the formation of citizen protection committees in the Greater Santiago Metropolitan Area, designed to create community alert systems and reinforce the protection of individual homes against crime. The Secretaría General de Gobierno (General Government Secretary) trained local leaders to spearhead these committees, encouraging them to network within their communities, as well as with the Carabineros and officials in municipal governments, on preventive crime measures (Dammert 2006). After the initial boost following implementation, these committees languished, and the program subsequently dissolved.

Perhaps one of the most systematic attempts to incorporate the voice of the community in policing has been through new performance measures designed to assess the Carabineros. To collect solid data on citizens' security needs and police performance, the Carabineros developed a series of new performance indicators in the early 2000s. In 2003, for example, the Ministry of the Interior conducted the Estudio Percepción y Evaluación de la labor de Carabineros de Chile (Study of Perceptions and Evaluations of the Work of the Carabineros of Chile), a survey to assess public perceptions and evaluations of specific police duties (Frühling 2009). Among the many concrete performance measures, the survey asked respondents to rank the duties they considered to be most important and then evaluate how well the Carabineros fulfilled those duties. While concerns and priorities did vary depending on the socioeconomic group, on average, respondents ranked the sale of illegal drugs as their first concern, followed by minors' consumption of alcohol and burglaries, respectively. When asked to evaluate how well the Carabineros responded to such security concerns, responses revealed a gap between public expectations and performance. For example, the public prioritized concern over the illegal drug trade and evaluated police performance in this area negatively. Such surveys are valuable tools for tailoring police performance to meet the needs of local communities.

This emphasis on performance and responsiveness to citizens intensified in 2006, with the appointment of a new General Director of the Carabineros, José Bernales. In 2006, the Carabineros launched the Quality Improvement Program for Police Services to the Community, which assessed citizens' satisfaction with police performance through a series of surveys of people who had visited police stations or called the police (Frühling 2009). The survey asked people how promptly the Carabineros responded to their concerns, how well the police treated them, and how they evaluated the police's response. After a 6-month period of data collection, the Carabineros' Office of Planning and Research used the survey data to develop performance targets for the police to meet, aiming to use community feedback to improve police performance. Through measures such as these, Chilean policing strategies have sought to respond to communities' needs. While, of course, policing strategies cannot merely bend to the will of the majority, the solicitation of community feedback and subsequent development of target goals for police performance encourage a positive feedback loop between police and the communities they serve.

Effectiveness of Community Policing

Chile has clearly emphasized the importance of the community in public security policy and prioritized preventive measures over repressive practices. This emphasis is particularly notable, as other Latin American countries have reacted to crime increases with punitive (and in some cases repressive) crackdowns on criminal acts. Still, it is difficult to assess the success of Chile's community policing initiatives. Data collection has been uneven, and crime trends can be difficult to gauge. For example, the data clearly indicate that the number of reported crimes has steadily increased over the past two decades. However, it is not clear if this increase reflects solely more criminal acts or is due to the fact that citizens trust the police more and are consequently more willing to report crimes. Victimization surveys are a useful tool for measuring crime trends; however, such surveys also face limitations in that they overreport property crimes, and changes in question wording can make it difficult to gauge longitudinal trends, for example. In addition to problems of data collection, in the case of Chile, it is difficult to isolate the impact of community policing initiatives as such practices have evolved simultaneously with a host of related reforms of the justice system and its corresponding institutions (Pásara 2009; Tiede 2012). It is difficult to assess the individual effects of so many different concurrent reforms (Dammert 2010).

Still, there are some indicators that imply that community policing practices have encouraged a pragmatic approach to crime control policy, in contrast to rash, repressive, and ultimately ineffective practices that have emerged elsewhere in the region. Public fear of crime in Chile has not translated into support for mano dura crackdowns. Indeed, some of Chile's recent justice reforms have strengthened the rights of accused and convicted criminals, yet their implementation has not prompted a sharp reaction against such reforms (Tiede 2012). This stands in marked contrast to other Latin American countries, where public fear of crime has led to a backlash against penal reform (Ungar 2009). It is not clear whether community policing programs reduce actual crime rates better than alternative models, but the evidence does suggest that a focus on community policing leads to public security policies that strengthen democratic norms rather than undermine them.

References

Ahmad, Nabeela, Victoria Hubickey, Francis McNamara, IV, and Frederico Batista Pereira. 2011. "Trust in the National Police," *Americas Barometer Insights*, Number 59, http://www.vanderbilt.edu/lapop/insights/I0859en.pdf (last accessed December 23, 2011).

Candina, Azun. 2006. "The institutional identity of the Carabineros de Chile," in *Public Security and Police Reform in the Americas*, edited by John Bailey and Lucía Dammert. Pittsburgh, PA: University of Pittsburgh Press.

Dammert, Lucía. 2010. "Análisis policial: de la difusión a la confusión de modelos," in *Crimen e Inseguridad: Políticas, Temas y Problemas en las Américas*, edited by Lucía Dammert. Santiago, Chile: FLACSO-Chile.

Dammert, Lucía. 2009. "Citizen (in)security in Chile, 1980–2007: Issues, trends, and challenges," in *Criminality, Public Security, and the Challenge to Democracy in Latin America*, edited by Marcelo Bergman and Laurence Whitehead. Notre Dame, IN: University of Notre Dame Press.

Dammert, Lucía. 2006. "From public security to citizen security in Chile," in *Public Security and Police Reform in the Americas*, edited by John Bailey and Lucía Dammert. Pittsburgh, PA: University of Pittsburgh Press.

Dammert, Lucía and Mary Fran T. Malone. 2003. "Fear of crime or fear of life? Public insecurities in Chile," *Bulletin of Latin American Research* 22(1): 79–101.

Frühling, Hugo. 2009. "Public opinion and the police in Chile," in *Criminality, Public Security, and the Challenge to Democracy in Latin America*, edited by Marcelo Bergman and Laurence Whitehead. Notre Dame, IN: University of Notre Dame Press.

Fuentes, Claudio. 2002. "Resisting change: Security sector reform in Chile," *Journal of Conflict, Security, and Development* 2(1): 121–131.

Oppenheim, Lois Hecht. 2007. *Politics in Chile: Socialism, Authoritarianism, and Market Democracy (3rd edition)*. Boulder, CO: Westview Press.

Orces, Diana. 2008. "Corruption victimization by the police," *Americas Barometer Insights*, Number 3, http://www.vanderbilt.edu/lapop/insights/I0803en.pdf (last accessed December 23, 2011).

Pásara, Luis. 2009. "Criminal process reform and citizen security," in *Criminality, Public Security, and the Challenge to Democracy in Latin America*, edited by Marcelo Bergman and Laurence Whitehead. Notre Dame, IN: University of Notre Dame Press.

Tiede, Lydia. 2012. "Chile's criminal law reform: Enhancing defendants' rights and citizen security," *Latin American Politics and Society* 54(3): 65–93.

Ungar, Mark. 2009. "La mano dura: Current dilemmas in Latin American police reform," in *Criminality, Public Security, and the Challenge to Democracy in Latin America*, edited by Marcelo Bergman and Laurence Whitehead. Notre Dame, IN: University of Notre Dame Press.

Weeks, Gregory. 2003. *The Military and Politics in Postauthoritarian Chile*. Tuscaloosa, AL: University of Alabama Press.

Mexico

12

ROY FENOFF
KARINA GARCIA

Contents

Background

Mexico is the fifth largest country in the Americas (761,600 mi.^{2}) and has a population of 113,724,226 with 76% of the people living in urban areas (U.S. Department of State 2011). Mexico is composed of three main ethnic groups, with the largest being the *mestizo* or people of mixed European and native heritage (60%), followed by the Indians (30%), the Caucasians (9%), and others (1%). It is a federal republic consisting of 31 states and a federal district, Mexico City, which is the country's capital. Mexico City has an estimated population of 22 million people, making it the second largest metropolitan area in the western hemisphere and the fifth largest urban agglomeration in the world (United Nations 2009; U.S. Department of State 2011). Geographically, Mexico shares its northern border with the United States (2,317 mi.); it is bordered to the east by the Gulf of Mexico, to the south and west by the Pacific Ocean, and on the southeast by Guatemala (541 mi.), Belize (156 mi.), and the Caribbean Sea (CIA 2011). Mexico is a country of fascinating contrasts. It has beautiful landscapes, a colorful cultural history, and it is the fifth most biologically diverse country in the world (Hyde 2010). Unfortunately, Mexico's rich history and biological magnificence have been overshadowed by persistent poverty and crime. The 2008 Report of the Consejo Nacional de Evaluación de las Políticas de Desarrollo Social (CONEVAL) states that 47.4% of the Mexican population lives in poverty (CONEVAL 2009), and several investigations have indicated that the amount of crime and violence has been increasing since the mid-1990s, with a recent surge in violent crime being attributed to several organized crime groups that have been warring for control over different drug trade routes and regions of the country (Stratfor 2009; Donnelly and Shirk 2010).

In an attempt to alleviate the growing crime problem, the Mexican government and several businesses have been actively searching for solutions. In 2003, a group of businessmen in Mexico City paid $4.3 million to former New York City Mayor Rudy Giuliani to develop a plan that would reduce crime in Mexico City (Dellios 2003). The Giuliani plan made 146 recommendations that were based on the "broken-windows" theory and focused on reforming the police in Mexico City. The plan claimed that if all of Giuliani's recommendations were implemented, the crime rate in Mexico City would decrease by at least 10% annually for the first 3 years (Taylor 2004; Gerson 2005). However, to date, only a few of Giuliani's recommendations have been followed. Additionally, over the years, the Mexican government has devised different police reforms to weed out chronic levels of police corruption and improve the community–police relationship. One such reform took place in Mexico City, where 4,000 male police officers were fired and replaced by women who are thought to be, by nature, more honest (LaRose and Maddan 2009). Although many of the reforms have been ineffective (Sabet 2010; Asch et al. 2011), some of the more recent ones such as improved training, increased pay, and developing a more selective hiring process (McGirk 1999; LaRose et al. 2006; Asch et al. 2011) appear to have been a step in the right direction. Unfortunately, reforming the police force in a country with a culture of corruption and a population that distrusts the police is a hurdle that has proved to be difficult to overcome.

Since 76% of the Mexican population is estimated to be located in urban areas, it is no surprise that investigations regarding the growing crime problem and the suggested police reforms have focused on these areas. However, rural areas that are primarily made up of indigenous groups have also experienced increasing levels of crime. Interestingly, some indigenous communities in Mexico have responded to the growing crime problem differently than their urban counterparts. Communities in the southern states of Chiapas, Guerrero, Oaxaca, and Puebla have established their own police force, which uses community-style policing and has yielded, by some accounts, successful results (Rowland 2005; Sierra 2005; Puaz 2008; Lucero 2011; Ramirez 2011). This chapter will briefly discuss the state of community policing in Mexico, and then it will describe how indigenous communities in the southern state of Guerrero, Mexico, have established and successfully maintained a community police force in one of the poorest and crime-plagued regions in Mexico.

Community Policing in Mexico

In Mexico, community policing is a relatively new concept that has been tried only in a few places throughout the country. In January 2005, a form of community policing was introduced into Ciudad Juarez in the state of Chihuahua, Mexico. The citizens of this city, which has a history of murders and kidnappings, responded to the vicious rape and murder of two young girls by establishing an "elder police force" or *Policía Adulto Mayor* to patrol outside of elementary schools throughout the city (Rodriguez 2005). According to Rodriguez (2005), this unarmed police force consisted of 35 retirees who were 59 years or older and were selected out of 300 applicants. The 35 chosen retirees attended a 2-week training course at the police academy, where they not only learned techniques of observation, description, and basic first aid, but also received some physical training. After completing the training, the group patrolled the city's elementary schools during the week and the city's three largest public parks on weekends. The members of the group worked in teams of two and were charged with alerting the police to any suspicious activities or problems. Each officer worked 12 hours a week and received a $185 check and $75 in groceries each month. This group was intentionally made up of retired schoolteachers and doctors with the hope that they would gain the support and trust of the community, which the city police had been unable to attain because of their ineffectiveness and corrupt practices (Rodriguez 2005).

In 1997, Mexico City's Secretariat of Public Security (Secretaría de Seguridad Pública del Distrito Federal [SSP DF]) selected various high-crime neighborhoods and provided police officers with a 3-month training course on how to work and interact with members of these communities. The officers were then given zones of responsibility; assigned patrol cars, which had the words "Policía Comunitaria" on the sides where they could be clearly seen; and told to maintain constant contact with community members. Unfortunately, the training and the new title were the only things that distinguished these officers from the regular police force because police–citizen interaction was rare (Juarez 2007). Following this initiative, the Mexico City mayor, Andrés Manuel López Obrador, started another community policing program on March 20, 2003 called *Policía de Barrio*. This program was established to build confidence and trust between the police and the community members while also encouraging citizens, community organizations, church groups, and police officers to work together to reduce crime (Juarez 2007). Additionally, López Obrador introduced local town hall-style meetings in which community members, academics from the Universidad Nacional Autónoma de México (UNAM), and police personnel would come together to discuss police–citizen activities and public security concerns (Larose and Maddan 2009). As might be expected, these meetings were well attended by members of the police force, but most community members were reluctant to take part in them. Those community members who did participate were hesitant to speak openly and honestly about police corruption and abuse in their neighborhoods because the police officers that they had problems with sat right across the table with paper and pen in hand (Davis 2006). Although community policing in Mexico City is found in various neighborhoods throughout the city, and it is said to operate under the community policing philosophy, the community police officers spend most of their time in their patrol cars, which results in a community policing style that is absent of any police–public interaction and a community that remains distrustful of the police force and unwilling to report any criminal activity (Uildriks 2010).

Although it appears that community policing may not be effectively implemented in Mexico until police corruption is reduced and the rule of law is strengthened, some rural indigenous communities have demonstrated that some forms of community policing can be implemented successfully to reduce human rights violations and provide their communities with security. One of the more developed and studied indigenous community-style policing programs in Mexico is the *Policía Communitaria* of the Costa Chica and Montaña regions in the state of Guerrero.

Origin of Community Policing in Guerrero

Guerrero is a rugged mountainous region located in Southern Mexico. It is bordered to the north by the Mexican states of Michoacan and Morelos, to the east by Puebla and Oaxaca, and on the west coast by the Pacific Ocean. The *Policía Communitaria*, which is an alternative form of local policing described in the following sections, has been implemented in the municipalities of the Costa Chica and Montaña regions located in the eastern part of the state of Guerrero. These regions are two of the most remote and poverty-stricken areas in Mexico, with a history of conflicts between indigenous groups and the government (Rowland 2005; Fox 2007). Although these conflicts have been ongoing for decades, the 1990s marked the beginning of a violent crime wave that can be partly attributed to an increase in guns and drug trafficking in the area (Rowland 2005). Furthermore, over time, the organized crime presence in the region infiltrated the police and military units, creating a corrupt and dangerous security force that became increasingly involved in crime and human rights violations (Rowland 2005; Sierra 2010). In response to this influx of crime and violence and a blurred difference between criminals and government officials, several community leaders representing more than 40 villages came together to devise a plan that would increase personal security among the residents of that region (Rowland 2005; Sierra 2005; Johnson 2007).

The *Policía Comunitaria* was formally established on October 15, 1995 during a meeting that took place in the village of Santa Cruz del Rincon, in the Montaña region municipality of Malinaltepec (De La Torre 2006). The meeting was attended by community leaders from Acatepec and San Luis Acatlan in the Costa Chica region, as well as various social organizations, which included coffee-growing organizations, the Ejido Union, the Farmers Union, local churches, indigenous groups, and school representatives (Rowland 2005; Puaz 2008). In that same year, three community meetings took place. According to the Regional Coordinator of Community Authorities (CRAC), during the third meeting, the participants noticed that government officials had not attended any of the meetings to which they were invited. Moreover, the government had done nothing to address the thefts, robberies, murders, and sexual assaults that had become all too common on their rural roads, which the residents depended on to travel to markets, schools, and hospitals. This proved to community members that the government was not interested in solving the crime problems that their villages were facing. As a result, the group agreed that a locally based volunteer police force would be the most effective way to alleviate the problem, and they created the Security and Justice Communitarian System or *Policía Communitaria* (Peréz-Rojas 2002; CRAC 2011).

The *Policía Communitaria* was created with government approval to operate in a collaborative capacity with official law enforcement personnel. This new partnership was publicly supported by the governor of the state of Guerrero, Angel Aguirre Rivero. Rivero provided the *Policía Communitaria* with training in the use of weapons; some equipment, including a truck and 20 low-caliber firearms; and financial resources (Rowland 2005; Johnson 2007). The group agreed that the role of the *Policía Communitaria* would be to guard the rural roads and footpaths that connected their communities and, when necessary, detain criminals and turn them over to the state prosecutor's office, who would be responsible for the administration of justice. Initially, the *Policía Communitaria* appeared to have achieved a significant decrease in crime; however, the crime problem persisted because criminals who were turned over to state authorities were released shortly after giving bribes to government officials (Cruz-Rueda 2000; Sierra 2005). State authorities claimed that criminals were released due to lack of evidence against them, but local communities dismissed this explanation since the *Policía Communitaria* had witnessed many of the crimes as they were being committed. As a result of the judicial system's repeated failure to prosecute detainees, community leaders came together in 1998 and formed their own regional authority, which was responsible for administrating justice (Sierra 2005; CRAC 2011).

The crime-fighting partnership between the local communities and the state soon turned into the local communities taking full responsibility for policing, administering justice, and punishing people who were found guilty of committing crimes within their villages. However, local communities did not seek the government's approval for expanding their policing duties, including the administration of justice, thus leading to tensions between the local communities and Guerrero's state government. In 2002, Guerrero's Secretary of Public Security announced that the *Policía Communitaria* had gone too far by creating its own extralegal community justice system (Rojas 2002). According to Guerrero's state government, the self-governing communities of the Costa Chica and Montaña regions were in direct violation of the law and were ordered to cease and desist (Johnson 2007). Predictably, the government's ultimatum was ignored, and the communities' extralegal justice system continues to exist. In fact, the success of the *Policía Communitaria* in the Costa Chica and Montaña regions has resulted in the establishment of several other community police forces throughout the area (Uildriks 2010).

How Does Community Policing Work in the Costa Chica and Montaña Regions of Guerrero?

Community police forces are under the control of the General Assembly of Community and Municipal Authorities, which is made up of authority figures from the villages participating in the system. There are two groups that operate under the General Assembly: the Regional CRAC, which consists of six community leaders who assist in the administration of justice and supervising the functioning of the system (Cruz-Rueda 2000; Peral-Salcido and Ortega-Dorantes 2006), and the Executive Committee, which is also composed of six community leaders who are elected by their respective communities and are in charge of coordinating police actions, maintaining the communities' radio communication system, raising money for training and policing activities, and representing the police forces when meeting with government authorities (Cruz-Rueda 2000; Rowland 2005; Sierra 2005).

The initial duties of the *Policía Communitaria* consisted of guarding rural roads and turning over apprehended criminals to the state prosecutor's office. However, it soon evolved into a more comprehensive community policing program, with villages taking responsibility for the administration of justice in the prosecution of suspected criminals (Rowland 2005). In addition to rural roads, the *Policía Communitaria* also patrols neighborhoods and schools and provides security for social organizations and community leaders who attend meetings with government officials (CRAC 2011).

In regard to the formation of the *Policía Communitaria*, each participating village selects eight to 12 police officers, depending on the village size and crime problems. The individuals who are selected volunteer for a 1-year term of service and work in 15-day rotations in different communities without pay. The officers instead receive support in the form of food, shelter, uniforms, and weapons and are excused from all community duties and payments (Sierra 2005; Johnson 2007). However, some community members argue that the volunteer-policing style should be replaced by a system based on full-time, year-round salaried positions, which would help lessen the financial burden that the families of the *Policía Comunitaria* members face since they have one less person contributing to the household income (Rojas 2005a). Conversely, other community leaders argue that the job is an obligation of service to the community by which each volunteer not only provides but also receives security. Additionally, by not paying the officers for their service, opportunities for corruption are significantly reduced, and community members are deterred from becoming career police officers, which would undermine the self-policing philosophy on which the *Policía Communitaria* is based (Rowland 2005; Sierra 2005; Puaz 2008). The new volunteers are trained by community leaders and current police officers in observational and intelligence-gathering skills, maintaining public order, and ways to apprehend and detain suspected criminals (Rowland 2005).

Once the suspected criminals are detained by the *Policía Communitaria*, they are placed in front of a community assembly, which determines their guilt or innocence. The community assembly is similar to a court but without lawyers and a judge. The arresting officers explain to the assembly the circumstances of the arrest and the charges against the suspect, who is allowed to present a defense with the assistance of friends and family. After both sides have presented their case, the assembly determines whether the suspect is guilty or innocent. If the suspect is found guilty, then the assembly members vote on the punishment, which is referred to as *reeducation* by community members. The punishment given is similar to a restorative justice model as it is focused on the rehabilitation and reintegration of the individuals into their communities. Consequently, punishments usually consist of community service with nights spent in jail (Rowland 2005; Sierra 2005). Typically, this community service consists of manual labor ranging from 15 days for minor offenses and up to 5 years, or more, for serious crimes such as homicide and sexual assault. Convicts travel from village to village working in 15-day intervals until the length of their community service is completed. The work consists primarily of public work projects such as digging wells and repairing bridges, roads, schools, and churches. Throughout their sentence, convicts are guarded by community police, and their meals are paid for by the village they are working in (Johnson 2007). Additionally, those individuals who are found guilty are counseled by village elders, who act as role models for the convicts and help them understand the negative effects that their actions had on the community. The information obtained from these counseling sessions is then presented to the assembly of authorities, which decides whether or not the sentence given should be reduced (Sierra 2005). In this regard, research completed by Johnson (2007) found that the elder-counseling aspect of the rehabilitation process is rarely followed. Instead, individuals who are found guilty are given a punishment based on the severity of their crime and are sent to the village where the crime was committed to complete their sentence. The Executive Committee oversees the process and makes sure that the punishment is carried out. At the end of the sentence, the Executive Committee evaluates the behavior and responsibility of the prisoners and determines whether or not their sentence is extended or if they are released. As part of the final act of the rehabilitation process, the freed prisoners are taken to their home villages and turned over to their family in the presence of the entire community (Rowland 2005; Sierra 2005).

Conclusions

Successful community policing programs depend on police officers who are intimately familiar with the neighborhoods they are assigned to patrol, and a trusting local community that accepts them as a legitimate force of public order. Furthermore, being easily accessible and frequently visible and having a close relationship with the local residents are necessary to detect and deter crime (Goldstein 1987). Conversely, if the social environment consists mostly of hostile police–citizen interactions that are based on distrust and fear, then the likelihood that the community will voluntarily assist the police in combating crime is significantly reduced (Uildriks 2010).

Community policing in Mexico City has experienced little success because its people distrust the police due to high levels of corruption and service inefficiency which hinders police performance. For instance, a 1999 survey of Mexico City residents reported that 90% of respondents had little or no trust in the police. A 2003 survey of law school students in Tampico, Tamaulipas, reported that more than 70% of the respondents viewed the municipal and state police agencies negatively (Brown et al. 2006). In 2004, the United Nations International Crime Victimization Survey found that from 1999 to 2003, 75% of all crimes in Mexico went unreported. The survey indicated that in the state of Guerrero, specifically, only one out of every 13 crimes was reported to the police (Johnson 2007). A more recent nationwide survey found that 88% of the population lacks confidence in the police (Reames 2007). Moreover, Transparency International's 2011 Corruption Perceptions Index ranks Mexico 100th worldwide in perceptions of corruption on a scale in which a ranking of 1 is given to a country that is considered highly clean and a last-place ranking of 182 is given to one that is considered highly corrupt. Furthermore, Transparency International estimated that in 2010, Mexicans spent $2.75 billion in bribes, which equated to the average Mexican household spending 14% to 33% of its income on bribes (Santos 2011).

In contrast, community policing in the Costa Chica and Montaña regions of Guerrero has been proven to be successful in reducing delinquency, violence, and insecurity. Testimonies collected from various community members in 2003 assert that crime has been significantly reduced and community members feel that the *Policía Communitaria* is effective in protecting them and making them feel secure so that they can move around freely without fear of being assaulted or killed (Rojas 2005b; Sierra 2005). The biggest difference between the community policing approach used in these regions and the one Mexico City officials have tried to implement is that the police officers in the Costa Chica and Montaña regions were selected by people who live in these crime-plagued communities. As a result, the residents were able to create a police force that they could trust and were willing to accept as a legitimate force of public order. Additionally, the *Policía Communitaria* is intimately familiar with the communities it patrols because its officers live in the villages and have a vested interest in the communities' safety and wellbeing.

Programs similar to the *Policía Communitaria* of the Costa Chica and Montaña regions may be successfully implemented in other indigenous communities and rural areas in Mexico if municipal and state governments accept this form of local policing and maintain a positive working relationship with these community groups. Although attempting to establish this kind of community policing in Mexico City seems unlikely given its complex social, cultural, and political fabric, if government officials in Mexico City as well as officials in other urban areas take a closer look at the kinds of community policing systems that have been successfully implemented by the various indigenous communities throughout the country, they might realize that communities who trust and accept their police force feel safer and more secure, and a reduction of crime and violence can be achieved.

References

Asch, B. J., Burger, N., & Fu, M. (2011). *Mitigating Corruption in Government Security Forces: The Role of Institutions, Incentives, and Personnel Management in Mexico*. Santa Monica, CA: RAND.

Brown, B., Benedict, W. R., & Wilkinson, W. V. (2006). Public perceptions of the police in Mexico: A case study. *Policing: An International Journal of Police Strategies and Management, 29*(1), 158–175.

Central Intelligence Agency (CIA). (2011). *The World Factbook*. Retrieved on November 20, 2011, from https://www.cia.gov/library/publications/the-world-factbook/geos/mx.html.

CONEVAL. (2009). *2008 Summary of Poverty Levels*. Retrieved on November 20, 2011, from http://www.coneval.gob.mx/cmsconeval/rw/pages/salaprensa/comunicados/comunicado_2009009.en.do.

CRAC. (2011). *Sistema de Seguridad y Justicia Comunitaria de la Costa Chica y Montana de Guerrero*. Retrieved on November 21, 2011, from http://www.policiacomunitaria.org/.

Cruz-Rueda, E. (2000). *Sistema de Seguridad Publica Indigena Comunitaria*. Retrieved on November 22, 2011, from http://biblio.juridicas.unam.mx/libros/1/91/4.pdf.

Davis, D. E. (2006). Undermining the rule of law: Democratization and the dark side of police reform in Mexico. *Latin American Politics and Society, 48*(1), 55–86.

De La Torre, R. J. (2006). *Sistema Comunitario de Justicia de la Montaña de Guerrero. Una Historia Actual de Derecho Antiguo*. Retrieved on November 22, 2011, from http://www.juridicas.unam.mx/publica/librev/rev/hisder/cont/18/pr/pr29.pdf.

Dellios, H. (2003). *Mexico City Urged to Overhaul Police*. Retrieved on December 12, 2011, from http://articles.chicagotribune.com/2003-08-08/news/0308080234_1_giuliani-partners-police-chief-marcelo-ebrard-anti-crime.

Donnelly, R. A., & Shirk, D. A. (2010). *Police and Public Security in Mexico*. San Diego, CA: University Readers, Inc.

Fox, J. (2007). Rural democratization and decentralization at the state/society interface: What counts as "local" government in the Mexican countryside? *Journal of Peasant Studies, 34*, 527–559.

Gerson, D. (2005). *In Mexico City, Few Cheers for Giuliani*. Retrieved on December 12, 2011, from http://www.nysun.com/new-york/in-mexico-city-few-cheers-for-giuliani/11973/.

Goldstein, H. (1987). Toward community-oriented policing: Potential, basic requirements, and threshold questions. *Crime and Delinquency, 33*(1), 6–30.

Hyde, T. H. (2010). *Reality of Mexico's Green Battle*. Retrieved on November 20, 2011, from http://www.guardian.co.uk/commentisfree/cifamerica/2010/feb/12/mexico-climate-change.

Johnson, J. L. (2007). When the poor police themselves: Public insecurity and extralegal criminal-justice administration in Mexico. In *Legitimacy and Criminal Justice: International Perspective*, edited by Tom R. Tyler. New York, NY: Russell Sage Foundation, 167–185.

Juarez, M. A. (2007). Evaluating the zero tolerance strategy and its application in Mexico City. In *Reforming the Administration of Justice in Mexico*, edited by Wayne A. Cornelius and David A. Shirk. Notre Dame, IN: University of Notre Dame Press, 415–438.

LaRose, A. P., Caldero, M. A., & Gonzalez-Gutierrez, I. (2006). Individual values of Mexico's new centurions: Will police recruits implement community-based changes? *Journal of Contemporary Criminal Justice, 22*(4), 286–302.

LaRose, A. P., & Maddan, S. A. (2009). Reforming la policía: Looking to the future of policing in Mexico. *Police Practice and Research, 10*(4), 333–348.

Lucero, J. A. (2011). The paradoxes of indigenous politics. *Americas Quarterly, 5*(2), 44–47.

McGirk, J. (1999). *City Life: Mexico City—All Women Force Drives Away Traffic Corruption*. Retrieved on November 20, 2011, from http://www.independent.co.uk/news/world/city-life-mexico-city-allwomen-force-drives-away-traffic-corruption-1111697.html.

Peral-Salcido, M., & Ortega-Dorantes, A. (2006). *Seguridad e Impartición de Justicia Comunitaria Regional en la Costa Montaña de Guerrero: La Policía Comunitaria*. Retrieved on November 20, 2011, from http://www.ciesas.edu.mx/proyectos/relaju/cd_relaju/Ponencias/Mesa%20Terven-Maldonado/OrtegaDorantesAmorPeralSalcidoMartha.pdf.

Peréz-Rojas, C. E. (2002). *Reclaiming Justice: Guerrero's Indigenous Community Police*. Video Distributed by Chiapas Media Project, Chicago, IL.

Puaz. (2008). *Popular Justice: Guerrero's Community Police*. Retrieved on December 12, 2011, from http://libcom.org/library/popular-justice-community-policing-guerrero-mexico-26032009.

Ramirez, G. M. (2011). *Mexico: Indigenous Communities Defend Themselves without the Government's Permission*. Retrieved on December 12, 2011, from http://upsidedownworld.org/main/mexico-archives-79/3214-mexico-indigenous-communities-defend-themselves-without-the-governments-permission.

Reames, B. N. (2007). A profile of police forces in Mexico. In *Reforming the Administration of Justice in Mexico*, edited by Wayne A. Cornelius and David A. Shirk. Notre Dame, IN: University of Notre Dame Press, 119–132.

Rodriguez, O. (2005). *Elderly Patrol Schools in Mexico City*. Retrieved on November 20, 2011, from http://www.globalaging.org/ruralaging/world/2005/patrol.htm.

Rojas, R. (2002). *Algunos Dicen Que la Defenderán Hasta las Últimas Consecuencias*. Retrieved on November 21, 2011, from http://www.jornada.unam.mx/2002/03/10/020n1pol.php?origen=politica.html.

Rojas, R. (2005a). *La Calma Uno de los Riesgos Para la Continuidad de la Policía Comunitaria*. Retrieved on November 21, 2011, from http://www.jornada.unam.mx/2005/09/28/index.php?section = politica&article = 022n1pol.

Rojas, R. (2005b). Reducen hasta 95% la delincuencia en seis municipios de Guerrero. *La Jornada* (Mexico), September 27, 2005.

Rowland, A. M. (2005). Local responses to public insecurity in Mexico. In *Public Security and Police Reform in the Americas*, edited by John Bailey and Lucia Dammert. Pittsburgh, PA: University of Pittsburgh Press, 187–204.

Sabet, D. (2010). Police reform in Mexico: Advances and persistent obstacles. In *Shared Responsibility: U.S.–Mexico Policy Options for Confronting Organized Crime*, edited by Eric L. Olson, David A. Shirk, and Andrew Selee. Washington, DC: Woodrow Wilson Center, 247–270.

Santos, A. M. (2011). *Bribes Cost Mexico $2.75 Billion in 2010, Says Report*. Retrieved on December 12, 2011, from http://latino.foxnews.com/latino/news/2011/05/11/bribes-cost-mexico-275-billion-2010-says-report/.

Sierra, M. T. (2005). The revival of indigenous justice in Mexico: Challenges for human rights and the state. *Political and Legal Anthropology Review, 28*(1), 52–72.

Sierra, M. T. (2010). *Indigenous Justice Faces the State: The Community Police Force in Guerrero, Mexico*. Retrieved on December 12, 2011, from http://www.highbeam.com/doc/1P3-2178079081.html.

Stratfor. (2009). Mexico in Crisis: Lost Borders and the Struggle for Regional Status. Austin, TX: CreateSpace.

Taylor, L. (2004). *Giuliani's Crime Plan for Mexico City a Work in Progress*. Retrieved on December 12, 2011, from http://seattletimes.nwsource.com/html/nationworld/2002002062_giuliani11.html.

Transparency International. (2011). *Corruption Perceptions Index 2011*. Retrieved on December 12, 2011, from http://cpi.transparency.org/cpi2011/results/.

Uildriks, N. (2010). *Mexico's Unrule of Law: Implementing Human Rights in Police and Judicial Reform under Democratization*. Plymouth, UK: Lexington Books.

United Nations. (2009). *World Urbanization Prospects*. Retrieved on November 20, 2011, from http://esa.un.org/unpd/wup/index.htm.

U.S. Department of State. (2011). *Background Note: Mexico*. Retrieved on November 20, 2011, from http://www.state.gov/r/pa/ei/bgn/35749.htm.

Peru

13

JOHN S. GITLITZ

Contents

Introduction: Rondas Campesinas

The rondas campesinas[*] or peasant patrols emerged among smallholding mestizo farmers in the second half of the 1970s in response to a double crisis: the collapse of the peasant economy combined with the inability of the Peruvian state, and particularly the judicial system, to provide for order in a way that protected even minimal peasant interests. Though initially a policing organization, the rondas rapidly adopted the much broader mission of creating order in the countryside, becoming at once a police, a judiciary, and a kind of local government. The patrols were an entirely informal organization, in the sense of being separate from the state institutional structure, and to a very large extent, they remain so today, despite some formal legal recognition. They were also informal in the sense that they did not develop highly institutionalized procedures. Their actions remain flexible with lots of local variations.

Though the patrols shared with the state an interest in order, and this enabled sporadic cooperation, they were in essence rivals to the state's judicial structure—police, public ministry, and courts—and each feared and distrusted the other. Politicians and local power holders responded by seeking simultaneously both to co-opt and to harass the patrols. Hence, the central question both have faced since the beginning has been how each could relate to the other, a question that, since 2000, at least one segment of the Peruvian state, the courts, has begun to wrestle with seriously.

---

[*] I explored the early history of the rondas in an article I published 30 years ago (Gitlitz and Rojas 1983) in which I not only presented the basic functioning of ronda justice (Gitlitz 2001) but also developed early ideas on the relationship between the rondas and the state (Gitlitz 1998). These ideas as well as the relationship of the rondas to the state, the dilemma of human rights, and the judiciary's response are further developed in a greatly expanded form in a forthcoming book yet to be given a title, to be published by the Instituto de Estudios Peruanos in the fall of 2012.

The Context That Gave Birth to Rondas

In the 1970s, the peasant economy of the mestizo, smallholding peasants of northern mountain Peru found themselves mired in deep crisis. A growing population, runaway inflation, and decreasing opportunities for urban employment were making family survival ever more precarious. Provincial power holders, particularly local merchants who have long exploited the rural folk, sought to protect their own wealth at the expense of the peasants. For the peasants, cattle, their traditional way of saving, were becoming ever more central, yet the peasants were simultaneously facing growing and more organized gangs of rustlers. Cattle theft had become an acute problem.

The state's judicial structure was incapable of providing an effective response. It was in part a problem of geography: rugged terrain, few roads, and relatively large distances made communications difficult. Partially, it was also the inadequacy of the police—few in number, poorly trained, poorly paid, generally located in urban centers, often corrupt, and, at least in the eyes of the peasants, more concerned with protecting the interests of urban power elites than the farmers. Partially, it was also the problem of the public ministry. Prosecutors too were few in number, located in the cities, arrogant and dismissive of the peasantry, and unwilling to make the effort to go out to the countryside to investigate (and often demanding payment to do so). The courts were no better. But to a very large extent, it was a problem of the law itself. Written by intellectuals in the nation's capital, it defined rules that were frequently inapplicable in the countryside and established complex and lengthy procedures and standards of proof the peasants did not understand. One example is as follows: theft under the law was not punishable by jailing unless the value of the theft exceeded a certain amount—perhaps not great in Lima but often more than the value of a peasants' cow. The result was a judicial system peasants found inaccessible, slow, expensive, and unreliable. The result was a judicial system peasants found inaccessible, slow expensive, unreliable and incapable of responding to the challenge posed by rustling.

Emergence of Rondas

In December 1976, thieves broke into the primary school of the hamlet of Cuyumalca, not far from the provincial capital of Chota in the northern Peruvian department of Cajamarca. In response, the hamlet's lieutenant governor, a local peasant appointed by the provincial sub-prefect, urged the peasants to organize a system of nighttime patrols, in which all village men would participate, to protect their homes, crops, and cattle. The patrols immediately demonstrated their effectiveness, and within 2 years, hamlets across the province and in neighboring provinces had organized their own patrols. Orin Starn estimated that by the 1980s, more than 1400 hamlets across northern Peru had organized patrols. Patrols now exist the length of the Peruvian Andes and in the Amazon jungles, although their structures vary widely with local conditions. The early patrols emerged in the smallholding mestizo areas that characterize large parts of the northern mountains. In the mountains farther to the south, which are more indigenous, the patrols emerged as ancillary to existing community structures mandated by law. In the jungles, where indigenous cultures are still stronger, they evolved in yet different ways.

The patrols emerged initially as policing organizations. They captured rustlers and handed them over to the police and public ministry. The state, however, seldom prosecuted. The peasants saw this as evidence of corruption; prosecutors say the peasants seldom provided proof. In response, by 1978, the peasants had begun to evolve a system for trying the thieves themselves. By the early 1980s, they were using the structures they had created to adjudicate all matter of disputes—both criminal and civil—within their communities. What they had created had become, in essence, a parallel, informal legal system.

How Does the System Work?

The rondas in northern Peru have evolved three basic structures: the patrols themselves, the community assembly, and an elected community ronda committee.

The patrols: All men between the ages of 16 and 60 are required to participate in rotation (usually once every 2 weeks) in nighttime patrols, which guard fields and trails within the community. They will stop anyone they encounter at night, inquiring as to their reasons for being out. If the person is known to the patrol group, he or she may be allowed to continue on or be escorted home. If the person is not known, he or she may be detained until morning and then allowed to continue on. If a theft or other major problem is discovered, the patrols will coordinate to carry out house-to-house searches, investigate, capture, and question suspects.

The committee and the assembly: When problems occur, whether civil or criminal, they will be brought to the attention of the committee. If relatively simple, the committee will seek to resolve them. If more serious, it will bring them before the assembly. In civil disputes (ranging from domestic violence to neighbor squabbles to things like inheritance or contracts), the assembly acts as mediator/arbitrator, seeking to bring disputants to some kind of reconciliation. It is successful mediation that is judged to constitute a just solution. The assembly will use social pressure and, if deemed necessary, physical force to push disputants to compromise and to guarantee the compromises reached. In criminal cases (most often theft, interpersonal violence short of homicide, and witchcraft), the aim is to reincorporate the person deemed culpable back into village society. To that end, the assembly will investigate, demand (and often coerce) confession, and require reparation. The process often involves physical punishment, for its utilitarian and cleansing value. Once the "guilty" party has been punished, confessed and begged forgiveness, and repaired the damage he or she has done, in a formal ceremony, he or she will be officially forgiven. In both civil and criminal matters, the goal is to "rebuild communal peace." It is reconciliation and the reconstruction of order, rather than carefully documented proof or "punishment fit the crime," which is deemed justice.

Effectiveness, Abuses

Research has been carried out reconstructing cases via examining minute books and through interviews with participants in four communities, revealing both strengths and weaknesses, as well as occasional abuses. In general, the author—and other commentators—have been impressed by how often assemblies have been able to achieve reconciliation. Yet the rondas have not always been successful. For disputes to be resolved, assemblies must be able to build communal consensus, and that may not be easily achieved. The patrols have had their greatest success addressing conflicts among neighbors, considerably less with family disputes.

There have also been abuses. Physical punishment is a constitutive part of the process, for without it, guilt cannot be cleansed. Yet it easily can cross the line into excessive, even on occasion brutal, vengeance. Community factionalism sometimes impedes impartiality, and leaders can be venal, power hungry, even corrupt. Finally, sometimes community values, however rooted in tradition, can be offensive to contemporary eyes: for example, discrimination against women, including but not limited to toleration of physical abuse or discrimination in inheritance disputes.

Relations with the State and Its Judicial Institutions

The rondas emerged independent of the state and remain essentially an informal institution, and the rondas and the state inevitably see each other as rivals. Yet both have an interest in order. The peasants know that order cannot be achieved without the support of the state, and the state has increasingly come to realize it cannot be successful without the rondas. For 36 years, that tension has shaped relations between the two: the state, rather than repress the patrols, has sought to control and co-opt them, while persistently harassing them as well, and the patrols have struggled to maintain their autonomy. During the 1980s and the early 1990s, the guerrilla uprising of the Shining Path made the ronda–state relationship particularly difficult.

During the late 1980s, the García government legally recognized the patrols, but in a way that narrowly circumscribed their functions, essentially seeking to bring them under the control of the Interior Ministry. The rondas simply and successfully refused to participate. At the same time, the government began bringing charges—for kidnapping when the patrols detained suspects, for assault when they used violence, and for usurping judicial functions—against numerous leaders. During the early 1990s, the Fujimori government issued decrees converting the patrols into "Civil Defense Committees," under the control of the military and with the mission of assisting the military in counterinsurgency. Again, with a few exceptions, the rondas simply refused to cooperate.

The first breakthrough came in 1993, when the Fujimori government promulgated a new Constitution, which affirmed that Peru was a "multicultural" nation and recognized the right of "Peasant and Native Communities" (terms referring to indigenous communities with a legally mandated structure in the Andes and jungles, respectively) to administer justice. To the rondas, however, it offered only a "supporting" role, perhaps because as the expression of a mestizo peasantry, the rondas were not clearly indigenous. For all of these, the Constitution qualified that right to administer justice upon respect for "fundamental rights." And it expressly left to Congress passing a law that would clarify what all of this meant, something that the Congress was unable to do. The new Constitution had little impact. By and large, prosecutors and courts continued to consider the patrol's administration of justice as illegal, just as they continued to bring charges against ronderos and their leaders.

Congress finally tackled the Constitution's challenge in 2002, adopting a new ronda law. Largely incoherent, with no clear delimitation of ronda authority, it did nothing to improve the situation. Again, charges continued to be brought against ronderos, in fact in increasing numbers as the exploitation of natural resources by international corporations became an increasingly conflictive local issue.

In 2002, the Ministry of the Interior stepped into the fray, proposing a convention between that Ministry and the patrols that would authorize the rondas to investigate, detain, and interrogate suspects as long as they were not physically mistreated and were then handed over to the judicial system. In exchange, the courts would promise to respect investigations and not to bring charges against the peasants. In short, it would authorize the patrols to act as police, but not as courts. The vast majority of the rondas rejected the convention, which was signed by only one provincial federation and has been in force in only one district of that province.

Since 2004, however, Peruvian courts, or at least some segments of the judiciary, have been wrestling with the dilemmas much more seriously. In that year, an appeals court in the high-jungle department of San Martin reversed the convictions for kidnapping and usurpation of a number of ronderos. In a carefully reasoned decision, the court argued that the rondas were an expression of indigenous culture, therefore were authorized to administer justice under the Constitution, and hence could not be prosecuted for doing what they were legally entitled to do. In 2009, the Supreme Court turned its attention to the question, issuing an opinion (Acuerdo Plenario) that reiterated the San Martin's court position and went on to tackle as well the very difficult question of fundamental rights, though in the opinion of many observers, unsuccessfully.

Conclusions

Under the Peruvian legal system, courts do not make law. Their decisions do not set binding precedents. Only Congress can make law. Since 2009, the Supreme Court has hosted a number of congresses, commissions, hearings, and so forth to develop proposals to submit to the Congress. In the process, they are examining a number of questions:

1. Are the rondas of northern Peru an expression of indigenous culture entitled to the Constitution's protections?
2. What does it mean to protect fundamental rights? The rondas do use physical violence, they do coerce confessions, they do not have clear standards of proof or a clear concept of due process, and so forth, yet these are concepts developed to further a system in which establishing guilt as a prerequisite for punishment is central. The ronda's administration of justice is shaped by a different logic. What can be demanded of them?
3. Are there any reasonable limits to the competence of ronda justice? Do they have jurisdiction over outsiders within the community's territory? Are there any areas over which state courts legitimately must maintain a right of review?

So far, this discussion has been limited to some segments of the courts and the not-for-profit community. The public ministry continues to maintain a much more hard-line position.

The rondas too are overcoming a generation of distrust. They know, however, that whatever conclusions are reached by the courts, these will include some limitations on the patrols. They will have to decide whether these are limitations they can accept.

References

Gitlitz, S. (1998). "Decadencia y supervivencia de las rondas campesinas del norte del Peru," *Debate Agrario* 28:23–54.

Gitlitz, J.S. (2001). "Justicia rondera y derechos humanos," *Boletin del Instittuo Riva Aguero (Lima)* 28:201–220.

Gitlitz, J.S. and T. Rojas. (1983). "Peasant vigilante committees in northern Peru," *Journal of Latin American Studies* 15(1):163–197.

Trinidad and Tobago

14

VAUGHN J. CRICHLOW

Contents

Background

In recent decades, the community policing movement has elicited a greater focus on the quality of community life and public safety. Still, it is not always clear what indigenous factors are salient for community policing to be successful, and this can be especially challenging in transitional societies. Despite its aspiration to developed country status, the Republic of Trinidad and Tobago is no exception. Regarding its characteristics and accomplishments, it is the number one exporter of ammonia and methanol in the world and the premier exporter of liquefied natural gas (LNG) to the United States. It has the largest economy in the Caribbean due to its rich oil and gas reserves, and it recently experienced a construction boom in which world-class centers for arts, entertainment, and business have been established.

Trinidad and Tobago consists of two islands with a combined population of approximately 1.3 million and lies approximately 7 mi. off the coast of Venezuela. Trinidad was named by Christopher Columbus in 1498, and it is roughly 1864 mi.^{2} in size, slightly larger than the state of Rhode Island; Tobago, the mythical setting for Daniel Defoe's *Robinson Crusoe*, is the less populous island, with approximately 300 mi.^{2}. In regard to their colonial history, the islands were most recently a British crown colony, though heavily influenced by Spanish, French, Portuguese, and Dutch colonizers who were part of an ongoing conflict that caused the islands to change hands several times between 1498 and 1802. Ultimately, the country gained its independence in 1962 and later became a republic in 1976.

The influence of diverse cultures is evident in Trinidad and Tobago's *Carnival*, one of the largest street festivals in the world, and also in the names of streets and towns throughout the country. It is also evident in the rhythmic English pidgin that is commonly spoken and in the many national holidays that are celebrated (Mendes 2006). East Indians and Africans are by far the largest ethnic groups; however, there are also highly influential minority groups such as the Chinese, Syrian, and Lebanese communities. Citizens of African origin are predominantly descendants of enslaved Black Africans who were brought to the islands during the trans-Atlantic slave trade, which ended in 1838, when slaves were officially emancipated (Brereton 1996). Citizens of Indian origin are predominantly descendants of indentured laborers who traveled from India to Trinidad in the mid-1800s to work on sugar plantations.

The earliest form of organized policing in Trinidad and Tobago can be traced to the late 1500s, when the Spaniards founded St. Joseph, San José de Oruña, where the Town Council controlled a police unit for many years that never exceeded 10 members. In the decades following the abolition of slavery in 1838, there was an increasing need for policing in rural areas, and this led to an expansion of the police force. The police headquarters was established in Port-of-Spain, the capital city, and 12 police stations were built to house more than 100 officers in the police force. Officers from the British Metropolitan Police were also well represented on the force, and the organization used a traditional policing model derived from the Royal Irish Constabulary. This model was principally concerned with suppressing protest and protecting the upper class (Trotman 1986).

Regarding racial tensions, scholars have argued that Africans from Trinidad, and neighboring islands, were deliberately chosen over East Indians as police constables because of their perceived greater physical strength and endurance (Segal 1993). It was suggested that this perpetuated a racial imbalance that persisted for more than a century, and some argue that this was compounded by ethnic niches and group-level perceptions of prestigious occupations. It is noteworthy that, policing is not traditionally deemed to be a prestigious occupation due to comparatively low wages, difficult work conditions, and minimal education requirements.

Origins of Community Policing in Trinidad and Tobago

In order to understand the origin of community policing initiatives in Trinidad, it is important to consider the structure of the organization, as well as the context of social unrest and rising crime rates. The Trinidad and Tobago Police Service (TTPS) is divided into two divisions of sworn ranks; the first division comprises the top-level managers, and the second division comprises the lower-level managers. These officers are dispersed throughout the country and assigned to police stations and branches. Traditionally, citizens were required to come to the stations to report crimes, and these stations were generally not required to send out patrols; and in this respect, there has been no significant change. On the other hand, branches are specialized units that are not bound by geographical lines and comprise about 50% of sworn personnel. They are designated for dispatched mobile response, homicide, fraud, anticorruption, organized crime, narcotics, dignitary protection, highway and traffic duties, and heavily armed patrols. The administrative branches include the training academy, finance, bands, transport, planning, and development.

After the passage of the Police Service Act in 1966, there was an organizational shift from a militaristic style to a more service-oriented approach (Government of the Republic of Trinidad and Tobago 2009). This transformation was preceded by some major civil disturbances such as the *Hosay* massacre of 1884, in which the police were ordered to fire on a procession of 6000 citizens, killing at least 20 and wounding many others. During the *Water Riots* of 1903, 13 men were killed by the police for attempting to destroy the main parliamentary building. After the process of transformation had already begun, the TTPS, along with the military regiment, dealt with a *Black Power* uprising in 1970, which led to civil unrest and a limited state of emergency. They also experienced a failed 1990 coup perpetrated by a group called the *Jamaat al Muslimeen*, which held the prime minister and other parliamentarians hostage for 6 days. This resulted in 24 fatalities and the total destruction by fire of the police headquarters.

These events can be juxtaposed with reports of major drug trafficking activity, a rising homicide rate, a spate of kidnappings for ransom in the early 2000s, and an increase in gang-related violence. There were also news reports of police corruption and inefficiency in the handling of serious crimes and a growing perception of police incompetence among citizens (Wilson et al. 2011). In an attempt to chart a new course, the state appointed two Canadian candidates to fill the positions of commissioner and deputy commissioner of police in 2010. This was the first time that foreigners held these positions since the nation gained its independence in 1962. The government also implemented a crime-fighting strategy, which principally involved a state of emergency for three consecutive months in 2011. These events were unprecedented and ought to be considered in light of contextual characteristics that could impact the nature and effect of community policing in the country.

Although the TTPS aspired to become more of a service-oriented organization in the 1970s, this ideal was difficult to sustain in an environment of racial and political tension. In addition, there was little evidence-based scholarship to inform and support organizational transformation, and there were no significant changes in police training. Moreover, there was no internal philosophical ethos to reflect some of the external signs of change, such as the construction of new police stations and the purchase of patrol vehicles and new police uniforms. It was not until the 1990s that the term *community policing* became popular, and in 1993, the Association of Caribbean Commissioners of Police (ACCP) decided to adopt community policing policy in 24 regional territories, inclusive of Trinidad and Tobago. This move highlighted the consensus that current law enforcement approaches were not gaining the desired results. Additionally, community policing ideals, particularly in regard to community involvement in order maintenance, offered very appealing prospects (Deosaran 2002).

In response, the government of Trinidad and Tobago made a bold statement regarding the restructuring of the TTPS and provided resources to implement a new community policing policy. Furthermore, in 2001, a series of seminars were organized for police officers of all ranks to be sensitized to the needs of the community with the hope that this would positively impact the delivery of service. Still, there were concerns about the readiness of the TTPS to implement community policing policy (Deosaran 2002). It is also noteworthy that, there was an effort to launch community outreach programs through a small unit of police officers in the late 1990s; however, a decade later, there was very little evidence to show that this approach had made any impact on crime. Therefore, although the concept of community policing was widely endorsed throughout the policing fraternity, there were no organizational changes or substantial program initiatives to capitalize on this support. In 2005, the government again announced plans to restructure the TTPS and streamline its capabilities for better service delivery. Within these plans, there was a proposal to amend the constitution regarding the powers of the government and the Police Service Commission to directly influence the Police Service, however, the bill was struck down due to the government's failure to secure a parliamentary majority. Alternatively, the government was successful in passing legislation that gave the commissioner of police greater authority in personnel matters such as promotion and termination.

There were some important additional changes that came on stream. The promotion process within the TTPS was adjusted from a seniority-based system to a merit-based system. The training facilities and curriculum for new recruits were overhauled, a crime analysis unit was created, and there were new procedures for crime scene management and homicide investigation. An additional change was the implementation of a pilot project in

2007 under a new initiative called *Policing for People* based on the recommendations of a team of scholars from George Mason University. The project was called the Model Stations Initiative (MSI), and it was designed to enhance the daily activities of police in five of Trinidad's 77 station districts (Wilson et al. 2011). Although results are still forthcoming regarding the long-term implications of these changes, they were arguably the strongest effort toward evidence-based community policing in the nation's history.

How Community Policing Works in Trinidad and Tobago

There is clearly no sustained program of community policing in Trinidad and Tobago. Rather, over a period of roughly 15 years, there have been a number of policy changes, along with short-term initiatives that have reflected the core principles of community policing. In 1996, Commissioner Noor Mohammed attempted to implement a community policing plan designed to strike a balance between the traditional methods of policing and a more community-oriented approach. As described earlier, this coincided with the government's announcement regarding a new commitment to community policing.

Local consultants described the initiative as a consultative process that would not involve the creation of "vigilante groups." There was also a perception that community policing merely involved increased neighborhood patrols and that a greater police presence in the community was tantamount to a community policing strategy. Nevertheless, the main goal of community policing initiatives in Trinidad was crime prevention rather than crime fighting or suppression. This new style of policing required a shift from the traditional "top-down approach" to one that was focused on police–citizen relations. Such a model would encourage citizens to articulate their problems, and ultimately, regional councils would be established to implement community policing in all police divisions— the equivalent of police precincts in the United States.

According to news reports in 1997, a paper was submitted to the TTPS by a local crime consultant that listed the organizations that should be involved in the regional councils to support community policing efforts. These organizations included women's groups, youth groups, religious groups, entrepreneurs, parent–teacher associations, and officials from the Magistracy—the judges who preside over the lower courts. In this way, it was suggested that each regional council would be empowered to address the problems in its specific catchment area, and this would avoid the "one-size-fits-all approaches" that ostensibly ignore the differential needs and cultures across communities (Bagoo 2008b).

The implementation process in the late 1990s proceeded fairly smoothly when a small section of the Police Service was responsible for community outreach; however, the initiative was doomed for failure when new plans were introduced to make every officer a community policing officer. The move was not well received within the TTPS, seeing that in addition to their regular duties, police officers would be required to perform "community policing duties." The TTPS was clearly not yet ready to integrate community policing into its reward structure; therefore, officers could not be expected to perform according to new policy directives. It is therefore not surprising that subsequent to Mohammed's tenure, his successor tried to sustain the initiative, but in spite of his efforts, the community policing unit was dismantled (Bagoo 2008a).

Some years later, opposition members of parliament called for the implementation of a community policing model that reflected approaches used in Kenya and South Africa but this suggestion was quickly rejected by the government. The attorney general presented the government's view that the type of community policing that the opposition called for was nothing more than vigilantism. This assertion did nothing to correct the fundamental misconception that community policing gives license for citizens to take crime fighting into their own hands. Still, it was acknowledged that if not implemented properly in transitional societies, the locales where community policing was intended to thrive could become the breeding ground for vigilantism. An additional risk was the creation of relationships of patronage between the police and citizens, which arise when the police take bribes in return for protecting and serving some members of the community over others.

Despite previous reform efforts, when scholars began investigating the TTPS in 2005, they found that police officers were isolated from the public in their barracks and spent limited amounts of time on service-oriented patrol and other forms of community outreach. Special anticrime units operated out of police headquarters or divisional commands and were often accompanied by soldiers. These were the most visible signs of police patrol, and this style involved neighborhood *sweeps* and *crackdowns*. According to news reports, those living in *hot spots*, such as the areas surrounding Port-of-Spain, as well as eastern towns such as La Horquetta and Arima, would often experience intimidation and aggressive police contact. This assertive style of patrol reflected the persistent need to control levels of violent crime. It also reflected the natural instinct of police organizations to revert to traditional methods when facing rising crime rates.

Little attention was given to programs that could increase perceptions of police legitimacy and citizens' cooperation with the police, despite the fact that through the news media, it was evident that people were calling for a more democratic style of policing that did not trample on the rights of citizens. The MSI, launched in 2007, was a response to this call, and it reflected the government's renewed resolve. The initiative was arguably the most novel attempt at fostering better police–community relations since the policy announcement of 1996. MSI was a demonstration project implemented in five police stations, selected because of their diverse needs, and the project was designed to impact the everyday duties of police officers. It was hoped that it would address three of the core principles of community policing—problem solving, organizational decentralization, and community engagement (Brogden 2005).

Professor Stephen Mastrofski, the leader of the foreign team of experts who recommended the project, claimed that they had the support of every organizational level of the TTPS when conducting their research. Trevor Paul, the commissioner of police at the time, supported this claim by expressing his full support for the idea of the police and community working together, and this reflected the general attitude toward the government's umbrella policy of *Policing for the People* that was previously proposed. In a 2008 speech, the minister of national security gave a report on the details of MSI and stated that the *Policing for People* approach required officers to build trust with the public by being attentive, responsive, reliable, competent, respectful, and fair.

Therefore, the MSI focused specifically on improving police infrastructure and resources and increasing citizens' cooperation and support through routine interaction. Furthermore, it was reported that the model stations divided their districts into patrol zones and officers were deployed more effectively to specific patrol duties within those zones. A Victims Support Unit was also created in each of the model stations, and trained professionals with counseling experience were recruited to work with Victims Assistance officers in each unit. This initiative also required personnel to follow up with victims as their cases progressed through the legal system.

Effectiveness of Community Policing

An important finding of a recent study was that the TTPS had a public relations problem and failed to effectively get the message out on the progress of the MSI (Wilson et al. 2011). Additionally, the institutions within the relevant communities were not called upon to make statements on their meaningful contributions to the initiative. The study involved a survey that addressed contextual categories ranging from public perceptions of policing to collective efficacy (Wilson et al. 2011). It should be noted that after 1 year, the MSI reported at least a 20% decrease in all street crimes in all of five of the experimental communities. There were also reports of reduced fear at night from residents, reduced concern about robberies and housebreakings, and improved police visibility.

Based on the results of the MSI, it was recommended that the TTPS develop more accurate and usable crime records, more evidence-based strategies, and an evaluation plan for community partnerships and crime reduction. It was also recommended that enhanced training and organizational accountability be implemented as well as the improvement of the police complaint process. Furthermore, it was expressed that the police force needed to develop a culture of integrity. On the heels of these developments, plans were made to launch the program in five additional stations (Joseph 2008).

Ironically, instead of actually expanding the MSI or the *Policing for People* efforts, the government implemented a new initiative called the Citizen Security Program (CSP) in 22 pilot communities, focusing on addressing the most proximal risk factors associated with crime by incorporating a "community action" strategy. Here, it was reported that 548 persons were trained in various communities across the country in a range of topics including domestic violence prevention, shelter management, and child abuse. In 2009, a progress report highlighted that there was a reduction in homicides and that sexual offenses and shootings were also down. It was not clear whether alternative explanations for these outcomes were explored across the target communities. Moreover, in 2011, the new top-level management of the TTPS proclaimed new efforts to transform police patrol and increase public confidence in the police, but there was curiously no mention of the specific initiatives discussed previously.

Conclusion

Clearly, no substantive community policing program has ever been implemented in Trinidad and Tobago. There were some policing reforms and initiatives that reflected a desire to adopt widespread change, but it was nothing more than a desire. A sustained commitment to a national community policing program over successive administrations has not been achieved. The possible reasons for this failure are complex, and in order to come up with best practices in the future for community policing in indigenous societies, it might be useful to address the following observations.

First, the problem in achieving continuity might be explained by an adversarial political culture that encourages leaders to discard all programs tried by previous administrations, even if the programs showed signs of success. An additional observation is the tension between short-term and long-term strategy proposals. This means that long-term community policing measures, which often require a significant political and organizational commitment, are more likely to fall by the wayside than the assertive tactical approaches designed to reduce crime levels in the short term. Furthermore, community policing has not yet become part of the rewards structure of the TTPS, and the problems posed by gang violence, drugs, and violent crime cause police managers to rely on traditional law-and-order approaches that foster an adversarial relationship between police and communities.

Another concern is the report that the number of sworn personnel currently deployed is far below the required level of 7500 officers. As of 2011, the TTPS comprised no more than 6000 officers, and this is an important consideration when it comes to implementing labor-intensive reforms. Moreover, achieving a more democratized style of policing might not be achievable if not supported by the full democratization of the Police Service itself. With the current centralized bureaucracy, it is not easy to delegate the responsibility of implementation to district managers and superintendents. It is an additional concern that neighborhoods in Trinidad and Tobago might not be used to taking responsibility for their own order maintenance, and there might be low levels of collective efficacy, which is also a concern in other developing societies. Therefore, despite public opinion to the contrary, the communities themselves might not be ready to embrace democratized policing approaches.

Trinidad and Tobago is a diverse nation in which there are some disadvantaged crime-ridden communities, such as those surrounding the capital city, and some upper-class neighborhoods that are relatively crime-free such as those along the western peninsula. Still, it is noteworthy that most communities are not divided along class lines; it is therefore ubiquitous that upper-class as well as lower middle-class homes exist in the same neighborhoods. Furthermore, it is not unusual to find Trinidadians of different ethnic origins, as well as political persuasions, living as neighbors. In this respect, the islands of Trinidad and Tobago can be contrasted as Tobago leans more toward homogeneity; however, it is reasonable to expect differential levels of preparedness for community and problem-oriented policing at the neighborhood and street-block levels. These issues are not only relevant to law enforcement. They are also salient for good governance in general, and it is clear that they increase the difficulty level when it comes to the implementation of national policies.

In summary, it is a positive indicator that politicians and other stakeholders are willing to consider the recommendations of researchers, and this could be a welcome sign for future analysis on community policing. In this respect, it will become increasingly apparent that a foreign model of community policing will not be effective if incorporated wholesale into a local context. Policing strategies must be cognizant of the indigenous nuances of Trinidad and Tobago's landscape, and all formal and informal institutions must be committed to long-term transformation.

References

Bagoo, A. 2008a. Community policing not new to Trinidad. *Newsday*, January 20, 2008. http://www.newsday.co.tt/news/0,71799.html (accessed August 2, 2011).

Bagoo, A. 2008b. To community police or not community police? *Newsday*, January 20, 2008. http://www.newsday.co.tt/crime_and_court/0,72228.html (accessed August 2, 2011).

Brereton, B. 1996. *An Introduction to the History of Trinidad and Tobago*. Oxford: Heinemann.

Brogden, M. 2005. "Horses for courses" and "thin blue lines": Community policing in transitional society. *Police Quarterly, 8*(1): 64–98.

Deosaran, R. 2002. Community policing in the Caribbean: Context, community and police capability. *Policing: An International Journal of Police Strategies and Management, 25*(1): 125–146.

Government of the Republic of Trinidad and Tobago. 2009. History of the Trinidad and Tobago Police Service. http://www.ttps.gov.tt/AboutTTPS/OurHistory/tabid/123/Default.aspx (accessed November 18, 2010).

Joseph, M. 2008. Address by senator the honourable Martin R. Joseph, minister of national security on the occasion of the Trinidad and Tobago Police Service passing out parade at the police training academy, St. James barracks, St. James, August 9, 2008 at 4:00 p.m. http://www.news.gov.tt/index.php?news=304 (accessed December 18, 2011).

Mendes, J. 2006. *Cote ci Cote la: Trinidad and Tobago Dictionary*. Caribbean: Medianet.

Segal, D. 1993. Race and colour in pre-independence Trinidad and Tobago. In *Ethnicity*, ed. K. Yelvington, 81–115. London: Macmillan.

Trotman, D. 1986. *Crime in Trinidad: Conflict and Control in a Plantation Society, 1838–1900*. Knoxville, TN: University of Tennessee Press.

Wilson, D. B., Parks, R. B., & Mastrofski, S. D. 2011. The impact of police reform on communities of Trinidad and Tobago. *Journal of Experimental Criminology, 7*(4): 375–405.

United States
Indigenous Communities

15

SUSAN GADE

Contents

Background

The United States is one of the largest and most populous countries in the world. Nestled between Canada to the north and Mexico to the south, the United States has an estimated population of 308 million and a land area of nearly 3.8 million square miles. There are five Great Lakes, including Lake Superior, Michigan, Ontario, Erie, and Huron, which account for one-fifth of the world's freshwater supply. The Atlantic Ocean is located on the eastern coast, while the Pacific Ocean is located on the western coast. In addition to US territories, there are 50 states, 48 of which are situated on the mainland. Alaska, the largest state, is bordered by Canada, and its geographic proximity is closer to Russia than the US mainland. Formed from volcanoes, the state of Hawaii consists of numerous islands in the Pacific Ocean and has a tropical climate. The District of Columbia, or Washington, DC, is home to the US Capitol and has the highest population density, comparatively. While there is no federally recognized official language in the country, English is the primary language spoken, followed by Spanish. Finally, Native Americans are the poorest ethnic minority in the country.

Often referred to as a "melting pot," the United States is considered a diverse, heterogeneous society rich in cultural traditions. The indigenous population of Native Americans, or American Indians and Alaskan Natives, first inhabited the US mainland at least 12,000 years ago. Many native tribes originally lived nomadic lifestyles as hunters and gatherers. Following European arrival and colonization, millions of Native Americans perished due to disease. However, initially, Native American tribes were considered sovereign nations, and later, semisovereign states, which fell under the auspice of the military arm of the government (Wells and Falcone 2008). This was followed by a period of displacement, confiscation of land, marginalization, alienation, and oppression by the colonizing government, which continues to impact native life in the United States today.

Policing in America

British tradition shaped the development of policing in America. Police departments began to emerge in major US cities during the 1860s (Monkkonen 1981). Unlike their British counterpart, early (and present) American police departments featured a decentralized system (Uchida 2005). Politics influenced police organizations, whose primary role was to maintain order and, later, crime control. Some elements of informal community policing may have existed during the late nineteenth century, although response was largely reactive. Corruption was widespread, a byproduct of the interdependency of law enforcement and the polity. This slowly began to dissipate during the era of police professionalism.

Police professionalism was as much an evolutionary process as it was an organizational strategy. An efficient, professional organization had to be free of political control, which influenced personnel and operations. It also required a shift in focus to increase legitimacy and citizen satisfaction (Schneider 2009). August Vollmer, Chief of Police in Berkley, CA, was instrumental in pioneering reform efforts as well as the field of criminal justice. He implemented educational standards, leadership, training, science and technology, and alternative forms of patrol (Uchida 2005). The advent of technology, including the two-way radio and motorized patrol, enabled greater efficiency in police response and led to reductions in crime (Uchida 2005). In essence, police professionalism led to a major transformation of US law enforcement.

Today, there are more than 16,000 police departments in the United States (Skogan 1995). The implementation of professional and ethical standards and training reduced corruption and graft to a minimal level. Most law enforcement agencies emphasize proactive policing strategies rather than reactive response. A variety of models, including community policing, problem-oriented policing, intelligence-led policing, hot spot policing, and data-driven policing, are used across the nation to prevent and combat crime, fear, and disorder. While many progressive departments utilize a hybrid approach, community policing is the most common policing strategy (Weisburd and Eck 2004; Thatcher 2001).

Policing in Indian Country

Tribal policing reflects the values and traditions of American law enforcement. Prior to (and immediately following) European arrival, order maintenance was the responsibility of individual tribes according to custom, which integrated informal social controls with elements of shaming to preserve wellbeing in the community (Wells and Falcone 2008; Barker 1998). Egregious offenses were dealt with informally by a warrior (Wells and Falcone 2008; Barker 1998; French 1982). The Lighthouse Guard, instituted by the Cherokee in 1808, was the first official tribal police force (Wells and Falcone 2008; Barker 1998). In 1824, the US government created the Bureau of Indian Affairs to "negotiate" treaties and trade with tribal nations (BIA 2011). The military usurped control over reservation policing with the goal of assimilation and acculturation under threat of force (Barker 1998; Lithopoulos 2007). While some tribes conformed to the traditions imposed by the colonial government, many rejected Euro-American social conventions.

During the nineteenth and twentieth centuries, legislation was enacted, which decreased rights to self-determination, resulted in involuntary displacement, and substantially reduced the area of reservation lands or Indian Country. In 1830, the Indian Removal Act was passed, which relocated and displaced Native Americans. The Major Crimes Act of 1885 transferred jurisdiction from tribes to federal authorities for serious offenses such as homicide, kidnapping, rape, and robbery (which were later expanded) involving Indians on reservations (Wakeling et al. 2001). This minimized the role of tribal authorities in policing and adjudication and led to inefficiencies in the federal courts (Wells and Falcone 2008). Finally, Public Law 280 (1953) stipulated that jurisdiction over native tribes in some states would fall under the scope of state and local governments, which eliminated federal funding and protection (Wells and Falcone 2008).

Over the past four decades, self-determination and governance have been the primary objective for indigenous people in the United States. In addition, attempts have been made to remedy historical wrongdoings on behalf of the US government. This has led to fundamental change in policing of tribal lands. In 1975, the Indian Self-Determination and Education Assistance Act (Public Law 638) granted increased control over law enforcement, the judiciary, governance, education, and policy by enabling tribes to contract with the federal government to provide these services (Lithopoulos 2007). Additionally, increased funding has been allocated for tribes to enhance support for these efforts.

There are approximately 2.5 million American Indians and Alaska Natives who reside in the United States (2000 US Census) and 565 federally recognized tribes (BIA 2011). There are more than 200 police departments ranging from two to 200 officers, which service tribal lands (Wakeling et al. 2001). Most police departments in Indian Country use either their own tribal police department or the Bureau of Indian Affairs (contract) for law enforcement (Donelan 2009). According to Lithopoulos (2007), there are five tribal law enforcement models: Public Law 638, Bureau of Indian Affairs, self-governance agreement, tribal control, and Public Law 280.

Outside tribal lands, the public remains largely unaware of the increasing violence, victimization rates, and social problems surrounding indigenous people. While alcoholism is problematic in many native communities, little attention is directed toward the root causes of substance abuse. According to the National Congress of American Indians (n.d.):

- Per capita rates of violence are higher for American Indians compared to the general population.
- Native American women have the highest risk of victimization by an intimate partner.
- American Indian violent crime victims are more likely to be victimized by someone of a different race (p. 1).

Despite a surge in crime, empirical research is lacking regarding the extent of crime and victimization among Native Americans (and in Indian Country) and the effectiveness of policing strategies in addressing these problems. Tribal forces often face limited budgets, which inhibit their ability to adequately police communities. Tribal police departments also have fewer officers, comparatively. Finally, the complexities of jurisdictional assumption (over cases) can impede investigations and hinder prosecutions (Donelan 2009).

Origin of Community Policing in United States

The 1950s and 1960s marked a defining period in US history. The civil rights movement led by African-Americans and the landmark Supreme Court decision of Brown vs. the Board of Education (1954) led to desegregation and afforded all citizens, including minorities, equal protection under the law. In the 1960s, crime swelled, drawing an increasing demand of police services (Uchida 2005). Political, economic, and social unrest ensued, leading to increased racial discord and, ultimately, violence. Between 1964 and 1968, riots broke out throughout the country, which were often precipitated by police incidents, discrimination, and injustices involving African-Americans (Uchida 2005). Thus, community policing as an organizational philosophy stemmed largely as a response to racial tensions, fragmented relationships between law enforcement and citizens, and challenges regarding the effectiveness of traditional methods (Forman 2004; see also Green 2004).

Community policing formally surfaced in the late 1970s but gained widespread popularity during the 1980s (Skogan 1995). A growing body of research indicated that increasing the number of police officers, rapid response to calls for service, and random patrol had little effect on reducing or solving crime (Forman 2004). Instead, scholars stressed the importance of adopting problem-solving techniques that incorporated the community as a resource (Weisburd and Eck 2004; Skogan 1995). Collaboration and partnerships are central to the core mission of community policing, which includes addressing social problems and neighborhood decay (Schneider 2009; Thatcher 2001; Trojanowicz et al. 1998). The federal government rapidly began funding community-based policing initiatives, and in 1994, the US Department of Justice established the Community Oriented Policing Services (COPS). COPS was designed to promote community policing strategies in local, state, and tribal agencies. Last year, COPS, in cooperation with the Office of Justice Programs and the Office of Violence Against Women, awarded $118 million to American Indian and Alaskan Native communities to address substance abuse, interpersonal violence, crime prevention, and other initiatives (COPS 2011).

Community policing was embraced by departments across the country. Networking among police professionals, scholars, and policy makers helped facilitate its growth (Skogan 1995). Police chiefs visited other departments to learn about strategies for implementation. Skogan (1995) suggests that aggressive marketing by the government and its brain trust played a significant role in its swift expansion. Indeed, during the 1990s, politicians publicly declared support for hiring more officers, and COPS funding provided an avenue to achieve this goal (Meares 2002). Thus, the rise of community policing may be explained, in part, by influential forces and the prospect of monetary gain for departments who lacked resources to exact organizational change. However, the country was moving in a direction in which many administrators recognized the need for restructuring and improving police services. Despite obstacles, community policing seemed a viable solution.

How Does Community Policing Work?

Community policing is rooted in the philosophy that communities and citizens are an integral part of crime control and public safety. That is, law enforcement simply cannot police an entire jurisdiction itself without the support and assistance of the public. Forman (2004) argues that communication with citizens to identify/solve problems and citizen involvement comprise the two key components of community policing. While law enforcement may already be aware of some of the crime and disorder problems in the neighborhood, this method generates regular communication and information sharing, which in turn fosters trust. Members of the community who are reluctant to call police may be more inclined to report crime if police are viewed as legitimate actors who identify with their concerns. Minority communities, particularly in tribal areas, may view law enforcement as "outsiders" and may be hesitant to engage police as witnesses or victims of crime. Intelligence derived from citizens may also lead to solving and preventing crime.

Partnerships and cooperation with community and tribal leaders, nonprofit and faith-based groups, and the criminal justice system are vital elements of successful community policing initiatives. Police typically have well-established partnerships with other local, state, and federal law enforcement agencies, as well as the District Attorney's Office, US Attorney's Office, probation and parole, and other agents of the criminal justice system, since they collaborate with them frequently on cases. However, relationships with non-profit and faith-based groups and leaders differ by organization and its investment in the community. In indigenous communities, tribal political leaders, village elders, the tribal justice system, and social service providers should also be consulted. Involving members of these groups in community policing programs can be extremely beneficial, since they often maintain strong ties to the communities they represent. Further, they are usually perceived as legitimate by the public and can serve as a buffer between police and citizens. As with any organizational strategy, success is dependent upon the commitment of senior officials. Leadership is essential in transforming the mission into organizational philosophy, which is embedded in the department's culture (Wakeling et al. 2001).

Although community policing is a dominant theme in law enforcement across America, the extent of its implementation varies significantly. As Forman (2004) points out, community policing has different meanings for different departments and may simply involve the use of tactics rather than an organizational philosophy that evolves into standard police practice. The extent to which this strategy is rooted in a community is highly dependent upon the relationship between actors and long-term support for the endeavor.

Some strategies have gained visibility due to their unique application of community policing concepts. For example, in Chicago, officers participated in a prayer vigil in a high-crime area that was organized by the police department. In a survey conducted following the vigil, many officers indicated that police–church collaboration not only was good for the community but also increased officers' job satisfaction (Meares 2002). One may expect that some officers may question the effectiveness of nontraditional measures on the overall objective of preventing crime and disorder. However, as Meares (2002) explains, community policing involves defining priorities that align with respective goals of the community.

Citizen police academies also surfaced in both small and large departments around the country. Designed to strengthen police–community relationships, citizen police academies consisted of volunteers who received training and education in basic law enforcement techniques. Officers take participants on ride-alongs; walk a beat in a high-crime neighborhood, or direct traffic. Residents returned to the community with a greater understanding of the role and function of law enforcement. Some participants became police recruits following the experience.

Neighborhood beautification projects also serve as a community policing strategy. This involves residents and youth in neighborhood cleanups (e.g., trash removal, painting, trimming branches that block lighting) and may be followed by a luncheon or special event with officers in their districts. These projects incorporate Crime Prevention through Environmental Design (CPTED) concepts aimed to deter potential offenders by decreasing crime opportunities and address physical decay. Other examples include neighborhood watch groups, foot patrols, domestic violence and substance abuse initiatives, staggered visits from police and probation/parole, meetings with youth to discuss violence and safety, loitering ordinances, ordering in known law violators and gang members, and strict enforcement and prosecution of lesser offenses (Forman 2004). While there is much discussion of community-oriented strategies in the United States, research is lacking on the type of strategies used in indigenous communities and how they may contrast with traditional community policing approaches. However, informal community policing in Indian Country is common among tribal law enforcement.

What Community Police Do

It is customary in large organizations to have community policing officers or community liaison officers. Depending upon the availability of resources, community policing officers may be assigned to each of the police districts or areas where their services are needed most. Liaison officers are usually freed from responding to calls for service and investigating crime, since they spend most of their time in the community. They also attend meetings with group leaders and develop outreach programs. Community liaison officers establish relationships with members of the public to discuss crime problems and neighborhood concerns. This information is shared with superior officers or command staff to develop strategies and solutions. They also conduct household surveys on crime, disorder, fear of crime, satisfaction with police, vacant properties, physical decay, or social disorganization. Other duties include dispute resolution or routine order maintenance. Officers typically walk a beat, which is supplemented with motorized patrol. Some may prefer to be dressed in plain clothes rather than uniform. To maximize effect, Goldstein (1987) emphasizes visibility and accessibility (see also Skolnick and Bayley 1988).

Smaller police departments may have one individual assigned to community policing due to budget and personnel constraints. This officer may work full time or part time on initiatives, depending on need. Officers in rural areas and tribal lands may have stronger relationships with citizens due to close ties with members of the community (Wakeling et al. 2001). Larger departments often have high turnover rates for officers, who may be promoted or frequently reassigned to different divisions to gain additional experience. Regardless, the role and function of these officers are similar, although community policing officers in smaller jurisdictions may be involved in other crime prevention/response efforts, including conflict resolution. It is important to note that community policing should be tailored to fit the dynamics of the neighborhood or tribal land. Social, religious, and cultural traditions should be observed by officers, if possible.

Effectiveness of Community Policing

There are few comprehensive studies that examine the effectiveness of community-oriented policing initiatives. Some research captures a singular aspect of community policing, which may not be sufficient in determining the efficacy of the overall program. Despite this, community policing efforts have enjoyed some success. According to Skolnick and Bayley (1988), benefits include increased crime prevention, police accountability, legitimacy of police, and officer morale. Many scholars agree that community policing has a positive effect on citizen satisfaction, particularly in minority communities (Skogan 1995).

In an experiment conducted in Madison, WI, community policing had a positive effect on officers and citizens (Meares 2002). However, foot patrol experiments, while often increasing public perceptions of police, cause little reduction, if any, on crime (Skogan 1995).

There are also challenges to implementing community policing initiatives. The primary obstacle to implementing community policing programs is limited resources in communities and on reservation lands. Program development and evaluation of community policing strategies can be costly, which many small departments cannot afford. In addition, the demands of community police officers may conflict with traditional norms and patrol strategies as well as emergency response to calls for service (Skolnick and Bayley 1988). For community policing to be successful, an organization must have commitment, leadership, and participation from residents dedicated to improving public safety.

Conclusion

Community policing offers a promising solution to the challenges experienced by law enforcement and native tribes. Historical approaches to policing Indian Country fostered mistrust, since the imposed models alienated natives from the process. Community policing provides an avenue for tribal departments to incorporate native approaches to identify and remedy problems. Joint cooperation between entities can lead to the development of a program based on tribal traditions and normative values. Community policing of reservation lands will likely differ from traditional, western community-oriented programs. One principle advantage of community policing programs compared to other crime control strategies is flexibility. Review and evaluation of strengths and weaknesses will serve to enhance the overall quality of the initiative. In summary, community policing serves to bridge the gap between law enforcement and tribes by focusing on mutual collaboration to prevent crime, fear, and disorder in Indian Country.

References

Barker, M.L. (1998). *Policing in Indian Country*. New York, NY: Guilderland, Harrow, and Heston.

Bureau of Indian Affairs (BIA). (2011). BIA—Who We Are. U.S. Department of the Interior: Indian Affairs. Retrieved on November 3, 2011, from http://www.bia.gov/WhoWeAre/BIA/index.htm.

Community Oriented Policing Services (COPS). (2011). 2011 Coordinated Tribal Assistance Solicitation (CTAS). Retrieved on November 3, 2011, from http://www.cops.usdoj.gov/Default .asp?Item=2489.

Donelan, B. (2009). Child victimization on South Dakota Indian reservations: An overview of jurisdictional policy. *Forum on Public Policy: A Journal of the Oxford Roundtable*, Spring Ed., 1–12. Retrieved on October 2, 2011, from http://forumonpublicpolicy.com/spring09papers/ archivespr09/donelan.pdf.

Forman, J. (2004). Community policing and youth as assets. *The Journal of Criminal Law and Criminology, 95*, 1, 1–48.

French, L.A. (1982). *Indians and Criminal Justice*. Totowa, NJ: Allanhald Osmun.

Goldstein, H. (1987). Toward community-oriented policing: Potential, basic requirements and threshold questions. *Crime and Delinquency, 33*, 6–30.

Green, J.R. (2004). Community policing and organization change. In W.G. Skogan (Ed.), *Community Policing: Can it Work?* Belmont, CA: Wadsworth, 30–53.

Lithopoulos, S. (2007). International Comparison of Indigenous Policing Models. Public Safety Canada. Retrieved on October 3, 2011, from http://www.publicsafety.gc.ca/prg/le/ap/_fl/ipm-eng.pdf.

Meares, T.L. (2002). Praying for community policing. *California Law Review, 90,* 5, 1593–1634.

Monkkonen, E.H. (1981). *Police in Urban America, 1860–1920.* Cambridge, UK: Cambridge University Press.

National Congress of American Indians. (n.d.). Violence Against Women in Indian Country—Fact Sheet. Retrieved on October 4, 2011, from http://www.ncai.org/ncai/advocacy/hr/docs/dv-fact_sheet.pdf.

Schneider, J.A. (2009). *In Pursuit of Police Professionalism: The Development and Assessment of a Conceptual Model of Professionalism in Law Enforcement* (Doctoral Dissertation). Pittsburgh, PA: The University of Pittsburgh.

Skogan, W.G. (1995). Community policing in the United States. In J.P. Brodeur (Ed.), *Comparisons in Policing: An International Perspective.* Aldershot, UK: Avebury Press, 86–111.

Skolnick, J.H. and Bayley, D.H. (1988). Theme and variation in community policing. *Crime and Justice, 10,* 1–37.

Thatcher, D. (2001). Conflicting values in community policing. *Law and Society Review, 35,* 4, 765–798.

Trojanowicz, R., Kappeler, V.E., Gaines, L.K., Bucqueroux, B., and Sluder, R. (1998). *Community Policing: A Contemporary Perspective,* 2nd Ed. Cincinnati, OH: Anderson Publishing Company.

Wakeling, S., Jorgensen, M., Michaelson, S., and Begay, M. (2001). *Policing on American Indian Reservations: A Report to the National Institute of Justice.* U.S. Department of Justice, Office for Justice Programs, Washington, DC.

Weisburd, D. and Eck, J.E. (2004). What can police do to reduce crime, disorder and fear? *Annals of the American Academy of Political and Social Science, 593,* 42–65.

Wells, L.E. and Falcone, D.N. (2008). Rural crime and policing in American Indian communities. *Southern Rural Sociology, 23,* 2, 199–225.

Uchida, C.D. (2005). The development of American police: A historical overview. In R.G. Dunham and G.P. Alpert (Eds.), *Critical Issues in Policing: Contemporary Readings,* 5th Ed. Long Grove, IL: Waveland Press, Inc., 20–40.

Asia and Oceania

III

Afghanistan*
Police e Mardumi,† Indigenous Civilian Policing at District Level

16

DOEL MUKERJEE
MUSHTAQ RAHIM

Contents

Background

Afghanistan, a landlocked country, due to its geopolitical location, has always been a route for invaders, while political powerhouses have tried to bring the country to center stage of regional, political, and military power struggles. The last 30 years of history in Afghanistan has been volatile, ranging from the Russian invasion to internal conflict and the latest intervention of the international community in the aftermath of 9/11 attacks on United States. The last conflict commenced after a calm royal regime of over 40 years. However, review of history reveals continuous instability and fighting both internally within the tribes and externally with neighboring countries or foreign invaders.

Islam is the main religion, which predominantly forms the social and cultural fabric of the country. Fundamentally, the traditions and religion are strictly followed by the population that is predominantly living in the rural and semirural areas. The centuries-old tribal system is intact and is a determining factor in the sociopolitical aspects of community,

---

* The authors developed this paper as a part of the work at UNDP Afghanistan in 2010 and 2011.
† *Police e mardumi* is a Dari term that people can associate with community-oriented policing.

society, and the country. Usually, major and minor decisions are made by the chief of the village with the help of the *shuras** or village councils.

There are predominantly four major ethnic groups, Pashtoons (Pathan or Pakhtoon) in majority, followed by Tajiks, Hazaras, Uzbeks, and many other smaller ethnic groups. The groups are geographically centered around certain areas, with Pashtoons heavily located in the east and south but also having a presence in other parts of the country, Hazaras in the central highlands and some parts of the north, the Tajiks mainly living in the northern parts and some parts of the west, and Uzbeks in the north.

The Afghanistan National Police is the primary civilian police organization in Afghanistan, which was established in 1960. However, during and after the Soviet occupation, the police was militarized as it not only was faced with challenges to maintain public order but also was the first line of control for internal insurgency. After the departure of Soviets until 2002, the policing system was further weakened due to internal and external insurgency, where several police personnel found that they were jobless and were compelled to take up other occupations while the "virtue versus vice police" (Murray 2007) governed. This disintegrated the civilian police and created a vacuum when the democratic government was established. In 2003, the Afghan National Police (ANP) was established by a presidential decree, and since that year, the police organization has been undergoing a reform process in its rank and file, pay structures, training, and so forth.

Since the Afghan Interim Authority first took office in 2002, international agencies have played a crucial role in enabling the Ministry of Interior (MoI) to begin the process of rebuilding the civilian police by working jointly with all stakeholders. The international agencies were involved in supporting the police salaries, training, constructing police facilities, and so forth. In particular, police training has been an assiduous task as in the early years of reconstruction work, there were only a handful of professional police who had been trained before the civil war. The vast numbers of newly recruited personnel were untrained and illiterate soldiers from the various regimes who lacked discipline, formal policies, procedures, facilities, equipment, uniforms, and, most of all, public trust. There was also ethnic imbalance; also, most of the provincial and local police commanders owed allegiances to local military commanders, and central control was virtually nonexistent. Some of the provincial police commanders were ex-warlords continuing their existence in a legitimate form, making the basic structure of the civilian police organization almost defunct (Wilder 2007).

The development and reform process of police has engaged a large number of international organizations in the police sector, with the North Atlantic Treaty Organization (NATO) Training Mission for Afghanistan (NTMA), led by the military, taking the lead on the tactical side of policing; the European Union Police (EUPol) Mission focusing on civilian policing through police experts; and United Nations Development Programme (UNDP) doing the payment of police remunerations, institutional development, and community policing using civilian capacities. Further, there are numerous other actors bilaterally contributing to police development and reforms requiring huge efforts and resources for coordination, cohesion, and building of synergies.

Since the Bonn Agreement (2001),[†] and further as articulated in the Afghanistan National Development Strategy (ANDS), the threat to national and personal security

---

* These are traditional local bodies that discuss and help leaders to make a decision.
† The Bonn Agreement was the initial series of agreements between some prominent Afghans and the United Nations, intended to re-create Afghanistan.

remains a major impediment to growth and poverty reduction and, therefore, overall development of the country. As a part of the Afghanistan's National Security Policy, the government's goal with the direct support of the international community aims to establish a legitimate monopoly on the ANP and the Afghan National Army (ANA) to provide a secure environment for the rights of the Afghan people, to foster freedom of movement for people, commodities and ideas, and social and economic development. As a part of this commitment, the MoI and ANP aim to meet the governance and security needs of the country through the development of a professional, competent, well-trained, human rights–respecting, ethnically balanced police force that over the years will become fiscally sustainable, and the emplacement of good governance processes that ensures best practice from the national to district levels in government. It was envisaged that among the prime policies, it would be important to (1) enhance legal and governance structures at provincial and district levels and (2) educate the public about the tasks and purpose of the ANP and the rights of the citizens, thereby increasing the trust of the Afghan people in their police.

In early 1389 Solar Year (SY 2010), the MoI with the support of the international community drafted the National Police Strategy (NPS) and the National Police Plan (NPP) for 5 years. It was clearly identified that in the next 5 years, the people of Afghanistan would get services from their police as honest, accountable, brave, and impartial, and who will strive to create a secure and lawful society. Through the long-term vision, the ANP will uphold the Constitution of Afghanistan and enforce the prevailing laws of the country to protect the rights of all its people by performing their duties in a professional, nondiscriminatory, accountable, and trustworthy manner. These are in consonance with the basic values of the international conventions and the commitment at the Bonn Agreement. Further, the NPP 1389 has clearly demarcated that the police would gradually move away from its militarized role and primarily be responsible for law enforcement. They would work with the people to actively combat crime. Under the priorities spelled out in the national interest, the MoI has set the period SY 1389–1394 (2010–2015) to gain the confidence of the public; protect Afghan national interests; eliminate corruption; improve police capabilities including leadership, command, control and communication, training, equipment, and weapons to counter the specific threats in Afghanistan; reform and grow the ANP *Tashkil** to improve quality and quantity of the service provided by the police; improve morale and quality of life for police personnel; and implement intelligence-led policing.

Origin of Community Policing in Afghanistan

A recent Police Perception Survey 2010 (Kumar and Behrendorf 2010) indicates that the Afghans are, in general, reluctant to engage with the ANP. Approximately half of Afghans report that they would take criminal matters elsewhere, for example, to tribal leaders. Of those who have been crime victims in the past year, fewer than six in 10 (58%) reported it to the police, and among those who did, 56% say that the ANP adequately addressed the issue. At present, there are varying degrees of confidence in the police as the communities

---

* Police strength from tooth to tail.

prefer to sort out their problems through traditional justice institutions,* making the formal justice process redundant in its present form. The police are viewed as an organ of the government or even, in some areas, that of a particular power group rather than a solution provider of the state for the people.

The security situation in Afghanistan has been a global concern with over 140,000 foreign forces situated in the country in early 2011 (Foreign Forces in Afghanistan 2012) and has led to several attempts in developing a sustainable local security model, which has been in various forms of local defense hybrid models with limited essence of community policing. As mentioned earlier, the local governance institutions, *shuras*, and the village chief have great powers in decision making in the community. There is a traditional form of security structure existing even today called the *Arabaki* or volunteer system widely prevalent in southeastern Afghanistan. They are not local militia or hired private security guards as they enjoy the support of the community and undertake the decisions of the community elders. Even today, young men in Paktika province are known to take up arms as an honor and travel in their village to keep away miscreants. In various communities, there may be different forms of *Arabaki*; however, they have certain common principles based on which they function: that they implement the decisions of the community elders to maintain law and order and defend borders and boundaries of the village community. This volunteer force is part of a traditional code of conduct and honor called Pashtunwali.

Based on this traditional structure existent in Paktia province, in early 2009, the international forces supported a program called Afghan Public Protection Force (APPF). This program was initiated on a pilot basis in two districts in Maidan Wardak province. All recruits were between 25 and 45 years old, fit, free of drug use, without a criminal record, and, from the district, recruited to serve in the same jurisdiction. The overall objective of this plan was not to place overt tribal or ethnic dimensions in the selection process. All recruits would be subjected to a background check. Each recruit would receive 3 weeks of training, which would include classes on values, ethics, police law, use of force, human rights, and first aid. As a part of this program, each recruit would be equipped with one assault rifle, ammunition, and a uniform, and each unit would be issued a white Ford Ranger pickup truck marked "APPF," plus communications gear. The weapons were provided by the Afghan MoI, and the recruits were paid US$100 monthly, rising to a maximum of US$250 for an APPF captain. This idea was further consolidated as the Afghanistan Local Police initiative in mid-2010 with little public support. It is believed that this process is yet to be evaluated.

Other community-oriented policing programs that were introduced in Kabul province in late 2010 with some preliminary start in the middle of 2009 have been under the supervision of EUPol Afghanistan with the MoI in its reform of the Afghan Uniform Civilian Police through a 1-year pilot project that lays the foundations of the future structure of civilian policing in the country. The concept was piloted in Police District 3 in central Kabul, which aims to implement, assess, and develop the principles of community policing. In the near future, the project will be expanded to the remaining Kabul districts and other provinces. One of the positive principles introduced in this program was the concept of Afghan ownership, which would secure the needs of the ANP as the way to succeed

---

* As per the Police Perception Survey, 2010 (UNDP), substantial numbers of Afghans say that they would turn to other actors, rather than the police, in various dispute-related circumstances. If they were a victim of a property dispute, most, 53%, say they would go to the local elders rather than going to the police (30%) or taking the matter into their own hands (15%).

in reforming Afghan Uniform Civilian Police (EUPOL 2011). The EUPol-led project is a cooperative effort between the Afghan Uniform Civilian Police, Kabul Police District 3, MoI, and ISAF Forces (NATO Training Mission–Afghanistan, International Security Assistance Force (ISAF) Joint Command, and Combined Security Transition Command in Afghanistan [CSTC-A]). In this entire program, the EUPol officers provide advice and mentoring on a daily basis to their local colleagues. The mentoring and training are conducted mainly by EUPol staff with support from NATO Training Mission–Afghanistan, ISAF Joint Command, and CSTC-A.

In early 2009, UNDP conducted a study on Prospects of Community Policing in Afghanistan (Mukerjee 2009). Interviews with the *local shuras,* parliamentarians, nongovernmental organization (NGO) representatives, media personalities, academicians, and police personnel at the operational level confirmed that when arming community groups in a complex security situation where there were both licit and illicit weapons, locally trained armed civilians would make the system more fragile. Most civil society groups in Afghanistan and human rights reports are in consensus that while self-defense is an important aspect of promoting relatively low-cost security, this aspect is a state obligation, which has to be fulfilled by the state with accountable, well-trained state forces. The argument is that if well-trained service personnel themselves sometimes lose control when provided with guns, how can poorly trained citizens remain under control when armed with guns? This will only take society toward more criminalization, and the innocent will always have to live under the shadow of the gun, which several programs have tried to dissolve in countries facing conflict. The study indicated that while people were open to the idea of capacity development, discussions within the community showed that they would not like outsiders to make decisions for them or the members of their community to be armed. To them, the term *community policing* was objectionable, but local terms, such as *police e mardumi* or *da toleni police*, were acceptable. With the mission that the efforts would be locally driven, owned by the people, and that the future of any innovative efforts in this direction would be dependent on the groundswell created, pilot *police e mardumi* was taken forward from 2009 to mid-2010 and has been extended as a full-fledged multidonor project across 65 districts since 2010.

The *police e mardumi* initiative follows all the principles expressed by the doyen of community policing, Dr. David Bayley, as building a police agency *that is accountable to the law, protects human rights, promotes civilian and intragovernmental oversight*, and *responds to the needs of the public*, which is promoted through engagement with the civil society, police, local governance councils, local community leaders, and the public. Further, the *police e mardumi* endorses the visions, benchmarks, and priorities set by the MoI and specifically focuses on the Afghan civilian police to bridge the gap between police, the ordinary people, and the governance institutions, creating an opportunity for the people not only to access the first rung of the criminal justice system but also to build a progression to bring them into the fold of the justice system. It provides space for people to articulate their aspirations to maintain the human security in their jurisdictions with state agencies. The mechanisms for *police e mardumi* facilitate due process, uphold human rights of people, and establish the rule of law at the local level.

Police e mardumi is based on the best practices in community policing practiced in South Asia* yet holds the essence of the existing traditional social structures. The concept

---

* Swiss Development Cooperation (SDC)-supported Commonwealth Human Rights Initiative (CHRI) implemented project with the Chhattisgarh Human Rights Commission between 2003–2006.

was first launched as a pilot across eight northern provinces in Kabul, namely, Guldara, Shakardara, Qarabagh, Istalif, Kalakaan, Mirbachkoot, Deh Sabz, and Police District 17. A multipronged approach was initiated with a vision to develop a deeper engagement to promote public confidence in the police.

How Does *Police e Mardumi* Work?

The *police e mardumi* program is based on two key strategies. The first is that there is a need for capacity development of a wide range of actors including the police, the local community leaders, and civil society organizations that would ensure that they were the catalysts for the change process. Capacity development of local traditional leaders was initiated to build the understanding of state and its various institutions and the roles and responsibilities of the most visible mechanisms of the state, that is, the police. The second effective strategy was that training by Afghan civil society organizations and lawyers helped in creating an enabling environment and capacity for the police and public interface meetings to take place on a bimonthly basis to identify problems and local solutions. The local Afghan NGOs and lawyers' groups were sensitized to be the catalysts, which enabled the local community and the police to develop crime and local security plans that outlined roles and responsibilities. The civil society agencies provided on-ground facilitation as trainers, monitors, and reporters. Also, such civil society interventions created public pressure on the police and established a process for a *lay visiting* system at the police stations, which was not open to public scrutiny.

The civil society groups and lawyers were mostly local people from the districts. In some cases, the NGO groups had been working at the district level for many years on health, literacy, or humanitarian projects with *shuras* and Community Development Councils (CDCs) of the National Solidarity Programme, which has resulted in reliable knowledge on the area, goodwill, and trust with the community leaders. At an orientation meeting, the police chiefs of the districts were introduced to the trainers and NGOs by the police chief of Kabul. Subsequently, the NGO workers and trainers visited the police station and also met some local community leaders, *shuras*, and the CDCs to introduce the concepts and to request for their views. At the meetings, the community leaders accepted the concept and set the date for the next meeting. It was documented that at the subsequent meetings, the people came in large numbers. The mobilization of the people was undertaken through phone calls, and the chief of the police station developed a full documentation of all these numbers to build communications for the future. A notable example of speedy communications was seen in the case of a helicopter that had crashed in the Deh Sabz district in mid-2010. The local people got in touch with the police chief within a few minutes of the incident. Several such quick communications had been documented during the implementation period of the project. During this period, in 2009 and 2010, the police and international forces have recovered a large cache of weapons based on information provided by citizens. None of the meetings provided any incentive in either cash or kind to the police or the community leaders who came together. Each group came to the meeting on their own on a bimonthly basis to provide their inputs and took part in decision making for the district similar to the process of decision making by the community of village elders or *shuras*. Some legal literacy was provided to the community leaders on governance, justice issues, roles and responsibilities of the police, how to engage with the information desks at the police station, and other practical aspects to build a strong police–citizen coordination.

The meetings did not discourage anyone from attending. Each meeting was open house, and at times, these had to take place at the nearest mosque to accommodate all those who were present. On other occasions, meetings were organized at the district *shura* halls. On some occasions, the district governors also attended the meetings and chaired them to take important decisions. On several occasions, it was documented that in district Istalif in late 2010, the women *shuras* also attended these meetings to voice their concerns on women's security. Sensitive social issues were also discussed at the meetings, such as how to prevent the atrocities on women as in the tradition of the *Baad*.*

Through a series of police public meetings, a written document was developed, which was facilitated by the NGO or civil society working as facilitators at the districts to develop a crime and security plan that outlined the areas required for police and public cooperation and the responsibilities of each stakeholder of the district. In areas where there was difficulty for the police to undertake patrol duty, the local people, as in districts in Shakardara and Kalakaan, undertook regular patrolling of public property, such as patrolling of water dams to prevent them from being destroyed by illegal quarrying.

Few Initiatives Established Locally under *Police e Mardumi*

Information Desks

While initiating the plan for implementation, it was clear that all efforts would have to be cost effective and would have to require a low budget so that many such efforts could be replicated across the country. A low-cost project was also one of the requirements of the MoI. It was observed prior to the *police e mardumi* program that there were no designated police officers to accept complaints or information from the people visiting the police stations, leading to wariness on the part of the clients. The police commandant played a central role handling all decision making. Therefore, information desks were established with basic furniture and one computer to initiate a database system of incidence recording. Some power back-ups with generator and solar sets were also provided as most of the police stations did not receive a regular supply of electricity. Prior to introduction of the concept, it was discussed with the local maliks, wakils, and so forth, who were at first hesitant but soon supported the efforts as they felt that they were involved in the decision making for their area. The police personnel were trained through a short course on communication skills, counseling and mediation, understanding legal issues (including police responsibilities and rights of vulnerable groups such as women and children), and how to register an incident, and so forth.

* A customary practice where women and girls are given as compensation for crimes committed by a male member of a family to the family of the person who is killed.

Sector Police Approach

In an environment where there are several strategies currently being used such as intelligence-led policing, COIN (counterinsurgency strategy), and so forth, the project used a traditional method of educating the neoliterate police personnel on their jurisdiction through map reading using both topographical sheets and Google Maps. This was learnt enthusiastically by police personnel along with basic information on how to undertake foot and vehicle patrolling. These basic components assisted personnel to identify potential resources in their jurisdictions. Further, although the police chief was encouraged to identify suitable staff to engage in regular duty, this was ignored by several commandants due to lack of inadequate *tashkil* (strength) at the police stations. As the police engaged with the public at the monthly meetings, at the request of the community members, timely patrolling was provided to schools and key installations such as electricity dams at the districts. It was observed that during the period of 1 year, the personnel appreciated the importance of the sector policing approach.

One complaint that most people have about the police is that they drive too fast and often dangerously on the streets. During discussions, it was evident that the police personnel were uncomfortable to drive slowly even during patrol duty in safe areas. The fear of being shot while patrolling has led to rash driving. Over time, it was reported that in market areas and near schools, the police had limited fast driving, and this was appreciated by the district governor at several districts.

Police Training

The development of interpersonal skills is also essential for the police personnel to interact and engage with clients visiting the police stations and community leaders to collect information. Experiential learning using adult education tools such as role plays, pictures, and so forth was undertaken to capacitate the police personnel of all ranks, and they readily associated with the program. Although multiple police reconstruction and specifically police training programs have been in place since 2002 in the country, supported by international agencies, it was felt that there was value in equipping police personnel with certain softer skills necessary for civilian policing especially while providing services to the people. A short 14-day training module was crafted, which included map reading, human rights (as per Islamic tenets), laws and legislations of the country, role and responsibilities of the police, rights of persons with special needs (women and children), communication skills, leadership skills, and conflict resolution methods. All these trainings were provided at the police stations to ensure the safety of the trainers and the trainees. Also, this allowed the flexibility of the police personnel to respond to local exigencies while the training was ongoing.

Public Education Campaign

As recorded in a baseline study initiated at the beginning of the project, police image and morale were at an all-time low coupled with the high level of attrition and 9% drug addiction in the police (SIGAR 2010a,b). Therefore, with the MoI and civil society, a rigorous media campaign was initiated using short 30- and 45-s jingles on the radio in drama format to bolster the image of the police with positive real-life stories. All the radio jingles were played on prime time. Information was provided to the public on how to use 119 (Crisis Response Service), on rights of people, and so forth. The public education campaign was designed keeping the cultural context that people in both rural and urban areas listen to the radio and are receptive to music and theater.

Relationship with Justice System

Police e mardumi linked the traditional justice institutions to support the development of the first rung of the criminal justice system. The police department has little crime data to report other than those collected in the cities such as Kabul. In rural areas, the people prefer to access the *shuras* to seek advice and receive expeditious judgments; these can be anything from theft, murder, and runaway girls. *Police e mardumi* initiated the process of creating an enabling environment through discussions with traditional leaders such as maliks, wakils, and local governance institutions such as the district governor, the District Development Assembly members, and some CDC members of the villages. Once their endorsement was received, planning process was initiated on when the legal trainers from Kabul would be sent to the police stations and districts to undertake training. Further, the availability of the 119 hotline service for complaints about crime, information sharing, and corruption reporting was promoted through radio jingles. The option that a person can report to an authority that will listen and take immediate action through coordination between the MoI and the district police instilled confidence in the leaders of the traditional systems.

At the beginning of the efforts on *police e mardumi*, it was benchmarked through a quick analysis of available crime data that the crime reporting was low. However, once the *shuras*,* *maliks*, and *wakils* were in agreement with the process that was being undertaken, including the police and public interaction, incidence reporting went up. Also, with the police trainings, it was evident that the police personnel were eager to execute their duties in documenting the incidences.

Incidence Reporting Increased with Implementation of *Police e Mardumi*

Prior to the implementation of the project, the average annual incidence reported at most of the police stations in 2009 was between 11 and 31 cases. Deh Sabz district reported 32 cases in 2009; with the implementation of *police e mardumi,* the incidence reporting increased to 88 cases. Similarly, in the Guldara district, where in 2009 there were only three cases reported, the number of incidences reported increased to 406. Most of these incidences were reported at the bimonthly meetings or were brought individually by the *shura* members or village *malik* with the community member. It was noted that some of the incidence reporting also improved with the police image improving among the community groups. In the Guldara district, while the police commandant was in one of the villages, he rescued a boy who was drowning in the river. It was observed that after this incident, several

---

* Traditional community leaders.

community leaders and ordinary people were proactively visiting the police station. One of the legal literacy workshops for the community leaders was also organized at the police station with the support of the police personnel who set up a tent to facilitate the training program.

Effectiveness of *Police e Mardumi*

After 14 months of on-ground operations, assessment by experts and joint stakeholder reviews were undertaken where some critical areas were identified as to what would work best across the country in the context of the current competitive police reconstruction, training strategies, and counterinsurgency programs. Stakeholder reviews and field visits by MoI and experts have unfolded that the pilot districts have faced an unprecedented upsurge of reporting of roadside bombs, intruders in the area, incidences of theft, and so forth. The following are some of the lessons and learning of *police e mardumi*.

Police e mardumi had been initiated on a small scale where acceptability of various activity components was discussed regularly with the stakeholders.

- The program activities were in keeping with the Islamic traditions, ensuring that each training program had a religious teacher, which greatly helped to gain the confidence of the local people, especially the community leaders. Also, the fact that the trainings and discussions were completely driven by local needs ensured complete credibility of the activities at the local level.
- That activities were often demand-based was evident from the implementation of *police e mardumi* in Farza and Khakejabber districts on invitation from the ordinary people who expressed interest to participate in police public forums, as they knew that these were locally driven, without any political dimensions or external mandates.
- Across international agencies, international trainers (mostly military, some contracting agencies with ex-military personnel, and some civilian police who are few in number) provide training to police personnel. The trainers operate with interpreters. Under *police e mardumi*, local civilian trainers were provided orientation to implement training to the police personnel, making them well accepted. An evaluation sheet was used to evaluate some of the trainings, which showed positive trends in grasping information. Most of the trainees had undergone a 6-week training program prior to this training. Only 10% of the trainees had not received any form of training before. It was evident from the evaluation that most trainees showed improved skills in understanding human rights, the constitution, and governance in the country.
- Low-cost engagement mechanisms were acceptable to the senior leadership of the Ministry for Interior as these could be replicated across larger areas without high-budgetary implications. Most of the training programs, including legal literacy classes, do not cost more than "a cup of tea" for the participants, making it a cost-effective and sustainable process.
- A crucial time when trust between the citizens and police is built is when a citizen requests for immediate response from the police. The Crisis Response Center (or 119 center) at the MoI was established in 2007. *Police e mardumi* provided

training to the 119 operators and has subsequently undertaken work of establishing regional hubs. A regional hub has recently been established at Kandahar for the south. Further media campaigns have been undertaken to advertise how 119 or 100* can be used to get response from the police.

- At the initial stage of *police e mardumi* work, several international agencies had expressed their skepticism[†] of civil society participating in security sector work. However, *police e mardumi* brought together a quick mechanism for capacity building of police personnel along with knowledge enhancement of civil society to play the role of oversight bodies in future. This process has helped to open up a closed institution in a small geographic area. Therefore, the role of civil society (CSO) especially in the Afghanistan context is important in building democracy through participation in governance and initiating the dialogue on accountability. By participating and knowing the police and the security sector, the civil society will be in a position to provide informed opinion in future.

- In the entire reconstruction process, there are multiple agencies with multiple mandates and strategies to mitigate the ongoing conflict. Although the police in the context of the NPS is seen as a civilian police body, in reality, the ANP are also the first lines of fighting force for the ongoing insurgency. Therefore, even through its 14 months' intervention on ground, *police e mardumi* has had modest success. The debate on whether a military approach should prevail to fight insurgency or whether the development approach is effective and sustainable in full-blown insurgency situations is ongoing. These differing mandates have deterred *police e mardumi* from being upscaled rapidly. The critical question on the minds of most Afghans and international experts is whether *police e mardumi* is more relevant in safe and swing (medium threat) areas only. Can there be a common strategy that is effective across the entire country? The answer is no. The strategies would have to change in the high-threat areas. Police–public contact through crisis response centers and the correct and timely response of the police to such calls may help in the trust- and confidence-building process. On receiving timely response, the people would value the need for state institutions and provide information, which is critical to fight insurgency. At present, the quality of information is often weak, making recovery of weapons and information on roadside bombs difficult to detect for the police. However, with enhanced response of the police, public support may be less challenging.

Conclusion

In early 2011, *police e mardumi* was institutionalized at the MoI, and at present, it is being implemented across 65 districts in Afghanistan covering eight provinces. The escalation of the efforts was based on the results received in terms of enhanced information flow

---

* As per Ministry of Communication, Government of Islamic Republic of Afghanistan (GoIRA), the number 100 can be used as an emergency number. The 119 was started with the idea of running an emergency response telephone similar to 911 in the United States. This was read in the Persian script from left to right and therefore became 119 in Afghanistan.
† In September 2009.

between the police and the people, through a series of coordinated activities in each district where a philosophy was introduced that was nonexistent before, within the Ministry, within the international community, and within civil society. A few contemporary community-oriented policing projects have been launched by bilateral agencies through pilot initiatives. *Police e mardumi* was initiated to trigger a ripple in informed quarters so that many more agencies recognize the concept and move the police from its present militarization to community-oriented, accountable, and transparent policing systems. The efforts were implemented with constant advocacy, with the international community, civil society, and government agencies providing information as to what processes were being undertaken; the partnerships developed, making it possible for the philosophy to be acceptable. It is certain that there is much work to be undertaken on the policy side, especially since there is urgent requirement to build civilian policing and focus resources on district stabilization. Yet the question as to how fast this model can be upscaled and ensure sustainable processes across large jurisdictions is something that requires greater coordination by government, civil society, and international community together.

References

EUPOL Newsletter, National Information System for PD 3, November 15, 2011, p. 5.

Foreign Forces in Afghanistan, BBC, May 17, 2012. http://www.bbc.co.uk/news/mobile/world-south-asia-11371138.

Kumar, S. and Behrendorf, B., Policing Best Practices in Conflict/Post-Conflict Countries, UNDP Afghanistan, 2010.

Mukerjee, D. Prospects of Community Policing in Afghanistan 2009 (unpublished), pp. 1–85.

Murray, T. Police-Building in Afghanistan: A Case Study of Civil Security Reform, *International Peacekeeping*, 2007; 14(1): 108–126.

Police Perception Survey, UNDP Afghanistan, 2010.

SIGAR, Actions Needed to Improve the Reliability of Afghanistan Security Force Assessments, June 29, 2010. http://www.globalsecurity.org/military/library/report/2010/sigar-audit-10-11.pdf

SIGAR, Quarterly Report to the U.S. Congress, July 30, 2010, p. 110. http://www.sigar.mil/pdf/quarterlyreports/2012-07-30.pdf

Wilder, A. Cops or Robbers? The Struggle to Reform the Afghan police, AREU, July 2007, p. 54.

Australia

ELAINE BARCLAY
JOHN SCOTT

17

Contents

Introduction

The policing of Australia's Indigenous people has a long and troubled history. Australia's police force began as a predominantly military organization to manage the convict population and overcome Indigenous resistance to the expansion of white settlement (Mazzerole et al. 2003; Cunneen 2001). In the later part of the nineteenth century and for most of the twentieth century, the police were involved in administering government policies of protection, which included maintaining order on Indigenous reserves or camps, removing children from perceived unsafe environments, and regulating Indigenous movements in rural towns (Cunneen 2001). This resulted in a lasting legacy for police–Indigenous relations reflected in the perpetual overrepresentation of Indigenous people within the criminal justice system. However, over the past two decades, community policing initiatives have been developed by Indigenous people to enable their communities to be more effective in preventing crime and provide effective models of sanctioning and rehabilitating offenders (Cunneen 2007). In this chapter, three of these initiatives are described, namely, Aboriginal courts, Aboriginal Community Liaison Officers (ACLOs), and community night patrols. These initiatives seek to heal and improve police–Indigenous community relationships and reduce the number of Indigenous people who come into contact with the criminal justice system.

Background

Before discussing these initiatives in full, it is worth noting the history, location, social structure, and socioeconomic profile of Indigenous communities in Australia, as these factors are likely to have a significant impact on matters of crime and justice. Australia has a land area of approximately 7.7 million km², which almost equates to the land area of the United States (ABS 2008). Yet, Australia has a population of only 21.5 million, and the greater proportion lives along the coast, mostly in the east, southeast, and southwest of the continent. The remaining population is scattered across a vast and remote interior

(ABS 2008, 2012). There are 548,360 Indigenous people in Australia: about 2.5% of the total population, and most of them live in rural and remote areas (ABS 2012). The geographical distribution of the Indigenous population is roughly the reverse of that of non-Indigenous Australians. Two-thirds of the former live in regional, rural, and remote localities, whereas two-thirds of the latter live in the capital cities. Generally, the greater the distance from the major urban centers, the bigger the Indigenous population relative to that of the non-Indigenous population.

At the time of European settlement of Australia in 1788, Indigenous people occupied the entirety of the continent. To the settlers, Australia was a *terra nullius*, an unknown and uncultivated wasteland, and the Indigenous inhabitants were considered inferior because they had not made productive use of the land. This justified the removal of Indigenous people to enable a swift uptake of the land to establish European models of order and productivity. The colonial police were central to the process of land dispossession as they were charged with ensuring the safety of the new settlers. At the same time, police were responsible for protecting Indigenous people. This involved surveillance of and intervention into family life, monitoring Indigenous movements, and management of finances and rations (Hogg and Carrington 2006).

Since that time, Indigenous people have been subjected to a plethora of policies and programs aimed at *fixing* the Indigenous problem. Protectionist policies introduced in the late nineteenth century brought intense surveillance and regulation of Indigenous people, which involved the removal of children, relocation of communities, suppression of traditional practices, and establishment of missions and reserves usually on the outskirts of rural towns. These policies were enacted by the police, which placed them at the forefront of state interventions that "criminalized" Indigenous people. This history of institutionalized and often legally sanctioned mistreatment of Indigenous people has left its mark on modern police–Indigenous relations. The police were seen as violent oppressors, while the police viewed Indigenous people as wild and uncivilized. In 1937, *Assimilation* policies were introduced, which expected Indigenous people to be absorbed back into "mainstream" Anglo-Celtic society. A system of town camps emerged. These town camps had permanent residents in addition to people coming and going from remote locations, often to access services. Today, individuals may spend time with extended family in both urban and rural locations and frequently move between the two. In addition, many country towns have Indigenous people living in defined areas, this being a product of the location of public (social) housing (Hogg and Carrington 2006; Cunneen 2007).

Indigenous Australians experience significant levels of disadvantage across a range of social, economic, and health indicators (Cunneen 2007). Factors contributing to the disadvantage of many Indigenous people include educational factors (such as poor levels of schooling); economic factors (such as low income and employment); physical environmental factors (such as inadequate housing due to overcrowded dwellings and substandard household facilities); and social factors (such as dispossession, dislocation, and discrimination). These disadvantages intensify with the remoteness of a community, underlie specific health risk factors (such as alcohol and other drug use, smoking, nutrition, obesity, and physical inactivity), and contribute to Indigenous overrepresentation within the criminal justice system (ABS 2009).

The Indigenous population has a much younger age structure than the non-Indigenous population; the median age for Indigenous people is 21 years in contrast to 37 years for the non-Indigenous population. Furthermore, Indigenous life expectancy is 10 years less than for other Australians (ABS 2009). The relative youthfulness of Indigenous people is important because reported crime is more likely to involve younger people aged between 15 and 24 (Cunneen 2007). Drought and economic decline in rural Australia over the past two decades have meant that many towns have lost population, services, and employment opportunities. Many young people aged 15 to 24 years, particularly talented youth, have moved from rural areas to urban centers. The exception to this trend is the Indigenous population. Many young Indigenous people find themselves trapped in towns with declining resource (service and recreational) infrastructure. The fact that older age groups are disproportionately larger in rural communities means that remaining youth are more easily identified, which can exacerbate intergenerational conflict. Geographic separation and, often, isolation have only heightened perceptions that Indigenous people constitute a specific law-and-order problem. This in turn has led to "overpolicing" of Indigenous people in some areas (Barclay et al. 2007).

Indigenous people despite their relatively small numbers, yet they account for over a quarter (28%) of young people in juvenile detention and more than one quarter (26%) of the total prison population (AIHW 2009). Overall, police data suggest an Indigenous offending rate of approximately 1 in 10, compared with 1 in 79 for the non-Indigenous population (Parliament of Australia 2010). Official crime statistics indicate that Indigenous offender rates for acts intended to cause injury tend to be around 10 to 16 times higher than for the non-Indigenous population. Much of this crime is related to violence within Indigenous communities—usually domestic violence (see Hogg and Carrington 2006). As the greater proportion of appearances by Indigenous people before courts involve children, Indigenous adults receive harsher sentences due to their prior convictions. The dramatically higher rates of criminalization and police intervention with Indigenous compared to non-Indigenous reinforce their exclusion from social and economic participation (Cunneen 2001).

Indigenous people come before the courts for more serious property offenses, including breaking and entering and stealing motor vehicles, and as perpetrators of all forms of violent crimes. Indigenous people are also more likely to come before the court for public order offenses and justice-related matters, and breaches of existing court orders, such as conditions placed on apprehended violence orders, bail, bonds, probation, or parole. However, Indigenous people are less represented for offenses relating to fraud, traffic matters, or illicit drugs (AIHW 2009).

Indigenous people are also vastly overrepresented as victims of crime in all Australian states and territories. With the exception of blackmail/extortion and robbery, Indigenous people had a higher victimization rate than non-Indigenous persons for all categories of offense (ABS 2010). Violent victimization is substantially higher in Indigenous communities, and Indigenous people are more than 12 times more likely than non-Indigenous people to be hospitalized as a result of violence. Rates of hospitalization resulting from domestic violence in the Indigenous population are 35 times higher than in the non-Indigenous population. Often, the violence in Indigenous communities is related to alcohol abuse, social inequality, mental health issues, and the role of violence in traditional Indigenous culture (Parliament of Australia 2010).

Explanations for Indigenous victimization and offending can be divided into sociostructural and behavioral categories, which are often interrelated. In terms of sociostructural factors, the legacies of colonization, dispossession, and child removal policies, such as psychological distress and social disorganization, heighten the risk of criminalization and victimization. Other risk factors include low educational achievement, unemployment, living in a crowded household, financial stress, living in an area with perceived community problems, and being a member of the "stolen generation" (those children who were taken from their families under previous protectionist policies). Policies of child removal and institutionalization have severely damaged the parenting capacity of many Indigenous people. Many parents are further incapacitated by their poor health, substance abuse, and imprisonment, and poor parenting is a significant risk factor for juvenile offending (Weatherburn et al. 2006). Of great concern is the identification of an intergenerational cycle of abuse and violence. Indigenous children frequently witness or experience violence, which is normalized and increases the risk that they themselves will use violence. A 2007 report into child abuse within Indigenous communities in the Northern Territory led to an Australian government intervention to combat high levels of drinking, drug use, sexual abuse, and lawlessness in Northern Territory Indigenous communities. This involved placing 51 extra police officers in remote communities; placing bans on alcohol, drugs, and pornography; providing health checks for Indigenous children under the age of 16 years; and quarantining 50% of welfare payments for the purchase of food and other essentials (Edwards 2008).

It is primarily young Indigenous males who are responsible for the bulk of criminal offenses (Hogg and Carrington 2006). Many offenses like theft and vandalism are committed in groups, simply to break the monotony of what is experienced as a highly circumscribed existence. Being sent to a detention center in another locality may be seen as an opportunity for new experiences and to gain access to resources that are not available in the local community. Incarceration removes young men from what should be productive work and family roles, teaches young offenders criminal skills, and distorts role models for young people growing up, where it is normal to have large numbers of people in prison; also, each contact with the criminal justice system further reduces the employability of individuals. As rural and remote communities are disadvantaged because of inadequate infrastructure and services, local residents may not have the capacity to address local crime problems (O'Connor and Gray 1989).

Policing in Indigenous Communities

Effective policing of Australia's Indigenous communities has been historically undermined by the highly centralized nature of police organizations in Australia. Australia has 55,387 full-time sworn police officers, working across eight police services, centrally controlled and organized by a single organization within each state and territory (AIC 2006). Each state and territory police service is divided into regions, which are subdivided into police districts or Local Area Commands. Each command has various police stations, with some small stations staffed by only one officer. But the centralized management system does not provide for diversity and localized approaches to community policing, particularly of Indigenous communities in rural and remote areas (Mazzerole et al. 2003).

Social disadvantage and prejudice lead to structurally discriminatory law enforcement against Indigenous people (Jobes 2003). For example, some rural community leaders have used law-and-order rhetoric to target Indigenous youth as lawbreakers (Jobes 2003). Consequently, police resources have been disproportionately allocated to racially segmented towns, in the same way that they have been in built-up urban enclaves with higher proportions of Indigenous residents. In such places, police often distinguish between "good" Indigenous residents (those who are usually well behaved, recognizing and adapting a subordinate role in the local social hierarchy) and those they perceived to be "bad" (defiant or disrespectful, refusing to assimilate into the dominant culture and hostile to law enforcement) (O'Connor and Gray 1989). Extreme polarization is the result, with each group (Indigenous and police) seeing themselves as victims, and the police casting themselves as having a difficult job with little support from the public and justice system (Scott and Jobes 2007). Officers in racially antagonistic communities have experienced strain in being a member of white institutional society in juxtaposition to the Indigenous social system. To avoid disrupting the dominant normative system, some officers practice reactive policing, which may involve prejudice, abuse of powers, and cultural insensitivity. Overpolicing, whether in rural or urban communities, has resulted in Indigenous people feeling harassed and resentful about the police (Scott and Jobes 2007).

Open-air spaces within towns are often places where Indigenous people congregate and drink, which conflicts with the commercial and service functions of a community. This results in high levels of policing, noncomparable with non-Indigenous populations, and high arrest rates for minor offenses, such as bad language (Hogg and Carrington 2006). Alcohol abuse among Indigenous people is of particular concern for police. Dealing with public drunkenness and associated violence for rural police can be grinding, repetitive work, requiring them to juggle responsibilities of being a social worker and law enforcer. The challenge for police is trying to assimilate the traditional patterns of behavior of local Indigenous people into the conventional concepts and procedures of criminal law. The process is confounded by communication and language barriers, the role of kinship, Indigenous customary law, multitribal and interclan conflicts, and substance abuse (Hogg and Carrington 2006).

The overrepresentation of Indigenous people in the criminal justice system and its effects on the Indigenous population have been a challenge for policy makers and a source of advocacy and concern for many, particularly Indigenous people themselves. The past two decades have seen strenuous efforts by Indigenous groups, the courts, law reform bodies, and the police to address these problems (Cunneen 2007).

The shift with regard to Indigenous policies can be traced back to a Royal Commission into Indigenous Deaths in Custody (1987), which was triggered by a series of deaths in police custody and prison in circumstances that raised concern among the families and the communities of those who died (Cunneen 2007). The commission found that Indigenous people were dying at the same rate as non-Indigenous people in custody, but the overrepresentation of Indigenous people in the criminal justice system led to a higher percentage of deaths. The commission's recommendations were to improve police–Indigenous relations, divert Indigenous people from police custody, and improve custodial health and safety. Since this inquiry, police agencies in partnership with their state governments have made significant changes to reduce the disadvantage experienced by Indigenous people within the criminal justice system. New programs include the adoption of community policing, diversionary programs, cross cultural training and education for police officers, a commitment to improve custodial health and safety, and greater Indigenous autonomy concerning justice issues. A concerted effort has been made to educate the judiciary to ensure a greater understanding of the complexity of the issues that come before the courts. More Indigenous staff have been employed in courts and prisons, and alternative forms of community-based sentencing have been introduced (Cunneen 2007; Mazzerole et al. 2003).

One response to the difficulties of policing rural areas has been to limit the periods in which officers are assigned to racially divided and underresourced (usually isolated) towns. In New South Wales (NSW), officers are rotated every 2 years. While such a system serves valuable functions in ensuring that such areas are adequately resourced and limits the possibility that a police culture which is antagonistic to the local Indigenous community may develop, a problem is that officers lack the time to embed themselves in the local community. Studies of policing indicate that officers living in rural areas often develop a "localistic" as opposed to "legalistic" approach to policing, which is based upon the likelihood that such officers will both reside and embed themselves in the communities they service. Having officers move on after a limited period of time may impact upon their ability to build trust and rapport with local populations (Scott and Jobes 2007).

Community Policing in Indigenous Communities

Key community policing strategies that have been successfully introduced include the following.

Aboriginal courts offer an alternative sentencing court for adult Indigenous offenders. Koori courts involve taking a sentencing court to the local Indigenous community, where the magistrate, the offender, the victim, their families, and "respected" members (often "Elders") of the local community informally discuss the matter and negotiate an appropriate sentence. The role of the court is to bring about rehabilitation, make the offenders more responsible for their behavior, and increase the offenders' awareness of the harm caused by their actions. The Koori court usually deals with nonviolent offenses such as property crimes, driving offenses, and drug offenses and is successfully diverting some offenders from prison (Parker and Pathe 2006; Marchetti and Daly 2004).

The sentencing of more serious or repeat offenders who are most likely to receive a prison sentence is addressed through circle sentencing (Marchetti and Daly 2004). This process involves Indigenous Elders, the magistrate, the offender, the support people, the victim and their supporters, the defense counsel, and the police prosecutor. It is a closed court, and all participants sit in a circle to discuss what would be an appropriate sentence for the offender. Circle sentencing has brought about real change because the Indigenous community is involved in the court processes and offenders have to face the Elders and other people from their community who they know and respect (Marchetti and Daly 2004). Although current research reveals that circle sentencing has no effect on the frequency, timing, or seriousness of offending, it still strengthens the informal social controls that exist in Indigenous communities and therefore has a role in crime prevention.

Aboriginal Community Liaison Officers (*ACLOs*) provide a link between the police and Indigenous communities. Liaison officers are unsworn employees, without police powers such as arrest, search, or use of force. They quintessentially represent community policing. Their roles vary across jurisdictions, but their core functions are similar and include the following:

- Building good communication and relations between police and Indigenous communities
- Resolving disputes between police and Indigenous people

- Improving understanding within communities about the role of police and encouraging Indigenous people to discuss crime problems with police
- Helping police and Indigenous communities work together on crime prevention solutions
- Identifying local crime problems and other issues impacting on police relations with the community
- Educating police to increase cultural awareness

Liaison officers work closely with Indigenous offenders during interviews and while in custody, as well as with victims and their families. In some cases, they advise Indigenous people on basic legal issues and justice processes and may contribute to government policy development (NSW Police 2011).

Indigenous community patrols or night patrols are community-based services that operate a safe transport and outreach service for people (largely juveniles) who are on the streets late at night (Blagg and Valuri 2004). Lack of transportation is a common problem in rural communities, but is acutely experienced by Indigenous people who are more likely to experience poverty and, as noted above, have higher proportions of younger people. We have also noted above how government policies have produced the geographic isolation of Indigenous people, many of whom remain on the fringes of rural communities or in poorly resourced and isolated settings.

Night patrols are an Indigenous initiative. Indigenous communities have played a key role in the management, staffing, and organization of such services. In this respect, this initiative differs from the previous two community policing initiatives, both of which have emerged within more formal criminal justice structures. The first night patrol was instigated by the women of Yuendemu in central Australia during the early 1990s to challenge violence and help protect the community in the absence of effective intervention from mainstream justice systems (Walker and Forrester 2002).

Night patrols perform a wide range of functions, according to the needs of their communities and the resources available. Typically, teams of local people patrol communities at night (mostly in vehicles but sometimes on foot) and assist community members who may be at risk of either causing harm or becoming a victim of harm. The approach is noncoercive, seeks to be culturally appropriate, and offers an alternative to police involvement. Common forms of assistance that a night patrol service might offer include transport to a safe place or sobering-up shelter; mediating potentially violent situations; moving youth off the streets; or referring clients to other community support services and acting as a nexus between police, courts, clinics, and family. In interrupting potential conflicts, taking responsibility for unprotected children, and removing drunkenness, Indigenous communities are empowered to act for themselves. With the support of local police, but often without their active engagement, the community relies on the resources of Indigenous people and their codes of conduct in this problem-solving work (Blagg and Valuri 2004).

As communities are not homogeneous, and neither is the structure of night patrols, reviews of the way night patrols operate throughout Australia reveal that relationships between police and night patrol staff also vary greatly. In many places, night patrols provide a strong support for police, providing intelligence. The police support the patrols and rely on them whenever possible for information and negotiation in situations involving Indigenous victims and offenders.

However, in some communities, night patrol staff report police to be non-cooperative. Problems may arise through personality clashes between individual officers and patrol staff or more deep-seated historical tensions, which have produced a lack of trust between Indigenous communities and police. Lack of communication may result in police moving on young people from patrol collection points, which may in turn place them at greater risk of criminal victimization.

Effectiveness of Community Policing

To be effective, community policing initiatives for Indigenous communities need to incorporate different strategies, be community driven, be culturally appropriate, and involve significant others such as family members and community Elders (Memmott et al. 2006). Rural and remote Indigenous communities are diverse and unlike other Australian communities, and therefore, programs must be designed for the specific circumstances of each community. Traditional and cultural value systems must be considered when planning activities. Programs have little chance of being effective if they are imposed upon an Indigenous community by external organizations. Similarly, problems can arise where a project has been developed by a small minority of community members in isolation and without input or support from the broader community. Unless the community develops solutions, they will not take ownership of the project or maintain a commitment to ensure it succeeds. Projects should be planned by people who have an intimate knowledge of the problem behaviors, the capacity of the community, and the solutions that are likely to work. Projects that are community driven and effective in one Indigenous community context are more likely to be adopted by other communities. Community consultation is therefore very important at all stages of the project, but this process can be time consuming and requires flexibility. The process can be confounded by local politics: the rules pertaining to kinship, Indigenous customary law, and multitribal and interclan conflicts (Memmott et al. 2006).

Some evaluations of the night patrol programs in Australia (Blagg and Valuri 2004), including a study in progress conducted by the authors and others, have demonstrated that the programs can achieve the following:

- A reduction in juvenile crime rates for offenses such as vandalism, motor vehicle theft, and street offenses
- An enhancement of perceptions of safety
- Minimization of harm associated with drug and alcohol misuse
- An encouragement of Indigenous leadership, community management, and self-determination
- An encouragement of partnerships and cultural understanding between Indigenous and non-Indigenous communities
- A means of promoting and demonstrating Indigenous leadership (Memmott et al. 2006)

The most common reason that young people in small remote communities are on the streets at night is boredom, which itself is a product of underresourcing in remote and isolated communities (Blagg and Valuri 2004). Some are there because the street is a safer place than home. In the warmer months where temperatures can be extreme in "outback" locations, the evenings bring cool relief and opportunities to escape from hot dwellings. Children who are picked up by the night patrols, taken to youth centers, and provided with sporting and creative activities are content to be driven home at the end of the evening and stay home. Nutrition, often provided by youth centers, can be a major incentive for using patrol services. In providing recreational and nutritional support, patrols directly address the material causes of much criminal activity involving Indigenous youth.

Conclusion

Indigenous Australians are chronically overrepresented within the criminal justice system. While Indigenous people remain the poorest sector of the community, compounded by the inevitable lower levels of education and employment that constitute the poverty cycle, poverty-based crime will continue to be a problem (Mazzerole et al. 2003).

Given some of the issues that we have noted above, especially problems with traditional forms of policing (officers adopting a legalistic approach to their work), community policing may prove successful in reducing crime because it adopts a proactive, preventative approach that draws on one of the most important forms of social capital among Indigenous people—strong social and kinship networks. The policing approach cited above has its roots in restorative approaches to justice community networks and the significance of trust and rapport. However, we also need to acknowledge the different capacity of groups to regulate conflicts, support victims and offenders, and resource reintegration. For example, high rates of offending prevent the recruitment of Indigenous people with criminal records to community policing, especially in smaller and isolated towns. Given that community policing also relies on different conceptions of community, we need to recognize that communities are not natural sets of relations but constructed on a broad terrain of history and politics. Indigenous communities are constructed from and through practices of colonizers, yet they are disrupted, dismantled, and destroyed as part of the colonial process. There are fundamental clashes generated by colonialism and neocolonialism, such as forced relocation of tribal groups. In such conditions, community has a special meaning and impacts differently on members. In this way, Indigenous communities consist of members and outsiders: traditional owners of the land and others who had come from other parts of Australia. Tension may exist between these groups because of competing claims to the area, displacement of families, and different values, and such processes can hinder the success of community policing.

References

Australian Bureau of Statistics (2008). Australian Social Trends, 2008, 4102.0 (Canberra: Australian Bureau of Statistics).

Australian Bureau of Statistics (2009). Experimental Estimates and Projections, Aboriginal and Torres Strait Islander Australians, 1991 to 2021, 3238.0 (Canberra: Australian Bureau of Statistics).

Australian Bureau of Statistics (2010). Recorded Crime—Offenders, 2008–09, Cat. No. 4519.0 (Canberra: Australian Bureau of Statistics).

Australian Bureau of Statistics (ABS) (2012). 2011 Census of Population and Housing, Retrieved 18th October 2012 from http://www.abs.gov.au.

Australian Institute of Criminology (AIC) (2006). Sworn Police Officers in Australia. Crime Facts Info, No. 116, 14 February 2006, Australian Institute of Criminology.

Australian Institute for Health and Welfare (AIHW) (2009). Juvenile Justice in Australia, 2007–2008. Retrieved 20 November 2011 from http://www.aihw.gov.au/publications/index.cfm/title/10853.

Barclay, E.M., Hogg, R. and Scott, J. (2007). Young People and Crime in Rural Communities, in Barclay, E.M., Donnermeyer, J.F., Scott, J. and Hogg, R. (Eds.). Crime in Rural Australia: Integrating Theory, Research and Practice (Sydney: Federation Press).

Blagg, H. and Valuri, G. (2004). Aboriginal Community Patrols in Australia: Self–policing, Self–determination and Security. Policing and Society, 14:4, 313–328.

Cunneen, C. (2001). Conflict, Politics and Crime: Indigenous Communities and the Police (Sydney: Allen & Unwin).

Cunneen, C. (2007). Crime, Justice and Indigenous People. In Barclay, E., Donnermeyer, J., Scott, J. and Hogg, R. (Eds.). Crime in Rural Australia (Leichhardt: The Federation Press).

Edwards, M. (2008). NT Intervention Head Says More Needs to be Done, ABC AM, Australian Broadcasting Commission. Retrieved June 2008 from http://www.abc.net.au/am/content/2008/s2270854.htm.

Hogg, R. and Carrington, K. (2006). Policing the Rural Crisis (Sydney: Federation Press).

Jobes, P.C. (2003). Human Ecology and Rural Policing: A Grounded Theoretical Analysis of How Personal Constraints and Community Characteristics Influence Strategies of Law Enforcement in Rural New South Wales, Australia. Police Practice and Research, 4(1), 3–19.

Marchetti, E. and Daly, K. (2004). Indigenous Courts and Justice Practices in Australia. Trends and Issues in Crime and Criminal Justice, 277, 1–6. Retrieved from http://www.aic.gov.au/publications/currentseries/tandi/261-280/tandi277.aspx.

Mazzerole, L., Marchetti, E. and Lindsay, A. (2003). Policing and the Plight of Indigenous Australians: Past Conflicts and Present Challenges. Police and Society, 7, 77–104.

Memmott, P., Chambers, C., Go-Sam, C. and Thomson, L. (2006). Good Practice in Indigenous Family Violence Prevention—Designing and Evaluating Successful Programs. (Sydney: Australian Domestic and Family Violence Clearinghouse, University of New South Wales). Retrieved from http://www.austdvclearinghouse.unsw.edu.au/PDF%20files/Issuespaper_11.pdf.

NSW Police (2011). Aboriginal Issues. Retrieved 20 November 2011 from http://www.police.nsw.gov.au/community_issues/aboriginal.

O'Connor, M. and Gray, D. (1989) Crime in a Rural Community (Annandale, NSW: The Federation Press).

Parker, N. and Pathe, M. (2006). Report on the Review of the Murri Court (Brisbane: Department of Justice and Attorney General). Retrieved 20 November 2011 from http://www.justice.qld.gov.au/files/Services/MurriCourtReport.pdf.

Parliament of Australia (2010). Indigenous Australians, Incarceration and the Criminal Justice System. Discussion paper prepared by the committee secretariat, Senate Select Committee on Regional and Remote Indigenous Communities, Canberra. Retrieved 20 November 2011 from http://www.aph.gov.au/.

Scott, J. and Jobes, P. (2007). Policing in Rural Australia: The Country Cop as Law Enforcer and Local Resident. In Barclay, E.M., Donnermeyer, J.F., Scott, J. and Hogg, R. (Eds.). Crime in Rural Australia (Sydney: Federation Press).

Walker, J. and Forrester, S. (2002). Tangentyere Remote Area Night Patrol. Paper presented at the Crime Prevention Division, Australian Institute of Criminology, Sydney, September 2002.

Weatherburn, D., Snowball, L. and Hunter, B. (2006). The Economic and Social Factors Underpinning Indigenous Contact with the Justice System: Results from the 2002 NATSISS survey, Crime and Justice Bulletin, 104. Retrieved from http://www.bocsar.nsw.gov.au/lawlink/bocsar/ll_bocsar.nsf/pages/bocsar_pub_byyear.

Bangladesh

18

M. ENAMUL HUQ

Contents

Background

Modern times have brought greater expectations from both the government and the community that the law enforcement agencies will provide a safe and secure environment. Many progressive police managers believe that the time has come to alter the policies and practices within their organizations to meet these expectations. These reasons are rooted in the history of policing and police research during the last quarter of the twentieth century, in the changing nature of communities, and in the shifting characteristics of crime and violence that affect these communities.

Even before the advent of formal public policing, communities policed themselves, and community members had norms and reinforced them. When Sir Robert Peel established the London Metropolitan Police, he set forth a number of principles, one of which could be considered the seed of community policing "to maintain at all times a relationship with the public that gives reality to the historic tradition that the police are the public and that the public are the police. The police being only members of the public that are paid to give full time attention to duties which are incumbent on every citizen in the interests of community welfare and existence" (The Police Act 1861). But the British colonial empire gradually shifted the public policing from community-based to a militaristic organization based upon the Royal Irish Constabulary model. In this system, the police agency has a regimented and militaristic rank structure; also, the agency has strong organization hierarchies based on the military model of authority and responsibility. The countries that are emerging to liberal democracy have the legacy of the colonial policing resulting in centralized police organization and the command structure isolating the police from the community.

Functioning of Community Policing

In these contexts especially, the historic legacy of the police therefore necessitates the adoption of a different philosophy of policing, removed from regime support and party politics and with a clear distinction of duties from that of the military. This philosophy is one of focusing on communities—the public—and their needs and on providing a more account-able policing service to the community combined with respect for human rights.

It is argued that the community policing strategy is both historically and practically the hallmark of good policing—technically and morally. The existing structure and functions of community policing prevailing in Bangladesh need to be reorganized. What is now lacking in Bangladesh is the strategic planning and desire to implement the appropriate community policing system in its true sense. It is, however, believed that community policing is quite feasible in Bangladesh, and to be implemented, it requires some modifications and basic structural changes in its system and operations.

Effectiveness of Community Policing Program

> Police is only one, even if an important limb of the criminal justice system and social defense system. Therefore, it is equally important that the other arms of these systems like prosecution judiciary, jail, correctional, and penal services are also modernized. (Huq 1992)

After all, the action of one infringes on the other. Further, unless laws keep pace with the needs of the times, all efforts would at best be an exercise in futility; otherwise, it would be like putting a jet engine on a bullock cart.

The Bangladesh police is primarily a reactive force with a philosophy of public control rather than community service. There is a considerable emphasis on solving crime after it occurs, rather than preventing it from happening in the first place. The abuse of human rights, corruption, politicization, little or no accountability, assumption of military-style roles, and exclusion of certain groups within the police are all characteristics that police services across the region have been blamed for at various points during recent years.

There is a dearth of information about community police; some indicators are poorly defined, and others have yet to be identified. In addition, the inferences regarding casualty may be weak because often, they are not based on empirical research. Further research and subsequent monitoring of community police is urgently needed; the present study aims to fill in this gap of information.

In policing a liberal democracy, with a diverse and energetic population, there are two broad strategies available to the police executive: the community policing approach and the law-and-order enforcement approach. These two are not so much exact opposites as they are points on a continuum. Community policing encompasses a variety of philosophical and practical approaches and is still evolving rapidly. Community policing strategies vary depending on the needs and responses of the communities involved; however, certain basic principles and considerations are common to all community policing efforts.

Community policing is a practical philosophy of policing in action aiming at strengthening trust and confidence in the police through a democratic process. In the policing system, police are viewed as a part of the community playing a major role for the achievement of safety and security of the community. It is a joint process in which both police and community people work together for the creation of a safe and secure environment of the neighborhood. Community policing is both a philosophy and an organization strategy that allows the police and the community residents to work closely together in new ways to solve the problems of crime, fear of crime, physical and social disorder, and neighborhood decay.

Police Organization of Bangladesh

Bangladesh, teeming with millions of people, is very densely populated. Underdevelopment with repeated natural scourge and rising expectation of democracy but with very limited resources and equipment pose a big challenge for the police to come up to the desired goal. Hence, voluntary organizations have undertaken the role of motivation for self-help by the community as a whole and the senior citizens in particular to supplement and augment the government efforts to ameliorate the suffering of humanity through sound economic growth as well as political and social stability because peace is the foremost prerequisite for development, and development fortifies peace.

Looking back to history when present Bangladesh was part of undivided India until 1947, and East Pakistan until its liberation war of 1971, the Rural Police was a very important organ for policing. The term "community policing" connotes the function and role of community in matters related to law and order. In my early career in the police department, I noted the role and importance of *Chowkidar* and their leader, called *Dafadar*, who were supposed to be the ears and eyes of the police station in their rural setting and kept informed of all important happenings in the weekly Chowkidari Parade. Besides, anything important, for example, arrival of strangers and departure of suspicious subjects from their jurisdiction, was to be reported then and there for updating the Thana (police station) records. During inspection of senior officers, this register was an important function of rural policing, that is, community's relation and cooperation, criticism and suggestions, and so forth, which used to reflect the idea of law enforcement from the very grassroots level.

Alternate Dispute Resolution

This is a practical to exercise community leaders in helping to mediate and negotiate between disputing parties to resolve issues locally instead of resorting to Thana (police station), court, and legal provisions. This has been practiced mainly in petty cases when both the parties consent to sit in *shalish*, which is arbitration through local leaders of acceptable integrity and impartiality for peaceful settlement of the aggrieved and accused parties who are bound to go by the decision taken thereof. These days, such emphasis is laid on this to reduce the number of innumerable cases pending in the court for years together, where justice is delayed and also financial constraints of both sides are really perturbing for indefinitely prolonging the compoundable petty cases. There should be training institutes for comprehensive alternative dispute resolution proceedings for increasing the professional acumen of the police, prosecutors, magistrates, Union Parisad chairman, and concerned lawyers and legal officials—in fact, all the stakeholders too. This will be a good example of community policing, and the end result will be to inculcate a better and peaceful atmosphere in the society to live in.

And to attain that peace, that outstanding problem of police administration in maintenance of public order, that is, internal security considered as mandatory obligation. In the backdrop of the above-mentioned factors in Bangladesh, this project is likely to continue the improvement of services to the community—strengthen police relation through community participation, help in the effective use of resources, and enhance cooperation among others. And the innovative approach is sure to promote quality and excellence in law enforcement by the police, which is supposed to stand for the following:

P: Polite
O: Obedient
L: Loyal
I: Intelligent
C: Courageous
E: Efficient

Recommendations

> Each new generation offers humanity another chance. If we provide for the survival and development of children everywhere, protect them from harm and exploitation and enable them to participate in decision directly affecting their lives we will surely build the foundation of the just society we all want that children deserve. (Huq 2009)

This is the preamble of the United Nations (UN) declaration of the human rights for children. This has been a central concern of the UN since its creation. In keeping with the idea of children's rights, perhaps it may be mentioned that, of late, there have been a good many efforts for welfare of a particular age group, for example, children, adolescents, and so forth. But regrettably, it may be pointed out that there are few tangible activities or even indications for doing something special for those who are on their last legs.

Loss of solidarity in a local community and changes in family structures, both contributing to accelerated urbanization, have weakened families and local communities in their inherent ability of problem solving, mutual assistance, and crime prevention. This in turn has brought about various changes, and the old are now exposed more frequently to such dangers as fraudulent persuasion, traffic accidents, senile dementia, habitual vagrancy, and so forth. Old people, with their abilities declined, are liable to be affected by the social changes, which are endorsed by an increase in absconsion and suicide.

The country's overall efforts against crime and offending will be only as intense as the public demand. It goes without saying that the government of a society is bound to act in response to the desires of the people. Therefore, in the ultimate analysis, the people and the rest of the law enforcement agencies will be effective only to the extent that the public would approve and demand. But one thing can be said with confidence, and that is, the police machinery has to be updated thoroughly if it is to meet the challenges of the twenty-first century.

In the context of the present-day situation of law enforcement, perhaps the majority of taxpayers do want a change, and that can be achieved if policing is given the attention that it deserves, the main idea being to help police to protect the citizen. This helping can only be beneficial not only through modernization of material and equipment only rather much depends upon the mental make up of the person in command of the country—be it legislator, bureaucrat, politician, or any other authority who should honor the rule of law in each citizen's life and foster an awareness of the heritage of individual freedom under the law, emphasize respect for law, and reaffirm the value of the rule of law. And to this end, the constitutional custodian of internal peace and order can contribute more effectively if every citizen, whatever might be his or her status or position in life, wants the police left alone to do their job without hindrance and holds the police accountable for their performance according to highest standards of professional propriety and integrity,

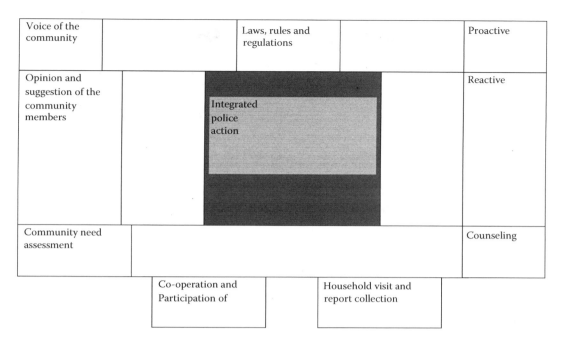

Figure 18.1 Conceptual framework Co-operation and Participation community policing in Bangladesh.

lest democracy is surrendered in favor of tyranny and repression. It is in the enlightened self-interest of the government (in whatever form) even at this late stage to let the police function by the law, under the law, and for the law before crossing the point of no return.

The existing structure and functions of community policing prevailing in Bangladesh needs to be reorganized. What is now lacking in Bangladesh is the strategic planning and desire to implement the appropriate community policing system in its true sense. It is, however, believed that community policing is quite feasible in Bangladesh, and to implement it here, one needs to bring some modifications and basic structural changes in its system and operations (Figure 18.1).

The vision and mission statement of the above-proposed community policing in Bangladesh would be to ensure the safety, harmony, and peace of community residents initiating immediate measures as an integrated action taken by the police with the help of the community. To make the community policing system more effective in Bangladesh, its origination needs to be remodeled both in urban and rural areas, keeping in view that *police is public and public is police.*

Acknowledgments

- Ain O Karjokrom (Bengalee Practical Handbook of Law): Dr. M. Enamul Huq (1986)
- APPL Publications
- Asia Crime Prevention Foundation—Resource Papers (periodicals published in between 1989–1990)

- Bangladesh Society of Enforcement of Human Rights
- Bangladesh Police Co-operative Society—The Detective-Monthly Journal of Police
- Bureau of Statistics—Government of Bangladesh
- Community Policing in Indigenous Community in India—Mahesh K. Nalla and Graeme R. Newman
- Community Policing in South Korea—Wook Kong and Mahesh K. Nalla
- Crime and Criminology—Reid Sue Titus
- Crime Index Bangladesh 2007—Omar Faruq and Nurjahan Khatun
- Criminal Justice System Administration—Dr. M. Enamul Huq
- Essays on Crime and Development
- HIV/AIDS—Drug Abuse—Dr. Aditi Titas Huq (2005)
- International Criminal Review
- International Institute of Security and Safely Management, India
- INTERPOL General Assembly Proceedings
- National Institute of Local Government—Government of Bangladesh
- Peace Now—Professor B. G. Bahar
- Poverty and Environment—Increasing Crime Incidences in Urban Area—Aneek R. Haque (2005)
- Prosperity Without Crime—Edited by Dr. M. Enamul Huq, ACPF Publications (2006)
- Retired Police Officers Welfare Association Bangladesh—Resource Materials
- UN Declaration on Basic Principles of Justice for Victims and Abuse of Power

References

Huq, M. E. (1992). Readings on Policing. Dhaka: Sumi Printing and Publications Ltd.
Huq, M. E. (2009). Best Interest of the Children. Dhaka: Academic Press and Publishers Library.

China

19

LENA Y. ZHONG
SHANHE JIANG

Contents

Background

The People's Republic of China (hereafter China) is the most populous country in the world, with more than 1.3 billion citizens. It covers approximately 3.7 million mi.[2]. Since economic reform commenced in 1978, China's gross domestic product has increased by an average of more than 9% annually. At the same time, China's crime has had a rather striking increase. In order to solve problems of soaring crime rates, the Chinese Ministry of Public Security in 2002 officially adopted community policing as a philosophy and strategy in crime control. Since then, various community policing programs have flourished in the nation. Because several publications have studied the historical background, philosophy, development, and general practice of community policing in China (Wong 2001; Wu et al. 2011; Zhong 2009; Zhong and Broadhurst 2007), this chapter focuses on Shenzhen, a city at the vanguard of the economic reform and openness in China, to investigate its implementation of community policing in depth.

Shenzhen is situated in the Pearl River Delta of the southeastern coast of China, part of Guangdong province, bordering Hong Kong in the south. It was established as the first Special Economic Zone (SEZ) in China in 1980. Designated as a laboratory and window for economic reform and openness in China, Shenzhen leads the inland areas in economic transition and social changes, with the slogan "Shenzhen today is the interior areas tomorrow." Over the past three decades, it has grown from a small fishing village into one of the major metropolises in China. In terms of administrative division, it includes six districts and two new zones (Luohu, Futian, Nanshan, Yantian, Bao'an, and

Longgang Districts and Guangming and Pingshan New Zones), 57 subdistrict offices, and 799 neighborhood committees (*Shenzhen Statistical Yearbook* 2010). Shenzhen now boasts itself as a high-tech and manufacturing hub in southern China, the worlds' fourth-busiest container port, home to China's fourth-busiest airport, and one of the most popular tourist destinations in China. The economic growth in Shenzhen ran parallel to an influx of migrant workers, mainly rural–urban migrants, from other parts of Guangdong province or other provinces in China. In 1980, its total population was only 333,900, with migrants accounting for 3.6%; in 2010, its total population rose to 10,357,900, with migrants accounting for 76.2%. Owing to its huge migrant population, the average age in 2010 in Shenzhen was under 30 years (Shenzhen Government Online 2011). The vibrant migrant population has been blamed for the growing crime rates in Shenzhen. In 1980, the total number of recorded criminal cases was 623, at a rate of 187/100,000 population; in 2008, it rose to 75,905, at a rate of 866/100,000 population (*Shenzhen Political and Legal Yearbook* 2009). Facing the rising crime problem, community policing became an important part of comprehensive management of social order in the early 1990s in Shenzhen.

According to the Police Law 1995, the Chinese police have five components: public security police, state security police, prison police, judicial police in people's courts, and judicial police in people's procuratorates. Public security police are the largest. For average citizens, police in China usually refer to public security police (Ma 1997). The Ministry of Public Security is the central agency of public security police. Local public security police departments are under the dual leadership of the superior-level public security organ vertically and of the local Chinese Communist Party committees and governments horizontally. The Shenzhen Public Security Bureau was established in March 1979. It has 14 subbureaus and 119 police stations. The size of the police force was 19,000 in 2010, at a ratio of 180/100,000, much higher than the national ratio of around 140/100,000 in China. Notwithstanding the low police–public ratio, Chinese citizens' satisfaction with Chinese police is generally positive (Jiang et al. forthcoming).

Origin of Community Policing in Shenzhen

Policing in China has long embodied the essence of community policing, although the concept of community policing *per se* was not imported to China until the early 1990s, when China was facing an escalating crime rate regardless of successive waves of crackdown campaigns (Zhong 2009). In 2002, the Ministry of Public Security decided to formally implement community policing in the cities throughout China, and 4 years later, rural areas followed suit (see Du 2009).

In China, the essence of community policing is manifested in the policing guideline of "mass line" and the general crime control policy of "comprehensive management of social order." The mass line refers to "for the masses, relying on the masses, from the masses, and to the masses." It embodies two layers of meaning. First, policing is based on the interests of both the state and the masses, with a focus on "for the masses." Second, policing relies on the masses and on the mobilization of the masses, and the police function to win the understanding and support of the masses (Yu et al. 1997, p. 152). The police–public relationship can be characterized metaphorically: the police are fish and the masses are water. The mass line was operationalized as "mass prevention and mass management" whereby the public, social forces, and government agencies were mobilized to combat crime and maintain social order.

One of the most notable mechanisms of "mass prevention and mass management" is the neighborhood committee, a mass organization of self-management at the grassroots level in urban areas. As prescribed by the Chinese Constitution, a neighborhood committee establishes subcommittees for people's mediation, public security, public health, and other matters in order to manage public affairs and social services in their areas, mediate civil disputes, help maintain public order, convey residents' opinions and demands, and make suggestions to the government. For example, the subcommittee of people's mediation is responsible for resolving conflicts and disputes between individuals, groups, and organizations in the neighborhood and preventing them from escalating into criminal cases. The subcommittee of public security is aimed to educate residents on safety and legal matters, to report to the police criminals and suspicious individuals in the neighborhood, to provide assistance to the police for local crime control and population registration, to reeducate juveniles with mild offenses, and to report major discontent among residents to appropriate local authorities, *inter alia*. It is notable that the police and the neighborhood committees work closely with each other. The police provide direct professional guidance to the neighborhood committees, and the subcommittee of public security is considered to constitute a link and bridge between the police and the masses and plays a key role in uniting and mobilizing the masses in crime prevention (Zhong 2009).

The general crime control policy of comprehensive management of social order emerged in the early 1980s, when the Party leadership was concerned about rising crime. The guiding principle of comprehensive management of social order combines punishment and prevention, with the focus on prevention, and its final goal is to "fundamentally improve social order." It has been summarized into six words: *strike, prevent, educate, manage, construct, and reform*. Basically, the six aspects represent the duality of punitive (strike and reform) and preventive (prevent, educate, manage, and construct) approaches (Zhong and Broadhurst 2007). By design, the focus of comprehensive management of social order should be on its preventive prong, but in reality, the punitive prong prevails, as shown in the launch of successive waves of strike-hard campaigns in China since 1983 to tackle the abrupt increases in crime.

The mass line in Chinese policing has its cultural embeddings, in contrast to professionalism in policing in the United States (Jiao 2001). Indeed, when comparing the community policing philosophy in China with the US approach to community policing, Wong (2001) concluded that there is much similarity in spirit amid drastic differences in practice between the two community policing models. In a general sense, social and crime control in China entails the integration of formal and informal mechanisms, which proved intriguing to Western observers (Clark 1989). Survey data showed that college students in China, compared with their counterparts in the United States, were more likely to view formal and informal crime control as important mechanisms and to highly rank the blending of formal and informal mechanisms in crime prevention and control (Jiang et al. 2010). The findings are in line with that of another survey: Chinese college students in general had positive attitudes toward the philosophy and practices of community policing (Wu et al. 2011).

As previously noted, Shenzhen has faced a serious crime problem, especially crime by migrants, since its establishment as an SEZ in 1980. The program of Building Little Safe and Civilized Communities (BLSCC) was used as one of the main approaches to control rising crime in Shenzhen. The Shenzhen police unequivocally declared that BLSCC drew on community policing as used in Western societies, while tracing its lineage to traditional crime control paradigms in China since 1949 (see Huang and Luo 1997). The program was piloted in several villages in 1992 and 1993 and was formally launched in full scale in 1994. BLSCC is still being implemented in Shenzhen nowadays, and over the years, it has gained unyielding support from the Shenzhen government, including the police.

BLSCC in Shenzhen

Historical Development

As shown in Table 19.1, BLSCC has gone through five stages: preparation (1992–1994), first 3-year plan (1995–1997), second 3-year plan (1998–2000), third 3-year plan (2001–2003), and first 5-year plan (2004–2008).

Establishment of a targeted number of Little Safe and Civilized Communities (LSCC) was planned for each year and each stage. At the end of the year and stage, a review was conducted to check if the target had been achieved. Over the years, regulations were made and revised to guide the development of LSCC. In 2002, the Office of the Leading Group on BLSCC was changed from an *ad hoc* agency to a permanent agency, affiliated with the Office of the Comprehensive Management of Social Order under the Shenzhen Party Committee.

Philosophy of BLSCC

Under BLSCC, the whole city is divided into small zones, and each zone is urged to meet the standards of LSCC. The division of the collective into small entities clearly designates individual responsibilities that are in turn linked to individual rewards. This divide-and-rule principle, coupled with the responsibility system, greatly motivates individuals. In Shenzhen, the demarcation of little communities is based on geographical boundaries. There are eight types of little communities in Shenzhen: (1) multistory residential areas; (2) natural villages; (3) industrial areas; (4) blocks of high-rise buildings; (5) warehouse areas; (6) tourist areas; (7) multiple-function areas; and (8) schools, hospitals, and government offices (see Shenzhen Political and Legal Yearbook 1999 for more details).

An LSCC is two-pronged: safety and civilization. Community safety is measured by whether residents have feelings of safety, very few serious public security cases occur, and general public security cases are kept under timely control. Community civilization is measured by (1) moral education, (2) harmonious relationships among residents, (3) healthy community culture, and (4) purification of the environment (Zhong and Broadhurst 2007). For a little community to be eligible to be an LSCC, it must meet certain criteria and go through a complicated rating process by designated agencies yearly. The rating scale consists of model, advanced, pass, and failure. If a community is rated as a pass in the first year but fails to meet the standards in the second year, it will be stripped of its original title. It can also strive to upgrade to a higher level in the subsequent years.

BLSCC Elements

BLSCC is a key indicator of the prevention prong of comprehensive management of social order. The important elements of BLSCC can be grouped into four categories: organization features, safety measures, civilization measures, and the BLSCC rating system.

Table 19.1   Development of BLSCC in Shenzhen: 1992–2008

Preparation	1992	Pilot study in Xianxi village and Nanshan village was started.
	1993	Essential concepts of little, safety, and civilization emerged.
	1994	Decision on the first 3-year plan was made.
First 3-year plan	1995	The regulation "Five Standards on LSCC" including "Eight Subjects and Forty-Five Measurement Indicators" was promulgated.
	1996	The above regulation was revised.
	1997	The Notice on BLSCC Funding and the principle of "four ones" were announced; 627 new LSCCs were recognized, reaching a total of 1499 LSCCs, covering 972.1 square kilometers and 3.35 million people, at a coverage rate of 50% and 92%, respectively.
Second 3-year plan	1998	Three regulations on management of floating population were promulgated, reaching a total of 1699 LSCCs, covering 1042 square kilometers and 3.58 million people, at a coverage rate of 53% and 94%, respectively.
	1999	301 new LSCCs were recognized, reaching a total of 2000.
	2000	369 new LSCCs were recognized, reaching a total of 2211.
Third 3-year plan	2001	166 new LSCCs were recognized, reaching a total of 2377.
	2002	160 new LSCCs were recognized, reaching a total of 2504; The Office of the Leading Group on BLSCC was formalized; the regulation "Five Standards on LSCC" was revised; the Implementation Measures for Demoting and Revoking BLSCC Titles in Shenzhen were announced; previously qualified LSCCs were reassessed (33 LSCCs were revoked, 1 demoted, and 64 given warnings for improvement within a specified period).
	2003	171 new LSCCs were recognized, reaching a total of 2675; suggestions on further strengthening BLSCC to plan the second stage of BLSCC were promulgated.
First 5-year plan	2004	154 new LSCCs were recognized, reaching a total of 2724; 138 LSCCs were revoked by the end of 2004.
	2005	146 new LSCCs were recognized, reaching a total of 2869; reassessed previous LSCCs, promoted 41 LSCCs, demoted 5 LSCCs, and revoked 1 LSCC.
	2006	154 new LSCCs were recognized, reaching a total of 2988; 174 LSCCs were revoked by the end of 2006; further revised "Five Standards on LSCC"; promulgated Notices on the System of Revoking, Demoting, and Rectifying LSCCs in Shenzhen.
	2007	155 new LSCCs were recognized, and 49 LSCCs were promoted, reaching a total of 3143.
	2008	170 new LSCCs were recognized, and 37 LSCCs were promoted, reaching a total of 3313.

Sources: Shenzhen Political and Legal Yearbook 1996–2009.
Note: BLSCC = Building Little Safe and Civilized Communities; LSCC = Little Safe and Civilized Communities.

Organization Features

They are demonstrated by the leadership responsibility system and measured by fundraising. The leadership responsibility system requires that leaders at all levels of government, agencies, companies, and organizations be held accountable for implementing BLSCC and maintaining social order. That is, "whoever takes charge is held responsible." This system directly links the evaluation of BLSCC with a leader's year-end assessment, eligibility for "model" titles, and promotion. In the official reports on BLSCC, the leadership responsibility system is always an important indicator of the successful implementation of BLSCC. Every year, the Office of the Leading Group on BLSCC would issue a list matching leaders at the city government level with the communities striving to attain LSCC status. District and subdistrict level leaders would also be matched with striving communities within their jurisdictions. For example, in 2006, 31 leaders at the city government level were each assigned a community to be in charge of its BLSCC task, and at the end of the year, all the 31 communities, except five, were awarded LSCC titles (Shenzhen Political and Legal Yearbook 2007).

The police are an integral part of the leadership responsibility system. For example, in the *Shenzhen Political and Legal Yearbook* 2001, every public security subbureau, as well as every local police station, assigned a leader to be in charge of BLSCC. The police at all levels played a major role in BLSCC by assisting the local Party committees and governments at the corresponding level in making plans, designing programs, and organizing resources for the implementation of those plans and programs.

Since 1997, funding for BLSCC in Shenzhen has come from four sources: (1) the city government, (2) the district/subdistrict governments, (3) the residents and households, and (4) charges on convenience services. For example, in 1997, a total of 420 million Chinese yuan were invested in BLSCC, including 18.18 million yuan from the city government, 15.60 million yuan from the district governments, 51 million yuan from the subdistrict governments, and 340 million yuan from the villages, units, and residents (Shenzhen Political and Legal Yearbook 1998). From 1994 to 2008, the Shenzhen City Government invested 114.98 million yuan in BLSCC (Shenzhen Political and Legal Yearbook 2009). The substantial investment from different levels of the government demonstrates the government's resolve to improve social order through BLSCC.

Safety Measures

The Shenzhen police have actively taken the lead in the BLSCC program. They have been involved in installing target-hardening crime prevention measures. They have played an important role in managing the migrant population. They have also managed the special professions, like entertainment venues (i.e., dancing halls, saunas, and massage parlors), hotels, secondhand dealers, and the publishing industry. The police also link BLSCC with wiping out pornography, gambling, and drugs. One of the important criteria for BLSCC is "no drug addicts, no drug abuse dens, and no drug abuse network" in a community. To better adapt to the tasks of BLSCC, the police have actively adopted a series of tactics. The officers at the local police stations have engaged in four *a*'s activity* and four *have*'s activity† in order to increase police–public contact and pledge good police service to the public. Consequently, local police officers have become one of the important assessment targets of BLSCC. The police have also become directly involved in managing the security guards, a prominent private policing force emerging in the reform era (Zhong and Grabosky 2009). The security guards contribute greatly to safety and civilization in the communities. All of the communities employed security guards—mostly decommissioned soldiers in the early years of BLSCC.

---

* The four *a*'s activity is literally translated as to have *a* walk household by household; to have *a* meeting with the male, female, the old, and the young; to say *a* hello when everything is under control; and to have *a* thorough handling when problems are detected.

† The four *have*'s activity is literally translated as to *have* a thorough understanding of the beat situation, to *have* a good relationship with the beat public, to *have* a stable team for the management of beat public security, and to *have* a fundamental improvement of beat public security.

Under BLSCC, a community is encouraged to organize its voluntary mutual-help groups in maintaining social order, along with the tradition of "mass prevention and mass management." For example, as noted in the *Shenzhen Political and Legal Yearbook*, 2004, some residential communities organized retired people to patrol the communities, and in other communities, the police guided the residents to establish social order committees. In one residential community, the staff members from the property management office and resident representatives formed a mediation group and resolved five conflicts between neighbors (Shenzhen Political and Legal Yearbook 2006). In another community, residents actively engaged in voluntary work by building the drainage system, cleaning the garbage, and monitoring the community affairs on a daily basis (Shenzhen Political and Legal Yearbook 2008).

Situational measures were adopted to minimize the opportunities for crime. Among the different types of communities, some are closed or gated style, others half closed, and still others open style. In BLSCC, measures such as defensible space and crime prevention through environmental design were carried out. Fences were built, community entry and exit points were redesigned and electronically controlled, and antiburglary doors, infrared detectors, and closed-circuit television cameras were installed in some communities. In the later years of BLSCC, all communities were urged to be enclosed by installing gates and fences, designed to keep out crime. Subsequently, communities were urged to employ professional property management companies to be in charge of community affairs. For example, a community in Luohu District was long mired in poor social order and hygiene standards. The police and local subdistrict office helped the community to bring in a property management company, and within 1 month, the situation inside the community changed dramatically.

The Shenzhen government has treated the management of migrants as its top priority. Managing the migrants was crucial to the success of BLSCC because they reportedly committed a disproportionately high amount of crime in Shenzhen and constituted a significant threat to social order. Apart from adjusting the household registration (*hukou*) system (for more information, see Zhong and Broadhurst 2007) to allow the admission of some migrants as permanent residents in Shenzhen, the police made great efforts in controlling the places where migrants accumulated. For example, the landlords were demanded to sign contracts with the police for monitoring the migrant tenants and were obliged to take certain responsibilities if their tenants committed crimes. Starting in 2004, the Shenzhen government has systematically strengthened the control of rented properties where a large number of crimes occur every year. Offices on managing the rented properties at the district, subdistrict, and local levels were set up, and a team of over 8000 members was established. As a consequence, in 2004, the number of crimes occurring in rented properties decreased 51.8% compared to that in 2003.

Civilization Measures

In BLSCC, the promotion of civilization is as important as that of safety. The official line is that if safety is overemphasized at the expense of civilization, there will be no long-lasting public security and stability. Moral education, one of the civilization elements, is focused on enhancing the individuals' awareness and compliance to socialist moral rules and the Party and government policies. It is also achieved through selecting model or exemplary individuals or organizational units. Crime is considered a result of lacking morality in China. Pornography, gambling, and drug abuse are indicators of the lack of morality and thus should be prevented and controlled. Harmonious relationships in a community are also part of civilization. Thus, BLSCC also promotes good relationships and mutual help between neighbors.

Building community culture seems to be an all-encompassing concept of civilization. At certain occasions, it appears to overlap with moral education. Building community culture aims to enrich community social life and enhance the residents' knowledge by organizing various recreational and educational activities. As stated in the *Shenzhen Political and Legal Yearbook*, 1999 (p. 225), in BLSCC,

> Every little community is a battlefield. If socialist culture, which advocates and extols "the true, the good and the beautiful," does not occupy it, ugly and corrupted ideology, and unhealthy trends and evil practices will get a chance to get in.

The civilization of community is also embodied in its physical environment. In BLSCC, measures were adopted to clean, improve, and purify the environment. For example, one of the achievements in BLSCC was improvement of the environment by creating greenbelts, paving roads, and removing rubbish. The stress on the improvement of the physical environment is based on the strong belief that the physical environment has a great impact on people's moral and mental health, consistent with the "broken windows" thesis (see Kelling and Coles 1996).

BLSCC Rating System

The last element of BLSCC is its rating system. The rating system of BLSCC was introduced in 1995 and revised in 1996, 2002, and 2006 in Shenzhen. As presented in Table 19.1, the rating of a community is not a one-time exercise, and periodical follow-up assessments have been conducted to review the communities' status. Over the years, a substantial number of communities were stripped of their status titles or demoted. This type of reassessment gives the communities constant pressure to maintain a good standard.

Effectiveness of BLSCC

The BLSCC reports regularly published by the Office of the Leading Group on BLSCC are full of yearly achievements and statistics,[*] including how many communities were rated pass or model, how much money was invested, how much hardware was installed, and how many people were deployed. The achievements are based on the information submitted by the local communities and governments at all levels. Given the leadership responsibility system, local leaders have a strong desire to portray a positive picture. There were two surveys conducted in 1995 and 1998 by the governmental agencies; however, details of the methodology were not available. The 1998 survey was summarized by the Shenzhen Deputy Party Secretary at the first 3-year plan meeting in April 1998:

> One of the achievements lies in the marked improvements of public security. In all the little communities built so far, all kinds of criminal cases decreased 50%, compared with the same

---

[*] No scholarly evaluation of the effectiveness of BLSCC is available; we used governmental reports here. Readers should read the reports with caution.

period prior to their being built. Inside 848 little communities, no criminal cases occurred. All these built a foundation for the stability and betterment of public security citywide. The masses' feeling of safety has greatly increased. We conducted a survey with a sample of over 30,000 people, and 95% of the masses and foreign businessmen felt safe. (Shenzhen Political and Legal Yearbook 1999, 225)

Such official rhetoric reoccurs in the reports and yearbooks. For example, in the *Shenzhen Political and Legal Yearbook*, 2007 (p. 12), it was reported that

Out of 25 newly built or promoted LSCCs in Nanshan District, 22 had no criminal cases, accounting for 88%, and among the 204 LSCCs built over the years, 130 had no criminal cases, accounting for 63.7%. A survey showed that over 95% of residents are satisfied with law and order situation in their LSCCs.

In later years, other measuring criteria were introduced, including the increase in the proportion of real estate rented out after a community became an LSCC and the increase in rental (e.g., see Shenzhen Political and Legal Yearbook 2007, 12, 2009, 11).

Conclusion

Chinese police have a tradition of working with local communities. Prior to China's economic reform, Chinese policing was featured with the mass line, along with the rigid *hukou* system and low levels of residential mobility. Crime rate was very low. After 1978, the Chinese government has gradually adjusted its *hukou* system to allow more people to move from place to place to meet economic development, resulting in high levels of mobility in China. A side effect of China's rapid economic growth is soaring crime, especially in cities with high levels of migrants and transient population such as Shenzhen.

In order to control and solve rising crime problems, on the one hand, Chinese police have adopted advanced technology, including increased use of motor patrol and setting-up the crime report hotline '110'; on the other hand, Chinese police have formally adopted the Western concept and strategy of community policing to strengthen its community involvement and mass line tradition. BLSCC in Shenzhen demonstrates and reflects this process. BLSCC has the element of community policing so that it has similarities to community policing in the West, such as stressing cooperation between police and community and police service to the community. It is also a feature of (Chinese) Shenzhen characteristics that do not exist in the West. (Chinese) Shenzhen community policing is part of comprehensive management of social order, which is under the leadership of the Party and government and is a multiagency approach including not only police and community but also various governmental branches, schools, private security agencies, and companies. BLSCC and community policing aim to maintain community safety as well as community civilization, including a high level of socialist morality and harmonious relationships among neighbors. (Chinese) Shenzhen government claims that BLSCC and community policing are effective in crime prevention and control, but more scientific research is needed for its validation.

References

Clark, J. P. (1989). Conflict management outside the courtroom of China. In R. J. Troyer, J. P. Clark & D. G. Rojek (Eds.), *Social Control in the People's Republic of China*, pp. 57–69. New York: Praeger.

Du, J. (2009). China (community policing). In A. Wakefield & J. Fleming (Eds.), *The SAGE Dictionary of Policing*, pp. 40–41. London: Sage.

Huang, Z. and Luo, J. (1997). Preliminary study of the new characteristics of the management of public security work in Shenzhen: Reflection on the experience of Building Little Safe and Civilized Communities. In *Shenzhen Political and Legal Yearbook*, 1997, pp. 2–10. Shenzhen: Haitian Press.

Jiang, S., Lambert, E., and Jenkins, M. (2010). East meets west: Chinese and U.S. college students' views on formal and informal crime control. *International Journal of Offender Therapy and Comparative Criminology*, 54 (2): 264–284.

Jiang, S., Sun, I. Y., and Wang, J. (forthcoming). Citizens' satisfaction with police in Guangzhou, China. *Policing: An International Journal of Police Strategies and Management.*

Jiao, A. Y. (2001). Police and culture: A comparison between China and the United States. *Police Quarterly, 4*: 156–185.

Kelling, G. L., and Coles, C. M. (1996). *Fixing Broken Windows: Restoring Order and Reducing Crime in Our Communities*. New York: Touchstone.

Ma, Y. (1997). The Police Law 1995: Organization, functions, powers and accountability of the Chinese police. *Policing: An International Journal of Police Strategy and Management, 20* (1): 113–135.

Shenzhen Government Online (2011). Available at http://www.sz.gov.cn/cn/zjsz/szgl/201107/t20110712_1675680.htm (retrieved January 30, 2012).

Shenzhen Political and Legal Yearbook, 1996–2009. Shenzhen: Haitian Press.

Shenzhen Statistical Yearbook, 2010. Beijing: Zhongguo Tongji Press.

Wong, K. C. (2001). The philosophy of community policing in China. *Police Quarterly, 4*: 186–214.

Wu, Y., Jiang, S., and Lambert, E. (2011). Citizen support for community policing in China. *Policing: An International Journal of Police Strategies and Management, 34* (2): 285–303.

Yu, D., Zheng, X., and Su, T. (1997). *The Encyclopedia for Chiefs of Local Police Stations*. Beijing: Red Flag Press.

Zhong, L. Y. (2009). Community policing in China: Old wine in new bottles. *Police Practice and Research, 10* (2): 157–169.

Zhong, L. Y. and Broadhurst, R. G. (2007). Building Little Safe and Civilized Communities: Community crime prevention with Chinese characteristics? *International Journal of Offender Therapy and Comparative Criminology, 51* (1): 52–67.

Zhong, L. Y. and Grabosky, P. N. (2009). The pluralization of policing and the rise of private policing in China. *Crime, Law and Social Change, 52*: 433–455.

India

20

MAHESH K. NALLA
GRAEME R. NEWMAN

Contents

Background

India, which is about a third of the size of the United States, is one of the largest countries in South Asia (3,287,590 mi.²) and has a population of nearly 1.2 billion, making it one of the most densely populated land masses (17% world population on 2.3% land) in the world. Geographically, India shares borders with Pakistan in the west, Bangladesh in the east, and Nepal and China to the north. The island nation of Sri Lanka is located in the southern tip of India. This inverted triangle-shaped country has the frigid snowy peaks of the Himalayas to the north, the Arabian desert to the west, the Bay of Bengal to the east, and the Indian Ocean to the south. The capital city, New Delhi, is one among four large metropolitan centers; others are Mumbai, Kolkata, and Chennai. India is a diverse country with a long history and a rich heritage, culture, and traditions. Indian culture is strongly shaped by the Indo-Aryans who settled on the area more than 3000 years ago, followed by subsequent settlements of Persians, the Dutch, the Portuguese, and finally, the British. As a secular nation, India prides itself in having a diverse population that practices many different religions—Hinduism, Christianity, Islam, Sikhism, Buddhism, Jainism, Zoroastrianism, and Judaism. While the Constitution of India recognizes 17 Indo-European and Dravidian languages (English is not included), a more recent yet comprehensive ethnographic study revealed 324 distinct languages (Norton 2009).

After more than two centuries of colonial occupation by Great Britain, India gained independence in 1947 and became a republic in 1950 with the accession of the 562 "princely states" that were tied to the British through an ingenious system of intricate alliances. India has 28 states and seven union territories, most of which have their own state language in addition to Hindi, which is spoken by more than 70% of its population. Though English is not an official language of India, with a whopping 54% of its population below the age of 25, it has an estimated 350 million speakers and users of the language. Today, India is an economically vibrant country, and it is the second-fastest-growing economy in the world.

Police Organization

Unlike the decentralized police organizations in the United States, in India, most states are responsible for their police and are guided by the Police Act of 1861. Police are the subject of individual states and territories, which handle a myriad of chores that include law and order, riot control, crime investigation, protection of state assets, traffic control, and protection of state VIPs. Typically, each state is administratively divided into various zones, ranges, and districts, with the director general of police acting as the highest authority. In 2007, there were more than 1.6 million civil police personnel (women police: 1.8%) assigned to more than 13,000 police stations and 7000 outposts (BPRD 2010).

While India has progressed in many spheres, its police system remains fairly archaic and heavily entrenched in the old colonial mentality, with an operational philosophy of state protection as its primary responsibility. Amid growing criticism of police ineptness, corruption, and police brutality, various commissions and committees have been constituted to make recommendations for police reform. However, not many of these recommendations have been considered by ruling governments. India's highest court—the Supreme Court—finally intervened and ordered reforms in 2007, with the primary goal to minimize political interference and corruption. In addition, social activists and nongovernmental organizations (NGOs) have joined forces to push an agenda of civil society, transparency, and accountability of police.

Origin of Community Policing in India

The Indian policing system evolved from the pre-Mughal period, and it has stayed close to the seat of power, therefore neglecting rural India, which forms the majority of the landmass. In preindependent India, the British also did not take responsibility for law and order in rural India. In its place and in the absence of regular police, the village head served in the capacity of *village patel* (headman) assisted by *Chowkidars* (security guards or personal body guards) who served as a civilian support system for the regular police forces (National Police Commission n.d.). The postindependent India continues the tradition of rural policing, but to some extent, it has diluted the powers of the *village patel*. The National Police Commission report (n.d.) in 1950 characterized the experiments of some states such as the state of West Bengal as having a program called the Village Resistance Group to deal with *dacoits* (armed bandits) and violent criminal gangs as a concept in self-policing. The earliest known community policing program, called *Gram Rakshak Dal* (Village Defense Party [VDP]), was established in every village in the States of Maharashtra and Gujarat. The Bombay Police Act of 1951 empowers the Superintendent, the highest police official at the district level, to constitute volunteers for VDPs to support and assist police officers in patrolling, resolving minor disputes among neighbors, and informing police of bootlegging, gambling, drug peddling, and other crimes (Maharashtra Police 2011). According to the Maharashtra Police Department's official website (2011) in the district of Nashik, nearly 35,000 local citizens volunteered for the VDP.

Other states had similar programs, which were precursors to community policing efforts. In 1963, the Police Commission noted that the state of Orissa dismantled its approximately 25,000 *Chowkidars*, replacing them with about 1500 police constables to cover 50,000 villages only to revert back to appointing more educated *Gram Rakhis* (village defense) who discharge responsibilities similar to the *Chowkidars*. The state of Karnantaka also established such a program with the enactment of the Karnataka Village Defense Parties Act of 3964 in 1964, and it became fully operational in 1975. The act empowers the local superintendent of police to constitute *dalapatis* (village heads) supported by VDP members (National Police Commission n.d.).

The Supreme Court's landmark decision has given much impetus to NGOs, as well as state police organizations, and has established a greater connection with the public in the urban settings. For instance, the Police Reforms–People's Perspective–Public is Police (PRPP-PP) Campaign was started at Sirsa, in the state of Haryana, in January 2010, with its primary objective of bridging the gap between grassroots realities and policymakers in an effort to overhaul the police in India, with active citizen participation in policy analysis based on empirical study (Team Nishan 2010).

Many programs—most of which were commonly referred to as community policing—were initiated by police departments from various states and were either at the state level or focused on specific cities, communities, or towns to establish closer contact with citizens to build positive police–citizen relationships across the country. While some programs are simply referred to as "community policing," others have adopted names that reflect the underlying philosophy of community policing (COP) in local languages (Mukherjee n.d.). These include the following: the Friends of Police Movement (FOP), which began in the Ramnad District in the state of Tamil Nadu (Philip 1996) and eventually spread to the rest of the state; the Samarth Yojna Community Policing Experiment (Coimbatore City, Tamil Nadu); Trichy Community Policing (Trichy, Tamil Nadu); the Tuticorin Experiment (Tuticorin, Tamil Nadu); *Prahari*—The Community Policing Initiative (Assam); Aaswas (Assam); Community Policing Initiatives (Himachal Pradesh); Community Policing Initiatives (Ludhiana, Punjab); Community Policing Initiatives (Amritsar, Punjab); Community Policing Initiatives (Kolkata, West Bengal); Community Policing Initiatives (Diamond Harbour, West Bengal); Community Policing Initiatives (Nadia District, West Bengal); Community Policing Initiatives (Pune, Maharashtra); Mohalla Committee Movement Trust (Mumbai, Maharashtra); Slum Police Panchayat [village council] (Mumbai, Maharashtra); Maithri, A Community Policing Initiative (Andhra Pradesh); Parivar Paramarsh Kendra (Raigharh District, Madhya Pradesh); Community Liaison Groups (Uttarakhand); and Gram/Nagar Raksha Samiti (Rajnandgaon, Chattisgarh). In addition, there are other programs in the cities of New Delhi (Neighborhood Watch Scheme) and Chandigarh, and the most extensive statewide program, Janamaithri Suraksha Padhathi, in the state of Kerala.

While these programs are varied and are designed to bring people together to address local problems as diverse as city vigilante committees, institution of complaint boxes, establishing community consultative groups, working with school children, introducing drug awareness programs, and creating blood banks and health awareness camps, among others, from the Indian police administrative point of view, the Bureau of Police Research and Development (BPRD), Ministry of Home Affairs, Government of India, 2002–2003, five aspects of community policing were highlighted based on literature drawn from international experiences and benchmarks developed in India. These include the following: strengthening the beat system; creating a structure for formal consultation with the community; creating community policing resource centers; integrating the above with existing police structures; and partnership and problem solving (Borwankar 2008).

How Does Community Policing Work?

Relative to the imagery associated with the general concept of community policing from the West that portrays uniformed police officers on beat or as riding a bicycle or driving around in the patrol cars, community policing is very diverse in India. This is further complicated by India's diversity in urbanism, economic disparities, and culture. In this section, we will provide examples of community policing from diverse communities and regions of the country.

Community Policing in Urban Centers

Approximately 360 million Indians live in urban areas, and according to a *Times of India* report, 14% of India's urban population (about 53 million) live in 2 of the 10 million-plus metro cities of Delhi, Mumbai, and Kolkata; 9% (32 million) live in cities with a population of 5 to 10 million; 27% (101 million) are in cities with half a million to 5 million; and the majority (51% or 181 million) live in cities with less than 500,000 (Varma 2010).

Though examples of community policing were seen as early as 1981 in one of the districts of New Delhi, which experimented with joint police–citizen patrols (Bedi 1981), many more innovative community programs of all sizes have emerged all over urban centers.

Samarth Yojna Community Policing Experiment

Coimbatore, a city in the southern state of Tamil Nadu, commonly referred to as the Manchester of South India, not only grew from a population of about 1 million in 2001 to 2 million in 2010 but also has seen its share of an increase in communal riots and violence. The major goal of community policing in Coimbatore was to "resolve communal problems and win the confidence and trust of the people" (Mukherjee n.d.). Several workshops were held for police personnel to bring an attitudinal change to interact with the community. Members meet regularly at designated forums with the local community policing officers in order to facilitate conflict resolution among groups of people from different communities. On occasion, local government agencies are included in these meetings to solve problems "through effective intra and interagency consultations" (Mukherjee n.d.).

Other dimensions of community policing efforts include city vigilance committees to tackle property crime, trafficking in illegal substances, and terrorism. As part of this program, local citizens actively participate as the "eyes and ears" of the police, and this has substantially increased the levels of seizure of contraband goods, explosives, and lethal weapons, among others. Students were recruited as deputies for regular police officers in assisting in traffic management and baggage checks at railway and bus stations (Mukherjee n.d.).

There is a wide diversity in the range of activities subsumed under community policing programs in various cities across urban India. These include citizen assistance in police beats, establishment of complaint boxes, slum adoption programs (citizen engagement in proactive policing to reduce crime and violence), domestic violence and conflict resolution, drug awareness programs, organization of blood drives, and free medical and eye camps.

Mohalla Committee Movement Trust

The Mohalla Committee Movement Trust, established in Mumbai (Maharashtra State), was formed in the wake of violent Hindu–Muslim riots that broke out in 1992 and 1993, which left more than 1000 people dead (Takkar 2004). There are more than 24 such committees in Mumbai and 30 in Pune, also a city in Maharashtra. *Mohallas*, or beat patrol with a police constable, are in charge of holding regular monthly meetings (Mukherjee n.d.). Committee meetings are also held regularly before and during Hindu and Muslims festivals, occasions that bring people together in large numbers, therefore creating opportunities for communal flare-ups. Not all *Mohalla* committees have the same agenda. Some of the goals include the following: focusing on complaints related to police work in the area; addressing community concerns relating to water, health, garbage disposal, and environmental issues, among others; enhancing educational opportunities for children and youth; and promoting communal harmony such as joint celebrations of Hindu and Muslim festivals by both groups and organizing cricket (a popular Indian sport) games with teams composed of members from different groups representing each of the two teams. Some *Mohalla* committees also serve as conflict resolution centers, with upstanding citizens drawn from both religious groups.

In the state of Kerala, as part of their Janamaithri Suraksha Project (JSP), the Kerala Community Policing Initiative was more innovative in its program development. Kerala has more than 600 km (370 mi.) of rich and luscious coastline, which makes it a vulnerable spot for terrorist attacks as well as a haven for illicit trafficking in contraband goods. Coastal Security Committees (Kadalora Jagratha Samithies [KJS]) are created by selecting partners from various stakeholders including local administration, leaders of various fishing villages that dot the coast, fisheries departments, and port and harbor engineering departments, and they partner with the police and coastal vigilance organizations (Government of Kerala 2010). These committees operate at both the district and the local police station levels and include at least 10 local residents. There were more than 76 such committees constituted along the coastline in 2009. Committee members received comprehensive training, video supplemental materials, and interactive sessions with key stakeholders. Members were given photo identification cards and free radios/telephones for better communication. In 2009, more than 480 such meetings were held by these committees, with more than 1000 members participating. Committee members who worked on shifts notified the coastal police, Indian Coast Guard, and the Joint Operations Control that was established as part of this operation if they saw anything suspicious. As part of a test of emergency preparedness, mock operations were conducted with the joint efforts of the Indian Navy, Coast Guard, police, ports, and fisheries and harbor management (Government of Kerala 2010).

Community Policing in Urban Slums

Policing urban centers also brings with it new challenges. Common to all Indian cities, as in many countries in Asia, is the presence of large segments of the city's population living in slums, which are characteristically small dwellings with no electricity, running water, or basic amenities. The percentage of the population in major metro cities that lives in slums ranges between 10% and 20% (Sud 2006). This translates to approximately a million and a half out of 14 million. Delhi alone has 10% of its population living in slums. The city of Mumbai has a significantly higher percentage of slum dwellers, estimated to be nearly 50%, with some families living in small spaces of about 50 ft.[2] and having a monthly income of US$50. As in all underdeveloped and poor areas, the crime problem is higher in slums than in the rest of the city, yet the police presence is minimal in these areas.

The community policing programs called Slum Police Panchayats (council) began in 2003 in five slums in the city of Pune in the State of Maharashtra. These programs eventually spread to Mumbai in 2004, and the total number of such programs stood at more than 200 in 2004 (Roy et al. 2004). These *panchayats* consist of seven women and three men called *sahayak* (helper) and have one police officer. The disparity in female representation in these *panchayats* stems from the fact that women are disproportionately more often victims of crime, particularly offenses related to domestic violence. Additionally, these programs were created by members of the National Slum Dwellers Federation or *Mahila Milan* ("women together"), a group that has a strong interest in building grassroots community-based organizations. Interestingly, in these programs, helpers are nominated by the residents' organization and not the police. All helpers wear photo identification cards. In addition, the community makes a room available for the council to meet.

The *panchayats'* primary responsibility is to patrol the neighborhood and liaise with the assigned police officers. *Panchayats* meet every day at the regularly scheduled council meetings where local residents bring their disputes for a hearing. Council members help resolve these disputes before they escalate into violence and result in criminal charges. Apart from domestic disputes, the majority of disputes arise due to a conflict over boundaries that demarcate their residential living quarters. Given the very small piece of land that these tenements occupy, and that there is little or no formal oversight by the housing authority, neighborhood quarrels over land issues constitute a majority of the disputes. For community residents, this form of dispute resolution for minor issues is more acceptable. Not only is initiating a formal process slow, but also it takes more than a day for people to travel to the formal organizations and lodge formal complaints, which are generally minor in nature, which means that they would lose their wages during the time it takes to lodge a formal complaint. The *panchayat* members are aware that they do not have the power that police do, that dispute resolution is normally done as a group, and that this leaves more law-and-order situations for police officers, thus relieving them of some burden. Each *panchayat* maintains a record of the members on duty and the disputes that are handled in the center.

Community Policing in Rural India

As noted, India's rural land mass and population is nearly 70%. The primary membership for village defense programs in rural India, as seen in examples from the urban community policing program, is drawn from the local community to serve and assist with community law-and-order issues. Most programs have minimum membership requirements. These include a membership status of good standing in the community (no prior civil or criminal case involvement) with age limitations in the range of 18 to 70 years.

In the predominantly rural district of Nalgonda (75%) in Andhra Pradesh, the project *Aasara* was introduced with its focus on reducing the illicit trafficking of women and children, rehabilitating the victims, and empowering them by offering employment opportunities or support of small business loans (Bhagwat n.d.). Bhagwat (n.d.) notes that many community groups representing the local governments and businesses, as well as many upstanding local residents, partnered with the police department to start a community policing program in 2005. These partners included government departments such as the Revenue Department; District Rural Development Agency (DRDA); State Government departments of Women and Child Welfare, Education, and Health; *Panchayati Raj* (local governments); elected representatives for the state assembly (members of the Legislative Assembly [MLAs]); members of national parliament (members of Parliament [MPs]); and businesses such as State Bank of Hyderabad and the BC Corporation. In addition, many NGOs, including the Child and Police (CAP) SARIQUE project, local chapters of the Red Cross organization, and the Prajwala women's organization are active partners.

A variety of activities by various partners was conducted under the auspices of *Aasara* (Bhagwat n.d.). One of the partners, CAP, offered a 3-month training for alternative sources of livelihood for sex workers in 2005. The *Velgu* (Shine) project personnel trained four self-help groups of 26 members for 2 months in the production of incense sticks, plates, bowls, baskets, and tailoring. The Red Cross conducted camps on social awareness and personality development through behavioral training. The local member of the State Legislative Assembly assured support for a donation of 20 acre homes and agriculture land for horticulture for victims rescued from illicit trafficking as an alternative means of employment, while the Red Cross sponsored numerous health camps.

Community Policing in Tribal India

India's rural population is also very diverse. Nearly 8% of India's population, or more than 70 million people, live in tribal areas. The distribution of the tribal population in India varies from one state to another. In some states such as Arunachal Pradesh, Meghalaya, Mizoram, and Nagaland, more than 90% of the population are considered tribal. Most of India's tribal population lives in forested areas that are characteristic of low political and economic significance, reflecting some of the most underdeveloped and poverty-stricken areas of the country. Policing tribal or agency areas, as they are commonly referred to, raises interesting challenges.

Project *Prahari* is a community policing initiative in the state of Assam (Mukherjee n.d.). As noted above, the majority of the population belongs to tribal groups, with community characteristics that include low education levels and marginal living conditions. The impetus to create *Prahari* came up when five people in a remote village were brutally killed. When the perpetrators were apprehended, they admitted to the killings and justified it as being an offering to the local gods who had taken away the lives of numerous young children in their village. Apparently, two of the goals of *Prahari* were to deal with shamans practicing witchcraft as well as use them as change agents to bring about the end of the practice of witchcraft in other neighboring villages. This involved working with both the villagers as well as the police officers.

The process began with the creation of Community Management Groups (CMGs), which were formed at the levels of district, state, and local police stations. Eminent members from local politically affiliated backgrounds were drawn into CMGs. These groups worked in close affiliation with police stations in 48 villages. Interestingly, the strategy of the CMGs was not to directly tackle the witchcraft issue but rather to approach it indirectly by community involvement in self-help projects, such as developing community wells and canals to obtain water for agriculture and sinking bore wells for community water needs, among others, as ways to establish community support. The police improved their image by repairing roads and bridges, constructing community centers, and generating employment activities for village youth.

A second example of community policing that exemplifies community policing representative of the tribal population is drawn from Adilabad in the state of Andhra Pradesh, a district with a high concentration of population that is socially and economically backward (Mukherjee n.d.). The district has a heavy concentration of villages badly affected by a lack of economic development and one that has been heavily hit by rebel groups backed by Maoist ideologists. The rebel groups who call themselves *Naxalites* (People's War Group) were in control of many of these remote villages and made them inaccessible to police. The people in these villages over time had developed an antagonism toward the state on the grounds of a perceived lack of interest on the part of the state toward the welfare of its constituents.

A program called *Police Mee Kosam* (Police for You) was introduced in 2001 in this district, which began as a community development program (Mukherjee n.d.). The police began by organizing village meetings (*grama sabha*), mostly in villages with a large number of active extremists. More than 1000 meetings were held, and they drew more than 125,000 residents of these villages. The major problems of each of these villages were first identified with the input of the local residents. The police officers established protocols with local residents by visiting their homes and adhering to local customs such as removing their shoes upon entering their homes and greeting them with the local prevalent rituals. Within this framework, the police, as part of *Police Mee Kosam*, conducted 110 free medical and health camps, which benefited more than 100,000 local residents. An eye camp was conducted where 1300 people received free cataract operations; *jalayagnams* (watershed development programs) were developed and involved water purification projects, the digging up of numerous bore wells, and the building of overhead water tanks; power supply lines were added to many villages that previously never had electricity; new bus terminals were built to connect many villages; youth were taken to the capital city of Hyderabad on site visits and excursions to expose them to the potential opportunities for tribal youth; and new roads connecting various villages in the region were repaired or built (Mukherjee n.d.). Though no systematic research was conducted to evaluate these programs, raw data on incidents of extremist violence suggest that over a 3-year period, *naxal*-related violence was reduced by 80% (Mukherjee n.d.).

Effectiveness of Community Policing Programs

It is unclear to what extent any systematic research has been attempted in order to evaluate community policing programs in India. Newspapers occasionally report concerns or anecdotes of specific instances of citizen concerns relating to community policing. For instance, in one of the *Times of India* reports (Prashar 2011), some citizens reported that, though the local police department had made plans to create community policing programs to involve senior citizens, not much has been done. These citizens viewed the police as perceiving senior citizens as more of a hindrance, while the police management reiterated that they have to focus "more on core duties rather than such activities," suggesting a disconnection between the two primary partners in community policing.

However, Borwankar's (2008) work on the assessment of community policing efforts in the state of Maharashtra showed very supportive findings. In her unpublished dissertation, she surveyed 360 field officers (subinspectors and inspectors) and 126 supervisors (deputy superintendent of police) from three cities: Mumbai, Pune, and Nagpur. Her findings suggest that an overwhelming percentage of field officers and supervisors were familiar with the concept of community policing and believed that the citizens were generally supportive of working with the police in Maharashtra. Junior officers felt appreciated by their supervisors for participating in community policing efforts, while senior officers noted that the effectiveness of community policing efforts could be impeded by excessive involvement by citizen groups in shaping the programs. Overall, Borwankar, the highest-ranked police officer in the state, concluded that community policing programs in the state appear to be functioning well.

Conclusions

To a large extent, community policing programs in India do not resemble those commonly seen in the developed Western countries. Civil society organizations and creative and driven chief executives and senior police bureaucrats have tirelessly worked at improving synergies between the community and the police. Apart from the traditional citizen–police partnerships to control and reduce street crime, many other examples of community policing (as discussed above) do not on any account resemble traditional policing activities. In fact, they appear to be more of a grassroots community organization. Clearly, in areas where police organizations have adopted a more "social work" approach to developing partnerships with local residents, it appears that community support for the regular policing efforts flows naturally. These examples also suggest that the concept of community policing needs to be revisited.

Additional Information

Tamil Nadu Police (n.d.) Reaching Out to People: Trichy Community Policing Experience. http://profit.ndtv.com/videos/beyond-business/video-community-policing-initiatives-work-miracles-in-trichy-3438. Accessed October 15, 2012.

Videos

Community Policing Initiatives Work Miracles in Trichy. http://profit.ndtv.com/videos/beyond-business/video-community-policing-initiatives-work-miracles-in-trichy-3438. Retrieved July 3, 2011.

References

Bedi, K. (1981). Community Policing: Joint Night Patrolling by Citizens, Police. http://www.kiranbedi.com/communitypolicing.htm. Retrieved July 3, 2011.

Bhagwat, M.M. (n.d). Project Aasara. http://humanrightsinitiative.org/new/project_aasara.pdf. Retrieved July 3, 2011.

Borwankar, M. (2008). *A Study of Community Policing and Its Administration in Selected Urban Centres in Maharashtra.* Unpublished Ph.D. Dissertation, University of Pune. http://117.240.228.70/handle/10603/1993?mode=full&submit_simple=Show+full+item+record. Retrieved July 3, 2011.

BPRD (2010). Data on Police Organisation. http://bprd.gov.in/administrations/data-police-organisations.html. Retrieved July 1, 2011.

Government of Kerala (2010). Community Policing: A Kerala Perspective. Global Community Policing Conclave, Kochi City, Kerala, November 3–4, 2010.

Maharashtra Police (2011). Village Defense Party (Gram Rakshak Dal). http://mahapolice.gov.in/mahapolice/jsp/temp/villagedefence.jsp. Retrieved July 1, 2011.

Mukherjee, D. (n.d.). Community Policing Experiments/Outreach Programmes in India. http://www.humanrightsinitiative.org/new/community_policing_experiments_in_india.pdf. Retrieved on July 1, 2011.

National Police Commission (n.d.). Third Report (Chapter XX). http://police.pondicherry.gov.in/Police%20Commission%20reports/3rd%20Police%20Commission%20report.pdf. Retrieved July 1, 2011.

Norton, J. (2009). *Global Studies: India and South Asia* (9th ed.). New York: McGraw-Hill/Dushkin.

Philip, P.V. (1996). The "Friends of Police" movement in India. *The Police Journal, UK, 69*, 126–130.

Prashar, A. (April 10, 2011). Community Policing Awaits Support. *Times of India.* http://articles.timesofindia.indiatimes.com/2011-04-10/chandigarh/29402952_1_crime-marshals-punjab-police-police-personnel. Retrieved July 3, 2011.

Roy, A.N., Jockin, A., and Ahmad, J. (2004). Community police stations in Mumbai's slums. *Environment and Urbanization 16*, 135–138. DOI: 10.1177/095624780401600205.

Sud, H. (2006). *Poverty and Slums in India—Impact of Changing Economic Landscape.* New Delhi: South Asia Analysis Group. http://www.southasiaanalysis.org/%5Cpapers18%5Cpaper1769.html. Accessed July 3, 2011.

Takkar, U. (2004). Mohalla Committees of Mumbai: Candles in Ominous Darkness. *Economic and Political Weekly, 39*(6), 580–586.

Team Nishan (2010). "Better Together" Initiative Begins in Haryana from Yamunanagar—25th November 2010—Nishan. http://nishanjustice.org/news-updates/better-together-initiative-begings-in-haryana-from-yamunanagar/. Retrieved January 4, 2011.

Varma, S. (March 27, 2010). 53% of Urban Population Lives in Small Towns. *Times of India.* http://articles.timesofindia.indiatimes.com/2010-03-27/india/28144641_1_urban-population-world-population-urban-areas. Retrieved July 3, 2011.

New Zealand

21

GREG NEWBOLD
L. THOMAS WINFREE, JR.

Contents

Background

New Zealand is an independent nation located in the South Western Pacific Ocean, 1200 mi. east of Australia. It has two main islands, known as the North and the South Islands, and an economy heavily dependent on exports from cattle and sheep farming, fishing, and forestry. Although both islands are roughly the same in area, more than 3 million of New Zealand's 4.4 million inhabitants live in the North Island, and 1.5 million of these live in its largest and fastest-growing city, Auckland. The capital city, Wellington, is second largest, with a population of 350,000, and is located at the southern end of the North Island. Approximately the same number of people lives in Christchurch, the largest South Island city. The national population is thus highly urbanized, with 86% living in urban areas of 10,000 or more. The population is also ethnically diverse, as 70% are classified as European, 14% as Maori, 10% as Asian, and 7% as ethnic Pacific Islanders, known generically as Pasifika.

New Zealand was one of the last major landmasses colonized by humans. Its first inhabitants were migrants from Eastern Polynesia, now known as Maori, who arrived by canoe about 900 CE. By the time of first European contact in the seventeenth century, the Maori population of New Zealand was estimated to be about 200,000. The land was discovered by the Dutch explorer Abel Tasman in 1642, was charted by James Cook in 1769, and began receiving its first permanent European settlers at the beginning of the nineteenth century. Most of these settlers were British, and in 1840, by way of a document signed by 50 Maori chiefs known as the Treaty of Waitangi, New Zealand became a British Crown Colony. After a period of vice-regal governance, in 1852, the colony began operating as a parliamentary democracy and became an independent Dominion within the British Empire in 1907. Maori have always had the same voting rights as non-Maori, and in 1867, Maori representation in Parliament was guaranteed with the creation of four dedicated Maori seats.

Today, although increasingly aloof from Europe, the nation remains a member of the British Commonwealth and recognizes the queen of England as the titular head of state. Thus, no law can become effective in New Zealand until it is ratified by the queen or her local representative, the governor general (see Newbold and Jeffries 2010). The country operates a unicameral parliamentary legislature with an independent judiciary and public service. Because both the nation's population and its physical area are relatively small, government departments are nationally administered and have their head offices in the capital city of Wellington. The primary policing authority is the New Zealand Police (NZP), which has its National Headquarters in Wellington, headed by an appointed commissioner. The commissioner of police is independent from, but responsible to, the minister of police, who is an elected member of Parliament. The commissioner is responsible for 11,000 sworn and nonsworn staff, assisted by two deputy commissioners, five assistant commissioners, and a number of managers in charge of areas such as road policing, ethnic services, and youth services. Geographically, the country is divided into 12 NZP districts, headed by district commanders. These officers manage the more than 400 community-based police stations that exist around New Zealand. Apart from law enforcement, the police work in a number of related areas such as traffic control, crowd control, counterterrorism, search and rescue, and diplomatic protection. Central to the business of the modern police is community policing. Today, the NZP Web site (New Zealand Police 2011a) states specifically that

> *Community policing* is at the heart of all police activity in New Zealand. It is a policing style which means we believe the people who live in a community know their crash and crime concerns best. Our staff listens to what local people say, then work with neighbourhoods, local authorities and other community groups to find long-term solutions that suit the particular situation.

Origins of Community Policing

When New Zealand became a Crown Colony in 1840, a number of untrained policemen were sworn by the governor to try and maintain order within the five European settlements then in existence. In 1846, these officers were supplemented by a nationally organized paramilitary body known as the Armed Constabulary Force. The Armed Constabulary performed both civil and military functions and during the 1860s had as its primary duty the pacification of warlike North Island Maori rebelling against colonialist land-grabbing and other breaches of the Treaty of Waitangi. In 1877, following the end of land-war hostilities, the 582 men of the Armed Constabulary combined with 330 provincial policemen to form the New Zealand Armed Constabulary. Nine years later, in 1886, civil and military functions were statutorily split; on September 1, 1886, the NZP Force came officially into existence (see M. Hill 1986; R. Hill 1986, 1989).

Based loosely on the model of the London Metropolitan Police, the NZP Force was primarily authoritarian and reactive in its official brief. However, the rural and isolated nature of New Zealand at the time meant that inevitably, local constables worked within the communities where they lived and thus performed a number of social functions, both formal and informal (Hill 1995). In particular, following the establishment of (the world's first) national probation system in 1886, police played an integral part in community supervision of convicted offenders. Probation at the time was an alternative to imprisonment for first offenders and required them to report regularly to an officer and keep him informed of their places of work and residence. These first probation officers were usually policemen who were thereby assigned the twin tasks of both crime fighting and crime prevention (Newbold 2007). Reinforcing these roles, in 1890, the inspector of prisons, Lieutenant Colonel Arthur Hume, who ran the prisons as well as the probation service, was also made commissioner of police.

Thus, from the time of the inception of New Zealand's first police force, statutory provision for community involvement existed. The police continued playing a significant role in probationary support until 1954, when the probation service was reorganized and professionalized as a stand-alone entity.

For the most part, however, the NZP maintained a reactive stance, with principal concerns lying in crime control and without an emphasis on crime prevention or community policing. The police were dispersed around the country in a large number of urban, suburban, and rural stations and offices, many of which were isolated and manned by only one or two staff, a trend that remained through to the end of the century (Winfree and Taylor 2004; Taylor and Winfree 2005). Designated crime prevention officers were established in 1965, but their duties had mainly to do with enhancing property security by promoting the use of locks and burglar alarms. In the late 1960s, in the face of rocketing crime statistics, and in the hope of enhancing efficiency and crime fighting potential, a comprehensive review of the police took place. A survey of policing activities between 1966 and 1969 identified many inefficiencies and archaic practices and led to a document known as *The New Method of Policing* in 1970. Influenced by contemporary developments in other parts of the world, *The New Method* became a template for the most radical transformation of policing strategy ever taken within the NZP. Fundamental to the new method was centralization. Because they were deemed inefficient, many small suburban and rural stations were closed and replaced with larger stations, which could be staffed around the clock. Motorized patrols and radio communications were increased and improved. Foot patrols were restricted to city centers and trouble spots. In 1976, responding to the International Criminal Police Organization (Interpol) suggestions for increased computerization, a highly sophisticated national law enforcement computer database was established in the town of Wanganui (Dance 1986; Butterworth 2005).

Although the new method was criticized by some for removing the familiar local "Bobby" and depersonalizing police relations, it was a necessary response to rising crime and the increasingly sophisticated nature of criminal activity at the time. Among other things, drug use, manufacture, and importation had arisen as a permanent problem in the late 1960s, and New Zealand's first example of major organized, international criminal activity emerged in the form of the "Mr Asia" gang in the early 1970s (Newbold 2000, 2004). In the face of such developments, a coordinated and technologically advanced approach to the task of crime control was clearly essential. This fact notwithstanding, services identified in *The New System of Policing* were not wholly reactive, and a number of proactive community initiatives were continued including Youth Aid (see below), Crime Prevention, and a limited number of beat patrols. In 1973, the first community constables were appointed, and in 1976, the position of community relations coordinator was created in all major centers (Butterworth 2005; Dance 1986).

Nonetheless, in the 1970s, community initiatives remained largely advisory and educational in nature and did not represent a major departure from the primary concern of crime control. During the 1980s, significant shifts toward community policing occurred, involving the adoption of a "problem-solving" model with intensified community liaison and proactive work (Winfree and Newbold 1999; Winfree 2004). By 1996, 19% of police appropriations paid for preventive services derived from formal contacts within the community or from work such as responding to disasters or giving advice in civil matters. In 1995, a program known as *Policing 2000* provided a blueprint for policing into the twenty-first century. In this vision, the creation of more effective police–community partnerships was a key component of the police's desire to increase the safety of citizens and the security of their property, to reduce the fear of crime, and to enhance public trust and confidence in the police (Winfree and Newbold 1999; Winfree 2004).

Today, the NZP continues actively to promote community policing through a variety of strategies and agencies. Indeed, the police Web site says that community policing remains at the heart of police activity in this country. The mission statement of the NZP states that

> The New Zealand Police seeks to be a world-class police service working in partnership with citizens and the community to prevent crime and road trauma, to enhance public safety and to maintain law and order.

The police vision slogan, which appears on the sides of police vehicles and on official documents, is *Safer Communities Together.* Community support and reassurance is one of its primary stated functions (http://www.police.govt.nz). A new initiative, announced in December 2011, is Prevention First. The Prevention First strategy is aimed at stopping crime before it happens. Prevention First aims to give all police greater opportunities to be proactive and innovative in their work, with frontline staff gaining better support during times of high demand. A shared sense of purpose will be encouraged to improve morale and operating efficiency (http://www.police.govt.nz).

Because modern-day community policing occurs in a number of areas and directions, our purpose now is to examine some of these areas individually in terms of their history and current profile.

Aspects of Community Policing Today

Community Police

Today, the NZP deploys approximately 1000 dedicated community policing personnel around the country. Contrasting with the regular mobile patrols, the role of the community policeman/woman is primarily interactive. The community police's aim is to be visible and accessible within designated communities. Officers do this via foot patrols in which they talk to business owners and citizens, meeting with community groups and organizations to build partnerships between the police and the community and generally identifying and responding to public concerns. Community police have operational bases in rural areas, in community centers, in city malls, and in prisons, universities, and schools.

Youth Aid

Although in 1954, the police lost the probationer supervision they had had since 1886, they continued in the role of traffic safety education, which had been undertaken in 1938. The first general contact between police and schools occurred in 1956, during a decade when the function of the police in preventing crime through community work was first becoming officially recognized. In the 1950s, there was increasing concern about rising levels of juvenile crime, in a decade that also saw the emergence of the first youth gangs (Newbold and Taonui 2011; Yska 1993). In 1957, in recognition of the problem and in response to an Interpol circular of the previous year, commissioner of police Sam Barnett (who was also secretary for justice) created a Juvenile Crime Prevention Section (JCPS) within the NZP. Patterned on a similar initiative in Liverpool, England, the objective of the JCPS was to divert young offenders from crime through police involvement in youth clubs and police talks in schools. To forestall possible resistance to the program, Barnett reminded controlling officers that "a fundamental duty of the Police is preventive work" (Butterworth 2005: 238). Throughout the 1950s, the "talks-in-schools program" continued, and youth activity increased. In 1959, police–citizen youth clubs began appearing, and in the mid-1960s, the commissioner himself was a member of the board of trustees of the largest youth club in the country, Auckland's Boystown. Seventy percent of Boystown attendees at the time were Maori or Pasifika—groups, which, since the onset of the post-World War II (WWII) urban drift, had started becoming increasingly prominent in crime statistics. In 1969, two constables were seconded to Boystown for permanent duty (Butterworth 2005).

In 1968, JCPS was reorganized and renamed the Youth Aid Section, with the appointment of a national coordinator, expanded capacity deriving from better officer training, better organization, improved coordination with other youth agencies, and an even more energetic proactive approach to intervening with young people at risk. The first head of Youth Aid, Senior Sergeant Brian Mooney, said in 1968, "The fundamental responsibility of the police is the prevention of crime.... Intelligent crime prevention must begin with delinquency prevention" (cited in Butterworth 2005: 239). Pleased with the progress taken by the new section, by 1972, police administration had expanded the number of fulltime Youth Aid officers from 15 to 46. In 1976, the talks-in-schools program was expanded into a Law Related Education Program (LREP) and became part of the school curriculum.

Working alongside Youth Aid in the 1970s were "J" (Joint) Teams. These were formed in 1971 as a combined initiative consisting of police, church groups, voluntary agencies, and the departments of Child Welfare and Maori Affairs. Attached to Youth Aid from 1974, J Teams worked within communities, particularly Maori/Pasifika, and achieved a considerable degree of success. Staffing cuts within government departments in the late 1970s, however, forced the disbanding of J Teams in 1980. Nonetheless, the Youth Aid program still continues, with officers drawn from the frontline of policing. Youth Aid officers receive special training in the handling of young people's problems and in the operations of the Youth Court and Youth Justice facilities. These officers visit video and games parlors and other places where youth congregate, in order to maintain a watch on youth activities in their areas. They work in conjunction with schools, churches, family counseling agencies, and other government departments in an attempt to divert young people from lives of crime. A particular focus of Youth Aid officers is the Maori and Pasifika communities, which have specific problems relating to cultural and sometimes language differences and which need to be approached in a strategic and sensitive way (New Zealand House of Representatives 2011*; Hill 1986).

Today, with almost a quarter of all police apprehensions involving people under the age of 17, youth intervention has become a priority for the police. At Police National

* This is the New Zealand Police's annual report to Parliament.

Headquarters, a division known as the Youth Services Group coordinates police activities in the prevention of crime among young people. Because young offenders do not attract general criminal liability until they reach the age of 17, a large proportion of police response activity involves pursuing time-consuming alternatives to prosecution, such as youth diversion or organizing and convening Family Group Conferences under the Children, Young Persons and Their Families Act of 1989 (see Winfree 2004). Only if they commit a crime that is automatically indictable do offenders aged 14–17 normally face trial and/or sentencing in adult courts. Because of this, approximately 80% of all youth apprehensions are dealt with by means other than formal prosecution (New Zealand House of Representatives 2011). Since implementation in 2009, a government initiative called Fresh Start has placed a total of 720 young people under police guidance and care, supplemented by the establishment of 22 child case managers within the police. In addition, in 2011, a Police and Education Partnership program commenced to supplement the Youth Education Service, which has existed since 1995. Both programs deal with issues designed to increase traffic safety, to reduce graffiti, and to deal with problems related to bullying, domestic violence, and child abuse. Youth development programs deliver interventions not only to children and young persons but also to their families. Currently, 35 such programs exist, involving 2500 youth and children, in an effort designed to divert young people from lives of crime as soon as practically possible (New Zealand House of Representatives 2011).

Policing Maori and Ethnic Communities

Because a large proportion of offending, particularly youth offending, involves citizens from the Maori/Pasifika communities, proactive interventions in these areas have become a priority for the NZP.

Prior to WWII, Maori lived primarily in rural communities that were often self-policing, and official crime levels were low. After the war, however, as young Maori joined the national drift to the cities in search of work, indigenous offending levels increased. Where in 1930, only 10% of all prisoners received were Maori, by 1960, the figure had grown to 25%. At this point, the Department of Justice recognized that New Zealand had a "Maori crime problem." From here, the number of Maori in prison continued to rise, stabilizing at the current ratio of 50% of all receptions in 1980 (Newbold 2007; Newbold and Jeffries 2010).

Although Maori were never prohibited from joining the police, for many years, cultural factors and prejudice prevented them from doing so. Before WWII, Maori involvement in law enforcement was largely restricted to part-time auxiliary native and district constables. In 1945, the Maori Social and Economic Advancement Act created Maori wardens, who are unpaid, uniformed volunteers operating as social workers in Maori-dominated areas. The principal role of Maori wardens, operating among Maori in conjunction with the police, is the control of disorder and alcohol abuse. The Maori Wardens initiative, which continues today, was the first attempt at community policing of the indigenous people of New Zealand (Butterworth 2005).

But Maori within the police itself were rare, and before 1950, only two Maori are known to have joined the regular force. In 1955, this changed, with D.G. Ball, director of police training, ordering that when the new police training school opened that year, 25 of the first 100 places would be reserved for Maori recruits. From here, the number of Maori in the police continued upward, and by the mid-1960s, Maori were being actively recruited to the profession. By 1969,

there were 69 Maori policemen, and several had risen to the rank of non-commissioned officer or sergeant. Other ethnic groups, however, were excluded, with the commissioner in 1965
declaring that ethnic Chinese and "Hindus" (Indians) were unsuited to policing. Unsuited also
were Pacific Islanders, and applications from them should "not be considered." Apart from
Maori, he said, policing should be done by the "white races" (Butterworth 2005: 243).

In the late 1960s, this attitude began to change. Efforts to recruit Maori police intensified, and in 1968, the first Cook Island recruit was hired. From here, the hiring of New
Zealanders from all parts of the Pacific basin expanded rapidly. In 2003, the position of
general manager, Maori, Ethnic and Pacific Services, was created "to provide strategic
advice and operational support to districts and to Police National Headquarters" (http://
www.police.govt.nz). In addition to a number of ethnic liaison officers deployed about
the country, ethnic representation of Maori and Pasifika within the police today roughly
approximates their composition within the community. Since Asian people are currently
underrepresented, active attempts are being made to hire and train Asian and, in particular,
Mandarin-speaking officers, to assist with liaising among citizens within this community.

Since the 1840 Treaty of Waitangi was legally ratified in 1975, the "first nation status"
of Maori has increasingly been recognized. The Maori translation of "New Zealand Police"
(*Nga Pirihimana o Aotearoa*) appears on the side of marked police vehicles, and under
their commitment to the principles of the treaty, police undertake to remain sensitive to,
and cognizant of, Maori issues. Consultation with Maori on strategic matters and formal
liaison with Maori *Iwi* (tribes), through Maori wardens and Iwi liaison officers within the
police, is a part of this process. Recruitment among Maori is now actively pursued, and all
staff, particularly in the frontline, are trained in the principles of Maori culture and protocol. Most recently, in 2011, the commissioner convened a Maori Forum with Maori leaders
aimed at reducing Maori representation in the criminal justice system and at improving
relationships with Maori (http://www.police.govt.nz).

Domestic Violence

Because of the devastating effect it can have on a child's development and future, and
because of its well-known links with adult criminality (see, e.g., Ayers-Counts 1990;
Fergusson and Lynskey 1997; Straus et al. 1980; Newbold 2000), dealing with domestic violence is a critical component of all policing. In common with most other countries in the
world, until the 1980s, the NZP adopted a "hands off," minimalist approach when dealing
with domestic violence. Violence in the home was not seen as "real" crime, and police were
encouraged to pacify and reconcile warring partners where possible, resorting to arrest
only in serious cases (Cross and Newbold 2010; Newbold and Cross 2008).

During the 1980s, largely as a result of pressure from feminist lobbyists, this began to
change. Women demanded that police take domestic violence seriously, and as a result,
a number of international studies were conducted, with some indicating that mandatory
arrest reduces the likelihood of secondary offending. Internationally, therefore, police
departments began ordering presumptive or mandatory arrest, and New Zealand soon followed. In 1987, a *Commissioner's Circular* required that, in the absence of strong extenuat-
ing circumstances, arrest should be made in all domestic cases of evidentiary assault. Thus,
proarrest became the official policy of the NZP in domestic violence cases. Although, as
Cross and Newbold (2010) report, the policy often proved difficult to implement, the presumptive arrest principle remained in moderated form. The police response to domestic

violence is now more sophisticated and more clearly recognizes the complexity of crimes in this area. Police attending a domestic dispute today are required to fill in a form known as POL FVIR, which includes nine pages of detailed information about the incident and the parties concerned. Three pages of instructions direct officers on how to respond. Officer discretion over arrest is recognized, with safety of the victim and other family members being paramount. Where charges are preferred, the charges are expected to accurately reflect the gravity of the offending (Cross and Newbold 2010). The major cities now have a family violence coordinator, whose job is to oversee and organize domestic policing procedures and to liaise with other agencies—such as Women's Refuge and the Department of Child, Youth and Family—operating in this area. Family Safety Teams work with high-risk offenders, and information is shared via the Family Violence Interagency Response System.

A new initiative introduced in July 2010 is the Police Safety Order (PSO). PSOs allow police to take action even when no assault has occurred but where they believe future violence is likely. If there has been an assault, the police may also decide to issue a PSO rather than to arrest. A PSO requires a person to leave a premise immediately, for a set period of up to 5 days. The PSO protects victims from immediate harm and allows time for police to arrange for support or for permanent protection by way of court-issued Protection Orders. Breaches of orders are treated very seriously by the police and the courts. In 2011, the police received over 65,000 calls for service in domestic disputes and issued 5242 PSOs (http://www.police.govt.nz).

Other Community Measures

In addition to the above, the police operate in a number of other areas involving community-oriented activity, which we do not have time to explore in detail here. In 1992, national traffic control, which hitherto had been run by the Ministry of Transport, became amalgamated as the Traffic Safety Service of the NZP. The police now have oversight or control of all aspects of traffic safety, control, and law enforcement.

A second area where police operate proactively is in the use of crime prevention cameras (closed-circuit television [CCTV]) in public places. These are an innovation of the 1990s and operate in conjunction within the limitations imposed by the Privacy Act of 1993. Areas where cameras are set must be clearly posted. They are installed strategically in places where crime levels are higher than average, and apart from their crime-solving capacity, they are seen as an important deterrent to illegal activity.

Finally, there is a variety of police/public partnerships in New Zealand, by which citizens and police work together in monitoring their communities. The first is Neighborhood Watch and Neighborhood Support. Soaring burglary and car theft rates, particularly in the cities during the 1970s, resulted in a police initiative to establish a Neighborhood Watch scheme in October 1980. Neighborhood Watch involved formally organized information sharing and surveillance of properties among residents of suburban localities. To start the scheme off, police distributed 50,000 Neighborhood Watch kits, and within a few months, 30,000 households had joined. Four years later, following the horrific beating of television producer Robyn Scholes by a serial rapist in her Auckland home in 1983, a related scheme, initiated by citizens themselves, commenced. This was known as Neighborhood Support. Then in 1989, Rural Support began to provide community protection to rural dwellers. Since 1985, these schemes have collectively been known as Community Initiated Crime

Prevention and have proven highly effective in bringing neighbors together in the reporting and prevention of crime in residential areas, supported by local police. Currently, there are over 5000 community crime prevention groups in existence, and they are held partially responsible for the 40% drop in reported burglaries that have taken place since 1992 (Butterworth 2005; Dance 1986; McNaughton and Woodhouse 1986; Newbold 2000).

A second version of police/public partnerships is Community Patrols. Unlike Neighborhood Watch/Support, which deals primarily with homes in suburban areas, Community Patrols operate in both residential and commercial localities. Established in 2000, supported by police liaison officers and funded by charitable grants, patrols involve motorized surveillance of crime-prone districts by civilian volunteers in marked or unmarked cars equipped with radio communication. Usually operating at night, Community Patrols have no official authority to arrest, but, when organized properly, have the potential to reduce crime through deterrence, intelligence gathering, and the reporting of suspicious activity. Currently, there are about 200 patrols currently in existence, about 70 of which are affiliated to a national body known as Community Patrols of New Zealand. Although the concept of Community Patrols is sound, a study by Cooper (2004) found patrols to be poorly organized, badly monitored, and largely noncompliant with national reporting requirements. This contributed to low levels of public awareness of the patrols and to the likelihood that they are operating well below their effective potential.

Discussion and Conclusion

Since independent civil policing commenced in New Zealand in 1886, a community component has always existed, although traditional, reactive policing remained the focus of NZP activity for the first 100 years of its existence. Since about the mid-1980s, however, a preventive agenda has been increasingly developed to the point that today, community-based initiatives lie at the very heart of the country's policing strategy. The three main thrusts of community policing in New Zealand are in the areas of preventing youth crime, liaising with ethnic communities, particularly the Maori, and dealing with domestic violence.

The extent to which community-based initiatives have actually reduced crime is moot, and in any case, the effect is almost impossible to assess. We have said that community approaches to crime prevention have assisted reductions in burglary, for example, but this is only a partial explanation for the fall. Better security systems and the greater use of electronic commerce are also part of the picture—and notably, crimes of fraud and identity theft have correspondingly increased. Where indigenous crime is concerned, in spite of the considerable energy devoted to it, Maori offending levels have not diminished, and Maori representation in criminal gangs, domestic violence, and imprisonment remains extremely high (see, e.g., Newbold and Jeffries 2010; Taonui and Newbold 2011). In the domestic arena, levels of offending are difficult to measure, but family dispute callouts have certainly not fallen either.

We do not argue that community policing has been a failure. As police inspector Owen Dance (1986) has acknowledged, policing strategy is only one of many factors affecting crime rates, and nobody knows what crime levels would be if policing strategy was different. If creating public confidence and engendering positive relations with the public are any measure of success, then the community orientation of the NZP has produced a high dividend. Independent Citizens' Satisfaction Surveys conducted annually over the past 3 years have found consistently high levels of trust and confidence in the police, high levels of satisfaction with service delivery, and high agreement that the police are responsive to the needs of the community (New Zealand Police 2011b). Field observations conducted by the current authors confirm that the police's overall relationship with the general public is relaxed and amicable. Use of the term "mate" is commonly used in verbal interactions between police and citizens; the term "sir" is comparatively rare. The reason for this situation, we suggest, is that, in maintaining close links with the community and engaging actively with the concerns of everyday citizens, contemporary policing in New Zealand has minimized the authoritarian barriers often associated with uniformed law enforcement and successfully engaged with the rank and file of the New Zealand public.

References

Ayers-Counts, D. 1990, 'Domestic violence in Oceania: Conclusion.' *Pacific Studies Journal*, v.13 (3): 225–254. Special issue.

Butterworth, S. 2005, *More Than Law and Order: Policing a Changing Society, 1945–1992.* Dunedin, University of Otago Press.

Cooper, R. 2004, '*Roving Eyes and Ears,*' *Community Patrols of New Zealand: A Comparative Analysis.* Unpublished MA thesis in sociology, University of Canterbury, Christchurch.

Cross, J. and Newbold, G. 2010, 'Presumptive arrest in partner assault: Use of discretion and problems of compliance in the New Zealand Police.' *Australian and New Zealand Journal of Criminology,* v.43 (1): 51–75.

Dance, O. 1986, 'The police and community policing,' in N. Cameron and W. Young (eds.), *Policing at the Crossroads.* Wellington, Allen and Unwin/Port Nicholson Press.

Fergusson, D. and Lynskey, M. 1997, 'Physical punishment/maltreatment during childhood and adjustment in young adulthood.' *Child Abuse and Neglect,* v.21 (7): 617–630.

Hill, M. 1986, *In the Line of Duty: 100 Years of the New Zealand Police.* Auckland, Endeavour Press.

Hill, R. 1986, *Policing the Colonial Frontier: The Theory and Practice of Coercive Social and Racial Control in New Zealand, 1767–1867.* Wellington, NZ Government Printer.

Hill, R. 1989, *The Colonial Frontier Tamed: New Zealand Policing in Transition, 1867–1886.* Wellington, GP Books.

Hill, R. 1995, *The Iron Hand in the Velvet Glove: The Modernisation of Policing in New Zealand, 1886–1917.* Palmerston North, Dunmore/Department of Internal Affairs.

McNaughton, T. and Woodhouse, A. 1986, 'Neighbourhood Support Groups and their impact on community policing.' In N. Cameron and W. Young (eds.), *Policing at the Crossroads.* Wellington, Allen and Unwin/Port Nicholson Press.

New Zealand House of Representatives. 2011, Appendices of the Journals of the House of Representatives G.6 (AJHR G.6). Wellington, New Zealand Parliament.

Newbold, G. 2000, *Crime in New Zealand.* Palmerston North, Dunmore.

Newbold, G. 2004, 'The control of drugs in New Zealand.' In R. Hil and G. Tait (eds.), *Hard Lessons: Reflections on Governance and Crime Control in Late Modernity.* Hants, UK, Ashgate.

Newbold, G. 2007, *The Problem of Prisons: Corrections in New Zealand since 1840.* Wellington, Dunmore.

Newbold, G. and Cross, J. 2008, 'Domestic violence and pro-arrest policy.' *Social Policy Journal of New Zealand,* (33, March): 1–14.

Newbold, G. and Jeffries, S. 2010, 'Race, crime and criminal justice in Australia and New Zealand.' In A. Kalunta-Crumpton (ed.), *Race, Crime and Criminal Justice: International Perspectives.* London, Palgrave MacMillan.

Newbold, G. and Taonui, R. 2011, 'Gangs.' In J. Phillips (ed.), *Te Ara: The Encyclopedia of New Zealand*. Wellington, Ministry of Culture and Heritage. http://www.teara.govt.nz/en/gangs.

New Zealand Police. 2011a, 'Community policing: How we police in New Zealand.' Retrieved at https://www.police.govt.nz/service/community on January 11, 2012.

New Zealand Police. 2011b, 'Citizens' Satisfaction Survey: Final Report for 2010/2011 Fiscal Year (July 2010–June 2011).' Retrieved at https://www.police.govt.nz/service/community on January 11, 2012.

Straus, M., Gelles, R. and Steinmetz, S. 1980, *Behind Closed Doors: Violence in the American Family*. Garden City, NY, Anchor Press.

Taonui, R. and Newbold, G. 2011, 'Maori gangs.' In T. McIntosh and M. Mulholland (eds.), *Maori and Social Issues*. Wellington, Huia.

Taylor, T.J. and Winfree, L.T. 2005. 'Strangers in a not-so-strange land: A response to Goddard and Jaeger.' *Policing*, v.28 (4): 662–669.

Winfree, L.T. 2004. 'New Zealand Police and restorative justice philosophy.' *Crime and Delinquency* v.50 (2): 189–213.

Winfree, L.T. and Newbold, G. 1999, 'Community policing in the New Zealand Police: Correlates of attitudes toward the work world in a community-oriented national police organization.' *Policing* v.22 (4): 589–617.

Winfree, L.T. and Taylor, T.J. 2004. 'Rural, small town, and metropolitan police in New Zealand: Differential outlooks on policing within a unified police organization.' *Policing* v.27 (2): 241–263.

Yska, R. 1993, *All Shook Up: The Flash Bodgie and the Rise of the New Zealand Teenager in the Fifties*. Auckland, Penguin.

Philippines

22

RAYMUND E. NARAG

Contents

Background

The Philippines is located in Southeast Asia, where neighboring countries include Taiwan in the north, Vietnam in the west, Indonesia in the south, and the Pacific Ocean in the east. It is composed of three major islands (Luzon, Visayas, and Mindanao), but a total of 7107 islands compose the entire archipelago. The Philippines has a current population of 95 million people, making it the twelfth most populous country in the world. Filipinos speak eight major languages and 87 dialects, and English is also considered as an official language. The Philippines was colonized for more than 300 years (1565–1898) by Spain, where the elitist political, economic, and social system originated. The Philippines was also colonized for 48 years (1898–1946) by the United States, where the modern form of government was patterned. The country practiced self-governance after World War II until 1972, when strongman Ferdinand Marcos declared Martial Law. When Marcos was toppled through "People's Power" in 1986, succeeding governments had initiated efforts to redemocratize the Philippine political system. Among the agencies that were democratized was the Philippine National Police (PNP), which had been used as an adjunct of the Philippine Military.

In the following sections, this paper will provide a brief description of the formal characteristics of the PNP and the efforts to introduce community policing in the Philippines. It will then highlight the challenges of implementing community policing in light of the formal characteristics of the PNP and the Philippine sociocultural context. Given these challenges, the paper will highlight the *barangay tanod*, an indigenous form of policing that is consistent with the tenets of community policing.

Organizational Structure of PNP

The formal organizational structure of the PNP is characterized as unitary, centralized, and top-down (Pilar et al. 2010; Varona 2010).* There is only one overarching national organizational structure, where a national director presides over the 140,000-strong police personnel. Under the national director are national-level officers that are assigned particular administrative tasks. Below the national level office are 17 regional offices headed by regional directors supported by their respective staff. Under the regional offices are 79 provincial offices headed by provincial directors, with their corresponding line officers. Supervised by the provincial directors are the city or municipality police departments headed by their respective chiefs of police. The size of the city or municipal police departments depends on their population and economic classification. In bigger cities, the police departments could be subdivided into police precincts or police stations that correspond to a cluster of *barangays* (the smallest political-administrative unit in the Philippines). This organizational chart is similar for the 16 administrative regions, except for the National Capital Region, which is not composed of provinces but is instead composed of highly urbanized cities. In the National Capital Region, there are five police districts, where cities like Manila and Quezon City, with populations exceeding a million people, have their own police districts. Other cities are clustered to create three more police districts (De Guzman 2004).

This unitary, centralized, and top-down setup suggests that the different local police departments have more-or-less similar personnel systems and goal-setting mechanisms throughout the country (CPRM 2005). For example, there is one major academic and training center, the PNP Academy (PNPA), where most of the "commissioned" officers (with the rank of inspector and above) are educated and trained.† Graduates of the PNPA can be assigned to any geographical area of the country. A police officer from the northern part of the Philippines, who is an *Ilocano* (one of the eight major ethnolinguistic groups in the country), can be assigned to the southern part of the Philippines, where the major language spoken is *Bisaya*. In terms of personnel promotions, police officers can be transferred from one city, province, or region to another, depending on where the current vacancy is (CPRM 2005). Early in their careers, the commissioned police officers are also promoted at least every 3 years and, as such, could be regularly transferred to different localities to assume higher posts (CPRM 2005). Therefore, all the local city or municipal police departments experience the same leadership and personnel policies: these units could be headed by police superiors who gained experience from a unit other than their own (CPRM 2005).

Having a unitary, centralized, and top-down setup, the local police departments reflect the formal goals of the national leadership. These goals and priorities are developed by a cadre of national-level staff officers who are technically trained for this purpose (De Guzman 2004). These national "peace and order goals," as commonly referred to in the Philippines, are usually designed to support the long term economic and social goals set

---

* The unitary, centralized, and top-down character of the PNP could be directly traced from its historical origins as an adjunct of the Philippine Military (De Guzman 2004).
† The PNPA is under the Philippine Public Safety College (PPSC), which also provides training for the Jail and Fire Bureaus. "Noncommissioned" police officers are trained in the 17 Regional Training Centers of the Police National Training Institute (PNTI), which is also under the PPSC.

by the national government (CPRM 2005). The national director of the PNP can issue a directive to the lower units for them to adopt these identified goals and priorities.

Community Policing in the Philippines

Like many countries in the world, the Philippines has been receptive to the tenets of community policing (ICPC 2005). Police scholars and practitioners from the United States visited the country to share and train Filipino police officers on the philosophy, goals, mechanics, and administration of community policing. A number of Filipino police delegates had visited US local police departments to have a feel of what this new policing paradigm had to offer (US Department of State 2010).* The National Police Commission (NAPOLCOM), a civilian body overseeing the PNP, through its Technical Committee on Crime Prevention and Criminal Justice System, pilot-tested community policing in the city of Valenzuela, Metro Manila, to determine its viability in urban settings (ICPC 2005). International agencies like the National Democratic Institute (NDI), with funding assistance from the United States Agency for International Development (USAID), had also coordinated with local governments in Mindanao to determine its viability in the rural and far-flung areas (NDI 2006).† As a result of these exchanges and pilot activities, the PNP has incorporated the tenets of community policing in its statement of philosophy and national goals. In 1993, the PNP and the NAPOLCOM launched the Community Oriented Policing System (COPS) as the overarching guide to the National Strategic Action Plan (ICPC 2005). The PNP had also developed administrative structures within its rank to be the forefront in promoting community policing ideas and practices. Depending on their sizes, local police departments (municipality, city, and province) have standing Community–Police Action Center (COMPAC) offices (CPRM 2005). Additionally, community members were incorporated as overseers of police misconduct through the creation of the People' Law Enforcement Board (PLEB) in every police department (De Guzman 2004). The PNP had also incorporated community policing as a basic course that all new recruits had to undertake before becoming a police officer (CPRM 2005). It was proposed that advanced courses on community policing had to be undertaken by police officers aspiring for promotions (CPRM 2005). Finally, local governments (municipal, city, and province) were mandated by law to develop their own Integrated Area/Community Public Safety Plan (IA/CPSP) in cooperation with their corresponding police units (ICPC 2005).

As such, it can be said that the "formal elements" of community policing are present, in some form, in the Philippines. The rhetoric of community policing was echoed in the pronouncements of different Philippine presidents, from the time of President Corazon Aquino (1986–1992) (ICPC 2005) up until the current administration of President Benigno "Noynoy" Aquino, III. The Philippine legislature also endorsed community policing when it mandated that the PNP be transformed into a community- and service-based organization with the passage of the PNP Reform and Reorganization Act of 1998 (ICPC 2005).

---

* One recent example is the 3-week exposure trip of nine police officers from Sulu province, wherein they visited police departments in Virginia and New York as part of a program sponsored by the US Department of State.
† Police departments in three municipalities in the Autonomous Region for Muslim Mindanao (ARMM) were recipients of this project from 2002 to 2005.

The different national directors of the PNP also made references to the community policing as the desired philosophy and way of doing things in the PNP (Sanidad-Leones 2006). Civic organizations, especially those that clamor for better peace and order situations in the country, are also very vocal in their advocacy that community policing be fully implemented (Sanidad-Leones 2006).

Challenges to Community Policing

Despite the formal adoption of the structures and rhetoric of community policing in the PNP, community policing, as originally envisioned, has not been fully implemented. This paper identifies two of the reasons why there are roadblocks in implementing the ideals of community policing in the PNP. First, this paper explains how the structure of a unitary, centralized, and top-down administrative setup of the PNP discussed above (De Guzman 2004; Varona 2010) creates a considerable restraint with the localized, bottom-up conceptualization of community policing (Goldstein 1987; Peak and Glensor 2002; Trojanowicz and Bucqueroux 1998). As will be discussed, this limitation operates at the formal level of the bureaucracy. Second, and more importantly, the political culture of the patron–client relationship (Hutchcroft 1998; McCoy 2009; Sidel 1996, 1997, 1999) that so pervades the Philippine social system makes the bottom-up tenet of community policing vulnerable to exploitation. In contrast to the first limitation, this roadblock operates at the informal level. On the other hand, while the elements and rhetoric of community policing may not be fully attained in the policing structures of the PNP, a more indigenous structure, called the *barangay tanod*, roughly translated as *village watchmen*, may be more consistent with the philosophy, goals, mechanics, and administration of community policing. Though the *barangay tanod* was originally conceptualized as an instrument of Martial Rule (Rüland 1984; Varona 2010) and is not immune to the problems that beset the PNP (Austin 1988), it is more rooted to the community, thus offering a better potential (Austin 1995). As such, this paper will also highlight the unique attributes of this indigenous structure and argues that the future of community policing in the Philippines, if there is one, should be drawn upon this locally embedded structure.

Challenges from Formal Setup of PNP

The unitary, centralized, and top-down characteristic of the PNP poses considerable restraint to the realization of the tenets of community policing at the formal level. For example, community policing emphasizes that the police personnel should be familiar with the local community conditions in order to effectively communicate with the people (Goldstein 1987; Peak and Glensor 2002; Trojanowicz and Bucqueroux 1998). Community policing also emphasizes that the police, as a department, and the police officers, at an individual level, need to be able to identify the most pressing problems in the community (Goldstein et al. 1990). While this community policing rhetoric is formally adhered to by the local police departments, and well-meaning efforts are instituted to meet this imperative, as described above, still, the realities of a unitary setup pose unique hindrances. For one, the leaders of the police departments (chief of police and the line staff) usually do not rise from the ranks of the unit but rather enter the police departments "laterally" (CPRM

2005). The leaders of the police department are, by design, "newcomers" on the job. As such, the police leadership usually does not have a working knowledge of the conditions of the local jurisdictions that they are administering. Common feedback from police officers is that while they may have knowledge about the general peace and order problems like drugs and *jueteng* (illegal gambling) that beset some communities, the knowledge they developed usually comes from jurisdictions that are not similar to their current appointments (CPRM 2005; NDI 2006).* Additionally, the recurrent shuffling of commissioned officers, in which they are regularly transferred to their next assignments, usually in a different city, province, or region, as part of their system of promotions, indicates that they usually do not mature in their jobs (CPRM 2005). A usual complaint among commissioned officers is that by the time they have learned about the ins and outs of their current assignment, they are transferred to a new one (CPRM 2005). Finally, there may be an ethnolinguistic mismatch, wherein the commissioned police officers do not speak the language of the local population. As previously mentioned, *Ilocano*-speaking police officers can be assigned in non-*Ilocano* communities. Though English and Filipino (based on Tagalog) had been generally accepted as the language of government offices, including the police, the local population still manifests preference for police leaders whom they consider to be part of their own ethnolinguistic communities (CPRM 2005). Given these inherent mechanics in a unitary, centralized, and top-down setup, the police departments may be continually challenged to establish relationships with the local communities they are serving. Local community leaders, on the other hand, need to continually adapt to the leadership style of a newly installed chief of police, whom they assume will not be staying long in their current appointments (CPRM 2005). Finally, the formal programs that are comanaged with the community leaders are disrupted midway in their implementation once the police leaderships are assigned to their new jobs (CPRM 2005).

Community policing likewise advocates that the goals set by the police departments must be articulated with the active involvement of the community members (Goldstein 1987; Peak and Glensor 2002; Trojanowicz and Bucqueroux 1998). Community policing encourages the community members to have an active ownership of where the police department is headed. Having an ownership of these goals will increase the community members' stake and will likely empower them to fulfill their roles in the informal control of the community. Again, this community policing rhetoric is formally adhered to by the PNP. For example, the police–community relations offices conduct regular meetings with the community leaders and seek their inputs in setting the goals and priorities of the police departments. The local chiefs of the police departments are also "ex officio" members of community-based "councils," "boards," and "committees" that intend to integrate the police with other local government agencies and civic organizations.† However, the extent to which these formal inputs from the community generally become part of the actual local police department agenda is stifled by the unitary, centralized, and top-down setup. As mentioned, police goals and priorities are identified at the national level, and they simply trickle down to the local level. While some police departments may be able to tweak the nationally imposed goals to meet the needs of the local communities, the national goals

---

* These claims are generally anecdotal. However, these are generally acknowledged in the Philippine media.
† One such mechanism is the Peace and Order Council that is organized in every municipality, city, and province.

and priorities, with their attendant funding and personnel, still become the de facto goals and priorities. Additionally, the formal merit and promotion systems are tied with the accomplishments of the national goals (e.g., number of arrests per month), giving the local police personnel more pressure to achieve the nationally identified goals. Also, the pool of leadership of the PNP is concentrated to the commissioned officers, a class of personnel who are groomed to occupy national positions. By virtue of the higher posts they occupy in the local police department hierarchy, the achievement of the national goals is, by default, the priority. Finally, the adherence to the national goals, where the emphasis is usually on crime reduction, can turn the elements of community policing to suit the aims of traditional policing instead. There are instances where community-based initiatives, like the Neighborhood Crime Watch, has been used by some police departments in their efforts to round up petty thieves and drug users. The police used the community volunteers as spies, or in Filipino parlance, *aset*, to dismantle the local crime organizations (Sanidad-Leones 2006). Instead of empowering the community members in addressing the issues that cause crime (i.e., improving social relations among the residents, developing the community's collective efficacy), volunteers are put in the forefront of directly combating crime, or volunteers are pitted against members of the insurgent groups, thereby promoting a heightened sense of community vigilantism (Austin 1995; Kraft 2010; Kowalewski 1992).

It must be noted that this unitary, centralized, and top-down characteristic of the PNP operates at the formal level. While this characteristic is important in understanding how the formal structures of the PNP collide with the localized and bottom-up tenets of community policing, a more important political–cultural trait that operates at the informal level poses a greater challenge to community policing.

Challenges from Culture of Patron–Client Relationship

While the formally defined unitary, centralized, and top-down characteristic of the PNP runs in direct contrast to the localized and bottom-up tenets of community policing, the political culture of the patron–client relationship that so pervades the Philippine society, on the other hand, makes the localized and bottom-up tenet of community policing vulnerable to exploitation by some favored sectors. To have a better grasp of this dynamic, a brief description of the Philippine political culture is provided.

While the police agency and other government entities in the Philippines are unitary and centralized, it is continually preyed upon by socioeconomic elites whose power lies outside the government bureaucracy. Centuries of colonialism under Spain and the United States created an elitist socioeconomic class based initially on ownership of vast tracts of land (Agoncillo and Guerrero 1974; Constantino and Constantino 1978; Sidel 1996). This landowning class eventually diversified into manufacturing and service industries as the country became integrated into the global economy (Hutchcroft 1998). Most historians and political scientists attribute the longevity of this elitist class on its ability to capture governmental positions, the presidency and both houses of congress in particular, through the electoral contests (Kerkvliet 1995; Sidel 1996, 1997). Once a particular elite segment is in power, it would aspire to control the governmental bureaucracy by appointing individuals who are sympathetic to its interests. To maintain power, elite families from different regions and provinces forge alliances with other elite families (McCoy 2009). In the process, a hierarchy of elite power, as manifested by whether a family is national, regional, provincial, or municipal elite, emerges. For aspiring bureaucrats, appointment to desired governmental positions depends on the strength of the endorsement they can muster from the elites who are dominant in a particular jurisdiction. To be appointed as chief of police of a municipality, for example, a police officer needs the personalistic endorsement of a powerful politician, usually a town mayor, the congressperson, or a provincial governor (CPRM 2003; NCPAG 2006). Without this favored political backing, the most meritorious applicant usually will not be able to get the job. In exchange for this political endorsement, the appointees are indebted to their patrons and will serve their patrons while they are in power (Sidel 1996, 1997). This is not to say that all appointees work as a minion of the political patron, and there are individual variations in how appointees pay back the support. In general, however, the common expectation is that the appointees will remember the political favor initially given when intraelite struggles necessitate the appointees to take sides. For some appointees, it is beneficial to nurture their relationships with the political elites since they can be assured of support as they aspire to go up in the administrative hierarchy. As they climb higher on the administrative totem pole, they can also develop the careers of lower-level officers by serving as their patrons. In the process, they develop their own political base that could even propel them to higher positions. This political culture of the patron–client relationship, while used to describe the PNP, can equally be used to describe other organs of the Philippine bureaucracy, including the judiciary and the military institutions (Bakker 1997; Hernandez 2002). In general, while Philippine bureaucracy has the formal outward appearance of being unitary, centralized, and top-down, the political, economic, and cultural base dictates that its informal structure is decidedly localized and bottom-up.

Given this patron–client relationship, local elites can manipulate the tenets of community policing to forward their particularistic interests. For example, a local city mayor may groom an aspiring police officer to be the chief of the city police department. Despite the passage of the PNP law that instructs the police hierarchy to appoint only from those who are qualified, the endorsement of the city mayor usually counts as the more dominant criterion for appointment (CPRM 2005; NCPAG 2006; Varona 2010). Not adhering to the endorsement of the local elites does happen, and a growing number of professionalized police officials are clamoring for independence of the police from political meddling (CPRM 2005). However, most police officers still report that they cannot afford to lose the support of local politicians. For one, the local city mayor may withdraw financial support to the police department, which may hinder the police from performing their day-to-day tasks (CPRM 2005). More importantly, a police provincial director who sidesteps the endorsement of the city mayor may have his attention called by the provincial governor or district congressperson, who is an ally of the city mayor. The police provincial director may then risk the relationship he had with his own patrons. Upon appointment of a favored official, the local politicians may now use the police in the furtherance of their political interests. The local politicians may use the strong arm of the police to harass the business interests of their competitors (Sidel 1996, 1997). For example, they can order the police to shut down known illegal gambling, prostitution centers, and drug dens owned or operated by their competitors but, at the same time, instruct the police not to meddle in their own illegal activities. In some extreme cases, the police serve as the personal bodyguards or private armies of the local politicians (Quimpo 2009; Sidel 1996, 1997). While there is wide variation on the involvement of local politicians in illegal activities, and there is also a growing number of "enlightened politicians" who aspire to implement a clean and honest bureaucracy (Santos 2010), still, the widespread acceptance of the patron–client relationship ensures that the police are at the service of the local politicians.

If the bottom-up tenet of community policing is adhered to, a more intractable problem of patron–clientelism is likely to evolve. For example, in community policing, police officers are encouraged to exercise discretion in the beat to which they are assigned. Community policing assumes that every situation is unique and that police officers are given wide latitude in finding solutions to the problems that they face (Goldstein 1990). Community policing encourages police officers to tie up with the local community members and work closely in the identification of problems and implementation of solutions (Trojanowicz and Bucqueroux 1998). While this setup works favorably in social systems that are more or less based on merit and rule of law, these tenets exacerbate the problems associated with patron–clientelism. For example, as police officers mingle with the community, they are likely to be enticed by some community residents to exercise favor on their behalf. Local business may provide gasoline for transportation, food, and other resources to the individual police officers (CPRM 2003).* In exchange for these personalized favors, the police officers can offer their individual informal protection to the businesses from competitors or to turn a blind eye to their illegal activities (Sidel 1996). Thus, in the guise of community policing, the individual police officers may develop favored relationships with certain members of the community and serve as their patrons. In the process, individual police officers can develop a power base of their own, which can now challenge the formal police hierarchy. Errant individual police officers, known locally as *scalawags* (Moratalla 2000), who have deeply embedded themselves in the protection of illegal gambling, drug dealing, prostitution, and other criminal activities, are quite difficult to be disciplined by the formal mechanisms of the police hierarchy.

Given the acknowledged political culture of patron–clientelism, efforts to reform the PNP entailed the strengthening of the unitary setup, centralization of power, and unweaning of the police from the local politics (see generally the recommendations in the Action Program for Judicial Reforms [APJR] of the Philippine Supreme Court, CPRM 2003, 2005, 2006). Advocates of professionalism within the PNP push for the regular shuffling of the chiefs of police and other heads of department with the assumption that regular transfer would shield them from the corrupting influence of the local politicians. Advocates of professionalism also call for the strict adherence to formal procedures and the lessening, if not removal, of police discretion. In the sociocultural context of patron–clientelism, therefore, there is an inherent assumption that to professionalize the PNP, it must strengthen the formal elements of centralization and the top-down approach. As previously discussed, these formal elements of the bureaucracy also collide with the substantive tenet of community policing.

Barangay Tanod as Indigenous Form of Community Policing

The structure of *barangay* was initially created by the Marcos regime in 1973 to strengthen the hold of the dictatorship among the local populace (Austin 1988, 1995; Rüland 1984). In the early 1970s, a social movement in the cities and in the countryside that clamored for

---

* One of the acknowledged problems facing the PNP is the lack of financial resources provided to its personnel, which forces them to engage in corrupt practices (CPRM 2005; NDI 2006).

reforms against the elitist nature of Philippine polity was threatening to topple the Marcos government. The Marcos dictatorial government countered by creating the *barangay* (villages) as the lowest political and administrative level of the government and used it as the mechanism to enlist the support of local community leaders (Rüland 1984). Political analysts concede that this ploy had been largely successful: it tapped the Filipino attachment to the *barangay*, where a cultural and religious identity had been previously fostered by centuries of Spanish colonialism (Austin 1988). A *barangay* is usually composed of tightly knit extended families, with its own patron saint and *fiesta*. Additionally, local landowning elites embraced the creation of the *barangay* as it provided them with the structure to provide altruistic services to the "masses." The *barangay* served as a structure to win over the hearts of the masses that had been politicized by the social movements that demanded for land redistribution (Rüland 1984).

The *barangay tanod*, on the other hand, was created as the police auxiliary of the *barangay*. As previously noted, the formal police structure was organized only at the municipal or city level, where services were largely concentrated at the *centro* or municipal or city proper. As such, the police presence could rarely be felt at the *barangay* level. During the Marcos dictatorship, however, the *barangay tanods* served not only as a police auxiliary but also as the eyes and ears of the military against the activities of the insurgent communist groups operating in the rural and urban areas (Rüland 1984).

With the toppling of the Marcos dictatorship in 1986 and the democratization efforts of the Corazon Aquino administration (Yu 2005), the *barangay* structure was weaned of its repressive role. The *barangays* were reconceptualized to be the grassroots arms of the new government to provide basic services to the local population. In this structure, a town or city may be composed of 10 to 100 *barangays*, with a population averaging around 900 to 1500 residents. The *barangay* officers were popularly elected rather than appointed by the town or city mayors as practiced during the Marcos time. The *barangay tanods*, officially renamed as *barangay* security and development officers (BSDOs), were volunteers recruited from among the residents of the community (Sanidad-Leones 2006). In most cases, they were representatives of the families or clans living in the *barangay*. The *barangay* chairperson usually selects the members of the *barangay tanod* (Austin 1995). To become a *barangay tanod*, community volunteers have to undergo a brief training and orientation on their roles and functions as a police auxiliary. The number of *barangay tanods* depends on the size of the *barangay* but cannot exceed more than 20 in each *barangay* (Caparas 2000). In bigger *barangays*, the *tanods* could be subdivided into *puroks* or neighborhood blocks. Most *tanods* are provided with a *chaleko* or vest as a basic uniform. Some *barangays* have also introduced a small allowance, which ranges from Php100 to Php500 (US $2 to US $10) per month. *Barangay tanods* are also allowed to carry a *batuta* or nightstick, usually made of rattan. They can conduct *ronda* or night watch and question strangers and teenagers roaming the streets (Caparas 2000). They are the first to respond in cases of medical emergencies, floods, and other disasters. They also assist the *Lupon ng Tagapamaya* or Peace and Order Committee, a special committee under the *barangay*, which is tasked to mediate conflicts among residents. They can effect citizen arrests against those actually committing crimes (Sanidad-Leones 2006). In urban areas, they are deputized to manage the flow of traffic (Caparas 2000). In rural areas, the *barangay tanods* are usually called upon to control the behavior of local drunks (Austin 1995).

In its post-Marcos Martial Law form, the *barangay tanod* is more consistent with the philosophy, structure, administration, and mechanisms of community policing. They are more likely to generate support from the community residents due to their intertwining family and friendship networks (Austin 1995). Unlike the PNP, the *barangay tanods* are considered members of the community and thus are more likely to be trusted. They can serve as articulators of the needs and aspirations of the community residents. With their rootedness to the community, the *barangay tanods* are more knowledgeable about the crime situations that beset the *barangays*. Thus, the *barangay tanod* can be considered as localized and bottom-up in formal structure, a structure that corresponds to the tenets of community policing.

Conclusion

The future of community policing in the Philippines must therefore incorporate this local structure. The PNP must design ways in which it can incorporate the *barangay tanods* in its organizational setup. Currently, *barangay tanods* are managed exclusively by the *barangay* leadership, and they coordinate with the PNP only on an intermittent basis. For example, while some *barangay tanods* do receive training from the PNP (conducting patrol, mediating conflicts, dealing with drunks, etc.), this training depends on the individual initiatives of the *barangay* leaders and local chiefs of police. What is needed is a systematic and programmatic approach that will make these initiatives sustainable. Institutionalizing a relationship with the *barangay tanods* will maximize the rootedness of these volunteers to the community, enhancing the community policing philosophy in the PNP.

References

Agoncillo, T. A., & Guerrero, M. (1974). *History of the Filipino People*. Quezon City, Philippines: RP Garcia Pub. Co.

Austin, W. T. (1988). Field notes on the vigilante movement in Mindanao: A mix of self-help and formal policing networks. *International Journal of Comparative and Applied Criminal Justice*, *12*(1–2), 205–217.

Austin, T. (1995). Filipino self-help and peacemaking strategies: A view from the Mindanao hinterland. *Human Organization*, *54*(1), 10–19.

Bakker, J. W. (1997). *The Philippine Justice System: The Independence and Impartiality of the Judiciary and Human Rights from 1986 until 1997*. Leiden, The Netherlands: Leiden University.

Caparas, D. L. (2000). Participation of the public and victims for more fair and effective criminal justice administration in the Philippines. *Resource Material Series No. 56*, 241.

Constantino, R., & Constantino, L. R. (1978). *The Philippines: The Continuing Past*. Quezon City: Foundation for Nationalist Studies.

CPRM Consultants, Inc. (2003). *The Other Pillars of Justice through Reforms in the Department of Justice*. Manila: Supreme Court Press.

CPRM Consultants, Inc. (2005). *Transforming the Philippine National Police to a More Capable, Effective and Credible Police Force*. Manila: Supreme Court Press.

CPRM Consultants, Inc. (2006). *Conduct of Further Study on Operations and Linkages of the Five Pillars of Justice*. Manila: Supreme Court Press.

De Guzman, M. C. (2004). One for all? Philippine police officers' perceptions of civilian review. *Policing: An International Journal of Police Strategies and Management*, *27*(3), 358–379.

Goldstein, H. (1987). Toward community-oriented policing: Potential, basic requirements, and threshold questions. *Crime and Delinquency*, *33*(1), 6.

Goldstein, H., Goldstein, H., & Hill, M. G. (1990). *Problem-Oriented Policing*. New York: McGraw-Hill.

Hernandez, C. G. (2002). Restoring democratic civilian control over the Philippine Military: Challenges and prospects. *Journal of International Cooperation Studies*, *10*(1), 25–48.

Hutchcroft, P. D. (1998). *Booty Capitalism: The Politics of Banking in the Philippines*. Ithaca, New York: Cornell Univ Pr.

International Centre for the Prevention of Crime (ICPC). (2005). *Urban Crime Prevention and Youth at Risk: Compendium of Promising Strategies and Programmes from Around the World*. Bangkok, Thailand: UN-HABITAT.

Kerkvliet, B. J. (1995). Toward a more comprehensive analysis of Philippine politics: Beyond the patron–client, factional framework. *Journal of Southeast Asian Studies*, *26*(02), 401–419.

Kowalewski, D. (1992). Counterinsurgent paramilitarism: A Philippine case study. *Journal of Peace Research*, *29*(1), 71–84.

Kraft, H. J. (2010). The foibles of an armed citizenry: Armed auxiliaries of the state and private armed groups in the Philippines (overview). Soliman M. Santos, Jr. and Paz Verdades M. Santos. *Primed and Purposeful: Armed Groups and Human Security Efforts in the Philippines*. 185–212. Geneva, Switzerland: Small Arms Survey.

McCoy, A. W. (2009). *An Anarchy of Families: State and Family in the Philippines*. Madison: University of Wisconsin Press.

Moratalla, N. N. (1999). Graft and corruption: The Philippine experience. *Resource Materials Series*, (56), 503–504.

National College of Public Administration and Governance (NCPAG). (2006). *Medium-Term Development Plan for the Criminal Justice System (2007–2010)*. Manila: Supreme Court Press.

National Democratic Institute (NDI). (2006). Philippines: Promoting democratic governance and enhancing community–police relations in the autonomous region of Muslim Mindanao. http://pdf.usaid.gov/pdf_docs/PDACJ506.pdf.

Peak, K. J., & Glensor, R. W. (2002). *Community Policing and Problem Solving: Strategies and Practices*. Upper Saddle River, New Jersey: Prentice Hall. ISBN 0-13-091270-0, 480.

Pilar, N. N., Rebullida, M. L., Lopez, J. P., Mariano, M. G., Santos, G. M., & Honorio, F. F. (2010). Civilianization and community oriented policing in the Philippines. *Kasarinlan: Philippine Journal of Third World Studies*, *16*(2), 143–180.

Quimpo, N. G. (2009). The Philippines: Predatory regime, growing authoritarian features. *The Pacific Review*, *22*(3), 335–353.

Rüland, J. (1984). Political change, urban services and social movements: Political participation and grassroots politics in Metro Manila. *Public Administration and Development*, *4*(4), 325–333.

Sanidad-Leones, C. V. (2006). Effective preventive measures for youth at risk in the Philippines. *Resource Material Series*, (68–70), 151.

Santos, A. (2010). Putting People Power to work in Naga City. Philippine Public Transparency Reporting Project. http://www.transparencyreporting.net/index.php?option=com_content&view=article&id=88:putting-people-power-to-work-in-naga-city&catid=55:background-papers&Itemid=94.

Sidel, J. T. (1996). Siam and its twin?: Democratization and bossism in contemporary Thailand and the Philippines. *IDS Bulletin*, *27*(2), 56–63.

Sidel, J. T. (1997). Philippine politics in town, district, and province: Bossism in Cavite and Cebu. *Journal of Asian Studies*, *56*(4), 947–966.

Sidel, J. T. (1999). *Capital, Coercion, and Crime: Bossism in the Philippines*. Palo Alto, California: Stanford Univ Pr.

Trojanowicz, R. C., & Bucqueroux, B. (1998). *Community Policing: How to Get Started*. Cincinnati, Ohio: Anderson Pub Co.

U.S. Department of State. (2010). Country assistance strategy Philippines: 2009–2013. http://pdf.usaid.gov/pdf_docs/PDACN452.pdf.

Varona, G. (2010). Politics and policing in the Philippines: Challenges to police reform. *Flinders J History and Politics*, *26*,101–125.

Yu, S. C. K. (2005). Political reforms in the Philippines: Challenges ahead. *Contemporary Southeast Asia*, *27*(2), 217–235.

South Korea*

WOOK KANG
MAHESH K. NALLA

23

Contents

Background

Korea is situated on the Korean Peninsula, which is in the northeastern section of Asia, surrounded by China, Japan, and Russia, and spans 700 mi. from north to south. The Korean Peninsula exits to the Pacific Ocean and to China and Russia, while it is the entrance to the Asian continent and to Japan. Although Korea withstood thousands of invasions over centuries, it was annexed to Japan as a colony in 1910. At the end of World War II (1945), Korea was liberated from Japan and the United States, and the Soviet Union decided to divide the Korean Peninsula into two parts: north and south. The Republic of Korea (ROK) was established in the southern half of the Korean Peninsula under the supervision of the United States, while a Communist-style government was established in the north by the Soviet Union, both in 1945. In 1950, North Korea (Democratic People's Republic of Korea [DPRK]) invaded South Korea (ROK) in an attempt to unify the Korean Peninsula. The United States and United Nations' forces intervened to protect South Korea from North Korean attacks, which were supported by China and the Soviet Union. An armistice was signed in 1953, splitting the Korean Peninsula along a demilitarized zone around the thirty-eighth parallel.

Confucianism, which is generally emphasized in eastern cultures, is strongly inculcated throughout Korean society (Kim 2007; Yang and Rosenblatt 2008). The central tenets of Confucianism are that individuals respect older people and seek harmonious relationships with others. Confucianism led to a vertical social structure, which emphasizes harmony among members and obedience to government authority. In addition to Confucianism, Koreans have maintained their unique language and characters with one ethnicity (Hangul).

The first specific police unit (Podo-Cheong) was created in the early Yi Dynasty (mid-fourteenth century). The Podo-Cheong worked similarly to the entire criminal justice sector as we know it today: they arrested criminals, sentenced them, and jailed them. The modern police (Kyungmu-Cheong) was established in 1894 (the late Yi Dynasty) under

---

* In this chapter, we use the terms South Korea and Korea interchangeably.

the direct control of the Ministry of Home Affairs (Lee 1990). The Kyungmu-Cheong was replaced with the Bureau of Police Affairs at the beginning of the Japanese occupation in 1910. During the 35 years of Japanese occupation, the Korean police was strongly centralized and nationalized, and its primary focus was the surveillance of citizens and the suppression of antioccupation activities (Lee 1990). Although Korea became independent from Japan in 1945, Korean police continued their highly centralized and authoritative policing style (Hwang 2008). They also interfered with the political process by manipulating various elections in the 1960s and were served by undemocratic and authoritative regimes in the 1970s and 1980s (Moon 2004). In 1991, with the enactment of the Police Act, the Korea National Police Agency (KNPA) was established in order to move the police out of the jurisdiction of the Ministry of Interior, which was also directly responsible for administration of national elections (Pyo 2000).

Administratively, the KNPA is an apex bureaucracy that oversees 16 regional police agencies (state police). There are a total of 248 police departments and 1,940 police substations (beats or Koban) spread throughout the entire country. Each state or regional police agency supervises anywhere from three to 41 police departments. The three levels of Korean police hierarchy (i.e., police headquarters, state police agency, local police department) enable the chief of Korean police to have an influence on all police officers (101,108 sworn officers, with 6.8% of them women).

Origins of Community Policing in Korea

The Korean police introduced community policing in 1999 as one of the many reform measures designed as part of what is referred to as the Grand Reform. The goal of the Grand Reform was to bring fundamental changes to police practices and cultures as well as to improve relations with citizens. The key units of community policing are police substations, which come under the direct control of the local police departments. A police substation (substation herewith) is a branch office of a police department. The number of substations for each police department ranges from five to 15 depending on the size of the community in which it is located. Each police substation has its own precinct and assigned area for patrols. Patrol officers work at substations, and they establish contact with citizens by visiting their homes (Hwang 2008). In general, about 20 to 40 officers are assigned to each substation. Officers are organized into three squads that cover two shifts per day. Each substation is supervised by an officer holding the rank of lieutenant or captain, which is determined by the size of the unit. Each police substation has several offices and a conference room that sometimes serves as a meeting place with community residents.

Ironically, substations were introduced by the Japanese during their occupation of Korea in 1910 and were primarily used for monitoring citizens to detect anti-Japanese activities (Hwang 2008). Japanese substation officers visited homes in their precinct for information gathering and surveillance purposes under the pretext of administering security surveys. While in principle, community policing was introduced by the Japanese, the underlying rationale was to achieve greater citizen compliance and social control, which was accomplished through the insidious practice of "eyes and ears" with and among local citizens. In Korea, all regional police agencies and local police departments conducted community policing under the direction of the KNPA, and their motives were not driven by the local community's needs. In addition, the Korean police did not establish special units for community policing but instead conducted community policing in various places around the country.

How Does Community Policing Work?

Korea is a largely homogenous culture with a single ethnicity, and most of its people share common Confucian values. In a Confucian society, moral order and ethics are very important, and they are preserved by community leaders who are mostly elders within their community. Misdemeanors are regulated through informal justice mechanisms. For instance, if a teenager is caught stealing, he or she and the parents are expected to admit the transgression in front of community members instead of reporting the crime to police.

The cooperation of patrol officers with community leaders is a very important element of community policing. The chiefs of substations meet community leaders in their precinct regularly to seek their cooperation. Although the rapid development of an economy can lead to the collapse of the traditional community in cities, a community leader's role is still considered critical. Meeting with community leaders is an effective way to disseminate the goals of community policing. These meetings are modeled along the lines of a beat meeting in the United States and are attended by patrol officers on duty along with some team members from other shifts, detectives from the police departments, and the chief of police for the substation. On occasion, the chief of the police department attends the meeting to receive the opinions directly from the residents. According to the KNPA (2004), in 2003, there were 20,088 community meetings attended by 155,600 citizens.

Substations located in cities hold some meetings on weekends to accommodate the schedules of working residents. Neighborhood crimes and other law and order issues that affect residents and businesses dominate discussions in the urban substations, while rural substations focus on crimes against the environment or crimes involving safety issues. With the aid of local media, substations announce community meetings in advance and encourage community members to attend these meetings. Meeting outcomes are shared with the local police departments as well as with the community. When issues emerge that have implications for other jurisdictions in the area, neighborhood members from other communities are invited to attend as well.

Police leaders consider officers' contact with residents as one of the core aspects of community policing. The introduction of community policing in 1999 also brought about a change in car patrolling strategies. Traditional car patrolling in Korea requires police officers to patrol their beat all day. However, in community policing, officers are required to patrol 40 minutes and then park their patrol car in an appropriate area. During the remaining 20 minutes, officers walk around and chat with local residents, and they are not limited to conversation relating to crime concerns.

The Korean police also conduct citizen surveys twice a year to assess citizens' perceptions of community concerns and satisfaction with police service. Police departments have used the feedback from these surveys to improve the quality of police service. In addition, the KNPA established Customer Satisfaction Centers (CSCs) in 2008. The CSCs call citizens on a random basis and interview them about their levels of satisfaction on various dimensions of police work. Survey results, which were organized as part of a joint effort by citizens and officer foot patrols (KNPA 2004), suggest that there is support for foot patrols as a component of community policing programs (Jaegal and Chang 2005).

In addition to activities such as the community meetings organized by substations, local police departments organize and conduct citizen police academies. These programs are conducted for a duration of 6 weeks, and participants receive certificates upon completion (KNPA 2004). Participants receive 3 hours of orientation one evening each week on topics that include basics of criminal law, criminal procedure, and patrol tactics. They participate in a ride-along with an officer and meet other officers such as patrol officers and detectives. The average class size is about 30 citizens. Admission to a citizen police academy requires a formal written application followed by a background check for any prior criminal record.

As noted earlier, historically, Korean police worked in isolation as an extension of the government in protecting state interests. As part of the community policing efforts, Korean police have recognized the need to build partnerships not only with the private sector but also with other government agencies. Consequently, Korean police created special units that systematically built partnerships with local fire departments, city governments, schools, and district prosecutors as partners in their community policing initiatives (KNPA 2002). The members meet every month to discuss and solve community problems. As in the case of the community meetings described above, the proceedings from the meetings with various community partners are shared with the local police departments, who in turn share these proceedings with the police headquarters. Information from these meetings is collated and analyzed at the police headquarters by combining it with additional data on local crime rates that the headquarters compiles to identify areas of concern, referred to as "hot spots." Based on these efforts, in 2009, a total of 598 areas were designated as hot spots (KNPA 2010) with some of these hot spots involving properties vulnerable to arson. In such instances, the local police department seeks cooperation with the local fire departments and holds a special-units meeting. Other examples of decisions made by special units created by the KNPA (2010) as a consequence of community policing efforts relate to school safety. Where school safety concerns are prominent, school principals are included in the monthly meetings and may be encouraged to hire more private security guards.

Community Policing Mandates

Foot patrol is one of the primary strategies adopted by the Korean police as part of the community policing mandate. Historically, foot patrol was conducted until the 1970s because before then, many areas could not be accessed by car. By the 1980s, new transportation infrastructure provided access to the most remote areas in the country. Principles of police effectiveness, as measured by the speed at which the police arrive at a crime scene, were popular in the United States and other developed countries and became popular in Korea as well. Consequently, Korean police placed more emphasis on car patrols as they enable officers to arrive at a crime scene more quickly. The efficacy of foot patrol as an important ingredient in many experiments in urban America gave much impetus to its reintroduction as part of Korea's community policing strategy. Further, it has been well established in research in the United States that foot patrol officers can improve the relationship with community members, while motorized officers have difficulty communicating with individuals (Skogan and Roth 2004). In addition and as noted earlier, research in Korea also established that citizens are supportive of foot patrols as they give the people easy access to the police (Jaegal and Chang 2005). As part of their foot patrol program, the Korean police organized citizen patrol units. Citizen patrol units consist of volunteer residents who, along with officers from the substation, conduct foot patrol with police officers, especially during the night shifts. As local members are more familiar with the more vulnerable areas of a community and know more of the local residents personally, these joint foot patrols have been found to be very effective. In 2006, there were 3889 citizen patrol units with an active participation of approximately 98,000 citizens, and it yielded 2964 arrests (KNPA 2007).

Second, another community policing mandate was to improve police response to citizen calls. Toward this end, the Korean police 911 call system was redesigned in 2009 in order to achieve a greater efficiency. This was the direct result of suggestions that came out of citizen surveys that revealed residents' dissatisfaction with delayed response times to crime scenes. In general, police officers are routinely dispatched to all calls irrespective of the degree of seriousness. However, as a result of the redesigned 911 call system, calls are now classified into three categories: (1) "emergency" for instances of violent crime (e.g., robbery, murder); (2) "general call" (e.g., misdemeanor); and (3) "noncrime related" (e.g., flat tire). Such modifications in the 911 calls resulted in a more efficient deployment of officers. In 2009, the new 911 call system was supplemented with Instant Dispatch System (IDS) to reduce dispatch time. In addition, global positioning systems (GPSs) and navigation devices were installed in all patrol cars; the locations of all patrol cars appear on an electronic map in the 911 report center and aid the dispatcher in dispatching calls that will have the best response times.

Third, the KNPA established the Night and Holiday Civil Petition Center throughout the country on 6 May 2008. One result from the citizen surveys noted that many citizens at meetings at the police substations complained about the inability of being able to obtain documents from local police departments. Local police departments issue several documents such as driver's license renewals and proof of stolen properties or traffic accidents. The division that issues those documents used to operate from 9 AM to 6 PM on weekdays, but residents now can receive documents at any time because the center currently operates 24 hours a day, 7 days a week.

Lastly, there was a change in traffic management from what was referred to as control-oriented traffic to field-centered traffic control in 2009. Control-oriented traffic focuses on strict enforcement of traffic rules with little or no discretion left to officers about whether to issue a citation or not. Under this style of traffic management, officers are required to offer no leeway for violators to explain themselves or to be able to only issue a warning to drivers. Field-centered traffic control, on the other hand, differs in its style. Traffic officers are dispatched to high-traffic areas at specific times to alleviate traffic congestion and prevent traffic accidents. Officers are given more leeway to either issue traffic citations or allow motorists to move on with a warning if the situation warrants it. This style of policing not only minimizes traffic hold up but also promotes more positive feedback from citizens.

Effectiveness of Community Policing

A comprehensive evaluation of community policing has not been conducted in Korea (Kim 2009). While the KNPA conducts citizen surveys twice a year, it is not one of its purposes to evaluate community policing. Despite a lack of systematic research, it is clear that citizens are more satisfied with the police since the implementation of community policing, as noted in the work of Jaegal and Chang (2005) cited above. Meetings with residents in substations, citizen police academies, citizen patrol units, and other community policing programs appear to have had an impact on citizen–police relations in many communities (KNPA 2007). In addition, through close participation in these programs, citizens appear to have more trust and less fear of police because they have a better understanding of how police work. One participant of a citizen police academy gave his impression of police when he graduated the academy:

> My image of police was shaped to a large extent when I witnessed police brutality in my child-hood. Since then, police remind me of violence and injustice. I was hesitant to participate in Citizen Police Academy due to my negative police image. The six weeks program changed my image of the police totally. I could understand through participation in the Citizen Police Academy how hard police officers work. I realized that police are here to protect us not to exploit. (KNPA 2007, pp. 85–86)

Police officers also have a positive attitude toward community policing. A survey of Korean police officers who attended training courses at the Korea National Police University and Police Comprehensive Academy (PAC) in 2008 suggested that they not only understand the concept of community policing but are also supportive of community policing activities (Nalla and Kang 2010). The reward structure for community policing involves incentives such as promotion and influences officers' attitudes. Moreover, officers often experience citizens' support and trust.

Despite the named benefits of community policing, there are also some concerns. First of all, the citizens' participation rate, a key factor for the successful implementation of community policing, is low. To some extent, citizen reluctance to participate in community policing programs is shaped by their imagery of past police brutality. In addition, there appears to be a limited number of incentives for volunteer citizen participation. For instance, citizen patrol units conduct night patrols for a 3- to 4-hour duration. Officers on the night shift can rest during the day, but citizen volunteers regularly have to go to work. Second, criteria for the evaluation of community policing have not been established. The KNPA has criteria to evaluate officers' performance in community policing, and as a result of these evaluations, the top three officers are promoted. However, some officers disagree with the established criteria for officer evaluations, and this leads to some officers resisting community policing. Last, frequent transfers of officers to other regions, a function of centralized police administration, weaken their relationships within communities. In general, police officers are transferred to other police departments when they get promoted or are disciplined. Moreover, the chief of the police station has the power to transfer police officers when it is deemed necessary. The frequent transfers make it difficult to build strong and sustained relationships with communities. Recently, the KNPA has started encouraging officers to work at one police department and allowing its officers with good evaluations to stay at their police departments even though they are promoted.

Conclusion

In this chapter, we explored community policing in Korea, from its background to many of its various programs. The introduction of community policing in 1999 was indispensable for the Korean police to acquire public support and legitimacy, and over 10 years later, community policing in Korea appears to be successful. Many community policing programs are conducted well, and citizens' satisfaction with police has increased. However, more systematic approaches for evaluating community policing are necessary. Kim (2009) indicated that studies on community policing have been descriptive and superficial. Empirical and comprehensive research is needed. In addition, Confucianism influences Korean society as well as the police. Future research should also address the extent to which Confucianism impacts the implementation of community policing. Though limited, research shows some modest improvements in this regard, but unfortunately, given the tainted history of Korean police that followed on the heels of Japanese police brutality, modern Korean police still have an uphill battle to garner citizens' acceptance and cooperation.

References

Hwang, E. (2008). Determinants of job satisfaction among South Korean police officers: The effect of urbanization in a rapidly developing nation. *Policing: An International Journal of Police Strategies and Management* 31(4): 694–714.

Jaegal, D., and Chang, S. (2005). The role of police for the successful implementation of community policing. *Korean Association of Public Safety and Criminal Justice Journal* 20: 415–447.

Kim, H. (2007). A party for the spirits: Ritual practice in Confucianism. In *Religions of Korea in Practice*, ed. R.E. Buswell. Princeton, NJ: Princeton University Press, pp. 163–176.

Kim, S. (2009). A content analysis of community-oriented policing researches in Korea. *Journal of Korean Police Studies* 8(4): 35–62.

Korea National Police Agency (KNPA). (2002). *Korean Police Annual Report.* Seoul, Korea: KNPA.

Korea National Police Agency (KNPA). (2004). *Korean Police Annual Report.* Seoul, Korea: KNPA.

Korea National Police Agency (KNPA). (2007). *Korean Police Annual Report.* Seoul, Korea: KNPA.

Korea National Police Agency (KNPA). (2010). *Korean Police Annual Report.* Seoul, Korea: KNPA.

Lee, S. (1990). Morning calm, rising sun: National character and policing in South Korea and in Japan. *Police Studies* 13: 91–110.

Moon, B. (2004). The politicization of police in South Korea: A critical review. *Policing: An International Journal of Police Strategies and Management* 27(1), 128–136. doi:10.1108/13639510410519958.

Nalla, M.K., and Kang, W. (2010). Police officers perceptions of community policing in South Korea: The influence of rank and organizational characteristics. *Annual Meetings of the American Society of Criminology.* San Diego, CA: ASC.

Pyo, C. (2000). Policing in Korea—The past, present and future. *The 1st Asian Association of Police Studies.* Seoul, Korea: AAPS.

Skogan, W.G., and Roth, J.A. (2004). Introduction of community policing. In *Community Policing: Can it Work?* ed. W.G. Skogan, xvii–xxxiv. Belmont, CA: Wadsworth/Thomson.

Yang, S., and Rosenblatt, P.C. (2008). Confucian family values and childless couples in South Korea. *Journal of Family Issues* 29: 571–591.

Thailand

24

SUTHAM COBKIT (CHEURPRAKOBKIT)

Contents

Background

Thailand, officially the Kingdom of Thailand and formerly known as Siam, is a country located in Southeast Asia. With a total land area of 513,115 km^2 (198,120 mi.^{2}), Thailand's size is equivalent to that of France and California in the United States. Thailand is the world's twentieth largest country in terms of population, with an estimated 67 million people in 2009. There are 76 provinces in Thailand. Bangkok is the capital city and has the largest population of about 9.6 million people, followed by Nakhon Ratchasima (about 2.6 million) and Chiang Mai (about 1.6 million). The terrain of the country varies according to the provincial groups. The north of the country is mountainous, while the northeastern part is plateau. The central region is predominately flat in the Chao Phraya river valley that connects to the Gulf of Thailand. The southern region consists of the narrow isthmus, which joins the land mass of Malaysia. The main local climate is tropical and characterized by monsoons.

Although established in the mid-fourteenth century, Thailand (then Siam) was recognized as a nation in 1783. It began diplomatic exchanges with the United Kingdom in 1826 and with the United States in 1833, the time period when European colonization invaded most countries in Southeast Asia. However, Thailand was the only country to avoid being colonized by a European power. This is reflected in the name "Thailand," which means the land of freedom. The official language of Thailand is Thai, and Buddhism is its national religion, with approximately 93% of the people being Buddhist, 5% Muslim, and 2% other. Buddhist temples are commonplace in Thailand, and they help serve several important purposes, including a place to hold social gatherings and spiritual and ceremonial occasions and, in the old days, for people's education. Thailand uses the Buddhist Era–based calendar, which is 543 years ahead of the standard Western calendar; therefore, the year AD 2013 is 2556 BE in Thailand.

As for its economy, Thailand is mainly an agricultural country with a high percentage of arable land that is used for rice production. Thailand is the world's number 1 exporter of rice. Other major exports include textiles and footwear, fishery products, rubber, corn, sugarcane, coconuts, computers, and electrical appliances. Tourism revenues are on the rise. In 2010, the gross domestic product (GDP) was about $317 billion, with an annual growth rate of 7.8% and per capita income of $4716.

The Royal Thai Police (RTP) is highly paramilitary and centralized. The RTP employs about 240,000 police officers (in 2007); 40,000 are commissioned officers whose ranks range from police sublieutenant to police general; the others are noncommissioned officers with a rank of police sergeant and below. The police–citizen ratio is about 1 to 260. The RTP consists of 29 police bureaus organized into the general staff, the technical and support, and the operation units. The key bureaus that interact directly with citizens are the Bangkok Metropolitan Police Bureau and nine provincial police bureaus, which are responsible for 1500 police stations nationwide. According to the RTP Human Resources Bureau (2004), the duties of the Thai police are (1) to provide the security of Their Majesties the king and queen; (2) to maintain order and peace within the country; (3) to protect security of life and property of citizens; (4) to prevent and suppress crime; and (5) to conduct operational duties stated in the criminal code and other related laws.

It is important to note that at present, the RTP has not yet fully adopted and integrated the community-oriented policing (COP) philosophy into police practice. Almost all police programs and activities with the people in the community can be considered as police–community relations (PCR), with the goal of creating good rapport with the public. The effort to fully implement the COP program took place once as a pilot study by former police chief Pongpat Chayapun of Bang Khunnon Police Station in Bangkok in 1996. The preliminary results of the study were satisfactory, but the program was discontinued after Chief Chayapun resigned. However, the RTP (via Police Commissioner Chayapun of the Central Investigation Bureau) has recently exerted efforts to institutionalize the COP philosophy and practice to all police agencies to give police officers guidelines and directions in implementing the COP strategy.

Thai lawmakers envision the essence of COP that emphasizes a working and trusting relationship between the police and the citizens in order to find innovative ways to solve and prevent crime and disorder when they drafted the Thai Constitution of 2007. Under the law and justice section, Article 81(1) states that the government must ensure justice to all people, and it must educate people about the law, perform all public duties in an efficient and effective manner, and allow the citizens and other professionals to participate in the justice system. Under the people participation section, Article 87(3) states that the government must encourage and support the participation of citizens in reviewing and monitoring the exercise of government authority at every level.

Origin of Community Policing in Thailand

COP is a new policing concept in Thailand, and most Thai police officers oftentimes misconstrue the concept as PCR (Chayapun 2011). In its effort to combat crime and disorder and build trust in the community, the RTP in 1988 developed the PCR policy in which the main objective was to cultivate good relationships between the police and the citizens. Although the RTP issued the PCR policy for all the police stations to implement, it did not provide clear and detailed steps or guidelines for police officers to follow.[*] The police

---

[*] While working as a deputy inspector at a police station in Bangkok in 1988, the author was ordered by the police chief to visit households within the jurisdiction two times a week in order to get to know the people as much as possible and create good rapport with them. Particularly, for each household, the author was advised to learn about the members of each family, their names, the types of vehicles and businesses they had, and their safety and crime concerns in their communities.

stations did not assign any officers to the PCR division. There was no program evaluation to measure the impact of the PCR program on crime or people's perceptions toward the police.

Although the origin of the PCR practice in Thailand is unclear, the initiative of the COP program was found to have originated in 1995, when the RTP announced its move toward adopting and implementing the COP philosophy (RTP 1995). The Royal Police Cadet Academy sent several police instructors to the National Center for Community Policing located on the Michigan State University campus, with the main goal of learning about the COP idea and incorporating it into the academy's curriculum for police cadets to study (Chayapun 2011). However, despite the mandate and plan to embrace COP into the training curriculum and, later on, police practice, the effort has not been implemented systematically or strategically. The curriculum change that reflects the adoption of the COP program can be considered superficial at best. As Singhsilarak and Cheurprakobkit (2007) stated, even though the RTP has directed all police agencies to emphasize the COP program in order to enhance a close working relationship between the police and the citizens to prevent and solve crime problems, the police training curriculum does not at all reflect the initiative.[*] Singhsilarak and Cheurprakobkit (2007, p. 67) concluded that, "The lack of such curricular changes indicates not only the failure to evaluate the program, but, more importantly, the lack of interest and concern in the programs from high-ranking police officials who could have easily initiated the assessment process."

In addition to the curriculum issue, the values and norms of the policing organization are also not conducive to the changing role of the police to be more service oriented, especially from the bottom-up perspective. The traditional role of police as crime fighting agents has been perpetuated by the reluctance on the part of police executives to change the status quo. The power of authorities and the paramilitary structure have silently subdued the voices of new ideas and the initiatives of educated thoughts from either midmanagement or front-line officers. This problem is mirrored by the finding of Puthpongsiriporn's (2004) study, which revealed that the majority of Bangkok metropolitan police officers did not believe that the RTP has the strong service culture needed for the success in implementing the COP program.

Despite the challenges and difficulties in fully implementing the COP program, most police stations, particularly in big cities, do embrace some COP ideas in their policy and practice. Dr. Purachai Piumsomboon, a former Thai police officer and a well-known police scholar, was the first to talk about Robert Trojanowicz's definition of COP and encourage the RTP to adopt the concept and put it into effect. As a result, police agencies in Thailand have developed and implemented a number of COP-related programs, including the following:

- The mobile police station
- Citizen input box
- The citizen patrol program
- The citizen household visit program
- Citizen review boards[†]

---

[*] Review of the recent program curricula of the Royal Police Cadet Academy showed inconsistent results, ranging from the absence of the community policing course to offering only the PCR course.

[†] Citizen review boards in Thailand differ from those in the United States in that the former review and monitor all police operations and management, while the latter review the investigation of complaints by members of the public regarding police misconduct.

First Community Policing Program: Bang Khunnon Police Station Model

Police Commissioner Pongpat Chayapun of the Central Investigation Bureau has been considered one of the most progressive police leaders in Thailand who has envisioned the quality of police service and law enforcement that the Thai police can and must deliver to the people they serve. Having received police training and education from various institutions both in Thailand and from overseas and having written several books on the fundamentals of crime investigation and investigation techniques, Chayapun has realized the increased importance of ever-changing advanced technology and tried to learn and apply such scientific knowledge and technical know-how to solve cases with more validity and accuracy. For example, during his tenure at the Crime Suppression Division, Chayapun created the Behavior Analysis Center to assist police investigators in solving cases using new technologically advanced techniques. Another good characteristic of Chayapun as a leader is his ability to teach and willingness to share his learned knowledge and skills with others.

After its modern roots in 1980s in the United States, the COP philosophy and practice have become popular in countries in many continents, including Asia. Chayapun learned about the paradigm shift in police macrostrategy in many countries, especially the United States, from traditional policing (being reactive to crime problems) to COP (being proactive to crime problems and neighborhood disorder). He also recognized the limited impact of the existing PCR programs in Thailand on crime problems. A key distinction between the PCR and the COP programs is the perception of the police officers. That is, to many Thai police officers, the PCR program is merely, as the program's name suggests, knowing and connecting with the people, and is not part of the crime prevention strategy. Chayapun (2011), then a police executive at the Bang Khunnon Police Station, learned about the potential benefits and advantages that COP has over the old traditional policing strategy and the PCR programs, and he decided to put the COP theory into practice for the first time as an experimental project.

The COP project implemented at the Bang Khunnon Police Station has the following characteristics (Chayapun 2011):

- The COP project was initiated by the assistance and with advice from several Thai police experts and international policing scholars and practitioners whose knowledge and experience helped to ensure that the development and implementation of the project were in line with the COP theory.
- The target area for the COP project was the Wat Bang Khunnon community, which is a community of about 230 households with approximately 1300 people.
- The Wat Bang Khunnon community was selected as the research site because of its optimal and manageable size. In the past, the community was plagued with several serious issues, including drug problems, gambling, robbery, burglary, and theft.
- The police station recruited two officers to be community policing officers (CPOs): Officer Trirung Boonchuay and Officer Wijarn Puthsiri. Therefore, Officers Boonchuay and Puthsiri were the first two CPOs in Thailand. Because there is confusion among police officers between the PCR and the COP programs, Chayapun has coined the term "community-serving officers (CSOs)" for those officers implementing the COP project.

- The project lasted 183 days starting from 31 May and ending on 30 November 1996.
- The two officers received training so that they would know about the history and philosophy of community policing.
- Before the project started, a survey study was conducted to learn about the Wat Bang Khunnon community and its members. The findings helped the police station and the officers involved in the project better prepare for the project and make it a success.
- A temporary house was provided for the two CSOs to stay in during the duration of the project.
- The CSOs' house was equipped with a telephone, a fax machine, and a computer for efficient communication with the main police station.
- While the project was in progress, the CSOs were supposed to stay and be a part of the community. The CSOs had four major roles while in the community: (1) educating people in the community about the COP philosophy and its impacts on crime and community disorder; (2) working with the members in the community to learn about criminal activities and their other concerns, the history of the community, and the behaviors and routines of community residents; (3) helping and working with the people on activities that would be beneficial to the crime prevention effort, such as neighborhood watch programs; and (4) regularly educating people and making them aware of their roles in protecting and preventing themselves from being victims of personal and property crimes.
- Program evaluation (i.e., a quasiexperimental study) would be conducted to measure the impact of the program intervention on crime and the community members' perceptions.

The effectiveness of the Bang Khunnon Model was also evaluated as planned, but not scientifically. Therefore, it is difficult to generalize the study's findings. A postproject interview study was conducted by three graduate students with 20 convenience samples from the community. There was no comparison group in the study nor was there preexamination and postexamination. Tape recorders and video cameras were used during the interviews. The interviewer asked each of the samples a set of eight open-ended questions, and the findings were very positive. The summary of the data is shown in Table 24.1.

Based on the comments from the table, it appears that the implementation of the COP program by the Bang Khunnon Police Station has revealed many of the characteristics of effective policing. First, by staying in and working closely with the people in the community, the police are able to create good rapport and build trust with the community's members. Second, police visibility and accessibility can not only minimize the response time to calls for service but can also reduce the crime rates and affect people's perceptions of safety. Third, police participation in the community projects is and can be beneficial in bridging the connection between the police and the public. Unfortunately, the project was discontinued after Chayapun was transferred to another post.

In 2011, 15 years after the first COP implementation at the Bang Khunnon Police Station in 1996, Police Lieutenant General Sanit Mahathavorn, who is police commander of Bangkok Metropolitan Division 3 and Chayapun's protégé, reintroduced the COP concept. Commander Mahathavorn improvised this project and turned it into an innovative police strategy called the "Bhan-si-khaao" project (meaning drug-free household) as a response

Table 24.1 Respondents' Comments on the Questions Regarding the Bang Khunnon's COP Model

Questions	Comments
(1) Did you know the CSOs in your community?	Yes. Most people in the community know the two officers whose names are Trirung and Wijarn.
(2) Were you satisfied with the job performance of the two CSOs?	Yes. Their work and presence helped reduce the problems of drugs, gambling, and crime in the community about 80%–90%.
(3) What did you see as collaborative projects between the CSOs and the people?	The CSOs helped with the community service projects, such as cleaning the street and areas in the community, fixing the sidewalk, and dredging a ditch.
(4) Could you compare the service given between the CSOs and the main police station?	Yes. The CSOs provided much better and faster service to the community because they lived there 24/7. People felt safer. The CSOs worked harder than the officers at the main station.
(5) Please describe any obstacles the CSOs had to confront.	The officers dealt with some resistance at the beginning while they learned to get to know the people. Later, people supported the officers well.
(6) Please suggest ways to improve the COP project.	The current practice is good. There is no need to change anything, except that police supervisors should have come and visited the CSOs and people in the community for moral support.
(7) Please suggest any service projects you would like to see.	No suggestion was given. However, one person said that if police officers at the main station are as good as the CSOs, there is no need to have CSOs.
(8) Do you like the concept of CSOs?	Yes. Every community should have CSOs.

to the increased drug problems in his jurisdiction's communities ("Community Policing: The Model" 2011). The project started on 1 March 2011 and ended on 31 September 2011. Groups of police officers and community leaders comprise subcommittees whose duty is to screen households that are not involved in drugs and put a sign that says "Bhan-si-khaao" in front of each of those houses. The households in which drug involvement is unclear do not receive a sign. Police Commander Mahathavorn stated that the households believed to be involved in drugs receive two pressures: (1) social sanctions from other members in the community and (2) the law enforcement strategy starting from warnings to strict enforcement of the drug law ("Community Policing: The Model" 2011). Mahathavorn further said that the outcomes of the Bhan-si-khaao project have been positive because people in the communities are receptive of and collaborative with the project, resulting in more than 10,000 signs being put up so far (about 30% of the total households).

How PCR Programs in Thailand Work

As mentioned above, the practice of COP in Thailand is in its incipient stage. With the exception of the two projects (the Bang Khunnon Police Station Model in 1997 and the Bhan-si-khaao project in 2011), almost all police–citizen interaction programs can be classified as PCR as opposed to COP. In other words, the program seems to focus more on creating police–citizen relationships than on building good partnerships with people in preventing and fighting against crime. Therefore, many police officers in Thailand perceive their PCR programs as the COP programs. This misconception will remain among the officers until they receive proper training and education on COP.

Presently, the implementation of the PCR programs may vary from one police agency to another, although not in a significant way. The characteristics of the PCR programs are as follows:

- The partnerships with the community leaders are through the citizen review boards, whose members are selected from the community.
- There are no guidelines about how community members are recruited to participate in the PCR programs, but usually, these program participants are those who already volunteer in other social charity functions.
- There are no reward structures given for member services.
- PCR officers do not have to patrol with the citizens unless there is a request from the community or a police supervisor. Their main duty is to build good relationships with the people through social activities such as playing in a band or giving away free items. After the activity is over, the PCR officers can leave the community. They do not have to remain in the community.
- The police dictate their policing roles and plan their own functions without the influence of or direct input from the citizens. The only group that can review police work is the citizen review board.
- As for responding to calls for service or calls on domestic disturbances, the main station will dispatch a patrol officer to the caller or the scene. The PCR officers are not responsible for these types of calls.
- Regarding directing and controlling traffic, the PCR officers have no role in this since it is the direct responsibility of the officers from the traffic division.

Conclusions

Given the fact that the concepts and practices of PCR and COP in Thailand have been adopted within a close time frame (1988 for the PCR program and 1995 for the COP program), the former seems to be institutionalized in the RTP, especially at the police station level, while the latter is much less popular. Most police officers mistake PCR for COP mainly because of the community component that is embedded in the structure of both programs. However, the effort to mobilize the Thai police officers and needed resources to adopt and implement the COP strategy as a way to increase police effectiveness is in progress and conceivably feasible.

There are three main factors that indicate the potential success of fully implementing the COP program in all police agencies in Thailand. First, the implementation of the Bang Khunnon and the Bhan-si-khaao projects is a testament to the success and promises of the philosophy of COP. Even though neither project can yet be considered as the best practice, the implementation of each project was carried out as a COP approach and could be used as a supportive model for future projects. Second, the RTP has good police leaders who have not only indicated their strong support of COP but also already brought the concepts into effect. Having good leaders to lead and initiate such a change in police practice is instrumental in the implementation process, especially for the RTP, whose organization is highly hierarchical and paramilitary in nature. Third, the constitutional mandates that require the roles of the citizens in both participating in the justice system and reviewing the government's performance should be conducive to the gaining of support from other government agencies and of resources needed for successful implementation of COP.

Despite the supporting factors, there are potential challenges that the RTP is facing in developing effective COP. One of the main issues is the lack of understanding about the COP theory and its potential benefits to improved police performance and the crime prevention strategy. This absence of insight into COP occurs among the majority of police officials (both low and high ranking) and other criminal justice practitioners. There also seems to be lack of participating researchers and relevant criminal justice and social workers in the process of the COP implementation. In the two COP projects mentioned earlier, there was no mention of either researchers or private businesses or other agency personnel who should have had vital roles in planning, monitoring, documenting, and evaluating the project. In summary, the COP effort in Thailand is in its beginning stage. In order to successfully implement this new policing strategy, the goal of the RTP must be to develop best practices in community policing that can be applied and replicated in police agencies throughout the country.

References

Chayapun, Pongpat. (2011). ทฤษฎีตำรวจผู้รับใช้ชุมชน: ทฤษฎีสำหรับศตวรรษที่ 21 [Community policing: Theory for the 21st century]. Bangkok: Central Investigation Bureau Printing.

ตำรวจผู้รับใช้ชุมชน โมเดลต้นแบบสร้างความสงบสุขให้สังคม (บทความพิเศษ) [Community policing: The model for society's peace and order (a special article)]. หนังสือพิมพ์แนวหน้า (2011). The Front Line Newspaper. Retrieved December 28, 2011, from http://www.ryt9.com/s/nnd/1242007.

Puthpongsiriporn, Sarit. (2004). Promoting a service culture for community policing in Thailand and a comparison study with Malaysia. Unpublished doctoral dissertation, Asian Institute of Technology, Thailand.

Royal Thai Police (RTP). (1995). Manual of Community Policing Officers. Bangkok: The Royal Thai Police's Publisher.

Royal Thai Police, Human Resources Bureau. (2004). The Royal Thai Police. Bangkok: The Royal Thai Police's Publisher.

Singhsilarak, Jakkrit; Cheurprakobkit, Sutham. (2007). Police education and training in Thailand. In Peter C. Kratcoski and Dilip K. Das (Eds.), Police Education and Training in a Global Society (pp. 57–70). Lanham, MD: Lexington Books.

Europe

IV

Croatia

25

KRUNOSLAV BOROVEC
SANJA KUTNJAK IVKOVIĆ

Contents

Background

Croatia (Republika Hrvatska) is both a Central European and a Mediterranean country with a territory of 56,594 km² (Croatian Bureau of Statistics 2010). Croatia shares its land border, 2375 km long, with Bosnia and Herzegovina, Hungary, Montenegro, and Slovenia (Croatian Bureau of Statistics 2010). It shares its sea border with Italy. Croatia spans from the Pannonia Valley in the northeast to the Adriatic Sea in the south.

On June 25, 1991, Croatia declared independence from the socialist Yugoslavia. On January 15, 1992, it became an internationally recognized independent country. Since the end of the war in Croatia in the early to mid-1990s, Croatia has been undergoing a transition. It became a member of the North Atlantic Treaty Organization (NATO) in 2009. After a 5-year long process, Croatia officially completed negotiations with the European Union in June 2011 and is scheduled to become its twenty-eighth member on July 1, 2013.

Croatia is a parliamentary democracy. It has three separate branches of government (legislative, executive, and judicial). It is divided administratively into 21 territorial–administrative units (counties), including the city of Zagreb. According to the 2011 Census, Croatia has 4,290,612 inhabitants (Croatian Bureau of Statistics 2011a). The overwhelming majority are Croats (90%; Croatian Bureau of Statistics 2011b), while Serbs, at 4.5%, constitute the largest minority (Croatian Bureau of Statistics 2011b). The official language is Croatian; in one county (Istria), in addition to Croatia, the official language is Italian. The script in use is Latin. The dominant religion is Catholic, with 88% of the population declaring themselves as Catholics (Croatian Bureau of Statistics 2011b).

The Croatian police was established after the elections in 1990, when the Republic Secretariat for the Interior Affairs of the former socialist Yugoslavia was renamed into the Croatian Ministry of the Interior.* The first several years in the history of the Croatian police were quite turbulent; at the beginning of the war in Croatia (1991–1995), the police were the only institution having the legitimate right to use force. The police role and the military role were intertwined (Kutnjak Ivković 2000). In April 1991, the Croatian Parliament passed appropriate statutory changes to facilitate the establishment of the National Guard Corps (NGC) as a police service within the Ministry of the Interior, with the primary mission to carry out the military function during the war. Police officers constituted a large portion of the manpower for the NGC, especially in the first few months following its formation. Seven hundred and fifty-five police officers died in the war, more than 3600 were wounded, and 31 are still missing (Borovec 2011a).

The transition period ensued as soon as the war subsided,[†] with a "war-is-over" attitude. Politicians and academics used buzzwords such as openness to the public, transparency, accountability, and rule of law, while, at the same time, police administrators focused on professionalism, depoliticization, education, courtesy, and politeness. In 1994, the Ministry of the Interior itself organized a seminar about the functions of the police in a democratic society (see Šintić 1994). In his opening speech, then Minister of the Interior Ivan Jarnjak discussed the balance between the protection of the rights of individual citizens and the protection of the interest of the society at large. The democratization process has focused on five key concepts: depoliticization, demilitarization, professionalization, demystification, and downsizing (Kutnjak Ivković 2000).

Today, the Croatian Ministry of the Interior Affairs is composed of two parts, the police and the sector for administrative and other professional affairs. Among about 26,000 employees of the Ministry, police officers constitute about 78% (20,697), making the police the most populous public service in Croatia (Borovec et al. 2011a).

The Croatian police are a centralized and hierarchical organization. The head of the Ministry is the Minister of the Interior, which is a political function. The police are a public service within the Ministry and are under the leadership of the Police Directorate (Ministry of the Interior 2011a). The director of the police is a professional function, which contributes toward depoliticization and professionalization of the police. The Directorate incorporates the police, criminal police, border police, special police, communication center, forensic center, police academy, and special safety affairs (Ministry of the Interior 2011a). The next layer in the hierarchy consists of 20 police administrations, corresponding to the 20 counties. At the bottom of the hierarchy are 186 police stations that perform regular police work on their territory.

Police work is regulated by the Police Law (2011) and the Law on the Police Activities and Rights (2009). Both of these laws regulate the organization of the police and the official rights and duties of police officers, as well as establish the rights and responsibilities of the police.

---

* The former socialist Yugoslavia was a federation. The military was established at the federal level and, when the war broke out, Serbia controlled the military. On the other hand, the police were decentralized at the level of republics. Thus, Croatia, as a former republic, had its own Republic Secretariat for the Interior Affairs (later renamed into the Croatian Ministry of the Interior).

† Most of the war activities subsided by the end of 1992, but about one-third of the Croatian territory remained out of the control of the official Croatian authorities. In 1995, after two military operations, most of the Croatian territory was reintegrated. Later in 1995, an agreement was signed allowing peaceful reintegration of the remaining Croatia territories in Eastern Slavonia.

Origin of Community Policing in Croatia

The Croatian version of community policing is grounded not only in the current social and political context, but also on historical legacy. The Croatian police inherited the system of the communist police, as established in the former socialist Yugoslavia. The primary role of the police was the protection of the state and the constitutionally protected socialist regime, while the rule of law and the protection of human rights were ranked low on the police priority lists. The disintegration of the former Yugoslavia and the establishment of independent Croatia resulted in numerous changes in the number and ethnic structure of the police employees. At the beginning of the war, many Serb police officers left their police posts,* and the rapid hiring—necessitated by the war—resulted in a large number of police, largely of Croat ethnicity, joining the police without undergoing adequate police training. The conditions at the time—the need to rapidly increase the numbers of officers to fight the war and thus put defense functions in the forefront (and the traditional police functions in the background)—necessitated such steps.

Since the end of the war (or, more precisely, the establishment of the Croatian military), the characteristics of the police have begun to resemble those of the traditional police organization, with the priorities now shifting to prevention and detection of crimes; apprehension of the offenders; maintaining the public order and peace; protection of people, places, and objects; and traffic control (Law on Internal Affairs 1994). The police primarily focused on its law enforcement function, fitting Wilson's legalistic model of police performance (Champion and Rush 1997). In this period, the police as an organization have had a strong centralized command and served primarily to enforce the law. Their activities have been almost exclusively reactive.

This legalistic model, dominant until the late 1990s, changed little from year to year. The changes included the introduction of new specialized units and sections, while its primary characteristics—the enforcement of the laws through beat officers' shift work and quick reaction to the indications of criminal activity—remained the same. The preventive function was performed exclusively through regular police patrols. The work of the detective units was also almost exclusively reactive, with the investigation of committed crimes and the detection and apprehension of the offenders. This model emphasizes the repressive and controlling role of the police in society (Cajner Mraović et al. 2003). In other words, the police have the "firefighter role" (Greiner 1997) because they react only when something occurs by dealing with the consequences of the crimes or violations of public order and peace, without questioning the reasons that led to them.

Led by the goal of effective control of criminal activities, police work is extensive, and it may violate the rights of many citizens. Police identity checks, rations, roadblocks, and routine checks of cars and drivers have been an everyday occurrence. These kinds of activities, when observed by the citizens, reinforce the perceptions that the police are repressive and that contact with the police results in a negative experience. Consequently, the level of support for the police and the cooperation between the citizens and the police

---

* When the war with the new, Serb-dominated Socialist Republic of Yugoslavia broke out in 1991, most police officers of Serb ethnicity left their posts in Croatia and fought against the newly established NGC. According to the 1991 Census, only 12% of the general population of Croatia was of Serb origin (Lajić 1995), while the percentage of ethnic Serbs in the old Croatian militia exceeded 70% (Jarnjak 1995), especially among the administrators and first-line supervisors.

weaken. In addition, the police typically cooperate neither with the other state public services nor with the local government. From the citizens' perspective, this state of affairs resulted in citizens either experiencing repressive police methods or frequently encountering the police shifting responsibility to other state public services without any attempts to coordinate with these services and work toward joint resolutions of problems in local communities.

The measures of police effectiveness during this period are indicative of the reliance on the legalistic model of police work. The primary measures of effectiveness and success are the official, police-generated crime statistics and other quantitative measures of safety. Because these crime statistics were used as the measures of police supervisors' success, a tendency developed to adjust and fix them (Cajner Mraović et al. 2003). Police work had not been validated externally at all; the discrepancy between the official crime statistics and the citizens' perceptions of safety started to widen. Individual citizens, the general public, and the media perceived the police as the only organization in charge of controlling crime, thus exclusively responsible for the perceived widespread crime (Cajner Mraović et al. 2003).

Cajner Mraović (2003), who conceived and developed the idea of community policing in Croatia, listed the following characteristics as typical of the police work at the time:

- The police are preoccupied with their own organization, internal procedures, and effectiveness to the point at which they are not able to confront effectively the important problems that are not crimes.
- The police invest the largest proportion of their potential into rapid responses to calls for service and devote too little time and resources to the development of their own initiatives in prevention or reduction of the problems existing in the local communities.
- The community is the primary source of enormous potential that largely remains unutilized for the resolution of various problems considered to be solely the police responsibility.
- The police have substantial potential in their patrol officers, whose time and talent are not completely utilized.
- The efforts put into the enhancement of police work typically result in failure because they are inadequately planned, monitored, or implemented.

Clearly, substantial and extensive organizational and structural changes were required to allow for the actual transformation of the traditional police model, used by the Croatian police at the time, toward the community policing model.

The beginning of community policing in Croatia dates back to 2003, when the Ministry of the Interior asked experts, headed by Cajner Mraović, to develop a new strategy of police activities and their implementation. The conditions for the new strategy had been established with the 2000 reform of the Police Law; the changed law contained new articles that paved the road for community policing (Veić 2001). The revised law encouraged police–public cooperation in pursuit of safety, as well as cooperation between the police and other institutions and organizations. To achieve these goals, the police have been given the right to establish coordinating committees or task forces (composed of citizen representatives and police representatives), and to determine community problems and establish priorities among them. A key challenge facing Croatian community policing was "to establish the idea that the people living in a particular community are responsible for the quality of life in that community" (Cajner Mraović et al. 2003, p. 53). Thus, necessary requirements are open communication among the citizens and their respect and cooperation in pursuit of common interests. Following this idea, community policing stops being exclusively a police project and instead becomes the project owned by the whole community, which, in turn, strengthens the community spirit (Cajner Mraović et al. 2003).

How Does Community Policing Work in Croatia?

The strategy of community policing was expected to influence positively public perceptions of the police, increase the ease of identifying and recognizing the local community policing officer, and develop close relationships between citizens and the police. All these effects should have had a positive effect on the quality and quantity of information received from the citizens, which would enable the police to become more effective in crime control and crime prevention. In addition, the successful partnership between the police and citizens, as well as other state, regional, and local institutions and organizations, would entice the police to be more effective in crime prevention. An active partnership with the media should result in an increase in public acceptance of, and respect toward, the police, as well as provide for better use of the media potential in the process of creation and implementation of preventive activities (Cajner Mraović et al. 2003).

To achieve a successful transformation of the police, the reform included several aspects that targeted all organizational levels, from individual police officers to the organization as a whole. In particular, the six projects were:

1. Reform of the uniformed police
2. Development and enhancement of criminal prevention
3. Organization of prevention in local communities
4. Reform of public relations
5. Reform of the system of police education and professional development
6. Internal democratization of the police

Reform of Uniformed Police

When getting in touch with the police, citizens most often interact with uniformed police officers. Consequently, their perceptions of, and support for, the police are influenced by their contact and experience with uniformed police officers. An increase in positive, citizen-initiated contacts with the police could improve the view of the police and reduce the need to rely on reactive police activities. Consequently, critical changes during the transition have to include the uniformed police. The Croatian police have recognized this and, accordingly, have placed emphasis on the transition of the uniformed police. The police were expected to become a public service and follow "the service model" (Modly 1996, p. 315). Faber and Cajner Mraović (2003) summarize the reasons for the reforms of the uniform police shortcomings as follows:

1. The police primarily use reactive and repressive methods.
2. The police work is routine and irrational.
3. Police officers do not have a steady territorial assignment and have insufficiently developed contact with community members.
4. The police do not utilize the community potentials fully.
5. The police devote insufficient attention toward the solution of the citizens' problems.
6. The police organization does not position police officers in patrol adequately.

Following these shortcomings, a new model of police work, including a new territorial division and a new organization within these territories, has been developed. The new territorial division introduces "contact districts" (*kontaktni rajon*). It is a part of the territory characterized by increased safety problems (e.g., crime rates, large number of calls for service, large number of police interventions); presence of an increased number of citizens (e.g., squares, streets, pedestrian areas, stations, terminals); and proximity of objects with special safety concerns (e.g., schools, banks, hospitals, sports arenas, state institutions, and organizations). Depending on the level of urbanization and population density, contact districts cover the areas populated by about 1000 to 2000 citizens.

To accompany the changes in territorial organization, a new police assignment was established within the sector of uniformed police—a "contact police officer" (*kontaktni policajac*). Contact police officers' primary function is proactive; they should develop proactive relationships with citizens and other key stakeholders (e.g., school principals, restaurant and store owners, heads of organizations and institutions) in their territory with the purpose of identifying and solving community problems (Faber and Cajner Mraović 2003). The work of these contact police officers is conceptualized as a public service and should contribute toward the enhanced quality of relationships between the police and citizens and other stakeholders.

About 700 police officers have been assigned this role and became contact police officers (Ministry of the Interior 2012). In addition, the Ministry created another new assignment—"preventive police officer"—and assigned 52 police officers to it. Preventive police officers' task is to serve as coordinators for contact police officers from the same police stations.

An important element of community policing is contact police officers' continuity on a specific territory, which allows them to get to know the local population, identify the problems in the community, and recognize and establish relationships with potential partners. The contact police officers' work hours have to be adjusted to cover the times during which the citizens are at home, thus making the contact feasible. Eventually, contact police officers should become the link not only between the local community and the police, but also between the citizens and other state organizations and services in charge of safety and quality of life in the community.

As the theoretical views about community policing in Croatia have been developed, the Ministry engaged in the pilot phase of the project. After the initial selection of future contact police officers as part of the pilot project, the officers were surveyed by Ministry of the Interior in March 2003 (Ministry of the Interior 2003a) with the purpose of assessing their readiness to embark on the new tasks. The results showed a high degree of agreement with the statement supporting the need to change policing from the traditional model to the community policing model; 92% of the surveyed police officers supported the view that it is necessary to engage in community policing reform, and about the same percentage indicated readiness to participate actively in the reform themselves (Ministry of the Interior 2003a). The establishment of the contact districts and assignment of contact police officers was supported by 91% of the surveyed police officers (Ministry of the Interior 2003a).

Six months later, in September 2003, the same police officers were resurveyed (Ministry of the Interior 2003b). The results showed an even higher degree of agreement with the need to introduce community policing, suggesting that even the minority of police officers who did not agree with the changes in the first place have appreciated the need for such changes (Ministry of the Interior 2003b).

According to the respondents participating in the March 2003 survey, the most critical threats to community policing come from the police administration and political structures; about two-thirds (64%) of the surveyed police officers agreed that the police management was not ready for the reforms, and about the same percentage (68%) supported the view that the political structures will interfere with the depoliticization and professionalization of the police because such changes will decrease their potential influence on police work (Ministry of the Interior 2003a). In the repeated survey conducted in September 2003, these views have been changed only slightly (Ministry of the Interior 2003b), with 51% of the respondents believing that the management was not ready for the reforms and 56% estimating that political structures will interfere with depoliticization and professionalization of the police. Finally, 80% of the surveyed police officers—future contact police officers—agreed that the public does not support the police and does not approve of the police methods (Ministry of the Interior 2003b). It is not surprising that, consequently, the overwhelming majority of the surveyed police officers (96%) agreed that the public opinion surveys and the surveys of the police officers should be conducted on a regular basis. The majority of police officers also agreed that public support is more crucial as a measure of successful policing than reliance on the police-generated statistical indicators is.

At the end of the pilot phase of the project, the Police Directorate—in charge of implementing and monitoring the community policing efforts—compiled the information from all 20 police administrations and summarized its findings about the implementations of the reform of uniformed police and the introduction of community policing (Police Directorate 2008). On the positive side, the Police Directorate noted an improvement in communication and cooperation with citizens, more focus on local community problems, increased emphasis on proactive activities, as well as decreased skepticism toward the community policing model and changed views about the role of the police officers in the community (e.g., contact police officers should focus on problems traditionally viewed as lying outside of police jurisdiction; contact police officers view themselves as helpers and friends of the law-abiding citizens). The Police Directorate (2008) also noticed that the proactive and preventive approach was particularly visible in several aspects of police work: children's traffic safety, prevention of drug use, and prevention of juvenile alcohol consumption. In addition, the report suggests that contact police officers were also active in vandalism prevention, prevention of bullying and violence among juveniles, and protection of senior citizens. According to the Police Directorate, contact police officers had engaged in numerous order-maintenance activities such as removal of abandoned vehicles, fixing of broken street lights, and control of abandoned animals. Police officers' engagement in these kinds of activities suggests that they have moved away from the traditional view of police work and expanded it to include the activities that directly affect quality of life. Police officers also applied the routine-activities approach by registering bicycles to prevent their thefts and installing video cameras in certain neighborhoods (Borovec et al. 2011b). Finally, to enhance their communication with the citizens, increase the level of confidence in the police, and improve data collection, contact police officers in Zagreb and four other cities (Rijeka, Vukovar, Novigrad, and Buje) established "mailboxes of trust" as a new way of communicating with the citizens that allows for anonymity.

On the negative side, the implementation of the pilot project was accompanied by lack of awareness displayed by some administrators and contact police officers about the possibilities and the importance of the project (raising red flags about the appropriateness of police administrators' education and contact police officer selection); the realization that, on average, contact police officers spend only about 60% of their time on the project; and lack of willingness of other institutions and organizations to develop partnerships (Police Directorate 2008).

Development and Enhancement of Crime Prevention

In addition to the reform of the uniformed police, community policing required changes in other aspects of police work and operation. One of the crucial aspects is the proportion in which crime prevention and crime repression are represented in overall police work. The Croatian police view crime prevention, one of the top priorities, as the totality of all state, private, and other measures and activities focused on prevention of criminal activity and reduction of crime consequences (Cajner Mraović et al. 2003). Yet, the police administrators recognize the need to develop and further enhance the crime prevention function. The overwhelming majority of police officers surveyed in 2003 (97%; Ministry of the Interior 2003a) agreed that there is a substantial need to develop and enhance crime prevention while, at the same time, recognizing that the level of current cooperation with the other organizations and institutions in charge of safety, public order, and quality of life is low (71%).

In 2010, after long preparations, crime prevention units were formed at the state, regional, and local levels. These efforts were carried out under the guidance and cooperation of the German police. A total of 58 police officers were assigned to these units, and they are expected to become the key personnel responsible for crime prevention.

The Croatian police embraced the situational crime prevention approach. Most of the projects initiated by the crime prevention units in Croatia belong to the category of situational crime prevention. For example, urban prevention projects in Zagreb include the relocation of newsstands to more visible and more heavily trafficked areas to prevent theft and robbery. Other situational crime prevention projects include the prevention of theft of items from cars in large parking lots and the reduction of bicycle theft through their marking and registration.

In addition, the employees in the prevention offices have engaged in other projects such as the prevention of drug use, juvenile violence, and domestic violence, all of which emphasized cooperation with the local community. For example, the project "I Know, I Can, and I Will" targets elementary-age children and their parents (Borovec 2009). In the first stage, the students, their teachers, and contact police officers visited the local police station and learned about its operation. The students were taught about the dangers of drug use and ways of self-protection. In the second stage, the parents, teachers, and contact police officers met in schools to learn about and discuss the prevention and legal consequences of drug use. The third stage of the program included lessons for students about the prevention of juvenile violence and bullying, vandalism, and drug addiction. Similarly, the project "Alcohol? No, Thanks!" sought to sensitize the public about underage drinking, reduce the availability of alcoholic drinks to juveniles, and promote the development of alternate ways of socializing (Ministry of the Interior 2011b). The partners in the project were the police, the city of Dubrovnik, the Office for Public Health, Family Center, and several elementary and high schools.

Organization of Prevention in Local Communities

In addition to a stronger emphasis on prevention in everyday police work, the Croatian model of community policing assumed that the community itself would embrace the preventive approach. Following the initiative by a few police experts (Borovec et al. 2011b), communities across the country have started establishing Crime Prevention Committees. Since 2004, 167 committees have been established in cities and communities across the country.

These committees, which can be viewed as interagency coordinating councils, community coalitions, or coordinating committees (Foster-Fishman et al. 2001), are composed of local public officials, members of nonprofit organizations, business leaders, and citizens who address questions of common interest and concern (Zakocs and Edwards 2006). These committees are coalitions, defined as groups of representatives of various organizations and institutions from the community who agree to work together to achieve common goals (Buterfoss et al. 2003). The establishment of crime prevention committees assumes that two conditions have been met: the political will to engage in prevention and the establishment of partnerships (Bynum 2005). The coalitions and partnerships in the community should have a positive influence on the development of the community (Granner and Sharpe 2004) and, thus, could be used to promote safety in the community.

The committees have been entrusted with fulfilling a number of different tasks (Cajner Mraović 2009). Their primary purposes are to stimulate and promote creative and innovative preventive ideas, short-term projects, and long-term preventive projects. Furthermore, they should provide leadership and support to the individuals and organizations performing preventive activities at the local level; coordinate activities of various institutions, organizations, associations, and groups of citizens; recognize and preserve best practices; provide training on partnerships and prevention; make prevention programs accessible to the members of the larger community; and provide continuity in preventive programs (see Cajner Mraović 2009).

In a joint evaluation by the United Nations Development Programme and the Ministry of the Interior, Bašić et al. (2011) evaluated two committees and their operation. They selected the crime prevention committees from Čakovec and Split. Based on the Community Readiness Model (CRM), developed by the Tri-Ethnic Center at the Colorado State University (Colorado State University 2011), Bašić et al. (2011) used a nine-point scale measuring the community's readiness for prevention, where 1 indicated that the community was not aware of the problems, did not know how to deal with the problems, or was tolerant of the problems. The results showed that the development of crime prevention committees is a slow process characterized by a number of drawbacks such as a low level of knowledge about prevention among the committee members, low group cohesion, and low visibility of the committee in the community. The authors concluded that the committees' activities would be more appropriately labeled as short-term preventive activities rather than long-term preventive programs.

Reform of Public Relations

Demystification of the police and greater openness to the public were some of the guiding principles of the police reforms in the 1990s. The idea was revived with the push for community policing in 2003. The strategy of community policing required changes in the way the police and public communicated; the dominant view was that, through their relationship with the public, the police must show their responsibility for the police work and can expect understanding and support from the public (Borovec, 2011b). Consequently, changes were required in the organization of the police.

In a 2003 survey of police officers, two-thirds of the respondents rated the organization and the quality of the Ministry's public relations as poor (Ministry of the Interior 2003a); the overwhelming majority of the respondents (90%) supported the reform of public relations. In a follow-up study, conducted 6 months later (Ministry of the Interior 2003b), virtually all (99%) respondents supported the reform.

In 2007, the position of the spokesperson for the police at the national and regional levels was established and professionalized. In addition, in 2010, public relations offices were established in all 20 police administrations; these regional offices are coordinated by the national Office for Public Relations. About 70 people were employed at both regional and national offices. These public relations offices represent the largest public relations service among the public services in Croatia (Ministry of the Interior 2010). Nonetheless, while it is the largest public relations service, it is a decentralized service.

In addition to the structural and organizational changes, the public relations service started engaging in public campaigns to improve safety in the community. One of the first campaigns, developed in 2007 and still ongoing, is "Fewer Weapons, Fewer Tragedies." Coordinated with the United Nations Development Programme, it invites inhabitants to voluntarily turn over the weapons and mines that they have kept illegally since the end of the war. With 64,271 pieces of weapons turned over to the police, this campaign was determined to be the most successful such campaign in the history of the United Nations (Ministry of the Interior 2011c).

In 2010, the Ministry initiated the campaign "Live Your Life Without Violence," teaching the public about domestic violence. The campaign brings together the police, social institutions, schools, and the court system. The campaign has won the Award for the Media Promotion of Safety via Facebook.

In 2011, the Ministry established a Web portal (http://www.nestali.hr) containing information about all missing persons in Croatia and instructions on how to report a missing person. The campaign, titled "National Registry of Missing Persons" educates the public about this service.

The Ministry also focused on improving internal communication. In addition to publishing the journal *Peace, Respect, and Trust* every month, the Ministry e-mails the weekly *E-Police Herald*.

Reform of System of Police Education and Professional Development

The reform of the police would not be complete without a reform of the system of police education and professional development. As Cajner Mraović et al. (2003)—the authors of community policing in Croatia—emphasized, the new role of a police officer in the community, that is, closeness with the citizens, focus on developing solutions for different community problems, group work, and constant need for communication, requires traditional police officers to develop new or rarely used skills and knowledge. The process of decentralization, which accompanies community policing, assumes that the police officers walking the beat, particularly contact police officers, are trained and prepared to make such complex decisions.

At the beginning of the reform (2003), a survey of police officers revealed that two-thirds of the respondents (64%; Ministry of the Interior 2003a) evaluated the system of police education as poor. The key aspects of the reform have been to change the ratio of theoretical to practical instruction; introduce new courses (e.g., social psychology, communications, ethics, and leadership courses); and develop courses on communication skills, management courses, and antistress training.

Internal Democratization of the Police

Democratization of the police is perceived as decentralization in decision making and participation of various parties, from both the police and the community, in making the key decisions affecting the police. However, the push toward community policing did not initiate democratization reforms; in the mid- to late 1990s, when the war had ended and the society started transitioning away from communist society, the Ministry engaged in democratization of the police as well (Kutnjak Ivković 2000). The key words, including transparency, partnership, and trust, are being explored and discussed. However, just as the process in the society at large is ongoing, it is continuing within the police as well. Police education and organization are trying to follow and adjust to the newly developed conditions in society. Recently, the Ministry introduced two substantial changes to the process.

The first is the development of the Reform Strategy of the Ministry for the Interior Human Resources System, 2009–2011. This reform strategy is the result of the Twinning project PHARE 2005 (Ministry of the Interior 2009), financed with European Union funds. The Ministry initiated the reform in four directions: development of an integrated human resources system; strengthening the role of human resources; enhancement of police officers' participation and motivation; and reform of the police academy.

The second is the enactment of the new Police Law (2011) and the related acts regulating continued professional development, establishment of professional standards, recruitment requirements, police officers' competencies, promotion, reassignment, police ranks, and police education. The new law, created after the public discussion of its norms, regulates these issues in a more transparent way.

Effectiveness of Community Policing

So far, there have been no attempts to provide an overall assessment of community policing in Croatia. However, some specific aspects of the reform have been evaluated (the findings were presented above as an illustration of specific components of Croatian community policing).

In 2003, immediately after the beginning of the implementation of community policing, the Ministry surveyed police officers about their views of the reform (e.g., the assessments of police work, support for the reform, views about community policing, overall effective-ness of community policing, police education, quality of public relations, and quality of cooperation with the local community). The overwhelming majority of the respondents supported the view that it is necessary to engage in the community policing reform and supported the establishment of contact districts and contact community officers (Ministry of the Interior 2003a). They also seemed ready to participate actively in the reform them-selves (Ministry of the Interior 2003a). In a 6-month follow-up, the surveyed police officers showed an even higher degree of support for the changes (Ministry of the Interior 2003b).

At the same time, the results showed that the police officers perceived that the most critical threats to community policing come from the police administration and political structures that were not perceived to be ready for the reforms (Ministry of the Interior 2003b). Police officers were also critical and emphasized that the politicians would inter-fere with depoliticization and professionalization of the police (Ministry of the Interior 2003a, b). Finally, the majority agreed that the police do not enjoy a high level of support and welcomed regular police and public opinion surveys (Ministry of the Interior 2003b).

In 2009, the Ministry conducted a public opinion survey for the first time. It was titled "Nationwide Study of Public Perceptions of Safety, Police Activities, and Cooperation between the Police and the Local Community" (UNDP and Ministry of the Interior 2009). The results showed that citizens expressed a great degree of safety in their communities; the overwhelming majority felt safe at home at night (93%) or when walking in the neigh-borhood at night (86%). The majority felt that they could defend their property (60%) and themselves against a violent threat (57%; UNDP and Ministry of the Interior 2009). The most significant problems in their communities include illegally parked vehicles, rude drivers, and intoxicated citizens.

When asked to evaluate the police, the evaluation results were mostly positive (UNDP and Ministry of the Interior 2009). The majority of the surveyed citizens evaluated the police as polite (68%), neatly dressed (82%), and effective in maintaining public order (61%). Police car patrols were perceived as the most visible part of the police; 77% of the citizens had noticed them (UNDP and Ministry of the Interior 2009). About one-half (47%) did not see a police officer walking the beat or patrolling their neighborhood on foot (UNDP and Ministry of the Interior 2009). When asked whether they had helped the police in the last year, about 16% responded affirmatively (UNDP and the Ministry of the Interior 2009), and 91% of the respondents expressed their willingness to assist the police in the future. The overwhelming majority (82%) of the respondents agreed that better cooperation between the police and the local community was required for order maintenance in the community.

Furthermore, about one-third of the surveyed citizens had contact with the police in the last year (UNDP and Ministry of the Interior 2009). Most of the people who had contact with the police last year evaluated the contact as positive because police officers devoted due attention to them (78%; UNDP and Ministry of the Interior 2009). On the other hand, about 22% of the surveyed citizens, their family members, or friends had at least one negative experience with the police in their lifetime (UNDP and Ministry of the Interior 2009). Those who personally had a negative experience with the police (12% over-all; UNDP and Ministry of the Interior 2009) either were stopped by the traffic police or encountered a police patrol.

Next, as part of the reform efforts targeting the organization of prevention in the local communities, the Ministry initiated an evaluation of crime prevention committees in two large towns (see Bašić et al. 2011). The report suggests that, while the older and more established of the two crime prevention committees was in the middle of the scale in its readiness, the younger of the two committees was almost at the beginning in terms of its readiness (Bašić et al. 2011). The current efforts performed by the two committees were evaluated by Bašić et al. (2011) more as short-term preventive activities than long-term preventive programs. The findings pointed out that more serious efforts—both by the police and by the local community—are necessary to create fertile ground for crime prevention committees to operate successfully.

Conclusion

The Croatian police have been going through a complex transformation from a police burdened with the communist heritage and a military role in the recent war into a modern democratic police organization. The strategy of community policing played a substantial role in the transition, fostering democratization, depoliticization, and professionalism. The programs and projects introduced as part of the community policing efforts have substantially changed the functions and the organization of the police.

Despite the positive trends, the Croatian police are still in transition, and the process is far from complete. The strategy of community policing—emphasizing the change in the way police officers see and perform their roles, accepting the view that the police are a public service, and changing the role of citizens and local communities in the creation and maintenance of safety—has not been completed. The road toward complete integration of the strategy of community policing among the Croatian police lies ahead.

References

Bašić, J., Novak, M., Mihić, J., and Grozić-Živolić, S. (2011). Unapređenje rada na izgradnji sustava prevencije kriminaliteta i podrška osnivanju koordinacijske jedinice za prevenciju kriminaliteta. Završni izvještaj eveluacijskog tima projekta. Zagreb, Croatia: Centar za prevencijska istraživanja. Unpublished.

Borovec, K. (2009). Role of the police in the prevention of drug abuse among youth. *Child and Society*, 11(1/2): 407–415.

Borovec, K. (ed.) (2011a). *Hrvatska policija u Domovinskom ratu*. Zagreb, Croatia: Ministarstvo unutarnjih poslova RH.

Borovec, K. (2011b). Strategija odnosa s javnošću Ministarstva unutarnjih poslova Republike Hrvatske. *Mir, ugled, povjerenje*, 53: 1–15.

Borovec, K., Balgač, I., and Karlović, R. (2011a). *Interna komunikacija u Ministarstvu unutarnjih poslova: Procjena zadovoljstva poslom i internom komunikacijom.* Zagreb, Croatia: Ministarstvo unutarnjih poslova.

Borovec, K., Balgač, I., and Karlović, R. (2011b). *Situacijski pristup prevenciji kriminaliteta, od teorije do prakse utemeljene na dokazima.* Zagreb, Croatia: Ministarstvo unutarnjih poslova.

Buterfoss, F., Morrow, D., Ardythe, L., DeWitt Webster, J., and Clinton Crews, R. (2003). The Coalition Training Institute: Training for the long haul. *Journal of Public Health Management and Practice*, 9(6): 522–529.

Bynum, T.S. (2005). Upute gradskim vijećima za prevenciju o provedbi prve faze komunalne prevencije: analiza stanja sigurnosti. *Izbor članaka iz stranih časopisa*, 3–4: 128–147.

Cajner Mraović, I. (2009): *Prevencija kriminaliteta u lokalnoj zajednici. Nova razina razvoja policije u zajednici.* Zagreb, Croatia: MUP, Policijska akademija.

Cajner Mraović, I., Faber, V., and Volarević, G. (2003). *Strategija djelovanja Policija u zajednici.* Zagreb, Croatia: Ministarstvo unutarnjih poslova,

Champion, D.J., and Rush, G.E. (1997). *Policing in the Community.* Upper Saddle River, NJ: Prentice Hall.

Colorado State University (2011). Tri-Ethnic Center. http://www.triethniccenter.colostate.edu/communityReadiness.htm.

Croatian Bureau of Statistics (2010). *Statistical Yearbook 2010.* http://www.dzs.hr/Hrv_Eng/ljetopis/2010/SLJH2010.pdf.

Croatian Bureau of Statistics (2011a). *2011 Census of Population, Households, and Dwellings, First Results by Settlements.* http://www.dzs.hr/Hrv_Eng/publication/2011/SI-1441.pdf.

Croatian Bureau of Statistics (2011b). *Croatia in Numbers.* http://www.dzs.hr/Hrv_Eng/CroInFig/croinfig_2011.pdf.

Faber, V., and Cajner Mraović, I. (2003). *Reforma operativno-preventivnog rada policije u odori.* Zagreb, Croatia: Ministarstvo unutarnjih poslova, Policijska akademija.

Foster-Fishman, G., Berkowitz, S.L., Lounsbury, D.W., Jackobson, S., and Allen, N.A. (2001). Building collaborative capacity in community coalitions: A review and integrative framework. *American Journal of Community Psychology,* 29(2): 241–261.

Granner, M.L., and Sharpe, P.A. (2004). Evaluating community coalition characteristics and functioning: A summary of measurement tools. *Health Education Research,* 19: 514–532.

Greiner, A. (1997). Was zur Aufgabenwahrnehmung des Streifendienstes bedacht werden muß. *Die Polizei,* 1: 1–2.

Jarnjak, I. (1995). Hrvati rado nose odoru. *Halo* 92, 44:7.

Kutnjak Ivković, S. (2000). Challenges of policing democracies: The Croatian experience. In Das, D. and O. Marenin (Eds.). *Challenges of Policing Democracies: A World Perspective.* Newark, NJ: Gordon and Breach Publishers, pp. 45–85.

Lajić, I. (1995). Demografski razvitak Hrvatske u razdoblju od 1991. do 1994. *Revija za sociologiju,* 26: 55–64.

Law on Internal Affairs (1994). *Narodne novine,* 96.

Law on the Police Activities and Rights (2009). *Narodne novine,* 69/09.

Modly, D. (1996). Pozornik danas. *Policija i sigurnost,* 3: 314–317.

Ministry of the Interior (Ministarstvo unutranjih poslova) (2003a). Istraživanje stavova policijskih službenika o provedbi Strategije djelovanja Policija u zajednici, na početku polot projekta. Unpublished.

Ministry of the Interior (Ministarstvo unutranjih poslova) (2003b). Istraživanje stavova policijskih službenika o provedbi Strategije djelovanja Policija u zajednici, na kraju polot projekta. Unpublished.

Ministry of the Interior (Ministarstvo unutranjih poslova) (2009). *Strategija reforme sustava upravljanja ljudskim potencijalima Ministarstva unutarnjih poslova za razdoblje od 2009. do 2011.* Zagreb, Croatia: Ministarstvo unutarnjih poslova.

Ministry of the Interior (Ministarstvo unutranjih poslova) (2010). Zavrsena 11. konferencija HUOJ-a. http://www.huoj.hr/konferencije/zavrsena-11-konferencija-huoj-a-hr181.

Ministry of the Interior (Ministarstvo unutranjih poslova) (2011a). Ravnateljstvo policije. http://www.policija.hr/25.aspx.

Ministry of the Interior (Ministarstvo unutranjih poslova) (2011b). "Alcohol? No, Thanks!" http://www.mup.hr/108692/3.aspx.

Ministry of the Interior (Ministarstvo unutranjih poslova) (2011c). "Fewer Weapons, Fewer Tragedies." http://www.mup.hr/main.aspx?id=96853.

Ministry of the Interior (Ministarstvo unutranjih poslova) (2012). Projekt "Kontakt policajci." http://www.mup.hr/1071.aspx.

Police Directorate (Ravnateljstvo policije) (2008). Izvješće o provedbi projekta "reforma operativno-preventivnog rada policije u odori" i radu kontakt-policajaca u 2008. godini. Unpublished.

Police Law (2011). *Narodne novine,* 34/11.

Šintić, J. (1994). *The Functions of the Police in a Democratic Society*. Zagreb, Croatia: Ministarstvo unutarnjih poslova Republike Hrvatske.

UNDP and Ministry of the Interior (Ministarstvo unutranjih poslova) (2009). *Rezultati istraživanja percepcije sigurnosti građana, postupanja policije te suradnje između policije i lokalne zajednice.* Zagreb, Croatia: Program Ujedinjenih naroda za razvoj u Republici Hrvatskoj.

Veić, P. (2001). *Zakon o policiji s komentarom i stvarnim kazalom*. II izdanje, Zagreb, Croatia: Ministarstvo unutarnjih poslova.

Zakocs, R.C., and Edwards, E.M. (2006). What explains community coalition effectiveness? A review of the literature. *American Journal of Preventive Medicine*, 30(4): 351–361.

Finland

SIRPA VIRTA

26

Contents

Introduction

This article deals with community policing innovations in Finland, in particular, in the Helsinki Police Department (HPD).* Discussing innovations does not mean that community policing has been reinvented in Finland. On the contrary, it means that its basic values (respect of human rights, deserved trust and confidence, good-quality police services for all, citizen-focused approach, multiagency cooperation) have been integrated into daily routine policing and police management in innovative ways and by innovative means like social media.

Helsinki is the capital of Finland. The number of inhabitants is 595,500. Finland is a Member State of the European Union (EU), which means that the police take account on the common European security and policing strategies and justice and home affairs policies. The National Police Board under the Ministry of the Interior, and the Police Commissioner, form the supreme command of the Finnish police organization. The police in Finland is a state authority. Currently, there are 24 local police departments. The recent organizational reform took 2 years (2009–2010); the Police Board was established, and the number of local police departments was reduced from 90 to 24.

The number of the staff of the HPD is 1386 policemen and 339 other staff (administration, guards). There has been a 5- to 15-person reduction of personnel in both groups every year since 2006, mainly due to the state's public sector cost-saving policy. The investments of the HPD for community policing have not been extra resources but rather in the form of improved police services, effective networking with strategic partners, and

---

* The data used in the evaluation of the community policing reform of the HPD: reports of the community policing team of Eastern Precinct 2008–2011, reports of virtual community policing team 2009–2011, statistics of the HPD, and self-assessments of the teams. In addition, the author would like to thank deputy chief of the HPD, Lasse Aapio, for information and interview on November 17, 2011, and Chief Inspector Veli Hukkanen (Chief of Eastern Police Precinct Itäkeskus) for pilot project documents and reports.

reorganizing tasks and rethinking duties inside the organization. In Finland, community policing means a good-quality, citizen-focused, and effective local policing. It is not a separate model; it is, rather, a way of thinking about local police services and the role of the police in neighborhoods. Like in Belgium (see Bruggeman et al. 2007), community policing in Finland is integrated in local policing.

However, in order to understand the way community policing policy has been translated into action, and the way it is today integrated in local policing, we have to look back. It has been argued that community policing research has tended to be ahistorical stories of organizational rearrangements and reforms without connections to wider sociopolitical developments (Crawford 1997). The contextual and ethnocentric character of community policing is an important factor in evaluations of significance and success of the policy and its implementation (Virta 2002b). Another special feature in adopting and adapting community policing in non-English-speaking countries is that in many languages, there are no exact translations for community policing. This means that, often, something has been lost in translation. Some translations, like the Finnish term *lähipoliisi* and the Swedish term *närpolis*, refer to neighborhoods and the police that are (physically) near people, and therefore, the terms lack the more communitarian connotations of the original policy. In Finnish, for example, the word *community*, translated literally, refers to some kind of suspicious subcultures, that is, it also has negative connotations.*

Since the 1960s, there has been a long tradition of the community policing style in Finland. A policeman lived in his or her own district and was familiar with the residents and local social norms. The informal duty of a policeman was also to mediate in minor conflicts between residents and prevent or reduce social and other tensions (Virta 2002a, 190; Brogden and Nijhar 2005). The modern police service is based on the "Principle of Prevention," and community policing can be seen as *the* way of implementing this principle today. The origin of this principle can be traced, for instance, to the influential writings like "A Treatise of the Police of the Metropolis" by Patrick Colquhoun in 1795. However, this was not a new idea even then. The old Anglo-Saxon methods of "keeping the peace" and the latter system of mutual pledging included the notion that crimes should be prevented by the vigilance of one's neighbors or by obedience to higher authority (Pike 1985). The roots of a policy of preventive policing of the nineteenth century were in ancient traditions of communal self-policing (Reiner 1985).

Anglo-American community policing has been implemented in Finland since 1996. The development of community policing was a consequence of international policy transfer processes rather than of an urgent need for reform. Finnish welfare society has been relatively stable and not very multicultural so far, but the situation is changing quite rapidly. Recorded crime rates are low. Both the adoption and the implementation of the community policing strategy have been a part of wider public sector modernization, and community policing was regarded as part of a natural process of police evolution and improvement of police services (Virta 2002a). In addition, as a principle of a welfare society and an

* For a teacher or instructor in European and other international police training and education projects, translation of Anglo-American terminology in general is very challenging. The author has been involved in community policing training in many European countries (e.g., in Greece, Belgium, Bulgaria, Latvia) and elsewhere (in Moldavia) and found out that the police in these countries use English terminology in strategies, due to the lack of proper translations. In police training, then, community policing must be explained and reinvented in their own languages.

integral part of welfare policies, it has been necessary to try to socially integrate the most marginalized groups of people by avoiding all rhetorical differences, and the convention by consensus to keep the community together should work without the exclusion of anyone. This principle is seen today in the Internal Security Program of Finland (2008) and in the (National) Community Policing Strategy (2010). Preventing social exclusion is therefore an integral part of community policing too.

Community Policing in Transition: Meeting New Challenges

Although crime prevention and preventive policing have a long tradition in Europe, it has been argued that over the past three decades, there has been another "preventive turn," and community policing and partnerships have become a defining attribute of contemporary crime control and its interface with wider social and urban policing (Crawford 2009, xv). In the broader social and political context, the growing sense of uncertainty surrounding the terrorism issue has resulted in a new mood of prevention, preemption, and precaution. The nature of policy-making processes follows the "Precautionary Principle." Terrorism has made the precautionary logic obvious after 9/11, and politics in general have taken a turn aimed at making precautionary logic part of everyday life (see, e.g., Virta 2008). The criminal justice model of countering terrorism in Europe and the main counterterrorism strategies of the EU count on preventive policing and especially community policing as a vital tool for local-level prevention of violent radicalization and homegrown terrorism.

Another significant element of contemporary community policing discourse and practice is that it has been "securitized." Crime has been reconceptualized as security risk (Zedner 2009). Community policing tends to be more and more about security provision and coproduction, security management, intelligence management, network management and local safety planning. Several elements turn community policing into a very challenging exercise for practitioners: the network structure and model of contemporary prevention, the nature of security knowledge (preventing the unknown or the unthinkable), the precrime logic of security, and the global and ambiguous nature of the threats and crimes to be prevented.

Intelligence gathering has become an even more important part of community policing than it was before. Intelligence-led policing (see, e.g., Ratcliffe 2008) has been reconciled with community policing in many countries. Intelligence-led policing is a way of doing police business; it is primarily a practical notion of how better to deliver police work. Community policing and intelligence-led policing are complementary (rather than competitive models). Intelligence management processes (intelligence gathering, community profiling, strategic analysis, targeting, and intelligence exchange) would be very valuable in improving the capacity of community policing initiatives. Community policing, and a good relationship between the police and the public, could play an important role in intelligence-led policing because trust and confidence toward the police is a precondition for successful intelligence gathering (especially for gathering community intelligence about community tensions and worries of people) (Virta 2008).

Perhaps one of the most promising fields in the development of community policing measures and means is social media and the emerging possibilities and innovations of the Internet and virtual community policing. Several police forces in the United Kingdom, United States, and Canada have launched profiles on social networking sites, providing a place where social network users can report crimes (often anonymously), chat with the police officers, and help fight crime. Using social networks, police can update their friends and fans in real time, while these same friends and fans are encouraged to use the system to report crime (Evans 2008).

The police in Finland now have strategies for the police to be represented on social networking Web sites such as Facebook, IRC-Galleria, Twitter, and MySpace. Because these are vibrant online meeting places, the police can meet young people and chat with them, give advice, and listen to their concerns. This is seen as a new complementary model of community policing, as the Internet is today a very popular community. Seventy-nine percent of young people under the age 17 in Finland use the Internet 2 to 3 hours every day (statistics from Helsinki Police Department 2011). Finnish police officers who work online on Facebook have their own personal profiles (picture, contact details, fields of interests). In August 2011, the police had 172,269 fans on Facebook, 25% of them under 18 years old (Helsinki Police Department 2011).

It has been argued that the Internet has the potential to transform police organizations by creating a new virtual police–citizen interface (Rosenbaum et al. 2011). The police in Finland have been active in this since 2008 by educating citizens about crime in their community; providing information about police programs, activities, and services; and engaging citizens in a two-way dialogue. For education purposes, the police have also put a lot of preventive material (videos, presentations) in its own forum on YouTube (http://www.youtube.com/suomenpoliisi).

HPD: Community Policing Innovations

The HPD started community policing reform in 2007 in the Eastern Police Precinct Itäkeskus as a pilot project. The main drivers for the reform were multicultural development, a growing number of immigrants and emerged crime problems. In addition, the reform was part of the implementation of the national Community Policing strategy 2007. The HPD Strategy for 2008 to 2012 had a special initiative of developing a new and innovative community policing model for the whole department and the city of Helsinki, based on the experiences and lessons learnt from the Itäkeskus pilot project in 2007 and 2008. City authorities have supported the initiative and have been active partners in safety planning processes.

The other significant HPD community policing initiative was launched in 2008 by three enthusiastic young officers who started to work on what they called "virtual community policing." The police in Finland did not have a social networking strategy at that time. Working online with Internet communities on Facebook and other forums is seen as vital when the police are aiming to actively engage with local communities. Social networks are also increasingly being accessed on the move via mobile phones, which has increased possibilities to be in contact with people, get real-time information, and give advice. The philosophy of virtual community policing in the HPD is mainly proactive: listening to young people's worries and chatting with them, helping and guiding in various security-related issues (e.g., how to report crime or suspicious behavior); and so on. It is seen as an innovation of good-quality and effective police service and a form of neighborhood policing where the police are near and accessible in a novel way.

Pilot Project Itäkeskus

Itäkeskus, the area of the Eastern Police Precinct, is the most multicultural area in Helsinki. There are approximately 150,000 inhabitants, of whom 12% are immigrants. The biggest immigrant groups are Estonians, Russians, and Somalis. The unemployment rate is higher than in other parts of Helsinki. In many respects, community policing reform was seen as the best possible police response to the problems of the area.

The basic idea of the reform was to integrate community policing style and thinking into all activities, including crime investigation, from management level to street level. The pilot project had three main objectives:

1. Organizational development (integration of community policing in daily police work, development of community policing capacity, teamwork and professional skills, and development of assessment and new measures for results and outcomes)
2. Networking with strategic partners (other authorities, residents' groups) in order to make a safety plan for the area together, to improve cooperation processes, to find effective problem solving mechanisms and models, and to create an integrated security coproduction model for the area
3. Citizen engagement (contacts, visibility, foot patrolling, involving people in safety planning processes, youth work, school visits, events)

The pilot project started in August 2007. It had a steering group of officers from the community policing team and the investigation and analysis team. The community policing team of five officers was established. The team was quite independent. They did not have to respond to emergency calls, so they had an opportunity to concentrate on networking, planning and creating their own ways of doing the job. The nature of leadership in the pilot project was facilitative; the team was equipped with a patrol car and other facilities, which made them easy to access 24/7 (one e-mail address, one mobile phone number). The total cost of the project (other than salaries) was approximately 25,000 euros.*

A big effort was made so that citizens, other authorities, and actors got to know the community policing team, their visions and duties, and contact details. There were many articles and news reports in newspapers and on the radio, and information sheets and other material delivered in public places like shopping malls. From the beginning of the project, the team was very active in contacting people, citizens' groups, and associations and networking with strategic partners. Patrolling by foot was one of the priorities all the time, and the target was to have contact, that is, to talk with 14,000 people during the 12-month project.

The objectives set for organizational development were not met completely, but this was due more to some structural and work conditional matters rather than implementation failures. The community policing team had too many tasks and responsibilities, and even if they were dedicated and committed to achieve everything they were expected to, there should have been more officers. Today, there are priorities and more defined tasks and duties, according to the HPD strategic priorities, and management of the community

* The results and outcomes of the pilot project are well documented in the project report of the HPD (September 30, 2009).

policing teamwork is better organized. Sixty percent of the work of the community policing team is patrolling (by foot when possible). In emergency situations, community policing teams can be used flexibly to other tasks too. Forty percent of the work consists of
"area-based problem solving," which means that community policing team members help,
for instance, shopkeepers in solving shoplifting problems; make risk assessments; and act
as "security consultants," encouraging, empowering, guiding, and advising people and
communities in solving their problems themselves. Police officers usually have a social
worker with them in patrols, especially when there are domestic violence cases. There are
also multiagency teams for aftercare (social and healthcare services, youth workers, victim
services).

However, the objective to get the community policing style integrated into routine
police work succeeded also in reconciling the intelligence-led policing approach and community policing. Community intelligence is shared with crime investigation teams and
is taken into account in operative and strategic management. Intelligence is also helping
community policing teams in targeting their patrolling (where and when) and other activities. Intelligence-led policing practices have led to more future-oriented decision making
too.

A safety plan for the Eastern Precinct area was completed in 2009, as a result of the
community policing team's work with strategic partners (social work, family work center,
health center, psychologist, urban planning and traffic authorities). The safety planning
process is well described and evaluated in the reports of the HPD. The safety plan is based
on several working papers, for instance, an assessment of safety and security in the area
(57 pages), many kinds of statistics and examples of good practices, and two citizen surveys
conducted in 2007. The safety plan includes four categories of objectives for working with
"problem" (vulnerable) families; working with children and young people (early intervention); preventing and reducing alcohol and drug problems; environmental safety and traffic conditions. The organization of safety and security cooperation has been renewed from
2010 onward; there is the steering group, which is not chaired by the police anymore, and
four subgroups (for the fields of cooperation above). Safety and security have become a
common shared agenda for the authorities and other actors in the area.

The objectives set for citizen contacts were met. The police had 14,000 contacts with
people. The number of contacts was actually counted by a very small calculator the officers
carried in their uniform pockets when they were patrolling by foot in the area and talking
to people. The community policing team visited kindergartens and schools and organized
a big event for schools. In this event, 3050 pupils, 150 teachers, and 50 police officers participated. Performance management for the community policing pilot project was planned
so that results and outcome were assessed monthly. For instance, in April 2008, the team
and individual officers attended 25 meetings with partners and five school visits. Statistics
of work hours for each task show how the community policing team spent their time: during the year from September 2007 until September 2008, the team used 4138 hours for
cooperation with partners and citizens, 2182 hours for planning and developing community policing initiatives and special projects, 1719 hours for patrolling, 403 hours for their
own training, 288 for management and administration, and 211 hours for investigation (of
minor crimes).

The most recent available statistics (June 1–30, 2011) from the Eastern Police Precinct
community policing team show no big changes; the time used for patrolling (foot patrolling, public order, traffic) was 60.55% of their work hours, and that for cooperation with the

partners and other preventive policing tasks was 39.45% (meetings, school visits, residents' associations' events, shopping malls consulting). The pilot project and its experiences and results have been taken into account in HPD tactical, operative, and strategic management.

Virtual Community Policing

A virtual community policing team of three dedicated officers of the HPD started its work in 2008, when an enthusiastic young police officer, Sergeant Marko Forss, had convinced his superiors and the commanding chief of the HPD that working online is the most promising new community policing method. The team created virtual community policing Web pages (http://www.facebook.com/pages/Suomen-poliisi/) and personal profiles for Facebook, IRC-Galleria, and Twitter (http://www.twitter.com/suomenpoliisi). The main task of the virtual community policing team is to work online proactively, so that it is very easy and convenient for people to contact the police. Virtual community policing is an interactive means to share and exchange information, to chat and get to know each other, and to create trust and confidence in the police. The police also inform people about criminal activities in social media (identity theft, credit card fraud, sexual abuse, wrong identities' risks), prevent school bullying, tell children what kind of behavior is against the law, and give advice (about driving licenses, driving regulations, how to deal with drug dealers, how to report crime online).

The three police profiles in IRC-Galleria received approximately 16,000 messages in 2010. Most of the messages were questions about various policing and security-related matters, but people also informed the police about criminal matters. Many of these led to a crime investigation process. The officers of the virtual community policing team use their Facebook profiles daily. In addition to informal chats, they receive approximately 80 questions or messages per month in their personal inboxes. When needed, the officers arrange personal meetings with people, go to schools and events, and give presentations and lectures to their colleagues and other audiences (Helsinki Police Department 2010). The team also investigates minor crimes and offenses and petty crime once a month for foot patrolling in the city center with a social worker. The officers are very popular among young people who know them from the Internet and like to chat face to face too. The most significant outcome of the work of the virtual community policing team is that they have created trust and confidence and provided safety and security both on the Internet and in real life.

It has been argued that community policing does have the capacity to affect petty crime and also serious crime (Connell et al. 2008). This could be the case in virtual community policing too. The main purpose of the virtual community policing team is to prevent crime and disorder, on the Internet and elsewhere, but they also inform crime investigators and report crimes conducted on the Internet (70 cases in 2010) and in the real world reported to them via Facebook, IRC-Galleria, or Twitter (43 cases in 2010). The crimes that happen on the Internet are mostly sexual abuse of young people or children. In a 7-month period (in 2010), the team had 36 sexual crimes reported; 27 of them happened on the Internet and nine of them were physical. In cases where children or young people are victimized, it seems to be easier for them to tell the police they know and trust, for instance, on Facebook or by e-mail, what has happened. There are no official survey results yet, but virtual community policing team officers have conducted minor Web surveys themselves. In one of them (during one day in September 2011), 97% of 156 persons who responded agreed strongly that virtual community policing is very-good-quality police service and that it is "so good to know that you are there for us."

The virtual community policing initiative of the HPD has been so successful and it has had so much positive publicity that the Police Board decided to invest in it, so that there were 13 new "Net cops" trained at the Police College in 2011. In addition to this, there are many police officers in local police departments who use various Internet channels daily but do not work online all the time. By participating in chats, for instance, the police can follow where young men with their motorbikes are going to gather and make friendly visits to their motorbike meetings. Early interventions are usually the best way to prevent crimes and disorder.

Community Policing in Prevention of Extremism

Preventing violent radicalization and recruitment and extremism in general is a huge challenge for the police. Many contemporary EU security and policing strategies rely on community policing. Reconciled with the intelligence-led policing approach, it is seen as a vital tool for local-level prevention in these issues too. The new challenges have been recognized by the police in Finland too. Integration of immigrants and general prevention of social exclusion have been seen as the most effective way of preventing extremism. The Finnish police have participated in the EU-funded project Community Policing on Preventing Radicalization (COPPRA), led by the Belgium Federal Police, since 2009.* The project has produced training material for street-level community policing purposes and front-line officers. In 2012, there were five training weeks, one week of training offered for five officers from each Member State.

There is already some research evidence that community policing can really work in prevention of extremism, but there is also opposite evidence (see, e.g., Spalek et al. 2008; de Kool 2008). However, according to the research results from the United Kingdom, the impact of counterterrorism strategies on local policing has not been significant. A very small part of routine policing tasks are related to counterterrorism (including radicalization prevention measures), even in high-risk areas (Tregidga 2011). In the United States, some research literature has suggested that homeland security appears to represent a potential threat to community policing, but, for instance, the research results of Jason Lee (2010) show that there has been no significant shift from community policing toward homeland security and that these two approaches are seen as complementary.

The HPD had special awareness training for community policing teams in May 2012. It will inform police not just about the European project but also about how to adapt means to prevent extremism in Finnish society and how to take account of these issues in community policing (both virtual and in the streets). Integration and intercultural dialogue will be the main means in the future too.

Organization Reform of the HPD

The organization and the management structure and practices of the HPD were reformed in the beginning of 2012. There will be no precincts any more when Eastern, Southern,

---

* The author is a member of the Steering Committee of the COPPRA II project (second phase, which started in 2010). There are 15 Member States' police organizations involved in the training project.

and Northern Precincts are to be fused. Community policing teams' management will be centralized to the new Preventive Policing Unit. Community policing will still be area based in practice, and teams will work in their own areas, but it will have more holistic and coherent strategic and operative management. The virtual community policing team will be more integrated in the work of the Preventive Policing Unit, so that online community policing will be one important element of prevention.

The aim of the reform is that there will also be more officers for foot patrols in the city center. The strategic objectives for visibility and accessibility mean that not just named community policing officers, but also other police officers, engage in foot patrolling when they are not engaged in emergency tasks or other duties. Police are also encouraged to develop ways of networking, community engagement, and citizen contact and to use discretion in solving problems with, for instance, social workers, shopkeepers, or traffic authorities.

Another improvement for services is the establishment of multiprofessional teams in the Preventive Policing Unit. There will be teams of police officers, social workers, and a psychiatric nurse. These teams are meant mainly for long-term solutions and problem solving (domestic violence, drug- and alcohol-related problems, vulnerable families). The HPD has had multiagency cooperation and team-based work with social and health services earlier too, but it will be more systematic and permanent in the future.

Conclusions

Evaluation of the community policing innovations and development in Helsinki is based on performance reports, self-assessment reports, and statistics of community policing teams and the HPD. It would be too early to assess results and outcome in detail. It is assumed, however, that community policing innovations have led and will lead to significant service improvements from citizens' point of view. Random Web surveys and other feedback indicate that people are very satisfied with community policing and innovative police services.

Community policing innovations have improved the image of police services in Helsinki. The police have moved more toward a "service-style policing" (see Hawdon 2008). Service-oriented police departments tend to have high regard for the opinion and the needs of community and administrators, and beat officers try to develop various procedures that make service a major concern to officers at every rank and in all tasks. The good practices of the Eastern Precinct pilot project have been benchmarked. Especially, the model of "empowering safety cooperation," which combines risk assessment, risk management, education of partners and citizens in problem solving, and the security expert role of the police is widely recognized.

References

Brogden, M. & Nijhar, P. (2005). *Community Policing. National and International Models and Approaches*. Willan Publishing. Cullompton.

Bruggeman, W.; van Branteghem, J.-M. & van Nuffel, D. (Eds.) (2007). *Toward an Excellent Police Function*. Politeia. Brussels.

Connell, N.; Miggans, K. & McGloin, J.M. (2008). Can a Community Policing Initiative Reduce Serious Crime? *Police Quarterly*. Vol. 11, Nr. 2. 127–150.

Crawford, A. (1997). *The Local Governance of Crime. Appeals to Community and Partnerships.* Clarendon Press. Oxford.

Crawford, A. (Ed.) (2009). *Crime Prevention Policies in Comparative Perspective.* Willan Publishing. Cullompton.

de Kool, W. (2008). The signalling of Islamist radicalism and terrorism by Dutch local police officers. In Virta, S. (ed.), *Policing Meets New Challenges: Preventing Radicalization and Recruitment.* Juvenes Print, University of Tampere. Tampere.

Evans, D. (2008). *Social Networks and Web 2.0 Policing.* Report. http://www.north-wales.police.uk .10.6.2009.

Hawdon, J. (2008). Legitimacy, Trust, Social Capital and Policing Styles: A Theoretical Statement. *Police Quarterly.* Vol. 11, Nr. 2. 182–201.

Helsinki Police Department. (2010). Annual report of the virtual community policing team. http://www.poliisi.fi.

Helsinki Police Department. (2011). Annual report of the Helsinki Police Department.

Lee, J.W. (2010). Policing after 9/11: Community Policing in an Age of Homeland Security. *Police Quarterly.* Vol. 13, Nr. 4. 347–366.

Pike, M. (1985). *The Principles of Policing.* MacMillan Press. London.

Ratcliffe, J. (2008). *Intelligence-Led Policing.* Willan Publishing. Cullompton.

Reiner, R. (1985). *The Politics of Policing.* Wheatsheaf Books. Brighton.

Rosenbaum, D.; Graziano, L.; Cody, S. & Schuck, A. (2011). Understanding Community Policing and Legitimacy-Seeking Behaviour in Virtual Reality: A National Study of Municipal Police Websites. *Police Quarterly.* Vol. 14, Nr. 1. 25–47.

Spalek, B.; El Awa, S. & Zahra-McDonald, L. (2008). *Police–Muslim Engagement and Partnerships for the Purposes of Counter-Terrorism.* Project report. University of Birmingham. Birmingham.

Tregidga, J. (2011). *The Securitization of Routine Policing? A Case Study on the Impact of Counterterrorism Policy on Local Policing.* PhD Thesis. University of Cardiff. Cardiff.

Virta, S. (2002a). Local Security Management: Policing Through Networks. *Policing: An International Journal of Police Strategies and Management.* Vol. 25, Nr. 1. 190–200.

Virta, S. (2002b). Local security networks as an outcome of community policing. In Van den Broeck, T. & Eliaerts, C. (eds.), *Evaluating Community Policing.* Politeia. Brussels.

Virta, S. (Ed.) (2008). *Policing Meets New Challenges. Preventing Radicalization and Recruitment.* Juvenes Print, University of Tampere. Tampere.

Zedner, L. (2009) *Security. Key Readings in Criminology.* Routledge. Abingdon.

Germany

THOMAS FELTES

27

Contents

Background

The Federal Republic of Germany is located in the heart of Europe, linking the west with the east, and the north with the south. The most densely populated country in Europe, Germany has been flanked by nine neighboring states since the unification of the two German states in 1990. Germany covers an area of 357,022 km².

For most of its history, Germany was not a unified state but a loose association of territorial states that together made up the "Holy Roman Empire of the German Nation." In 1871, the "German Reich" was founded. Nowadays, the Federal Republic of Germany is divided into 16 federal states (*Laender*), each responsible for the government of its own state (see chart). The states that exist today were established after 1945, but have in part, retained their old ethnic traditions and characteristics as well as their historical boundaries.

There are currently 82.6 million people living in Germany, about 15 million people with migrant background, mainly from Turkey and also from the former Union of Soviet Socialist Republics (USSR).

After the World War Two (1945), the German police was under the supervision of the military regional governments of the Allies. With the new German constitution of 1949 and the foundation of 11 states in the early 1950s in West Germany, these states got the power to establish their own police forces. In East Germany, formerly the German Democratic Republic (under Russian government), one central police force was established. Each of the 16 German states has its own police law and its own police force. Furthermore, there are the Federal Police, the Federal Criminal Police Office (BKA), and the federal customs. The police laws of the 16 states deal with the prevention of crime, the preservation of public security and order, and the warding off of impending danger. This is the main reason why there is no single strategy or philosophy for community policing (CP) in Germany: each state and even each local community can decide on its own way on whether and how to implement CP. Both patrol police (uniformed) and detectives (plainclothes) are working together in the same force. The uniformed or patrol police deals mainly with general public security functions, with traffic problems and accidents, and with minor crimes. Detectives or criminal investigation police are responsible for all other crimes. The total number of police officers on duty is 265,000 (2010), resulting in one officer for 330 inhabitants. In fact, if one calculates losses due to transfer, illness, training, administrative tasks in ministries, and so forth, the "real" number is about one officer available for between 8000 and 10,000 inhabitants at a given moment.

It is difficult to decide what "indigenous people" or "indigenous communities" in Germany are and whether such a differentiation makes sense in terms of policing the community. If we define "indigenous" for Germany as being German (coming from the Germanic peoples and tribes), nobody can say what the influence of the emigration of nations over the centuries has been. Nowadays, many people have a German passport but have a non-"German" background: overall, some 20% of the population, but if we look at given age groups and special parts of Germany, for example, bigger cities, this percentage goes up to 50% and more.

The Migration Period, also called the Barbarian Invasions (*Völkerwanderung*, "migration of peoples"), was a period of intensified human migration in Europe that occurred from around 400 to 800 CE. The migrants at that time came from parts of Europe, nowadays known as France, Italy, and Scandinavia, but also from Eastern Europe. Later migrants came, for example, from Poland during the eighteenth century. During the transformation of Germany from an agrarian to an industrial society, many Poles migrated to the rapidly transforming areas around the Ruhr River, because the expansion of the coal mining industry of the area required manpower, which could not be supplied from the nearby regions. From the 1870s, a large wave of migration of the aforementioned groups started to settle in the Ruhr area. Nowadays, about 2 million people with Polish background live in Germany. Later on, in the 1960s, a large-scale immigration of Turkish workers occurred, due to the demand for labor in Germany. Nowadays, about 4 million people with Turkish background live in Germany.

The question of whether something like the *Urheimat* ("homeland") of Germans really exists is still unsolved. Profound changes in culture (and language) occurred over centuries, resulting in the fact that an indigenous population in Germany exists only in the minds of some Germans, which is a result of discussions about the "foreign infiltration" during the 1990s, when Germany had high numbers of asylum seekers. The resulting xenophobia and aversion against non-Germans peaked in 2010, when a controversial book *Deutschland schafft sich ab* (Sarrazin 2010) was published, saying that people with Turkish background are less intelligent than (biological) Germans and sparking a nationwide controversy about the costs and benefits of the ideology of multiculturalism.

Another issue is the loss of cultural identity to modernism with the younger generation, especially young people with Turkish background. They are now the third generation, after their grandparents came to Germany in the 1960s as *Gastarbeiter*. By law, every German citizen (indigenous and minorities included) has the unrestricted right to form political parties; stand for office; and vote in federal, regional, and local elections. Some states also allow people with European Union citizenship to vote for local governments. Members of migrant minorities, as well as Jews and Roma/Gypsies, have faced considerable racist violence in Germany in recent years. NGO's estimate that nearly 150 people have been killed by right extremists since 1990 (unification). After a series of killings by a group of right extremists, discovered in 2011, which remained unsolved for years, the cooperation between German police and secret services was discussed. The three members of the so-called Zwickau cell murdered nine people from a non-German background and one policewoman, despite being watched by police and intelligence agents for years. It became obvious that the authorities had failed but also that many fellow citizens and even neighbors looked away during this period of 10 years, while the three lived underground. Besides that, the German majority see immigration as a threat to high wages, employment, the welfare state, and ethnic and religious homogeneity. Tough policies on immigration and security against terrorism have been vote catchers in recent elections.

Origin of CP in Germany

In contrast to theoretical and political discussions on police and police functions and to many studies in foreign countries, empirical police research was very rare in Germany until the beginning of this century. Police in Germany is—like in other countries—an unspecified agency, used by citizens for various purposes, which exceed by far the much-specified duties named in the German Law. Unlike other police forces, German police do not have any discretionary power in criminal cases. Every offense noticed by or brought to the notice of a police officer must be registered and prosecuted. The state attorney only may dismiss cases and use discretionary power. Nevertheless, in neighborhood disputes, family conflicts, and minor offenses, police officers have possibilities of discretionary decisions in everyday conflicts. They use techniques like immediate conflict solution and take immediate actions to help people in everyday conflicts. Further, police play an important role in the settlement of conflicts and in the redress of various molestations (disturbances, brawls). In these fields, their work is relatively effective and efficient. But these services have only partly to do with their legal task. In the field of prosecution, however, police work is rather ineffective. Citizens call the police to solve very different problems more often than in earlier times. Victims call the police in order to find an institution and people in this institution who are able to help them and to support them emotionally (mostly) and financially (sometimes). Just putting a few more police officers on the street has no impact on both the crime rate and the clearance rate, which is determined by a lot of different factors besides policing. The police are less and lesser able to cope with the very different and difficult tasks of policing a modern, complex society.

CP as a solution for the problems mentioned and as a reaction to the increase in registered crimes in the 1970s and 1980s has been discussed in Germany since the beginning of the 1990s (Dölling and Feltes 1993). Since then, more and more communities have implemented some kind of "community policing," although there is no nationwide understanding of what that really means and whether CP is a new strategy, a philosophy, or just new wine in old barrels (Feltes 1995a). CP in Germany is largely an outgrowth of a community concept of crime prevention. German concepts of CP emerged from the new crime prevention philosophy, both social and situational. German states have tried out various policing theories or working philosophies over the past two decades, including what can be called "citizen-friendly policing," which evolved into today's community crime prevention. Thus, CP in Germany is not a single organizational feature of German police forces but rather an applied philosophy that can be used in specific neighborhoods, in specific instances, and for achieving clearly defined results. In most states, police either take the initiative in organizing CP boards or councils in their town or city, or cooperate with the mayor or city council by participating on a local Crime Prevention Council (Jones and Wiseman 2006; Pütter 1999). Indigenous groups, minorities, and especially communities with a high percentage of migrants are until now not a target for CP, although some states now try to increase the very low percentage of police officers with migrant background (between 1% and 2% in most of the states and 9% in Berlin) (Hunold et al. 2010). Some police education institutions focus on policing minority groups of migrant communities, but until today, nearly 30% of people with Turkish migrant background have the feeling of discrimination by police (Sauer 2011).

How Does CP Work?

In Germany, CP is also known as district policing, aiming to gratify the citizens' needs for a visible police that is openly present in their surroundings and among the people living there. The officer should talk to the people, be a direct partner for their requests, and have knowledge of their concerns and emergencies. The district police officers should provide close and trustful contacts. In doing so, they should increase the overall feeling of security, enhance the understanding of police actions, and influence the relationship between police and citizens in a positive way. In particular, the officers shall initiate and keep up contacts in their district. This applies to official bodies, businesspersons, institutions, and organizations, but specifically, contact with citizens is voluntary. The district police officers' scope of duties is vast. They deal with aspects of traffic, crime prevention, and tracking. The officers' specific knowledge of a place and its people can furthermore add to crime investigation.

Usually, only a few officers perform such a task; a ratio of 1 officer per 15,000 inhabitants is not unusual. Officers responsible for the city center usually work on their own responsibility; however, often, relationships are built with other persons or organizations. District officers generally are on foot patrol; sometimes, they use public transport. Police cars are used only in exceptional cases. Usually, the officer is on an early shift, starting at 7 AM. Regularly, however, late shifts also have to be carried out. For financial reasons, the number of district officers has been more and more reduced in many cities. Naturally, district policing should be without any operational specifications so that the officers can concentrate merely on their district, de facto; however, each officer has to fulfill a number of orders every day. The tasks are summarized as follows:

- Foot patrols; making contact with the citizens and businesspeople; keeping informed about the happenings, areas of problems, and conflict
- Taking youngsters to court, the youth welfare office, or the prison
- Investigations of wanted persons for other services (other police services or the office of the public prosecutor)
- Taking young men to the recruiting office, in case they do not appear voluntarily (this is due to the liability to a military service in Germany)
- Victim support after break-ins, robberies, and thefts
- Giving statements for requests
- Cooperation with the crime prevention unit
- Working with kindergartens and primary schools (e.g., information, pedestrian training, bicycle training, checking child safety seats of parents who take their children to school by car, etc.)
- Investigating motorists with radar photos
- Checking of persons with regard to the law on firearms
- Small investigations supporting the emergency patrol unit
- Research on false alarms caused by private systems
- Everything that occurs on the spot or what the officers observe

While on duty, the district officer is connected to the overall radio traffic of the main police station and is able to react when he or she is close to an incident. Direct orders from the radio communicator to the district officers are rare and occur only when all patrols are engaged elsewhere. The district officers have the same information technology and databases on their display as their colleagues from the emergency patrol. Other cooperation concerns municipal and public organizations. An official partnership between police and the city government, for example, considers regular joint patrols of district officers and officials from the municipal department for public order. These are occasionally accompanied by the security service of the public transport company, who are responsible for safety and order around the central station and the bus and tram stops. Information exchange between these parties is regularly initiated.

Most police forces have some kind of community beat patrol (CBP). In a recent study, we observed incidents in which two patrol police officers and CBPs were involved. Police officers in city A deal with 1.3 incidents per hour, and their CBP colleagues deal with 2.1 incidents per hour. Calls per hour were 0.8 for emergency patrol and 0.2 for CP. However, the numbers do not include incidents that involved answering questions from the public or chatting with citizens, which accounted for high numbers of incidents. With regard to the total numbers, traffic seems to be an issue of emergency patrol rather than CP. For the total number of observations, the highest numbers related to "maintaining the law." However, the community police work in one of the cities differs substantially from the other: 21.9% compared to 34.0%. Accordingly, very few incidents relating to serious crimes were observed by CBP. Also, internal tasks seem to play a relatively minor role for CP. The CBP work is largely concerned with "networking" and "giving assistance," particularly answering questions from the public. As Tables 27.1 and 27.2 show, there are significant differences between the two cities, which make clear that local and regional decisions vary and result in a kind of "local police culture," equivalent to the already-described local legal culture (Church 1985). In city A, on the other hand, figures for "giving assistance" differ significantly from the average with regard to the work of the emergency patrol. Officers here were, for the most part, engaged in recording accident data, assisting persons requiring help (see example below), or helping out during riots, for example, at psychiatric departments. Particularly during night shifts, the officers assisted in cases of disturbance of the peace.

Incidents involving marginalized persons, such as alcoholics, drug addicts, or homeless people, are more likely to occur in nontraffic situations. Of these, most incidents are

Table 27.1   Patrol Work Subdivided into Main Categories (%)

	N	Maintaining the Law	Maintaining Public Order	Giving Assistance	Networking	Internal Job	Other
			Emergency Patrol				
A	129	47.3	3.9	** 38.8	1.6	1.6	7.0
B	167	61.1	8.4	22.2	3.0	0.6	4.8
			Community Beat Patrol				
A	162	34.0	9.3	17.3	22.2	14.2	3.1
B	196	** 21.9	4.6	** 32.7	* 31.6	** 1.5	7.7

$* p < .01; ** p < .001.$

Table 27.2 Patrol Work Subdivided into Subjects (%)

	Traffic				Law		Order/Assistance					Other		
	Collision	Violence	Check	Other	Serious Crime	Other	Social Problem	Questions from Public	Troublesome Youth	Public Order	Other	Networking	Internal Job	Else
Emergency Patrol														
A	** 17.8	25.6	5.4	3.1	10.1	3.1	13.2	3.1	0.0	0.8	10.1	1.6	1.6	5.4
B	* 12.0	28.1	13.2	4.2	14.4	3.6	4.2	1.2	0.6	4.2	7.8	3.0	0.6	3.0
Community Beat Policing														
A	0.6	15.4	** 9.9	4.9	5.6	1.2	1.9	13.0	0.6	6.8	3.7	22.2	14.2	0.0
B	1.5	15.8	3.6	3.6	** 1.0	0.5	2.0	** 27.6	0.0	4.6	4.1	** 31.6	** 1.5	2.6

* $p < .01$; ** $p < .001$ (with respect to total PSE).

Table 27.3 **Proportion of Incidents in which Officers Took Oppressive Measures—All Incidents**

	N	Warning	Summons	Arrest	One of These
			Emergency Patrol		
A	129	22.5	** 20.9	3.1	46.5
B	167	21.6	** 22.8	4.8	** 49.1
			Community Beat Patrol		
A	162	** 6.2	1.9	0.6	** 8.6
B	196	18.4	1.5	1.0	20.9

$* p < .01; ** p < .001.$

dealt with by the officers working on CBPs. District officers seemed to have very good knowledge of the marginalized persons in their district. When patrolling, they proactively approached and talked to marginalized groups or individuals. The encounters were always friendly, even when the officers had to ask them to leave certain places. They knew the people by name, and the officers were known to them and accepted by them, as their orders were generally complied with. On several occasions, the observer noted that CBP officers went up to persons they did not know, introduced themselves and their job, and asked for the person's name. Nearly all incidents that involve marginalized persons were initiated by the officers. The outcomes of incidents have been measured in terms of measures taken by the officers (see Table 27.3), divided into warnings, summons or tickets issued to citizens, and arrests. Considering the overall numbers, German emergency policing looks rather repressive, as many summonses are issued.

Besides that, special CP projects focus mainly on crime prevention: local or regional councils with representatives from social institutions, churches, public administration, business, and so forth analyze the local situation (usually by using victim surveys) and develop strategies for prevention (Dölling et al. 2003; Feltes 1995b). Very few of these activities are evaluated.

Relationship to Criminal Justice System

The police laws of the 16 states deal with the prevention of crime, the preservation of public security and order, and warding off impending danger. Further police tasks arise out of the criminal procedure code, which deals with prosecution of crimes as well as laws arising out of or existing next to it. The criminal justice code applies to the whole Federal Republic. The authorities and officials of the police force must investigate crimes and take all measures necessary to collect evidence. This principle of legality is the most unique regulation: neither the police as an institution nor the police officer himself or herself is allowed to dismiss a case. This can be done only by the office of the public prosecutor, where every case has to be reported. According to the criminal justice code, the police are assistant public officials to the state attorney's office. The public prosecutor is solely responsible for prosecution of crimes. However, individual measures (arrests, searches, impoundments) can be authorized by the police if there is no time to contact a public prosecutor or a judge.

The attorney of state also may give orders to the police. But in most investigations (especially concerning minor and medium crime), the necessary measures are taken without the cooperation of the state attorney; the case is merely sent to the state attorney's office, once the police investigations are completed. The state attorney makes the decision on whether or not to prosecute the case.

Effectiveness of CP

CP is a philosophy rather than a new strategy. As a consequence, the training and the management of police need to be adjusted to this new approach (Greene and Mastrofski 1998; Greene 1993; Feltes 2002).

The cooperation of the various actors in the field of community crime prevention is the most crucial point. Local crime prevention through CP needs crossdepartmental collaboration and networking with particular agencies and those who have the local expertise and the environment knowledge within police, law enforcement, social services, and other stakeholders in the community. They have to exchange and compare their individual and institutional resources and expertise and concentrate on bureaucratic obstacles in the control and prevention of crime. This happens, for example, in community prevention bodies, where communication has a key role in coordination and cooperation between the actors. The question of whether the programs implemented in fact have the desired effects on the local situation is difficult to decide because too many variables influence the result (changes over time and space). The prevention discourse sometimes gets (too) close to "law and order" concepts (such as "broken windows" or "zero tolerance"; see Dreher and Feltes 1998) and sometimes tries to implement solutions that really focus on the local rates of crimes. It very often also misses the necessary broader public impact, especially due to the fact that the crime rate in Germany has been decreasing since the late 1990s. The Ministries of the Interior and Justice document the prevention programs on the Internet and in brochures. In North Rhine-Westphalia (the biggest of the German states), over 900 partnerships between police and the public have been started since 1999, addressing situations of public fear and disorder in the communities. Nationwide, one estimates that 2000 municipal bodies do at least some kind of prevention work, but very few are evaluated in the sense that the situation before starting such a project is compared with the situation afterwards.

Conclusions

CP is based upon the idea that the activities of the police have to be extended in the communities for them to become an institution that cares and coordinates efforts to improve social cohesion (Weitekamp et al. 2003). But in Germany, crime control in general and the idea that fighting crime is the core task of police still remain prevalent. As CP has its main focus on keeping the public peaceful, on mediating conflicts, on coordinating efforts to improve the whole quality of life in the community, and on crime prevention (Feltes and Gramckow 1994), it still lives a quiet life within the German police and tends to be sidelined. CP in Germany is mainly regarded as district policing or as a tool for prevention, working with joint crime prevention bodies in cities.

References

Church, Thomas (1985): Examining local legal culture. In: *American Bar Foundation Research Journal*, 10, 3, pp. 449–518. Available at http://www.jstor.org/pss/828165.

Dreher, Gunther, Thomas Feltes (eds.) (1998): *Das Modell New York: Kriminalprävention durch "Zero Tolerance"?* Holzkirchen, Felix.

Dölling, Dieter, Thomas Feltes (Eds.) (1993): *Community Policing—Comparative Aspects of Community Oriented Police Work.* Holzkirchen, Felix.

Dölling, Dieter, Thomas Feltes, Wolfgang Heinz, Helmut Kury (2003): *Kommunale Kriminalprävention—Analysen und Perspektiven.* Holzkirchen, Felix.

Feltes, Thomas (1995a): Bürgernahe Polizeiarbeit—neuer Wein in alten Schläuchen? In: *Jahrbuch Rechts—und Kriminalsoziologie*, pp. 125–148. Baden–Baden, Nomos.

Feltes, Thomas (1995b): *Kommunale Kriminalprävention in Baden-Württemberg.* Holzkirchen, Felix.

Feltes, Thomas (2002): Community oriented policing in Germany. Training and education. In: *Policing: An International Journal of Police Strategies and Management*, 25, 1, pp. 48–59.

Feltes, Thomas, Heike Gramckow (1994): Bürgernahe Polizei und kommunale Kriminalprävention. In: *Neue Kriminalpolitik*, 3, p. 16.

Greene, Jack R. (1993): Community policing in the United States: Historical roots, present practices and future requirements. In: *Community Policing—Comparative Aspects of Community Oriented Police Work.* Dölling and Feltes, pp. 71–92. Holzkirchen, Felix.

Greene, Jack R., Stephen D. Mastrofski (1988): *Community Policing: Rhetoric or Reality.* Westport, Greenwood Press.

Hunold, Daniela, Rafael Behr, Daniela Klimke, Rüdiger Lautmann (2010): *Fremde als Ordnungshüter? Die Polizei in der Zuwanderungsgesellschaft Deutschland.* Wiesbaden, VS Verlag für Sozialwissenschaften.

Jones, Arthur A., Robin Wiseman (2006): Community policing in Europe: Structure and best practices. Sweden, France, Germany. Available at http://www.lacp.org/Articles%20-%20Expert%20-%20Our%20Opinion/060908-CommunityPolicingInEurope-AJ.htm.

Pütter, Norbert (1999): *Community policing. Alternative zu herkömmlicher Polizeiarbeit?* In: *Bürgerrechte und Polizei/CILIP*, 64, 3/1999, pp. 6–16.

Sarrazin, Thilo (2010): *Deutschland schafft sich ab. Wie wir unser Land aufs Spiel setzen.* München, Deutsche Verlags-Anstalt.

Sauer, Martina (2011): *Partizipation und Engagement türkeistämmiger Migrantinnen und Migranten in Nordrhein-Westfalen. Ergebnisse der elften Mehrthemenbefragung 2010.* Essen, Zentrum für Türkeistudien und Integrationsforschung.

Weitekamp, Elmar, Hans-Jürger Kerner, Ulrike Meier (2003): Problem solving policing: Views of citizens and citizens expectations in Germany. In: *Social Work and Society*, 1, 1, pp. 52–77. Available at http://www.socwork.net/sws/article/view/253/428.

Italy

STEFANO CANEPPELE

28

Contents

Background

Italy is a peninsula in Southern Europe. Geographically, it borders France (northwest), Switzerland (north), Austria (north), and Slovenia (northeast) along the Alps, one of the greatest mountain range systems of Europe, but most of its territories are surrounded by the Mediterranean Sea (7375 km). Because of its proximity to Africa (the closest Italian island, Lampedusa, is only 113 km from the Tunisian coast), Italy occupies a strategic position and is considered a gate to Europe. From an administrative point of view, Italy is now organized in 8092 *Comuni* (municipalities) grouped into 110 *Provincias* (provinces), which, in turn, are grouped into 20 *Regioni* (regions). In Italy, 44.6% of the population lives in municipalities with high urbanization (more than 500 people per square kilometer in contiguous areas with more than 50,000 inhabitants). Only two cities have more than 1 million inhabitants (Rome, 2.8 million, and Milan, 1.3 million).

Historically, the Italian Country was first established as a Kingdom in 1861, after the inclusion of the Kingdom of the Two Sicilies, which at that time included the southern part of Italy. The so-established Italian Kingdom was governed by the former king of Sardinia, Vittorio Emanuele II of Savoy, member of the royal family who ruled Italy until 1946 and who extended his model of government, a centralized one based on the French experience, to all the rest of the country—an approach adopted also for the police forces.

The former Kingdom of Sardinia, in fact, extended its police model to the rest of the country. At that time, the law enforcement agencies were mainly of three types: *Arma dei Carabinieri Reali* (Royal Carabinieri Corps) or, simply, *Carabinieri*; *Corpo delle Guardie di Pubblica Sicurezza* (Public Security Guards Corps); and *Corpo della Regia Guardia di Finanza* (Royal Guardia di Finanza Corps). All of them were centralized, and only the latter had a delimited and specific role related to the protection of the financial interests of the State against fraud (e.g., illegal smuggling of goods). The other two police forces had a general mandate related to the enforcement of the law and the maintenance of public order. The main difference between the two corps was the governance: the *Carabinieri* corps was headed by a general commander, and it was more autonomous, whereas the other, the public security guards corps, was under the direct command of the Ministry of the Interior.

Moreover, at a local level, in the most populous urban areas, an indefinite number of city councils decided to employ local wardens, who, under the direction of the municipalities, controlled public order in the streets.

In 1890, the Italian government decided to reform the *Corpo delle Guardie di Pubblica Sicurezza*, instituting the *Corpo delle Guardie di Città* (City Guardian Corps) with the intention of unifying the public security guards with the local police guards working in the urban areas. This reform worked only partially, and, in 1907, the Italian government officially recognized that municipalities could keep their own guards with functions related to enforcement of the local administrative regulation.

During the fascist regime (1922–1943), the leader of the National Fascist Party, Benito Mussolini, increased his control over the police forces. In 1922, the government incorporated the City Guardian Corps (since 1919, *Corpo della Regia Guardia per la Pubblica Sicurezza* [Royal Guardian of Public Security Corps]) into the *Carabinieri* corps, but this attempt failed in 1925. After the end of the Second World War, the Italian Republic (1946) reformed also its police force system. The Public Security Corps turned back to its former governance model, and only in 1981 did the Parliament pass a milestone law (Law 121/1981, *Nuovo ordinamento dell'Amministrazione della pubblica sicurezza* [New order of the Administration of Public Security]) revising profoundly the architecture of the police forces in Italy. In particular, the former *Corpo delle Guardie di Pubblica Sicurezza* (Public Security Guards Corps and a military corps) turned into the actual *Polizia di Stato*, a non-military police corps. The law also codified a new governance model in the field of public security acknowledging the plurality of actors that operated in the field of public security on the one hand, and calling for a coordination of policing at local and national level, on the other hand. In 1986, the reform also involved the local police. The government passed Law 65/1986, called *Legge Quadro sull'Ordinamento della Polizia Municipale* (Framework Law on the Organization of the Municipal Police), which stated how local police should be structured.

From the 1990s, a new wave of reforms involved public policing. Local authorities increasingly demanded to be not just a spectator but also an active participant in the security policies in which the words "crime prevention policy" started to be interpreted not only as "police patrolling and police arrests." In 1999, the Italian Parliament amended Law 121/81, also including in the governance model the representatives of the local authority. A new era of cooperation between national and local agencies had started with the experiences of *Patti locali di sicurezza* (local security agreements), a sort of contract among national and local actors to reduce crime and increase perception of safety at a local level.

Police Organization

Nowadays, the Italian police system has several police forces. The *Polizia di Stato* has around 115,000 police officers, and it is mainly concentrated in the city areas with its 103 *Questure*. Each *Questura* is organized into two divisions: *Polizia Anticrimine* (Criminal Police) and *Polizia Amministrativa e Sociale* (Administrative and Social Police). Other highly trained police officers belong to special centralized task forces.

The *Arma dei Carabinieri* is a military corps that functionally depends, only for public security, on the Italian Ministry of the Interior. It numbers approximately 100,000 people, and it is homogenously distributed across all the country, in rural and urban areas.

Approximately 80% of the police staff is deployed on the ground. It has 4675 *Stazioni* (police stations) presiding over the 8092 Italian municipalities. The police stations are hierarchically and geographically grouped into 539 *Compagnie* and 102 *Comandi Provinciali* (Provincial Commands), 19 *Comandi di Legione* (Regional Commands), and five *Comandi Interregionali* (Interregional Commands). The remaining staff is assigned to special task force groups. Both *Arma dei Carabinieri* and *Polizia di Stato* have a general and overlapping competence in the field of crime control and public security. The *Guardia di Finanza* has, instead, exclusive competence on financial crimes, although with its 65,000 officers, it is also engaged in crime control and public security. It is a military corps, and it has a hierarchical and geographical structure similar to the *Carabinieri*. The *Polizia Penitenziaria* (around 40,000 officers) is in charge of managing the 207 Italian prisons, while the *Corpo Forestale dello Stato* (about 8500 officers) specializes in the protection of the natural environment and in the prevention and repression of environmental crime. Finally, the *Polizia Locale* (local police) depends on local authorities (municipalities and provinces). Geographically, the *Polizia Locale* has a competence limited to the administrative boundary of the local authority. Functionally, the *Polizia Locale* has a major role in traffic regulation and in many areas covered by administrative sanctions. Usually, it is not involved in serious criminal investigations; it is very fragmented and not homogenously distributed across the country. The *Polizia Locale* is mainly concentrated in the cities situated in the north and central parts of Italy. Although it is hard to provide an accurate figure, the number of officers is around 60,000. All of these police forces have a different chain of command; however, Law 121/81 has instituted the *Comitati provinciali per l'ordine e la sicurezza pubblica* (Provincial Committees for public order and safety), also with the intention of facilitating the coordination among police forces. Those committees, chaired by the *Prefetto*, who is the authority of public security representing the State at a provincial level, have increased their role in the last decade and promoted an integrated approach toward crime and disorder problems in the communities. At the same time, the cooperation between national and local authorities has been further strengthened through protocols signed by different national and local actors in a specific geographic area (*Patti locali di sicurezza*).

Origins of Community Policing in Italy

The discussion on community policing in Italy began relatively late, compared to the US and other European experiences. In fact, during the 1970s and 1980s, the attention of the Italian security policies was focused on combating domestic terrorism (e.g., Red Brigades) and serious organized crime (the Mafia in Sicily, the Camorra in Campania, the Sacra Corona Unita in Puglia, and the Ndrangheta in Calabria). Only in the early 1990s, with the end of the so-called First Republic and the direct election of the mayor in the city council, did the issue of urban security become a major topic in the Italian political scene. At the regional level, local governments have begun to claim a role that previously had never been granted in security policies (Braccesi 2004). One of the ways through which local authorities sought to affirm the importance of their role in crime prevention was to develop the local police.

In the second half of the 1990s, some regional governments passed laws to support the development of the local police. The resources allocated were used to (1) enhance the professionalism of the operators through training, (2) purchase equipment and technologically appropriate instrumental equipment, (3) build new local police stations, (4) promote the creation of bodies of local police with a minimum number of employees, and (5) encourage initiatives of cooperation between local police and the community. At the same time, it also developed a debate on the type of police work and the importance of collaboration with citizens in order to have a safer society and less crime. This debate has produced a common tension to what has been called *Polizia di prossimità* (proximity policing). The experiences of proximity policing derive from the French experience of *Police de proximitè*, and, despite some criticism (Bertaccini 2011), it is intended as the European continental version of community policing. Officially, the term appeared in 2002, when the Minister of Interior chose the *prossimità* as a strategic priority. He updated the "coordinated plan to control the territory" and introduced the theme of "proximity services on foot" with "the objective to test the methods of control of the territory through daily contact between the police forces and the citizen" (Corte dei Conti 2009, p. 6). Generally speaking, this new approach from the Italian point of view has been considered a way to reestablish a daily relationship with the citizens, emphasizing the importance of dialogue between police officers and people.

In this context, the two largest national police forces (*Polizia di Stato* and *Carabinieri*) introduced proximity policing in their strategies to keep pace with the demands that come with the territory. Moreover, also at a local level, the concept of proximity policing has been used by the most inspired regional governments as a new tool for interpreting the activity of local police. Italy seems to have produced a double version of proximity/community policing: one performed by the national police forces and the other performed by some regional local authorities. The most advertised national initiatives were *Poliziotto di quartiere* and *Carabiniere di quartiere*. The aim of these two projects, launched in 2001, was to patrol neighborhoods on foot, introducing one or two police officers, immediately distinguishable by a special uniform, who should interact with the community. However, it quickly became evident that the term *Polizia di prossimità* was intended more as a container of initiatives, even very different ones, that could have better satisfied the citizens' crime and disorder problem. At a municipal and regional level, the experience of proximity moved forward to a direct involvement of citizens in neighborhood watch initiatives, also because in many situations, local police were already organized in neighborhood patrolling (Carrer 2003).

How Does Community Policing Work?

As previously mentioned, at the beginning of the 2000s, national police and regional authorities decided to perform proximity/community policing.

In 2002, the Ministry of the Interior launched the new initiative of *Polizia di prossimità*. The service had an experimental period of 12 months. In 2003, the service was gradually extended in the urban centers included in the project. The Ministry of the Interior had planned to allocate about 6000 police officers (4500 from the *Polizia di Stato* corps and 1500 from the *Carabinieri* corps) for more than 1000 zones by 2006. In January 2006, there were about 3700 police officers for 750 urban areas. On December 31, 2008, the service included less than 3900 operators (2274 and 1620 police officers) in approximately 800 areas. The destination of more police officers to the *Polizia di prossimità* program was suspended because of budget limitations. The patrols were usually composed of two operators wearing a special uniform. The staff were equipped with a radio transmitter, a mobile phone with predetermined numbers to call, and a handheld computer connected to the control room for data transmission and radio location. The service was provided mainly on foot and sometimes by bicycle. Each patrol covered an urban area of approximately 10,000 inhabitants, organizing the service in two shifts per day (8 AM–2 PM, 2 PM–8 PM). A significant number of services have been provided to the metropolitan areas of Rome, Milan, Naples, and Turin. As mentioned before, the strategy of proximity also included other initiatives to foster citizens' safety and their confidence in the police. In particular, the Italian government funded programs that made it easier to report a crime (collection of reports of crime at home for the elderly and handicapped, possibility of reporting a crime via Web) and facilitated the relationships between police forces and citizens through the Web and the institution of Public Relations Offices in each *Commissariato* of *Polizia di Stato*. Also included under this strategy of proximity is the neighborhood watch strategy adopted by the Italian government in 2009. Law 94/2009 mentions the possible involvement of groups of citizens (volunteer observers) in order to report to police forces events that can cause damage to urban security or situations of social disadvantage. This initiative was preceded by a strong political controversy. At that time, in fact, the Ministry of the Interior was a member of a separatist right-wing party that in the past had already instituted voluntary patrols. The fear of a violent degeneration was eliminated by the Decree, issued by the same Minister, which regulated the activities of volunteer observers. The associations, which cannot be the expression of a political party, must be non-profit, and they must be registered in a provincial register maintained by the *Prefetto*, who annually checks if the registered associations still have the necessary requirements. The individual requirements to become observers are as follows: (1) being 18 years or older, (2) being in good health and having no dependence on drugs (medical certificate is required), (3) having no criminal records, (4) not having joined any racist or extremist group, and (5) having successfully attended a training course. The observation activities can be carried out only in groups of up to three people, including at least one person aged 25 years or older, without the use of motorized vehicles or animals. During the service, volunteers should wear a distinctive uniform, should have a valid identity document, and should not bear arms. Their report of activity can be carried out only through mobile phones or radios.

After more than 2 years, the national neighborhood watch experience is still rare. The number of associations registered is less than 20 across the whole peninsula (Cherchi 2011). Ultimately, this national initiative was not effective, probably because it was excessively regulated by the State. However, this does not mean that in Italy, there is not a tradition of citizen volunteers in safety policies. At the municipal level, many experiences coexist, and local police established different forms of cooperation with citizens (Nobili 2009). The initiative of the so-called *Nonni Vigile* is, for example, very popular. In this experience, municipalities hire groups of retired people (in some cases, former police officers) in order to support local police in controlling pedestrian crossings near schools or monitoring public parks or streets. The myriad of initiatives—which blossomed in the last 10 years—describes the dynamism of the Italian local communities. All of them share the idea that the prevention of crime and disorder as well as the promotion of a safer environment are collective tasks. In this sense, not only local police but also *Polizia di Stato* and *Carabinieri* can operate better if properly supported by the citizens. Creating a safer society means promoting joint action between different national and local agencies, especially in a historical moment where budget cuts push toward optimization of resources.

Effectiveness of Community Policing

It is unclear whether community policing is effective and under what circumstances it could be considered effective. There is a dearth of systematic research studies on this topic because the experience of community policing is relatively young and evaluation studies are expensive and politically risky. The Ministry of the Interior had initially assigned a monitoring role on the experience of *Polizia di prossimità* to an observatory, which did not produce any report on the experience. In 2003, *Carabinieri* published the findings of a short Computer Assisted Telephone Interview (CATI) survey (sample of 1980 people) on the service of the *Carabiniere di quartiere*. Among the interviewees, 48.4% thought that it was an effective initiative, although only 8% declared that they had personally met the officer. The only public document available is the report written in 2009 by the Italian Corte dei Conti on the experience of *Polizia di Prossimità*. The magistrates observed that "the analysis of results [...] is complex because the effects of prevention activities are measurable in the medium/long term [...]. Despite the limitations of project implementation, the signals seem to suggest [...], as reported by the competent administrations, a growth in public confidence [...]" (Corte dei Conti 2009, p. 31). To support its positive judgment, the Court cites information provided by *Carabinieri*, which is not scientifically robust. In one case, the positive assessment comes from an online questionnaire that can be voluntarily filled out by any citizen. In another case, it is not possible to say that the program was effective only because there was a "moderate reduction of crimes (theft, robbery, and extortion)" (Corte dei Conti 2009, pp. 31–32) observed from 2006 to 2008 in the areas patrolled by the *Carabiniere di quartiere*. The other neighborhood watch initiative, promoted by the government in 2009, did not have any success because it was labeled as politically right wing oriented. But, as we have noticed before, neighborhood watch/neighborhood warden schemes have been carried out in many Italian municipalities. Also, the initiatives promoted by the local authority were not submitted to a rigorous evaluation. Due to the scarcity of funds, evaluation is neglected in favor of assigning more resources to the intervention. This lack of scientific evidence does not represent an issue, and the effectiveness of those policies is taken for granted. Generally, common sense suggests that the more eyes watch the street, the safer you are. And this is good enough to avoid opening Pandora's box through an expensive evaluation study, especially because police forces are already quite popular in the Italian public opinion. According to the crime survey carried out by the National Institute of Statistics (ISTAT 2010), the percentage of people satisfied with the Italian national police in 2008/2009 was 61.6%.

Conclusion

In this chapter, we explored community policing in Italy from its background, presenting some of its programs. In 2001, the introduction of community policing at a national level aimed at being an innovative strategy for increasing satisfaction with police activity. Unfortunately, this strategy was only partially implemented and poorly evaluated due to budget limitations, which probably will also affect the future of the Italian police.

Other initiatives, such as neighborhood watch groups, grew spontaneously at the local level but did not develop homogenously across the country, and any central attempt to regulate the phenomenon failed. Voluntarism of regional and local authorities provided positive leverage for promoting community policing, but the inner risk resides in not having a national strategy on this topic, although it is true that today, national police also pay much more attention to citizen needs than in the past.

In view of this, what will be the future of *Polizia di prossimità* in Italy? Hopefully, the financial crisis could be the opportunity for a global reorganization of the national and local police system. The budget cuts should lead to a reduction of overlapping competences between national and local police forces and to a more effective cooperation among agencies and with citizens. The direction taken by *Patti della Sicurezza* seems to celebrate a new season of fruitful cooperation between local and national authorities. The years to come will prove if this direction will turn into a new era for Italian policing.

Web Sites

Arma dei Carabinieri, http://www.carabinieri.it.
Corpo Forestale dello Stato, http://www.corpoforestale.it.
Guardia di Finanza, http://www.gdf.it.
Polizia di Stato, http://www.poliziadistato.it.

References

Bertaccini, E. (2011). *I modelli di polizia*, Bologna: Maggioli Editore.

Braccesi, C. (2004). Lo sviluppo delle politiche di sicurezza urbana, in Selmini, R., *La sicurezza urbana*, Bologna: il Mulino: 261–272.

Carrer, F. (2003). *La polizia di prossimità: la partecipazione del cittadino alla gestione della sicurezza nel panorama internazionale*, Milano: Franco Angeli.

Cherchi, A. (2011). "Il fallimento delle ronde: al Nord sono solo dieci." Sole 24Ore [Milan, Italy], 11 April 2011 [online edition]. Available at http://www.ilsole24ore.com/art/notizie/2011-04-18/fallimento-ronde-nord-sono-063802.shtml?uuid = Aav29rPD (23 January 2012).

Corte dei Conti. (2009). *Relazione concernente l'attuazione del progetto "Polizia di prossimità,"* Rome, Italy. Available at http://www.corteconti.it/controllo/finanza_pubblica/programmazione_monitoraggio/delibera_10_2009_G/index.html (23 January 2012).

ISTAT (Italian Institute of Statistics). (2010). *Reati, vittime e percezione di sicurezza*, Rome, Italy. Available at http://www.istat.it/it/archivio/4089 (23 January 2012).

Nobili, G. (2009). Ronde cittadine: una nuova strategia di sicurezza urbana? *Autonomie locali e servizi sociali* (3): 487–497.

Romeo, V. "I carabinieri di quartiere e la ricerca della loro identità." Effettotre [online blog], 4 February 2010. Available at http://www.effettotre.com/archivio_effettotre/arsenio_la_pen_colpisce_ancora.pdf (23 January 2012).

The Republic of Moldova

29

EVGHENI FLOREA

Contents

Background

The Republic of Moldova is landlocked, bounded by Ukraine on the east and Romania to the west, and occupies most of what has been known as Bessarabia. It is the second-smallest country of the former Soviet republics. Moldova is slightly larger than Maryland, with its official population at 3.56 million people.*

The country's location has made it a historic passageway between Asia and Southern Europe, as well as the victim of frequent warfare. Greeks, Romans, Huns, Goths, and Avars invaded the area throughout its history. An independent Moldovan state emerged briefly in the fourteenth century and grew in territory under its celebrated leader Stefan the Great in the fifteenth century but subsequently fell under Ottoman Turkish rule in the sixteenth century.

After the Russo–Turkish War of 1806–1812, the eastern half of Moldova (Bessarabia) was ceded to Russia, while Romanian Moldavia remained with the Turks. Romania took control of Russian-ruled Bessarabia in 1918 but was forced to cede it to the Union of Soviet Socialist Republics (USSR) in 1940, when the Soviet leader Joseph Stalin established the Moldavian Soviet Socialist Republic by merging the autonomous republic east of the Nistru and the annexed Bessarabian portion. Stalin also stripped the three southern regions along the Black Sea coast from Moldova and incorporated them into Ukraine.

After the proclamation of its independence in 1991, Moldova confronted a series of obstacles, including an ineffective parliament, the lack of a new constitution, a separatist movement led by the Gagauz (Christian Turkic) minority in the south, and unrest in the Transnistria region, where a separatist movement declared a "Transdniester Moldovan Republic." The Russian Army intervened to stem widespread violence and support the Transnistrian regime. In 1992, the government negotiated a cease-fire arrangement with Russian and Transnistrian officials, although tensions continue, and negotiations are ongoing. The conflict with the Gagauz minority was defused by the granting of local autonomy.

Like many other former Soviet republics, Moldova has experienced economic difficulties. Since its economy was highly dependent on the rest of the former Soviet Union

---

* This figure does not include about 0.533 million residents of a secessionist region, Transnistria, as well as an estimated 0.750 to 1 million people who work outside the country.

for energy and raw materials, the breakdown in trade following the breakup of the Soviet Union had serious economic and social effects, exacerbated at times by drought and civil conflict. Currently, Moldova is one of the poorest countries in Europe. Its industry accounts for less than 15% of its labor force, while its agriculture share is more than one quarter. The biggest ethnic groups are Moldovans (75.8%), Ukrainians (8.3%), and Russians (5.9%). Other present nationalities are Gagauz, Bulgarians, and Romanians. The dominant religion is Orthodox Christianity to which adhere 96% of inhabitants.

During the Soviet period in the territory of Moldova, police did not exist. Its functions were performed by the militia. It should be noted that differences between these two concepts (police and militia) in the Soviet Union were mostly ideological, rather than substantive in nature. It was believed that the police, this instrument of the arm of the exploiting class, was used to suppress discontent among the exploited workers and peasants. But militias, for their part, were proclaimed a truly people's formation, which was intended to implement real protection of public order. For this reason, bodies under the name "police" were never and could never be, not just in Soviet Moldova but also in any other state or republic of the Soviet bloc. But in fact, their Soviet militia was the police and exercised police duties.

With the approach of the collapse of the USSR, some of the Soviet Republics began to demonstrate some ideological independence from the weakening central powers. This was shown in the inclusion and adoption of laws that do not comply with communist ideologies. So, on December 18, 1990, in Moldova, the law "On Police" was accepted, which applies still today. According to this law, "Police of the Republic of Moldova represent their armed law enforcement body of public authority, designed on the basis of strict compliance of laws to protect lives, wellbeing, rights, and freedom of citizens, interests of society and the state from criminal and other illegal encroachments, and is a constituent part of the Ministry of Internal Affairs (The Law of the Republic of Moldova, December 1990)." As a law enforcement body of public authority, police of the Republic of Moldova are divided into state and municipal. State police perform their duties in all of the territory of the Republic of Moldova; municipal police perform their duties in the territory of the relevant municipal administrative unit.

If one tears away from the dry legal language and appeals to public opinion, it is necessary to admit that Moldovan police are not trusted by the population. Thus, the police and the bodies of justice are located at the top of the list of institutions that the citizens of Moldova trust the least. Sociological studies show that the population believes that the representatives of these institutions are the most corrupt public servants (Furtseva 2011).

Origins of Community Policing in Moldova

Since during the revolution of 1917, Moldova was a part of Russia, all the events associated with the coming to power of the Bolsheviks bear the most direct connection to the history of Moldova, including the process, emergence, and development of community policing in its territory.

At the legislative level, first amateur formations of workers for the protection of public order were created in Soviet Russia through the decision of the People's Commissariat of Internal Affairs (NKVD) on October 28, 1917, "On the workers' militia." The decision placed in the local bodies of government authorities the responsibility to organize the workers' militia. The legal power of this document consisted primarily in securing the rights of the workers to take part in the protection of public order. Since this ruling did not specify the organizational form of the workers' militia, creative initiative and revolutionary individual initiative of workers, united in Soviets (councils), were, in the first months of the Soviet authorities, the basis of construction of amateur groups for the protection of public order.

Thus, the militia was established, but the militia agencies did not have a permanent staff structure and were actually voluntary groups. In other words, for nearly a year, the militia, as a state organization, in Soviet Russia did not exist. In places where earlier formations of police existed, they were sometimes disbanded, sometimes reorganized. Local Soviets created and supported their own militias. Very soon it was realized that the system of law and order could not exist and effectively function as an assortment of volunteer units. Therefore, in 1918, the Soviet government reconstructed militias in the capacity of a state agency. At the same time, parallel with the state's militia, but under the control of the state authorities, they continued to operate voluntary organizations, such as public order squads, groups for police and criminal investigation assistance, support brigades under police bodies, and so forth.

The most famous voluntary organization in the USSR, rendering help to state militias in protection of public order, was the Voluntary People's Squad *Dobrovolnaia Narodnaia Drujina* (DND). The first Voluntary People's Squad for the protection of public order was formed in 1955 by the groups of workers of several enterprises in Leningrad, and in 1958, the movement received support from the party and state structures and became widespread. Later, these squads were created in other major industrial centers, including the capital of Moldova.

Based on this experience, the Soviet government, on March 2, 1959, adopted a resolution "about participation of workers in the protection of public order in the country." This resolution became the main legal–regulatory document that defined the tasks, powers, and forms of organization of DND.

Usually, vigilantes with red armbands on their sleeves in small groups of tree-four people, often with a police officer, walked around the streets of Soviet cities and kept order. They had fairly broad powers; particularly, they had the right to detain persons and bring them to the militia station. Thus, a few people without problems dealt with persons involved in disorderly conduct, drunkards, violators of peace, and so forth. Identification signs for the vigilantes were red armbands and badges, which were issued (or were given) together with certification of membership in the Voluntary People's Squad.

Due to the fact that in the period after 1960, the frequency of cases of violent resistance to the vigilantes by the offenders increased, in 1962, the Resolution of the Presidium of the Supreme Soviet of the USSR "on strengthening the liability for the attempt on the life, health, and dignity of the workers militia and people's squad" was adopted.

Participation in the DND was considered social work and was encouraged by the leadership of enterprises and organizations, the party, and the Young Communist League. On January 1, 1979, in the republic, with a population just under 4 million people, there were over 3000 squads, which included more than 115,000 vigilantes (Vartichyan 1979a).

Noticeable decline in DND participation began in 1989. By this time, the traditional Soviet organizational forms of public participation in the struggle against violators of the law were becoming ineffective due to the changes that were occurring in society. Serious blows were the transfer from commercial entities, the placement of posts for community policing of law and order, and the privatization and closing of large enterprises (from labor groups, which previously made up many DNDs) due to lack of funding.

At the time of the collapse of the Soviet Union, there had been serious changes in the motivations of the vigilantes. In modern conditions, the problem of involving citizens in law enforcement activities is that it has to address the lack of enthusiasm and, on some other basis, such questions as material compensation for participation in the protection of public order, above all.

How Does Community Policing Work in the Indigenous Community?

The Republic of Moldova, being an independent state, is still experiencing colossal negative impacts from the collapse of the Soviet Union. Last but not least, the collapse of the USSR also affected the system of protecting public order. By the beginning of the 1990s, the categorical rejection of everything, which was associated with the Soviet past, resulted in the country almost entirely destroying the entire extensive and well-honed structure of interaction between civilians and law enforcement in the protection of public order. For all their ideological richness and often-ostentatious character, it worked out. In the Soviet Union system, public participation in law enforcement was really massive and extremely effective. Today, this is acknowledged by even the most anti-Soviet Moldovans. Therefore, the recovery process of community policing is slowly gaining momentum but is still very far from the performance of the Soviet period. At the present time, in Chisinau, there are 58 units of the organization "Garda Populara"—the people's guard. They include 1004 civilians of the country: students, professors, workers, and retirees (mostly former law enforcement officers) (Nezavisimaya Moldova, February 21, 2006). In total, according to the Ministry of Internal Affairs of the Republic of Moldova, in the country, with a population of 3.5 million people, there are 1220 operating units of the people's guard, which includes in its membership 15,000 people (Nezavisimaya Moldova, March 24, 2009).

The legal basis for the activities of voluntary associations of civilians for the protection of public order was adopted by the Moldovan parliament in the 1997 Law of the People's Guard. Under this law, the main tasks of the people's guard are providing security and protecting the legitimate interests of civilians, assisting law enforcement bodies in the maintenance of public order, and preventing and suppressing violations of the law.

The people's guards can be created in enterprises, institutions, and organizations, and also by place of residence of citizens by decision of the local public administrative authorities. Citizens of the Republic of Moldova no younger than 18 years of age, of an able condition of health, able to do their business, and possessing moral qualities to fulfill the tasks set before them can join the people's guards by voluntarily submitting a personal statement. The foundation of the people's guard constitutes students, professors, workers, and retirees (mostly former law enforcement officers). A member of the people's guard who committed an offense incompatible with his presence in an arm of the people's guard or who neglected his duties was eliminated from the people's guard. This decision was adopted at a general meeting of the members of the people's guard. Enterprises, institutions, and organizations, which created the people's guard, provided the necessary facilities, telephone connections, furniture and inventory, transport, and other technical means. Costs for the maintenance of service space, acquisition of furniture, inventory, specialized literature, visual aids, forms of identification, armbands, and telephones, mail, and other expenses necessary for support of the activities of the people's guard were also paid for through resources of enterprises, agencies, and organizations that created the guards. The people's guard created by place of residence of citizens is provided with everything necessary for its activities by the relevant local authorities, at the expense of the allocated local budgets.

Every people's guard was headed by the commander of the guard and his deputy, elected at a general meeting of members of the guard for a term of 1 year.

The administration of enterprises, institutions, and organizations that created the people's guard could introduce a paid position for the commander of the people's guard or establish an additional payment to his official salary.

The general management of the people's guard was carried out by local authorities, which organized and directed their activities, took adequate measures to ensure compliance with the rule of law, and coordinated and improved cooperation of the people's guard with the public authorities, with authorization to protect the rule of law, hear reports on the work of the guard and records of the commanders of the guard, and solve issues of logistics.

The people's guard, jointly with law enforcement agencies, carried out the following functions:

- Participate in the protection of order and the overseeing of compliance with the law in public spaces (in buildings, on the street, in the markets, in parks, etc.) and also in monitoring of the maintenance of order during the conducting of meetings
- Take part in the struggle against hooligans, drunkenness, alcoholism, theft of property, and other offenses
- Jointly, with the agencies of internal affairs, perform preventative work with individuals released from penitentiary institutes as well as persons convicted of conditional punitive measures
- Participate in the struggle against homelessness, juvenile crime, and adults who involve juveniles in drunkenness and criminal activities
- Adopt measures to provide emergency services to citizens and victims of accidents or crimes and be present in public spaces in helpless states, participating in rescuing people and their property and maintaining public order during natural disasters and other emergency situations
- Implement measures to protect and conserve the environment and natural resources
- In conjunction with the traffic police, carry out measures for compliance of citizens with the rules of the road

Members of the people's guard perform their duties, usually, during their time off from work/study.

To help them carry out the above functions, the law empowers members of the people's guard with the following rights:

- To require from citizens compliance with public order and termination of offenses
- To require offenders to present identification documents in cases, when the establishment of identification is necessary to determine the details of the offense or involvement in it
- To detain and deliver to the police, when all other measures have been exhausted, those who violate public order or commit crimes, in order to establish their identities and prepare statements

- When suppressing crime, to confiscate weapons used by offenders in committing offenses, followed by immediate transfer to the police
- To use all possible means of active defense
- To have free access to the clubs, cinemas, stadiums, sports grounds, and other public places in pursuit of fugitive offenders, or to prevent crime, as well as to perform the duties of maintaining public order
- To have free use of city passenger transports (except taxis) in the manner determined by the local public administration
- To use, in nonurgent cases, any vehicle (except for diplomatic vehicles) for delivery to hospitals of persons affected by accidents or crime and in need of emergency care, as well as citizens in public places in a state of helplessness
- To have free use of telephone enterprises, institutions, and organizations

In addition to the rights of members of the people's guard, they have performance obligations, which is a necessary condition for their effective work. Otherwise, it is easy to blur the lines between street gangs and groups monitoring the social order. Among the most important obligations of a member of the people's guard are the following:

- To defend the honor, dignity, rights, and lawful interests of citizens, be tactful and courteous in the performance of their duties, and be determined to take legal action to stop any antisocial activities
- To work diligently for the entrusted site and to fulfill the requirements of the commander of the guard and its staff as well as instructions of law enforcement officers in carrying out joint activities to maintain public order
- To know and comply strictly with applicable laws, to study and apply forms and methods to combat crime, and not to divulge information obtained during or in connection with the performance of their duties that is protected by law
- To promptly report to the headquarters of the guards, police agencies, and other law enforcement agencies one's well-known facts about statements or committed crimes, natural disasters, or other emergencies that threaten the safety of citizens, enterprises, institutions, and organizations, as well as take measures to prevent such situations and to eliminate their consequences
- During the performance of their duties, to wear an armband and to carry an identification badge of a member of the guard
- At the request of citizens and police officers, to assist them in the prevention of crime
- To report periodically to the labor collective in which the people's guard is included

Members of the people's guard, who are active participants in the struggle against crime, are encouraged by local public authorities, law enforcement bodies, administrations of enterprises, institutions, and organizations, which created the people's guard, through:

- Announcements of gratitude
- Awarding valuable gifts or cash prizes
- Providing additional paid leave for up to 5 days
- Providing preferential treatment in health resorts and rest homes

According to the press services of the General Commissariat of the Police of Chisinau, at the end of the year, the work of the people's squads was found to be satisfactory. And the best vigilante squads were awarded valuable gifts and prizes. Thus, a squad of vigilantes who took first place was presented with a refrigerator, second place received a television, and third place received a stereo system (Nezavisimaya Moldova, February 21, 2006).

For outstanding achievements in combating crime and maintaining public order, members of the people's guard were presented through the established procedure for the state awards.

The members of the people's guard, in good faith relating to the performance of their duties, may apply to address the general assembly or the headquarters of the guard concerning the following sanctions:

- A warning
- A reprimand
- Exclusion from the guard

Besides the people's guard in the Republic of Moldova, there are other forms of participation in the protection of public order, which have not yet received widespread support. In its initial phase of existence is the community police, which should become the intermediary between the population, police, and branches of local authorities. In the opinion of the European organizations sponsoring this project, the competence of the community police will be to prevent crime, to assist citizens in resolving small everyday crimes, and also to monitor the activities of the state police. Last but not least, members of the community police will pay attention to how the population relates to the activities of the state police. This structure will obey the branches of local authorities and, by its nature, will think not as an oppressor but as a helper of the people. To date, the community police are active in two communities in Moldova (one is in a city and the other is in a rural region), and in the case of positive results in its activities, similar structures will be created throughout the country.

Individual participation of citizens of Moldova in law enforcement is carried out as follows:

- Announcement to the law enforcement agencies of the known facts concerning the offences inchoate or committed, causes, and conditions conductive to the commitment of these offenses
- Assisting law enforcement in the prevention and suppression of offenses

It should be noted that a very low level of public confidence in the police clearly had an extremely negative effect on the individual activities of the citizens in the region fighting against crime. Today, the people of Moldova call the police only in extreme cases, when there is some kind of serious offense, or when the callers themselves are the direct victims of such acts as burglary, carjacking, or robbery. The most active in supporting the police are retirees, whose trust in the state's law enforcement agencies and willingness to provide help to police had been formed during the Soviet times. In this context, the Moldovan police have a saying: "grandmother, a policeman's best friend."

Relationship to Criminal Justice System

After the collapse of the Soviet Moldova, as well as almost all other former Soviet republics, Moldova refused practically all forms of participation in the fight against crime that had been used during the Soviet period. The independent Moldova did not need comradely courts, exemptions from criminal liability with a transfer to the labor collective on parole, off-site meetings of courts, and other public activities along these lines. Since in this case, instead of the Soviet forms of fighting against crime, nothing appeared for a long time, there was a defined vacuum in the relations between the police and the public. This vacuum reflected extremely negatively in the perception of the public eye of the Moldovan justice system as a whole and also the police in particular. According to some opinion polls, about two-thirds of Moldovans do not trust the state's Justice Department (Furtseva 2011).

The Moldovan government adopted several measures designed to change the situation. The most important measures in this sense should be recognized: the development and consolidation of the Criminal Code of the Republic of Moldova in 2002 and the implementation of the institute of reconciliation with the victim, as well as the adoption of Law on Mediation in 2007. According to the mentioned law, mediation is an alternative way of resolving a conflict between parties by way of a mutual agreement with a third party. This method is based on the trust of the parties in the mediator, as the person intended to facilitate negotiations between them and to assist them in resolving the conflict by finding a mutually acceptable, effective, and lasting solution.

Parties can voluntarily resort to mediation on any stage of criminal procedure before the sentence is pronounced, if they reached an agreement on the criminal law issue that they had.

The main advantage of this method of resolving a conflict lies in the fact that during the mediation session, the parties can communicate in a way that is impossible in the courtroom. This is not a semiofficial situation but a frank discussion of the parties that are initially conflicting but willing to compromise. And a mediator is impartial and ensures confidentiality.

The results of the steps of the Moldovan government to implement elements of restorative justice did not take long to appear. So the Institute of Penal Reform (IRP) was established to manage the mediations and the workers who help reconcile the offenders and the victims. Representatives from the institute learn about cases of violations from the prosecutor. All of the information about the defendant and the victim is then carefully studied. In the event that the employee managing the mediation concludes that reconciliation is possible between the conflicting parties, they are invited to meet, so they can talk to each other. Under the named project, out of 79 attempts to reconcile victims and perpetrators, done over a time period of a year and a half, in 55 cases, the parties reconciled and found an understanding of each other (Calac 2006). Here is one of the best examples of the work of the IRP staff:

> … Maria is extremely tired of her husband's drinking. After drinking, he would become insane and beat her… After the next conflict and beatings, she went to the police. Her husband was waiting for punishment and a further life together would not be happy. Together the couple agreed to go to mediation. And it changed everything. After living together for so many years, they only found out during the session, that the true cause of discord was not drinking but the head of the family's children from previous marriages, to which he devoted

much more attention than their common children. After resolving this issue, relations between the spouses have changed (Komsomolskaya Pravda v Moldove, October 21, 2006).

Of course, it must be understood that mediation is not a cure. Reconciliation is not possible in all cases. For example, staff of the Institute does not attempt to reconcile the parties involved in such crimes as rape or armed attack. However, in cases of petty theft, family conflict, and violence in schools, mediation is a very effective way to reduce the number of prisoners.

Effectiveness of Community Policing

It is difficult to judge the effectiveness of community policing in Moldova. This is explained by the fact that this question is not given much attention by both scholars and the Moldovan Justice Department. Apparently, this is the first attempt at a general analysis of community policing in the post-Soviet period of Moldova, as I was unable to find any detailed scientific research that was devoted to this question. Leading domestic criminologists with whom I was able to speak on this subject matter recommended to him as sources of information, papers published also in the USSR, laws adopted in this area, as well as police reports and newspaper articles.

Certain conclusions about the effectiveness of certain types of community policing in Moldova can be made based on indirect evidence. As in the capital in the period from 2000 to 2004, the number of reported crimes decreased almost twofold, and recorded street crime, over the same period of time, decreased almost fourfold. The conclusion suggests itself concerning the apparent success of the police and street patrols in cooperative activities for the protection of public order. However, one should not rush to such assessments. The fact is that the Moldovan police in this period were characterized by artificially low numbers of reported crimes. This was done for public authorities in order to create among the population the illusion of success in combating crime and maintaining public order. In addition, I believed that the number of vigilantes according to the authorities (16,000 people) is not the actual number of people carrying out the activities of the Garda Populara. The work of national teams is constructed in such a way that enterprises, agencies, and organizations in which there are guards must provide progress reports to the local authorities. That is why guards often exist just on paper, for the report, or they operate from time to time in periods when some control of their activity from public authorities is expected.

The most productive work is the activity of nongovernmental organizations, which at the time of the grant were actively promoting such forms of community policing as community police, mediation, the establishment of telephone hotlines for victims of trafficking, the holding of seminars, round tables, and so forth. But after the financing, most of the time, all this activity ceases.

Conclusions

The Republic of Moldova is a classic example of Durkheimian anomie. Society is divided between those who are nostalgic for Soviet stability and those who share Western values. The existing social norms and ideals are extremely controversial. The primary laws only slightly correspond to the realities of life. On paper, they look thoughtful and accurate, but the population, in particular, does not observe them, and some (e.g., paying taxes, the ban on corruption) are actually sabotaged by a majority of citizens because of their mistrust of authority.

The experience of post-Soviet Moldova in the field of community policing is hardly positive. Most of Moldova is an example of how *not* to build relationships between police and citizens. During the transition from a totalitarian system to a democratic one, the entire system of citizens' interactions with law enforcement was almost completely destroyed. In this case, the authorities did not make sure to replace the old forms of public participation in order to protect the social order with something new. Nongovernmental organizations operating in the country are working in some highly specialized segments of the maintenance of public order. And ordinary citizens, wrongly assimilated to the philosophies of individualism, guided by the principle "I do not care," are showing indifference to what is happening in society. The work of the police in Moldova is one of the most unprestigious because of meager salaries, the risks to their lives, and lack of support from the general population.

In general, it should be noted that community policing in Moldova is in its infancy. The easiest way to remedy the situation is to return to the invaluable positive experience that was gained in the country during the Soviet period and use it while taking into account current realities. It was on this path that the other former Soviet republics went. For instance, Belarus has kept forms of citizens' associations participating in community policing such as the following:

- Councils for crime prevention under district administrations, as well as enterprises, institutions, and organizations
- Commissions to combat alcohol abuses
- Home, quarterly, and street committees
- Citizen courts
- Operational youth teams that are created on the initiative of the police, in cooperation with the local administrations and the rectors of higher educational institutions (Postnikova 2005)

It appears that the experience of Belarus can really help Moldova to establish cooperation between the police and its citizens, which ultimately will have a positive impact on the perceptions of public law enforcement and enhance public safety in the country.

References

Calac T. (2006). V Moldove zhertvy miriatsia s prestupnikami [In Moldova victims get reconciled with criminals]. Komsomolskaya Pravda v Moldove, October 21, 2006.

Furtseva E. (2011). Dve treti jitelei Moldovi ne doveriaiut politsii i sudam. [Two thirds of Moldovan citizens do not trust police and courts]. http://www.nr2.ru/economy/342306.html/print/ [accessed January 17, 2012].

Gutu Z., Vidaicu D. (2011). Raport de monitorizare privind implementarea legii rm nr. 134 din 14.06.2007 cu privire la mediere [Report on monitoring of implementation of the law of the Republic of Moldova on mediation]. Chisinau. http://www.justice.gov.md/pageview .php?l=ro&idc=103 [accessed January 17, 2012].

Hriptievschi N., Munteanu V., Vizdoga I., Redpath J., Smith R. (2009). Criminal justice performance from a human rights perspective: Assessing the transformation of the criminal justice system in Moldova. Soros Foundation, Moldova. http://www.soros.md/files/publications/documents/ CRIMINAL%20JUSTICE%20PERFORMANCE%20FROM%20A%20HUMAN%20RIGHTS%20 PERSPECTIVE.pdf [accessed January 17, 2012].

Institutul Reformelor Penale (IRP) [Institute of Penal Reforms (IRP)]. Moldova. http://www.irp.md [accessed January 17, 2012].

Legea Republicii Moldova nr. 134 cu privire la Mediere din 14 Iunie 2007 [The Law of the Republic of Moldova nr. 134 on Mediation from 18 June 2007]. Monitorul Oficial nr. 188-191. 7 December, 2007. Art. 730. http://lex.justice.md/index.php?action=view&view=doc&lang=1&id=326080 [accessed October 14, 2012].

Legea Republicii Moldova nr. 416 cu privire la Poliție din 18 Decembrie 1990 [The Law of the Republic of Moldova nr. 416 On Police from 18 December 1990]. Monitorul Oficial nr. 17-19. 31 January, 2002. Art. 56. http://lex.justice.md/index.php?action=view&view=doc&lang=1&id=312894 [accessed October 14, 2012].

Nezavisimaya Moldova, February 21, 2006. A ty zapisalsya dobrovoltsem? [Have you signed up for volunteering?].

Nezavisimaya Moldova, March 24, 2009. Dobroe imya narodnih drujin [The good name of popular guards].

Postanovlenie CK KPSS i Soveta Ministrov SSSR № 218 ot 2 marta 1959 goda "Ob uchastii trudia-shikhsia v okhrane obshestvennogo poriadka v strane" [Resolution of the Central Committee of Communist Party and Council of Ministers of the USSR nr. 218 from 2 of March 1959 "On the participation of workers in the maintenance of public order in the country"]. Spravochnik partiinogo rabotnika. Nr. 3. Moscow 1961, p. 577–579.

Postanovlenie Narodnogo Komissariata Vnutrennikh Del (NKVD) RSFSR ot 28 Oktiabria 1917 goda "O rabochei militsii" [The Regulation of the People's Commissariat of Internal Affairs (NKVD) of RSFSR (Russian Soviet Federative Socialist Republic) 1917 "On the workers' militia"]. Sobranie uzakonenii I rasporiajenii rabochego I krestianskogo pravitelstva. 1st December 1917. Nr. 1.

Postanovlenie Plenuma Verkhovnogo Suda SSSR 1962 goda ob usilenii otvetstvennosti za posiaga-telstvo na jizni, zdorovie i dostoinstvo rabotnikov militsii i narodnikh drujinnikov [Resolution of the Presidium of the Supreme Soviet of the USSR in 1962 to strengthen the responsibil-ity for the attempt on life, health and dignity of police officers and people's squad members]. Vedomosti Verkhovnogo Suda SSSR, 1962 Nr. 17, Art. 177.

Postnikova A. (2005). Voprosy vzaimodeistvia organov vnutrennikh del s grajdanami, uchast-vuiushimi v ohrane pravoporyadka (na primere opita Respubliki Belarus) \\ Regionalnaia prestupnosti: problemy i perspectivy borby. Materialy mejdunarodnoi nauchno-practicheskoi konferentsii [Issues of cooperation of Internal Affairs with the citizens involved in law enforce-ment (on the example of the Republic of Belarus) in Regional crime: Problems and prospects of the struggle. Materials from the International Scientific–Practical Conference]. Chisinau, pp. 479–483.

Redpath J. (2010). Victimization and public confidence survey. Benchmarks for the development of criminal justice policy in Moldova. Soros Foundation, Moldova. http://www.soros.md/files/publications/documents/Victimisation%20Survey.pdf [accessed January 17, 2012].

Spoiala L. (2010). Criminality in the Republic of Moldova. National Bureau of Statistics of the Republic of Moldova, Chisinau. http://www.statistica.md/public/files/publicatii_electronice/Infractionalitatea/Criminalitatea_editia_2010.pdf [accessed January 17, 2012].

Vartichyan I. C. (1979a). Dobrovolnie Narodnie Drujiny (DND) [Voluntary People's Squads (DND)]. In Moldavskaia Sovetskaia Entsiklopedia [Moldavian Soviet Encyclopedia] Vol. 8. Chisinau, p. 212.

Vartichyan I. C. (1979b). Tovarishcheskie Sudy [Comrade's courts]. In Moldavskaia Sovetskaia Entsiklopedia [Moldavian Soviet Encyclopedia] Vol. 8. Chisinau, p. 212.

Vartichyan I. C. (1979c). Drugie Samodeiatelnye Organizatsii Trudiashchikhsia [Other ama-teur workers organizations]. In Moldavskaia Sovetskaia Entsiklopedia [Moldavian Soviet Encyclopedia] Vol. 8. Chisinau, p. 213.

Netherlands

30

ARIE VAN SLUIS
PETER VAN OS

Contents

Background

The Netherlands (literally: the "low countries") derives its name from its geographical position, which is well below sea level in some parts. The Netherlands borders the North Sea to the north and west, Germany to the east, and Belgium to the south. It is considered the biggest of the small countries in Europe, and with an estimated population of 16 million, it is the thirtieth most densely populated country in the world. The majority of the population is of Dutch origin, but there are significant numbers of ethnic minorities from Indonesia, Turkey, Morocco and Surinam, Antilles, and Aruba. The Randstad, located in the west, is the country's largest conurbation, containing the Netherlands' four largest cities: Amsterdam, Rotterdam, the Hague, and Utrecht. It is the sixth largest metropolitan area in Europe.

The Netherlands is a parliamentary democracy with a constitutional monarchy. It has an elected government and a head of state, the queen (Queen Beatrix). The Dutch style of policymaking is sometimes labeled the "poldermodel," referring to the age-old tradition of consensus-based maintenance of the dykes in Dutch polders. These dykes required constant pumping to prevent flooding, and their maintenance fostered a decision-making style characterized by the recognition of cooperation despite differences. Corporative solutions were strongly preferred, and many traits of this poldermodel still have a strong influence on political processes and institutional arrangements, even in the fields of public security, criminal justice, and the police system.

Dutch Police Organization

From 1945 to 1993, the Dutch police was composed of the *gemeentepolitie* (municipal police) and the *rijkspolitie* (state police). In 1993, a new Police Act was introduced and accepted by the Dutch Parliament. From then on, the Dutch police was organized into 25 regional forces and one national force (Korps Landelijke Politiediensten, Klpd) that supports the regional forces while also assuming several important national-level tasks. As a consequence of the reform, the size of the smallest police force went up from maybe 30 police officers to approximately 700. The largest police force (Amsterdam-Amstelland) has about 7000 officers.

The regional police system is a decentralized system, and like its predecessor, it reflects a broadly shared view that the police should be oriented primarily toward the delivery of services to the general public, and not mainly be the central government's "strong arm." Article 2 of the Police Act stipulates the core tasks of the police: "The police have the task, subordinate to the competent authority and in accordance with the applicable rules of law, of ensuring effective law enforcement and rendering assistance to those who need it" (art. 2, Police Act 1993). Accordingly then, police work in the Netherlands consists of maintenance of public order, the enforcement of legal orders through an adherence to criminal law, and the performance of policing duties for the justice authorities (Ministry of the Interior and Kingdom Relations 2004).

As a rule, regional forces are subdivided into a number of districts (territorial) and divisions (functional). A large part of the police force works in basic units such as neighborhood teams where they serve in close proximity to the general public. A basic unit operates from one or more police stations, and its duties consist of many territorially bound activities such as daily patrols, dispute mediation, and keeping in touch with the happenings and sentiment of the general public, business institutions, neighborhood associations, and other interest groups. Functional units specialize in different aspects of policing, with some of them operating on an interregional basis (Ministry of the Interior and Kingdom Relations 2004, 16). Examples of specialized units are emergency services, arrest teams, police infiltration teams, and criminal investigation support teams. After 1994, many police forces had to adjust their organizations and their methods of policing. The most prominent of these efforts were the attempts to remedy the negative effects of increasing scale by reintroducing the tradition of community policing under the label of "area-bounded policing."

Origins of Community Policing in the Netherlands

In 1977, a milestone document called "A Changing Police" was published. This document was the starting point for Dutch community-oriented policing (from now on: COP) (see Cachet et al. 1998)* as it clearly stipulated that police work should be done by well-educated policemen oriented toward the good of the community. The mandate laid out in the document was for members of a community policing team to cover the whole spectrum of police work.

---

* Before 1977, only a few municipal police forces in big cities like the Hague and Amsterdam had started experimenting with beat officers.

Before 1977, the police officer's role was mainly to enforce the law and to make arrests as necessary. Police discretion was neither acknowledged nor accepted, and tasks were simplified and standardized by the use of standard operational procedures.* But this traditional ("professional") model of policing was incapable of dealing with the more complex and dynamic problems faced by Dutch society. The 1960s saw the Dutch police suffer gigantic losses in their legitimacy when rigid and repressive policing practices adopted in relation to the widespread student protests of the period drew bitter criticism. The Dutch police at the time then set itself a goal of reintegrating the force into the society and regaining the trust of the citizens (van Sluis et al. 2010). This period provided the impetus for the landmark 1977 document, after which the Dutch police started experimenting with COP.

By the 1980s, COP became the standard way of delivering basic policing, and it became the new orthodoxy of policing (Punch et al. 2008). However, in the 1990s, new developments took place in the field of public order. The squatter movement grew significantly and presented a new challenge to the police, as did football hooliganism and a vast increase in the number of petty crimes. The Netherlands also experienced the emergence of more professionally organized and more international crime, all of which served to undermine the predominance of COP. To meet these challenges, the Dutch police expanded its repertoire in the 1990s to include ideas such as "zero tolerance," "broken-windows policing," and "hot spot policing." While COP was still a cornerstone of the force's philosophy, there was, at the same time, a distinct move toward hard-line policing. These shifts in focus occurred at a time when there was a growing sense in the Netherlands that the Dutch tradition of tolerance had gone too far (Das et al. 2007; Punch 2006).

It is not surprising then that the police reforms of 1993 favored a model that was based on a larger, more centralized police force and greater distance between the police and the public. However, not long after the police reform of 1993, COP was once again revived as a foundational philosophy. In an effort to strengthen the bonds between the (regional) police and local communities, new community officers were introduced who were made responsible for organizing security in their area in a much wider and more permanent sense (Punch et al. 2008).

In the early twenty-first century, a new vision of COP was articulated in the strategy document called "Police in Evolution" (PIE) that was published by the Dutch board of chiefs of police. PIE stayed true to the values of COP by once again focusing on the local community and stressing community policing. However, the document also advocated for the greater involvement of community officers in crime fighting and for more assertive and firmer enforcement of laws.

Most recently, the Dutch board of chiefs of police has developed a national program for the development of area-bound policing with specific standards for COP. This strategy aims to enhance professional competence by disseminating the national standards through educational programs provided by the Dutch Police Academy (Vlek and van der Torre 2010). Each year, police forces are audited to measure their realization of these standards. Among the aims of this program is to have one community officer per 5000 inhabitants.

The Rutte cabinet that came into power in the Netherlands in October 2010 made the unambiguous choice of having a single, unified national police force spread across a consolidated number of regions (10 versus the existing 25). This aim is to be realized in 2013.

---

* However, in practice, police officers had an enormous amount of freedom to act as they saw fit.

As a result of this, COP will remain the cornerstone of Dutch policing at the local level, but the police officer will become a member of a robust, geographically organized team consisting of about 200 police officers representing all policing disciplines and carrying out all policing tasks under the auspices of the local government.

As this latest round of adjustments to Dutch policing demonstrates, the role of a Dutch beat officer is a resilient one. It has never completely disappeared from prominence in the Dutch police force. Even when its position seemed threatened, it always managed to fight its way back even if its profile was subject to significant changes.

Community Policing in Practice

Jack of All Trades

COP is currently the guiding principle of the day-to-day police work of all 25 Dutch regional police forces, and community officers are common across all forces. They have to contribute to law and crime investigation by taking on criminal investigations, conducting law enforcement activities, providing emergency services, and participating actively in citizen networks. Their role requires that they cooperate with professional agencies such as schools and municipalities as well. Community officers also have an important "signal and advice" function in that they are responsible for providing administrative authorities with information and early warnings about significant societal trends, emerging problems, signs of terrorism, and radicalization (van Os 2010).

"Knowing and Being Known"

It is not surprising then that "knowing and being known" is seen as the key role of community officers. Proximity and visibility are necessary if vital information is to be obtained from citizens and if the police are to restore the citizen's trust in them. The strategies they adopt to get involved with the community are wide. These include weekly open consultation hours in community centers, regular features in the local newspapers, visiting youth hangouts, participating in activities at the local schools and citizen panels, and simply chatting with people on the street (Terpstra 2008, 2009). But community officers do not only perform "soft" policing tasks. They also take on more repressive actions and frequently deal with social disorder caused by youth, road safety issues, and petty crime. Rule enforcement has also become an important part of the work of community officers. As a result, not much time is spent on social service (Stol et al. 2004; Terpstra 2008).

Balancing Horizontal and Vertical Dimension of Policing

Van der Torre (1999, 2007) characterizes this combination of soft and hard policing as the pragmatic policing style, which has now become the prevalent style among community officers. The increased influence of managerialism and top-down steering can be traced, in particular, to the result-based agreements that were made by police with the government (van Sluis et al. 2008). This style has also evolved as a result of mandatory involvement in the policing of areas such as public transport and in the fight against drugs and domestic violence. This has undoubtedly led to less professional autonomy for community officers

(Van Os 2010, 267) and to more uniformity in policing styles. Such an increase in the influence of top-down steering poses a threat for the professional practice of community policing as tailor-made solutions and specific security problems tend to require that the police be given greater room to maneuver and cooperate with other agencies.

Gaining the Trust of Citizens

This shift in the orientation of community officers also mirrors the shift in the public's attitude toward community policing. The public judges the police mainly on their performance and not on their philosophy. They are interested in particular on their success at catching criminals and fighting crime. Citizens demand that the police focus more on enforcement rather than on prevention (Egelkamp et al. 2003; Vlek and Loef 2007) and that they adopt a firm style of policing. They demand also that police officers have a fighting spirit and that they are not afraid of using coercive force in a professional way if necessary. Notwithstanding the changes in the public beliefs, Dutch police have enjoyed a high level of trust from citizens over the years, as successive Eurobarometer results show. This can largely be attributed to Dutch COP.

According to van der Torre (2011), the changes in the work of community officers are very much in line with the officers' own feelings about the true nature of police work. The balance between "empathy" and law enforcement had previously been eroded but now appears to be restored (van den Brink 2010). By acting vigorously, the police are able to foster respect among citizens and build their own credibility.

Problem-Oriented Policing

Systematic problem solving (problem-oriented policing) is increasingly also becoming an indispensable tool for community policing in the Netherlands (van Os 2010). Problem-oriented policing is high on the agenda of the Dutch Police Academy, and the Crime and Disturbance Area Scan has recently been launched. This scan is a standardized instrument that helps community officers to analyze and solve local security problems.

Time Spent in Neighborhood

The intentions outlined in COP's original framework state that community officers should spend much of their time on community policing. Bron et al. (2010) observed that community officers spend about 65% of their work hours on neighborhood-related activities. The major part of their nonneighborhood-related actions (32%) consists of emergency response, surveillance, and order maintenance work conducted outside of their designated neighborhood. This smaller percentage also covers administrative tasks like maintaining contact through email and writing Web logs to keep in contact with the neighborhood. The remaining 3% of time is spent attending briefings.

Balancing Community Policing, Crime Control, and Emergency Response

Community officers have to participate in criminal investigations in one way or another. Van der Torre (2011) advocates strongly that the Dutch COP go back to basics and strengthen its ability to do basic groundwork such as catching criminals, dealing with incidents, and maintaining public order. Over the years, adjustments have been made also to the proportion of time spent on community policing and crime investigation (Zoomer 2006). Special crime investigation teams have been set up in most districts to help community officers deal with both demands. During such criminal investigations, the community officers serve as experts in community affairs.

According to the Dutch COP philosophy, responding to emergency calls is also an integral part of the work of community officers. Because of their key role, community officers can call upon other officers for emergency responses as well as for support and backup during criminal investigations. Nowadays, emergency response is organized into separate units outside of neighborhood teams, and such responses are directed out of a central (integrated) control room. Thus, only calls for assistance that are less urgent are left to the community officers.

Networking

Generally speaking, the Dutch police are reasonably well integrated in neighborhoods, professional networks, and local government (Straver et al. 2009). Much of this cooperation is initiated by the community officers themselves, and they generally work well with other agencies. In fact, local security networks in the Netherlands simply cannot function (Terpstra 2009) without the specific expertise, dedication, support, and symbolic role played by the police or without the police's ability to use force in the last instance (see also Terpstra and Kouwenhoven 2004).

Citizen Involvement

Citizen participation is an important part of the integrated approach to local security. Van Steden et al. (2011) estimated that about 100 security-related citizen projects have been operational in the capital Amsterdam alone. For example, citizens participate voluntarily in neighborhood watches, and some boroughs have neighborhood parents providing active surveillance. These citizens commit themselves to patrolling their neighborhood because they feel that problems have gotten out of hand. Such instances of active citizenship are not possible, however, without the backing and coaching of the police and government authorities (van Steden et al. 2011).

Assessment

Dutch COP has made enormous progress over the years. However, it is still a work in progress. Not all of the above features are fully crystallized or problem-free at this time. From the point of view of national standards, there is still too much variation between and even within forces with regards to the organization and practice of COP. But as illustrated, many of these problems have their roots in the historical development of Dutch policing.

Some aspects of the community officers' work like prevention and networking, which are rather time consuming and do not often present measurable results, tend to come under threat as a result of managerialism within the police and the public urge for quick results. Consequently, it is difficult to retain citizens' trust. Citizens are very demanding and want value for money, and their trust is easily lost when the police do not fulfill their expectations (Terpstra 2010). The media play an important role in this respect. Security threats and police actions are often placed under a microscope, and it is sometimes a struggle to create a good public image. The legitimacy and authority of community policing have thus become an area of key importance.

A topic of frequent debate is whether the skills and competence of community officers are sufficient to allow them to fulfill all their tasks satisfactorily. The criticism is that their problem-solving capacities are still underdeveloped, and problem-oriented policing is not a common practice, even though it is said to be an indispensable tool for community policing (van Sluis 2002). Terpstra (2008, 2009) found, for example, that community officers' analyses of local problems of crime and disorder are often rather unsystematic and lacking in explicitness. They prefer to act on information they receive from personal contacts ("street knowledge") rather than information gained from research and science. This tendency is furthered by the fact that community officers tend to distrust standardized instruments that are developed by their colleagues in the police force.

Another criticism is that community officers spend much time in their neighborhood but still not enough. Officers themselves report that they often feel overruled by their managers in setting their priorities and executing their roles. This prevents them from spending more time on tasks they see as critical to the security of their neighborhoods (Bron et al. 2010).

A third criticism is that there are persistent problems in balancing the demands of community policing with those of crime control and emergency response. Because of their key role, community officers should call upon other officers for emergency responses as well as for support and backup during criminal investigations. However, in practice, community officers tend to lack the necessary power and authority to play all such roles well (van der Torre 2007). Further, police managers tend to see emergency responses as being more critical for gaining the trust of the public than community policing and so tend to prioritize them accordingly (van Os and Gooren 2010). Van der Torre avoid and many other researchers also observe a lack of crime investigation skills. Despite the large number of initiatives undertaken, only 12% of the community officer's time is spent on criminal investigations. This is far less than would be expected given the current "crisis" in crime investigations (van Os and Gooren 2010).

Community officers nowadays often experience role conflicts. Their new role in intelligence-led policing sometimes comes into conflict with their mandate to solve problems by cooperating with representatives of the community (Bervoets et al. 2009). Community officers often report that this dual role harms the relations they have developed in their neighborhoods as it muddies trust (Kool 2007). Sometimes community officers also experience difficulties with the new repressive demands that are made upon them, for example, a recent demand that they write tickets in order to meet arbitrary performance targets (van Sluis et al. 2008).

In general, community officers have greater difficulties supporting or even participating in initiatives that are undertaken by citizens (van Os and Tops 2010). Community officers are still rather "police centered" in their orientation (van Os 2010). The role of citizens appears to be limited in their view to that of providers of information, or "the eyes and ears of the police" (Terpstra 2008). The police are thus inclined to erect "professional barriers" in safety programs and to keep their distance from citizens who run up against a "bureaucratic ceiling" (van Steden et al. 2011, 14).

Conclusions

Inevitably, Dutch community officers fall short of the high expectations placed upon them. The community officer has become a jack-of-all-trades. However, things are progressing, and Dutch COP as a profession is still in its early stages. Although COP will likely be molded and remolded again and again to adapt to changing needs, it will continue to be a key feature of Dutch policing in the near future, as it has been in the past.

Many of the challenges that face COP are familiar ones, such as the need to reconcile the many claims that are made upon community officers, while moderating the sometimes unrealistic expectations of citizens and stakeholders. Other challenges include the need to balance COP with emergency response and crime control priorities, the need to improve the community officers' professional skills in problem-oriented policing and in crime investigation, and the continuing need to involve citizens more actively in COP.

New challenges likely to come up in the near future are serious cuts in the police budget and a more centralized system of policing. The questions that arise then are whether the Dutch COP will be resilient enough to counter the strong centralization tendencies and if the so-called robust teams will be strong enough to safeguard the provision of tailor-made local policing. This is also dependent on the local government. The bigger the role the local government takes in directing local security, the greater the freedom beat officers will have to tackle local security problems together with others in an integrated way instead of acting as mere implementers of national policing policies.

References

Bervoets, E. et al. (2009). *Bij de tijd: wijkagenten in Hollands Midden. Beschrijving en analyse van dagelijkse praktijken.* COT, Boom Juridische Uitgevers, Den Haag.

Bron, R. et al. (2010). *De tijdsbesteding van wijkagenten.* COT Instituut voor Veiligheids- en Crisismanagement. Andersson Elffers Felix, Den Haag/Utrecht.

Cachet, A. et al. (1998). *De blijvende betekenis van Politie in Verandering.* Elsevier, Den Haag.

Das, D. et al. (2007). The changing "soul" of Dutch policing. Responses to new security demands and the relationship with Dutch tradition. *Policing: An International Journal of Police Strategies and Management*, Vol. 30, No. 3, pp. 518–532.

de Kool, W. (2007). Mission Impossible?: Het signaleren van islamitisch radicalisme en terrorisme door Nederlandse wijkagenten. *Het Tijdschrift voor de Politie*, Vol. 69, No. 3, pp. 4–8.

Egelkamp, M. et al. (2003). *Naar een nieuwe barsheid! Beelden van dienders binnen en buiten de politie.* ES&E, Den Haag.

Ministry of the Interior and Kingdom Relations. (2004). *Policing in the Netherlands.* The Hague, Ministry of the Interior and Kingdom Relations.

Punch, M. (2006). *Van "alles mag" naar "zero tolerance": Policy transfer en de Nederlandse politie.* P&W Verkenningen, Apeldoorn.

Punch, M. and C.D. van der Vijver. (2008). Community policing in the Netherlands: Four generations of redefinition. T. Williamson (ed.), *The Handbook of Knowledge Based Policing: Current Conceptions and Future Directions.* Chichester, John Wiley & Son Ltd., pp. 59–78.

Stol, W.P. et al. (2004). *Politiestraatwerk in Nederland. Noodhulp en gebiedswerk: inhoud, samenhang, verandering en sturing.* Politie en Wetenschap No. 14., Elsevier Overheid, Den Haag.

Straver, R. et al. (2009). *Integratie van Nederlandse politie in wijken, netwerken en lokaal bestuur.* Stichting SMVP Producties, Dordrecht.

Terpstra, J. (2008). *Wijkagenten en hun dagelijks werk*. Politie en Wetenschap No. 46. Elsevier Overheid, Den Haag.

Terpstra, J. (2009). Community policing in practice: Ambitions and realization. *Policing*, Vol. 4, No. 1, pp. 64–72.

Terpstra, J. (2010). *De maatschappelijke opdracht van de politie. Over identiteit en kernelementen van politiewerk*. Boom Juridische uitgevers, Den Haag.

Terpstra, J. and R. Kouwenhoven. (2004). *Samenwerking en netwerken in de locale veiligheidszorg*. IPIT, Enschede.

van den Brink, G. (2010). *Empathie en handhaving*. Politieacademie, lectoraat gemeenschappelijke veiligheidskunde, Apeldoorn.

van der Torre, E.J. (1999). *Politiewerk: Politiestijlen, Community Policing, Professionalisme Politiewerk*, Samson, Alphen aan den Rijn.

van der Torre, E.J. (2007). *Lokale politiechefs. Het middenkader in de basispolitiezorg*. Politie en Wetenschap 38, Elsevier Overheid, Den Haag (typologie van wijkteamchefs en van operationele chefs).

van der Torre, E.J. (2011). *Politiewerk aan de basis: stevig en nuchter*. Lectorale rede, Politieacademie.

Van der Vijver, C.D. (2004). 'Kerntaken, sturing en professionaliteit.' B. van Stokkum and L. Gunther Moor (ed.), *Onoprechte handhaving? Prestatiecontracten, beleidsvrijheid en politie–ethiek*, SMVP, Dordrecht.

van Os, P. (2010). Community-oriented policing in the Netherlands: A process with many obstacles. *Cahiers Politiestudies*, Vol. 10–3, No. 16, pp. 261–268.

van Os, P. and W. Gooren. (2010). *Operationalisering referentiekader gebiedsgebonden politie; de tweede oogst*.

van Os, P. and P. Tops. (2010). Actief burgerschap en veiligheid. I. Helsloot et al. (eds.), *Zelfredzaamheid. Concepten, thema's en voorbeelden ander beschouwd*. Boom Juridische Uitgevers, Den Haag.

van Sluis, A. (2002). *Van "planning and control" naar strategische beleidsvorming. Een onderzoek naar beleidsvorming bij de politie*. Doctoral Thesis, Erasmus University Rotterdam.

van Sluis, A., A. Cachet, and A.B. Ringeling. (2008). Results-based agreements for the police in The Netherlands. *Policing: An International Journal of Police Strategies and Management*, Vol. 31, No. 3, pp. 415–434.

van Sluis, A., A. Cachet, P. van Os, M. Prins and P. Marks. (2010). Community policing in the Netherlands: A continuously changing constant. Paper delivered at the IPES conference in Kochio, India.

Van Steden, R., B. van Caem and H. Boutellier. (2011). The hidden strength of active citizenship: The involvement of local residents in public safety projects. *Criminology and Criminal Justice*, Vol. 11, No. 3, pp. 433–450.

Vlek, F. and K. Loef (ed.). (2007). *Burgers over blauw: een lastige klant gehoord; beelden, verwachtingen en ervaringen van burgers met betrekking tot de politie nader belicht*. Politie en Wetenschap, Apeldoorn.

Vlek, F. and E.J. van der Torre. (2010). De Nederlandse politie sinds 1993: Een wereld van verschil. Beelden over en uit de praktijk. *Cahiers Politiestudies*, Vol. 2009–4, No. 13, pp. 229–286.

Zoomer, O. (2006). *De opsporingsfunctie binnen de gebiedsgebonden politiezorg*. Zeist, Kerckebosch.

Northern Ireland

31

GRAHAM ELLISON

Contents

Background

Northern Ireland is situated on the western edge of Europe and shares a land border with the Republic of Ireland. According to the 2011 census, the population of Northern Ireland is approximately 1.8 million. In terms of community background, 48.3% of Northern Irish-born residents identified as having a Protestant community background and 45.1% a Catholic community background. In racial terms, the population of Northern Ireland is almost exclusively white (98.2%), with minority-ethnic groups comprising less than 2% of the total population. In racial terms, the population of Northern Ireland is almost exclusively white (99.1%), with minority ethnic groups comprising less than 1% of the total population. Life expectancy is broadly in line with the Western European average at 76.4 years for males and 81.3 years for females. The average gross domestic product (GDP) per capita income is $30,763.

Northern Ireland has a national police: The Police Service of Northern Ireland (PSNI) was established in November 2001 as a successor organization to the Royal Ulster Constabulary (RUC) that had policed Northern Ireland since the creation of the state. Currently there are 7500 officers in the PSNI. Recruitment changes brought about as the result of the report of the Independent Commission on Policing (ICP 1999), discussed below, have resulted in Catholic membership of the force (historically a sticking point) increasing to nearly 30% (compared to 8% in the RUC). The percentage of female officers has increased to 25% (compared to 12% in the RUC). Recent outreach work by the PSNI has made considerable strides in recruiting officers from the gay, lesbian, bisexual, and transgender (GLBT) community as well as those from minority ethnic backgrounds. The force is organized on a regional basis and further subdivided into districts and sectors for operational reasons.

Politically and administratively, Northern Ireland is governed as a constituent region of the United Kingdom along with Wales, England, and Scotland. However, Northern

Ireland's constitutional status has always been disputed in historical terms. Until 1920, the island of Ireland formed part of the British Empire and was governed as a colonial outpost from Dublin Castle by the British authorities. Following, a bitter War of Independence (1919–1921) fought against the British, the country was partitioned into 26 counties that were to form the Irish Free State with a majority Catholic population (later the Republic of Ireland) and six counties in the northeast that were to form the new state of Northern Ireland with a majority Protestant population. Northern Ireland was to continue under British rule, whereas the Irish Free State eventually declared independence. However, over one-third of the inhabitants of Northern Ireland were Catholics who, from the outset, deeply resented being coerced into the new (mainly Protestant) northern state. Thus, the inherently unstable nature of Northern Ireland's creation as a constitutional entity was later to sow the seeds for the violent sociopolitical conflict that erupted at the end of the 1960s (Weitzer 1995; Ellison and Smyth 2000).

Origin of Community Policing

Historically, Northern Ireland displays many of the features of a "divided society" model of policing (Brewer and Magee 1991; Weitzer 1995). Following the adoption of a new security strategy from the mid-1970s onward, the RUC was pushed to the forefront in counterinsurgency "war" with the Irish Republican Army (IRA). To facilitate this, the RUC underwent a wide-ranging program of technical professionalism (access to improved weaponry, counterterrorism, covert operations training, and so forth) and, given its mandate to defend the state, became embroiled in a number of controversial incidents and practices to "defeat terrorism" that had the effect of further estranging Catholics of all social classes and backgrounds from the structures of state policing. These included allegations of torture in obtaining confession evidence, collusion with loyalist paramilitary organizations, a differential attitude toward loyalist and nationalist dissent, as well as the use of plastic bullets (Weitzer 1995; Brewer and Magee 1991). In addition, there were concerns about the unrepresentative nature of the RUC (the force was majority Protestant), weak oversight, governance and accountability mechanisms, its overwhelmingly "British" cultural ethos and identity, and its emphasis on counterterrorism that became the normative framework for policing and impacted on the milieu within which officers came to perceive their role (Mulcahy 2006).

Several attempts were made at reforming the RUC during the 1970s and the 1980s, but these were not particularly efficacious, and throughout the duration of the conflict (1969–1998), the reform of policing structures in Northern Ireland was a key demand of nationalist/Catholic politicians in Northern Ireland. In 1994, the IRA declared a halt to its military campaign that was followed by a similar announcement 6 weeks later by a number of loyalist* paramilitary organizations. After a period of torturous political negotiation, the paramilitary ceasefires culminated in the Belfast Agreement (1998)—a constitutional settlement for the governance of Northern Ireland—and resulted in the return of a devolved political administration, the Northern Ireland Assembly. As we discuss below, a

---

* Loyalists are typically Protestants who advocate the use of violence to maintain Northern Ireland's constitutional status and link with Britain.

key component of the Belfast Agreement, however, was reform of the RUC that was opera-tionalized via the ICP (ICP 1999).*

Community policing has been described by some commentators as one of the most vacuous concepts in policing studies and is notoriously difficult to define (Brogden and Nijhar 2005). By the mid-1970s, the RUC had established a "Community Relations" branch, although arguably, it was merely a presentational device designed to cultivate a user-friendly image for the force. Substantively, it amounted to little more than the RUC organizing so-called "Blue Lamp" discos and cross-country rambles for young people (albeit overwhelmingly in Protestant areas). However, leaving aside problems of actual definition, it is perhaps easier to postulate what community policing is not: it is not, for instance, the centralized, militarized, hierarchical, reactive, command-and-control model of policing found in Northern Ireland historically that placed more emphasis on counter-terrorism than "ordinary" crime and that was both unrepresentative and distanced from local communities.

Given the spatial distribution of violence, the RUC could patrol relatively normally in many areas of Northern Ireland (although officers always had access to firearms and trav-eled in armored cars). However, from the mid-1970s, working-class republican[†] areas across Northern Ireland had effectively withdrawn their consent for state policing, which led to a number of self-policing or civil policing initiatives being established (discussed below). Such areas became extremely dangerous for the RUC (and other state security forces) to patrol in, with the risk of ambush by republican paramilitary organizations high. In such an environment, routine policing was all but impossible (McEvoy and Mika 2002), com-munity policing doubly so. Politically, however, neither the RUC nor the British govern-ment could admit that there were areas of the country that were effectively no-go areas for the police. Consequently, there was the bizarre spectacle of having three four-man "bricks" (teams) of British Army soldiers replete with armored personnel carriers or armored Land Rovers to provide cover for two equally heavily armed RUC officers "walking the beat" in staunchly republican areas. The RUC may have claimed that this represented "community policing," but it is a semantic smokescreen that owes more to the political exigencies of conflict management as interpreted by state authorities rather than any normative com-mitment to community policing.

Community Self-Policing and Informalism

Being thrust in the front line against IRA violence meant that the RUC quickly lost any vestige of legitimacy in working-class republican areas, and from the mid-1970s, there was a complete withdrawal of consent for state policing.[‡] Out of this policing vacuum emerged a form of civil policing practiced by republican organizations such as the IRA (McEvoy and Mika 2002). However, following a serious breakdown in relationships between the RUC

---

* It should be noted, however, that a parallel review of criminal justice was undertaken at the same time. The Northern Ireland Criminal Justice Review made sweeping changes to the nature of the prosecution system, youth justice, judicial reform, prisons and prisoner release, and the probation service.
† Republicans are drawn mainly from the Catholic community. Traditionally, republicans have differed from Irish nationalists insofar as they have advocated the use of violence to force a British withdrawal from Northern Ireland.
‡ Increasingly, the RUC was viewed equally problematically in working-class loyalist areas too.

and loyalists in the mid-1980s, self-policing and associated punishment violence became the dominant practice in loyalist areas also. There is now a general acknowledgment that the existence of informal nonstate-ordering mechanisms and structures is a common feature in those societies undergoing political schism or where the legitimacy of the state and its agencies is contested (Eriksson 2009). In this sense, the situation in Northern Ireland has been little different from many other transitional societies such as South Africa, where similar nonstate structures were mobilized in opposition to the apartheid-era justice system (Brogden and Shearing 1993).

In Northern Ireland, it was republican paramilitary organizations that came closest to establishing informal policing structures that existed in opposition to the state system. From the mid-1970s, the IRA had established a Civil Administration Unit that investigated complaints, gathered evidence, collected witness statements, passed a sentence, and carried out a designated punishment (McEvoy and Mika 2002). The "punishment" operated according to a tariff system and involved warnings, enforced exclusion from the locality or even Northern Ireland, beatings, shootings, or assassination. In practice, particularly for repeat offenders, the punishments were brutal and involved the "offender" being beaten with iron bars or hurling sticks (similar to a hockey stick) or shot through the thighs, elbows, or kneecaps with a low-velocity handgun. The specialist orthopedic unit at Belfast's Royal Victoria Hospital was to garner world-leading expertise in treating such injuries over the years. By and large, though, such activities were at variance with the ethos of the developing peace process, not to mention human rights concerns, and from the 1990s, they were dramatically curtailed and, as far as mainstream republicans are concerned, have now ceased.* The newly reformed PSNI was supposed to provide for an effective means of community crime control, but as we shall discuss shortly, the organization has faced difficulties and continues to lack widespread institutional legitimacy, and arguably, a formal social control vacuum continues in staunchly republican areas (McEvoy and Mika 2002; Eriksson 2009). In such areas, ex-combatants are still involved in the informal management of crime through Restorative Justice (RJ) initiatives (particularly with young people), and arguably, given the continued difficulties with state policing, it is ex-combatants and associated RJ schemes that still provide the closest approximation to what might be regarded as community policing in urban working-class loyalist and republican areas. Indeed, in such areas, the PSNI will often advise a member of the public to contact an RJ scheme in the first instance.

How Does Community Policing Work in Indigenous Community?

A core aspect of the negotiated political settlement in 1998 was that an ICP (see ICP 1999) would be established to make recommendations for the reform of the structures of state policing in Northern Ireland. The Commission reported in 1999 and made over 200 recommendations for reform. Among the key recommendations were changes in recruitment to increase the number of Catholic officers; changes to the symbolism and culture of the force such as changing the name to the Police Service of Northern Ireland; introducing enhanced oversight, governance, and accountability structures such as a fully independent police complaints machinery; and proposing a new community policing strategy—"Policing

* Although recently, dissident republican groups have been responsible for a rising number of such punishment attacks.

with the Community"—that was underpinned by the principles of public consent, human rights, democratic accountability, and organizational decentralization (see Ellison 2007 for a detailed exposition of the key ICP recommendations).

The development of community policing in Northern Ireland between the publication of the report of the ICP and the situation currently can be outlined in terms of three phases.

Phase One: Policing with the Community

A key reform strand in the ICP report (warranting an entire chapter) was "Policing with the Community," whereby a number of structures and institutional mechanisms were established to make the new PSNI responsive to local community inputs. Furthermore, recognizing that the police in many jurisdictions—including repressive ones—pay lip service to a form of "community policing" that has no substantive basis in reality, the ICP argued that policing needed to be structurally grounded in a human rights discourse. For the ICP, the protection and promotion of human rights was the core point of policing, and as it suggested, "There should be no conflict between human rights and policing. Policing means protecting human rights" (ICP 1999: 18). An emphasis on human rights protections rather than glib assertions about the merits of community policing was woven into the structural and institutional fabric of police governance.

In terms of community policing itself, in their report, the commissioners recognized that the "term community policing... has many definitions and has become somewhat devalued by frequent and indiscriminate use" (ICP 1999: 40). It was therefore taken as a working definition of community policing

> ...the police working in partnership with the community; the community thereby participating in its own policing; and the two working together; mobilising resources to solve problems affecting public safety over the long term rather than the police alone, reacting short-term incidents as they occur. (ICP 1999: 40)

As Topping (2008) argues, the aim of the ICP report was twofold. First, given the widespread levels of public alienation from the police, its proposals were an attempt to "reconnect" the police to the communities that they served. Second, it sought to resolve a number of issues around the provision of state policing that historically framed the dynamics of sociopolitical conflict in Northern Ireland.

Compared to the situation elsewhere in the United Kingdom (England, Wales, and Scotland), the changes brought about by the ICP have established structures for police accountability, oversight, and governance that are arguably more robust than those found elsewhere. The Northern Ireland Policing Board (NIPB) is composed of democratically elected politicians and independent members and performs a number of broad functions in relation to police governance such as setting funding requirements, monitoring performance, holding chief officers to account, and initiating inquiries into police actions, but importantly, it also draws up policing plans yearly and every 5 years that set priorities for the PSNI across a number of strategic areas (dealing with youth crime and domestic burglaries, for example) as well as convening public meetings whereby community members can question the PSNI on their performance.

The effective operation of the Policing Board has been beset by a number of political problems (arguably not of its making) that have severely impacted on the ability of the PSNI to "police with the community." The first major problem concerned the refusal of Sinn Féin*—currently the main nationalist political party—to take its seats on the Policing Board. Ostensibly, Sinn Féin argued that the implementation of the reforms in legislative terms did not follow the "spirit" of the ICP recommendations, but in reality, the party was extremely concerned about how a grassroots republican electorate would react to its participation in the new structures for police governance.† Following another round of cross-party talks and negotiations that led to the St. Andrew's Agreement signed in 2006—which promised the devolution of policing and criminal justice powers from London to Belfast—Sinn Féin finally agreed to take its seats on the Policing Board and local District Policing Partnerships (DPPs; discussed below)‡ in May 2007. Given the sectarian dynamics of Northern Irish society, the absence of a key political player (Sinn Féin) for such a long time did little to "reconnect" the police to the community in the ways envisaged by the ICP.

The story at the local level mirrored that occurring at the national level. The ICP recommended that 26 DPPs be established to provide a conduit between the police and local communities. DPPs are coterminous with electoral districts and are composed of local politicians and independent members, and their role is similar to that of the Policing Board— albeit within smaller geographically defined areas. They perform various functions such as drawing up local policing plans with the PSNI area commander that are focused on areas of community concern (such as, e.g., youth crime, thefts of farm machinery from rural areas, and so forth) and monitor the PSNI's adherence to these plans in terms of clear-up rates and other performance criteria.

Admittedly, starting from a rather low baseline (and expectations), the operation of the Policing Board and DPPs has proved to be competent rather than outstanding (were they a student, one would be tempted to award them a C or C+). As central planks in the PSNI's "Policing with the Community" strategy, both play a key role in acting as a communicative conduit between the police and local communities, particularly those most alienated by police actions in the past. However, in practice, the degree to which they have done this is debatable (Topping 2008; Ellison and O'Rawe 2010). The operation of DPPs in particular is constrained by the problems that are manifest in all such shared-governance relationships: There is a tendency for them to be police led; their membership is invariably middle-aged and not particularly representative of the wider community; and public meetings are not particularly well attended (Brunger 2011; Topping 2008). More generally, the operation and performance of DPPs at the local level were also undermined by Sinn Féin's unwillingness to take its seats (until 2007), which again meant that police engagement within republican communities, in particular, was limited.

Phase Two: Neighborhood Policing

Northern Ireland as an administrative region of the United Kingdom is subject to broader UK-wide policing trends and influences, particularly those initiatives that stem from the

---

* Traditionally the political wing of the IRA. More recently, it has embraced constitutional politics and is now the largest nationalist political party in Northern Ireland.
† In many respects, the reforms were not "sold" on the ground in republican areas (discussed further below).
‡ DPPS are due to be renamed 'Policing and Community Safety Partnerships' (PCSPs).

Home Office in London. As such, the second major incarnation of community policing (from 2003 on) saw the nomenclature used to describe community policing shift to what was termed neighborhood (or reassurance) policing (Mackenzie and Henry 2009). The Home Office stipulated that each territorial police force in the United Kingdom should implement a Neighborhood Policing Strategy together with Neighborhood Policing Teams (NPTs), who were to be responsible for a particular geographical sector. To facilitate dialogue between the police and local communities, neighborhood policing was incorporated within a Partners and Communities Together (PACT) strategy. Neighborhood police are the "partners" in this relationship together with local community representatives, politicians, and representatives of local statutory and nonstatutory agencies. PACT is a form of police–community consultation that has its origins in North American communitarianism (Brunger 2011), and one of its key roles is to act as a conduit between the police and the community by organizing public meetings and so forth.

The emphasis on neighborhood policing and PACT as a key component of the then New Labour administration's crime and disorder reduction efforts was the result of the realization that in spite of historically low levels of crime in the United Kingdom, confidence in the police nationally had taken a nosedive (Gray et al. 2010). As illustrated by successive British Crime Surveys, "fear of crime" and community concerns about low-level disorder (teenagers hanging around on the street, public drunkenness, and so on) were becoming a more salient concern among the public than crime itself (Gray et al. 2010). Neighborhood policing—or "reassurance policing"—as it is sometimes referred to, was seen as the new panacea and incorporated in the National Reassurance Policing Programme (NRPP) that operated between 2003 and 2005. Drawing upon the work of Wes Skogan in Chicago and Martin Innes in the United Kingdom, the NRPP put the onus on the police to identify those "signal crimes" (cf. Innes 2005) that were spatially variable and that caused high levels of community anxiety and concern (Mackenzie and Henry 2009). NPTs were to be established in order to do the following:

- Develop problem-solving policing strategies to identify and tackle signal crimes and disorders within neighborhoods and communities
- Emphasize community involvement and local partnership approaches involving a range of statutory and civil society actors/agencies in order to provide "local solutions to local problems"
- Emphasize the presence of dedicated officers in local neighborhoods who would know the area and its inhabitants and who could be regarded as the first port of call for a member of the public to contact

As Mackenzie and Henry (2009: 20) note, "the difference between the NRPP and previous iterations of CP [community policing] is largely one of degree and emphasis." However, as they acknowledge, neighborhood or reassurance policing is concerned with measurable "outcomes," community consultation, and police/public coproductive activities (Mackenzie and Henry 2009: 20) and, as such, is linked to New Public Managerialism (NPM) discourses that have become prominent in the public sector over the course of the past decade. It also reflects to a certain degree that there often exists a fundamental chasm between police priorities and those of the wider public, and this is something acknowledged by policing scholars. For the police, a high-profile murder investigation may assume priority and convey prestige and status on their detective work. However, for the members of the public, it is the teenager kicking a football against the gable wall of their house that epitomizes the "someone had better do something now!" aspect of Egon Bittner's aphorism regarding public expectations of the police.

In Northern Ireland, PACT and neighborhood policing are organized in local council wards, and according to the official guidance provided to the PSNI, the PACT model is "the minimum expected standard means of community engagement" (cited in Brunger 2011: 107). However, in spite of the rhetorical push for NPT and PACT, the implementation of both has been relatively slow to get off the ground and, during the first few years of operation, was confined to a number of relatively affluent middle-class neighborhoods (Community Foundation 2012; Topping 2008). In recent years, there has been considerable effort made to extend these initiatives to so-called "hard-to-reach" communities, but the impact here has been marginal, and there remains a widespread public view that the PSNI is failing to adequately tackle issues around neighborhood crime and disorder (Community Foundation 2012; Topping 2008; Ellison et al. 2012). In some areas, this has resulted in widespread disillusionment with the overall reform process but, more seriously, has generated support for a return to the informal justice and paramilitary punishment violence that were dominant features of the conflict years. As Topping and Byrne suggest, "PSNI inertia in the delivery of effective, community-based police services in loyalist and Republican areas has created a policing vacuum that is being filled by paramilitary activity" (cited in Community Foundation 2012: 4).

However, the successful implementation/operation of neighborhood policing depends on having police who, first, are seen to command community legitimacy and, second, can freely patrol without risk to themselves in particular areas and neighborhoods. In the case of the former, it is debatable to what extent this has occurred within staunchly republican communities, and in the latter, the resurgence of dissident republican activity by armed groups opposed to the peace process has already resulted in the deaths of two Catholic police officers.* Policing once again is proving to be a rather risky occupation in Northern Ireland that undoubtedly limits the degree to which the police can respond effectively to neighborhood crime and disorder.

Generally, though, the operation of neighborhood policing across many areas of Northern Ireland reflects the age-old adage that community policing works best where it is least needed. In middle-class residential areas, public satisfaction with the PSNI is generally high (almost 80% according to some studies—see Ellison et al. 2012). In urban working-class areas, the story is different. These areas have seen a proliferation of crime and antisocial behavior (disorder) in recent years, ironically as a side effect of the peace process and political transition (Ellison et al. 2012). However, there is a widespread perception in such areas that the PSNI is unwilling to take low-level crime and disorder seriously. As one community activist cited in Topping (2008: 790) argues:

It's [policing] non-existent... Nobody really sees any difference. In fact they'd [the community] probably argue they see less police on the ground than there used to be... it's definitely gotten worse.

* Dissident republican groups are opposed to the peace process and Sinn Féin's participation in the government of Northern Ireland. While their numbers are small, they have nevertheless embarked on numerous shooting and bombing missions in recent years. Two British soldiers have also been killed by dissident groups.

Phase Three: Policing with the Community 2020

In 2011, the chief constable of the PSNI and the NIPB wheeled out their new community policing strategy—Policing with the Community 2020. As the title implies, this is intended to provide a blueprint for the organization and operation of community policing until the end of the current decade. According to the chief constable, the new strategy seeks to consolidate the gains made over the previous 10 years. The strategy in many ways combines elements of the first two phases and attempts to integrate community policing into the gamut of policing practice across the organization, rather than particular specialisms. Broadly, however, the emphasis is on local problem solving, partnerships with statutory and nonstatutory agencies, local sector policing, and enhanced levels of communication with the public (such as providing mobile telephone numbers for "beat" officers and so forth). It also introduces an element of individual responsibilization insofar as it is managerially driven with targets and performance appraisals set for individual officers: policing with the community has thus moved from an organizational goal to an individual one.

Effectiveness of Community Policing

Comparatively speaking, the policing transition in Northern Ireland has been relatively successful, at least by the standards of other international efforts (see Ellison 2007 for a full discussion). However, whether this is due to the huge amount the British government spent on the reform program, which thus far has cost over £1 billion ($1.58 billion),* or to a normative commitment of the various actors to operationalize and implement the reforms is debatable. In any case, these "successes" have been most visible at the level of structures and institutions: establishing the Policing Board and the DPPs, for example. Where the reforms have been less than efficacious has been in terms of operationalizing these structures on the ground, that is, in fostering crosscommunity support for the PSNI and enhancing the legitimacy of the force among previously alienated and marginalized groups and communities. It is here that the PSNI has really struggled in spite of the rhetorical commitment to "policing with the community" and "neighborhood policing." The problem (or blame) does not lie solely with the PSNI, however.

Of course, there were numerous organizational difficulties in relation to the force making the adjustment from its traditional counterterror role to one typified by civil policing, not to mention the ambivalence to the reform program by some (albeit older) officers who were less than enthusiastic about what they perceived as the sacrifice of the RUC for politically expedient reasons. Nevertheless, the PSNI as a societal actor cannot operate independently of political context and the stop–start nature of the peace process, and the refusal of Sinn Féin to participate from an early stage in the working of the new policing structures undoubtedly led to a degree of inertia and the creation of a vacuum that impeded future progress. This has been compounded by a number of other factors: the resurgence of dissident republican activity and the targeting of police officers

---

* The corporate financial services firm Deloitte has conservatively estimated that the reforms have cost the UK government £100 million each year from 2000. This is over and above the £1 billion annual spent on policing in Northern Ireland. By the end of 2013, the reforms will have cost £1.3 billion.

have inevitably restricted the ways that the police can patrol and engage in neighborhood policing duties in certain areas. In many respects, this has resulted in a classic no-win situation for the police. In some areas, officers need to conduct a threat assessment before they respond to an assistance call, but a delay in responding merely confirms to residents the view that the PSNI is not taking issues of crime and disorder seriously in their area. Confidence in the police is therefore further eroded, and this is replayed endlessly in a vicious cycle.

More generally, though, the reform process in Northern Ireland points to the limits of police reform in a society where ethnic tensions and divided constitutional allegiances continue to be politically salient factors in impeding the pace and nature of change. It also points to the existence of diverse "communities" that often have competing interests and demands. The reality is that in spite of the progress thus far, there remain fundamental political obstacles to the attainment of a normatively ordered society in Northern Ireland. It is debatable, therefore, whether "community policing"—however defined or expressed—can paper over the cracks in the structural edifice. In this sense, Northern Ireland problematizes how far police reform, or the introduction of a meaningful variant of community policing, can be introduced unless the larger structural factors that go to the heart of police–public relations in a divided society are also addressed at the same time.

It would be wrong, however, to paint too bleak a picture. Bayley (2005) argues that a successful police reform program takes time (not to mention money and effort!). He estimates that it can take at least 10 years before the new structures of policing become embedded and another 10 years until they become fully institutionalized and legitimated. Northern Ireland is currently entering the second phase. As such, we should remain optimistic that the next decade will show demonstrable progress on the police reform front. This, however, is contingent on a stabilization in the political situation and, in particular, a reduction in the threat from dissident republican activity. In transitional societies such as Northern Ireland, police reform and political reform are often two sides of the same coin. In many ways, however, it is the police that are left to deal with the fallout from failures, obstacles, and hurdles elsewhere in the political realm, which invariably impact on the practice of policing in the short to medium term.

Conclusions

Much has changed in relation to policing in Northern Ireland. In many respects, the report of the ICP proposed a blueprint for police reform that is applicable to many transitional states and established democracies also. The emphasis on human rights protections embedded in the conduct and practice of police work; the establishment of robust oversight and governance structures including a fully independent police complaints machinery; changes to the cultural ethos and symbolism of the police so that they are not perceived to be "owned" by any one group; as well as decentralization and localism in police organization and practice are all a sound footing from which to construct a policing service with a strong community orientation. However, as the lessons from Northern Ireland demonstrate, reforms need to proceed in tandem with political efforts at conflict resolution.

References

Bayley, D.H. (2005). Police reform as foreign policy. *The Australia and New Zealand Journal of Criminology*, 38, 206–215.

Brewer, J.D. & Magee, K. (1991). *Inside the RUC: Routine Policing in a Divided Society*. Oxford: Oxford University Press.

Brogden, M.E. & Nijhar, P. (2005). *Community Policing: National and International Themes and Perspectives*. Cullompton, Devon: Willan Publishing.

Brogden, M.E. & Shearing, C. (1993). *Policing for a New South Africa*. London: Routledge.

Brunger, M. (2011). Governance, accountability and neighbourhood policing in Northern Ireland: Analysis of the role of public meetings. *Crime, Law and Social Change*, 55, 2–3, 105–120.

Community Foundation [Community Foundation for Northern Ireland] (2012). Community Policing: the Challenges from a Community Perspective. January, Issue 3. Belfast: The Community Foundation.

Ellison, G. (2007). A blueprint for democratic policing anywhere in the world?: Police reform, political transition and conflict resolution in Northern Ireland. *Police Quarterly*, 10, 3, 243–267.

Ellison, G. & O'Rawe, M. (2010). Security governance in transition: The compartmentalizing, crowding out and corralling of policing and security in Northern Ireland. *Theoretical Criminology*, 14, 1, 31–57.

Ellison, G., Shirlow, P. & Mulcahy, A. (2012). Responsible participation, community engagement and policing in transitional societies: Lessons from a local crime survey in Northern Ireland. *The Howard Journal of Criminal Justice*, 51, 5, 488–502.

Ellison, G. & Smyth, J. (2000). *The Crowned Harp: Policing Northern Ireland*. London: Pluto.

Eriksson, A. (2009). *Justice in Transition: Community Restorative Justice in Northern Ireland*. Cullompton, Devon: Willan Publishing.

Gray, E., Jackson, J. & Farrell, S. (2010). Feelings and functions in the fear of crime: Applying a new approach to victimisation insecurity. *British Journal of Criminology*, 51, 1, 75–94.

ICP [Independent Commission on Policing] (1999). *A New Beginning: Policing in Northern Ireland*. Belfast: Northern Ireland Office.

Innes, M. (2005). What's your problem: Signal crimes and citizen-focused problem-solving. *Criminology and Public Policy*, 4, 2, 1201–1215.

Mackenzie, S. & Henry, A. (2009). *Community Policing: A Review of the Evidence' Scottish Government Social Research*. Available: http://www.scotland.gov.uk/Resource/Doc/292465/0090209.pdf.

McEvoy, K. & Mika, H. (2002). Restorative justice and the critique of informalism in Northern Ireland. *British Journal of Criminology*, 42, 3, 534–562.

Mulcahy, A. (2006). *Policing Northern Ireland: Conflict, Legitimacy and Reform*. Cullompton, Devon: Willan Publishing.

Topping, J.R. (2008). Diversifying from within: Community policing and the governance of security in Northern Ireland. *British Journal of Criminology*, 48, 778–797.

Weitzer, R. (1995). *Policing Under Fire: Ethnic Conflict and Police-Community Relations in Northern Ireland*. Albany: State University of New York.

Poland*

32

EMIL W. PŁYWACZEWSKI
IZABELA NOWICKA

Contents

Background

Poland lies at the physical center of the European continent. Its population is 38.3 million, and the total area is 120,727 mi.^{2} (312,683 km^2). Its capital is Warsaw. Its current frontiers, stretching for 2198 mi. (3538 km), were drawn in 1945 and presently border six countries in the west. Poland borders Germany along the Oder and Lusatian Neiss rivers. In the south, the borders mainly follow the watershed of the Sudeten, Beskid, and Carphatian mountain ranges, which separate Poland from the Czech and Slovak Republics. In the northeast and east, Poland borders Russia, Lithuania, Belarus, and Ukraine. The Baltic coast forms the northern frontier. From the standpoint of nationality, Poland is a country that is almost uniform. There are relatively few ethnic minorities, about 1.5 million in all, mainly Ukrainians, Byelorussians, Germans Czechs, Slovakians, Lithuanians, Jews, and Gypsies.

Poland is a unitary republic, and its most recent constitution is from 1997. The nation's political system is based on the division into the legislative, executive, and judicial branches of government. The legislative branch is made up of the *Sejm* and the Senate. The 460 *Sejm* deputies and the 100 senators are elected in popular elections for a 4-year term. The main function of the *Sejm* is to legislate laws that the Senate can confirm, amend, or reject. Another important role of the *Sejm* is to conduct parliamentary control over activities of the executive branch of the government as well as to participate (sometimes with the Senate's role as well) in designating officials for some of the state's highest offices.

In 1990, Poland rejoined the International Criminal Police Organization (Interpol). Polish presence in international police organizations goes back to 1923, when Interpol was established, but in 1952, for political reasons, the Polish government broke off all relations

---

* This chapter partly uses the paper by Emil W. Pływaczewski that was presented in session 1 of the IPES Global Community Policing Conclave 2010, Kochi (Kerala), India, November 2–6.

with the organization. In 2004, Poland became a member of the European Union. In the second half of the year 2011, Poland occupied the presidency in the European Union.

The Polish Police is a uniformed and armed force, established to protect the security of the people and to maintain public safety and civil order. The police carry out the following tasks specified in Chapter 1 of the Police Act, adopted by the Polish Parliament on April 6, 1990:

- Protecting the people's life and their property against lawless assault
- Ensuring public safety and civil order in public places, means of public transportation, road traffic, and waters
- Initiating and arranging actions aimed to prevent crimes and misdemeanors in cooperation with state and local authorities and public organizations
- Detecting crimes and misdemeanors and pursuing the offenders thereof
- Supervising municipality (city) guards and private security companies
- Controlling whether codes of order and administrative regulations are observed in public places
- Cooperating with police services of other countries and their international organizations

Origins of Community Policing in the Indigenous Communities

At the beginning of the 1990s, democracy spread to vast new territories, mainly as a result of the fall of communist governments in Eastern and Central Europe (Brand and Jamróz 1995; Pływaczewski 2000). The changes that were introduced in Poland after the year 1989 involved the transformation of the political system, the beginning of a market economy, and the reformation of the legal system. Thus, Polish society of the 1990s was affected by dramatic political, economic, and social changes. Reforming policing systems, which had served primarily to protect the party–states from their opponents, into a system that serves and protects civic society has come to be seen as an essential prerequisite and concomitant of the democratization process in transitional countries (Caparini and Marenin 2004; Vogel 1994).

The time of transformation in Poland, like in other Central European countries, witnessed great organizational changes, which had objective consequences in many areas of social life. The police had to adapt to the changes in their organization, legal regulations, and professional awareness; they had to keep up with societal changes and, consequently, had to undergo a transformation themselves. Especially important was the issue of how to design police training and work in such a manner that the public could feel assured that police are for the society and not against it.

In 1990, the Parliament passed a new Police Act, which sought to create a police organization that would be adequately prepared to fight crime within the new democratic political framework. The new management of the Ministry of Interior and Administration realized that the Civic Militia, the armed force of the Polish United Workers' Party (in the communist period), would have to be transformed into a modern, apolitical police in a very short time if Poland were to become the democratic country it aspired to be after 1989. It was not an easy task for, on the one hand, the people's confidence in the new police had to be gained, and, on the other hand, the police had to be taught their new roles in the new constitutional order, that of public servants under the law and protectors of society.

Despite the objections of various political circles and public opinion at the time, the decision was made to introduce into the newly created police profound organizational changes, including shifts among managerial staff and the dismissal of discredited people who were unable to work within the new framework. This policy resulted in a shortage of manpower at all levels and reduced police efficiency, which was lowered further by a lack of senior officers to occupy managerial posts in the basic organizational units of the police (Plywaczewski and Walancik 2004).

The police must cope with even greater problems in trying to ensure the safe functioning of the society. The basic tasks of a democratic state with regard to the police are the following:

- To maximize their capacities to prevent and fight crime and other socially harmful phenomena
- To minimize the chances that their powers are used in conflict with democratic principles

Community policing as a concept and philosophy of preventive activities was first used in Poland at the beginning of the 1990s. It became particularly popular within some scientific circles and with those police officers who were involved in prevention. Community policing created new ways of solving problems in relations between the police, society, and different institutions. It also resulted in a new way of looking at such traditional police tasks as crime control, participating in law enforcement through reacting to the cases of breaking the law, helping endangered citizens, and helping citizens in other situations, when there is no direct threat.

Police officers' involvement in decreasing fear of crime has been forced by the necessity to do the following:

- Shift from the incident-oriented police model to the problem-solving oriented model
- Work out new criteria for assessing cooperation with the public, according to which a police officer not only prosecutes offenders but also prevents illegal acts

The key to community policing is the degree of social confidence in law enforcement agencies. Since the creation of the police in 1990, a continuous growth of such confidence could be observed. In 1993, it reached the peak level of 74%, slightly lowering to 70% in the following years. Compared to the other criminal justice and law enforcement agencies, police enjoy much better public approval than do public prosecutors, courts, and the prison service. According to 1995 surveys, as many as 49% of Poles were not willing to support the police in their work, which particularly applied to inhabitants of big cities. So, the question applies: why is there such a big discrepancy between the theoretically postulated public support for the police and actual cooperation? The reason for this situation can be persistent passivity of many people and the widely propagated philosophy of individualism. In such conditions, it is difficult to create proper communication mechanisms between polarized society and the police undergoing personnel and organizational transformations (Misiuk 1998).

In Poland, community policing has become a nationwide movement for fighting and preventing crime at a local level in the following areas:

- Preventing and combating crime
- Reducing threats to the public order, such as prostitution, vandalism, drinking alcohol in public places, and so forth
- Increasing people's feeling of safety
- Improving the standards of living in local communities as a final outcome

In 2001, an attempt to catalogue preventive programs was made, which revealed that there had been 438 programs, divided into the following categories:

- Person and property protection (63 programs)
- Traffic safety (926 programs, among them 19 aimed at children and youngsters)
- Pathologies (101 programs, among them 99 aimed at youngsters)
- Crime victims (5 programs concerning the problem of helping victims)
- General aspects of security

According to the above specification, 101 programs concerning preventing and combating social pathologies might suggest a growing number of pathological incidents in local communities. On the other hand, the vast majority of the programs deal with general aspects of security.

How Does Community Policing Work?

Preventive programs implemented by police units appeared to be particularly important undertakings as far as realization of community policing philosophy is concerned. In 1995, the National Police Headquarters launched the "Safer Town" program. A few years after its inauguration, several weak points were observed:

- Hasty, "occasional" attention paid by representatives of public administration to the problem of threat prevention
- Lack of coordination among institutions responsible for public order and safety prevention
- Minimal interest of social institutions and organizations in cooperation with police forces in the scope of public safety and order protection
- Lack of formal, systematic solutions on the level of "police-institutional and social environment"
- Poor quality of police units' technical equipment, insufficient involvement of prevention police officers in order tasks (such as escorts), lack of respect for law enforcement officers
- Lack of clear criteria for evaluation of preventive actions

Constant interest of the police in the program's implementation was accompanied by hasty, "occasional," and often chaotic actions undertaken by other institutions. Such a situation eliminated the chance for cooperation in numerous preventive undertakings, caused dispersal of actions and means, and led to decreased efficiency of actions.

In connection with the reform of the administration in 1999, the police is not the only entity responsible for security and public order. Local government bodies are also responsible for security, which under local laws are to initiate and engage in activities to improve the safety of citizens (Laskowski 2005). The aforementioned regulations are reflected in local programs for security developed on the basis of disaster management programs, which are to be implemented in every county. Local authorities, who have extensive knowledge of local conditions, needs, and characteristics of the county, as well as the types of hazards occurring in it, have participated in the development of these programs. All these factors were taken into account while developing the programs. Then, local security programs were approved by the governors (prior to the relevant resolutions being carried out by the county councils) and thus became part of local law. The development of these programs and their use in subsequent tasks will certainly have an impact on the cooperation of the police and local government bodies. Another important factor is the appointment of municipal police by self-government authorities. In recent years, the level of cooperation between the police and the municipal (urban) police has been increasing and is assessed by the police as satisfactory. This cooperation is mainly based on the agreements signed by the commanders of the police units and representatives of the local government administration.

The process of getting citizens to work toward security and public order is difficult not only because of the problems of mobilizing local communities and the emergence of their leaders but also because of the risk of incorrect forms of social participation (Łojek 2008). According to B. Hołyst, there are several reasons to hinder public participation in crime prevention: (1) If crime prevention is reaching too far and turns to repression, it precipitates many difficult problems; (2) selection of areas of crime, in which it is intended to maintain preventive actions with the participation of the public, requires thorough research; (3) citizens participating in the implementation of prevention programs must be properly chosen and characterized by socially valuable traits (objectivism, interest in public welfare, integrity, impeccable reputation, etc.), and persons employed in various civic committees should be independent from state institutions, which will enhance their confidence among the public; and (4) crime prevention actions must stay within the control of official authorities. The point is to eliminate the danger of abuse of power by certain social groups to meet their own interests (Hołyst 1999).

An example showing the involvement of citizens in solving local with security problems is the Group of Certain Persons,* the first contact with a group of active young people established by K. Lojek in January 2007. The desire for closer cooperation resulted from the civic action to combat the illegal placement of posters, conducted by the Action for Lodz. This action drew attention through its creative form, self-developed campaign in the media, and determination of the involved people. Impressive was the fact that, with their own ideas (filming and publishing on the Web civil detentions of flyposting people and the process of handing them over to the city guards) and using the resources available to every citizen, the action's organizers achieved results, which may arouse envy among

---

* The achievements of the Group of Certain Persons are available on the Web sites: http://www.dlalodzi .info, http://www.gpo.blox.pl, http://pl.youtube.com/user/grupapewnychosob, and http://pl.youtube.com/ user/tvlodz.

costly public campaigns and prevention programs. In response to a proposal of collaboration sent by e-mail, the representative of the group informed people of the need to make a team decision about the future of team collaboration. To dispel any doubts right at the outset (e.g., those associated with a request to K. Lojek for access to movies of civil detentions), he explained: "We are not supporters of the description of handing over of the caught fly-posting people to the Municipal Police. We have already got an opinion of ORMO (Polish acronym for Paramilitary Organization Supporting the Civic Militia), and we really only wanted to draw attention of the media (such films are, after all, 'sensational'), because with the use of them it is easier to put pressure on officials."*

Another example of community involvement is "Neighborhood Watch Patrol." Between 1998 and 2002, the number of burglaries in holiday cottages and shops in the Spychowo area increased. Crime prevention activities and investigations carried out by the police led to detection and detention of only a small percentage of all perpetrators. Such a situation was, among other things, due to the fact that the crime activity centered around holiday cottages located in poorly populated areas and left unattended after the summer time (e.g., Koczek, Kierwik, Połom). As a result, on January 10, 2003, an initiative of "Neighborhood Watch Patrol" was taken. A group of volunteers was formed. Today it consists of 60 members. The group acts in accordance with the rules and a description of relevant duties. The Neighborhood Watch Patrol's activities consist of night patrols, during which the members monitor the town, driving their own cars marked with a magnetic plate reading "Patrol." The "patrolman" reports to the duty officer in the County Police Headquarters in Szczytno the time of beginning and finishing his patrol. They stay in contact all the time, making phone calls when they notice anything in relation to security and safety. Moreover, in cases of emergency, they inform local police about the incident. Since the beginning of these actions, the number of crimes committed in the patrolled area has been systematically reduced.

An essential element of cooperation between the police and the communal (municipal) police consists of deployment coordination of police units and municipal police in the form of joint patrols. The deployment of patrols depends on the size of public order threats that occur in a particular area. The municipal police and the police can also create a local cooperation mechanism (e.g., there exists a team for prevention and counteraction against pathologies among young people in the municipal police in Oświęcim) (Laskowski 2005). Furthermore, units of the police and communal (municipal) police take part in various preventive programs.

Monitoring, used by the police and the communal (municipal) police, also plays an important role in the protection of public order and security. These law enforcement agencies also cooperate with the local governments in the field of dissemination of information among the citizens concerning security and avoidance of dangers or behavior in traffic. Local governments support in this field the printing of informative–educational materials, such as leaflets and brochures. It is of particular importance for children at the kindergartens and schools, who, thanks to these materials, know how to contact the police in case of an emergency.

As much as possible, local governments also support the police through such actions as car purchase, participation in renovation of the rooms, or purchase of information

---

* Personal e-mails of Krzysztof Łojek.

technology (IT) tools, as well as exemption from paying some taxes. Formation of a commission for public order and security is also an essential issue of police functioning within the structure of local government administration. These commissions are formed in the Polish administrative units, and their task as statutory institutions is to work out a county program project of crime prevention as well as security of citizens' safety and public order (Art. 12 point 9b of the Local Government Act).

National Police Headquarters also conducted a program, the objective of which was "Together Safer." The program concerns teamwork for the improvement of life quality in terms of safety and better access to public good, which is safety and security. In the first half of 2007, the National Police Headquarters accomplished several tasks in the following areas.

Security in Public Places and the Place of Residence

Analysis and assessment reports on uniformed police actions were drawn up. They were handed in to the Minister of Internal Affairs and Administration. Integrated organization and deployment of patrols was introduced by the National Police Headquarters Decision No. 152 of March 17, 2006. Also, a police program, "Safe Towns," on limiting crime and antisocial behavior in small and average-sized towns was implemented. The number of police and other law enforcement agencies' patrols was increased in places and at the time in which they were needed the most due to the more effective use of police human resources, and the force and resources of the Military Police, Border Guard, and prison service.

Safety at School

Information on structure and scale of juvenile delinquency, including that taking place at schools, was systematically prepared. Moreover, cooperation with the Ministry of Internal Affairs and Administration concerning competition of offers for nongovernmental entities on "counteracting aggression and violence among children and teenagers especially in peer groups" was established. The National Police Headquarters as an entity supporting the Ministry of Education in task performance was an initiator of working out specific guidelines for the competition "Safe School."

Safety in Public Transport

Preventive and operational actions on the main railway routes of the Polish State Railways (PKP) were based on the guidelines of June 20, 2001, prepared by the National Police Headquarters and included in the "plan of cooperation between various Regional Police Headquarters in preventive and operational security of trains in domestic and international communication." Tasks resulting from the strategy of actions leading to improvement of security in railway areas, which came into existence under the Agreement of July 6, 2004, between the National Police Headquarters, Border Guards Headquarters, Military Police Headquarters, and Polish State Railways PLC (PKP SA), were carried out.

The activities were also undertaken in order to improve security in the railway areas by the Central Unit for Security administered by the Head Deputy of Prevention and Road Traffic Office, which includes representatives of the agreement, and presently, works are being conducted that aim at developing the analysis of dangers in public transport, especially concerning buses, trolleybuses, and trams.

Safety in Road Traffic

While implementing tasks concerning this area, Police Headquarters inspired and supervised the realization of cyclic activities of control and preventive character, such as "Speed," "Sobriety," "Seatbelts," "Unprotected Road Traffic Participants (Pedestrians)," "Route E-30," "Minibus," "Taxi," and "Truck," as well as "Safe Weekend," "Safe Holidays," and "Safe Winter Holidays." The Chief of Police ordered his regional police commanders to intensify police activities in the main traffic routes by increasing the number of road traffic patrols, paying special attention to the dynamic form of supervision. Additional financial means were allocated for fuel for vehicles with video recorder—a 24-hour limit of 500 km for each Regional Police Headquarters. Cascade speed measurements were also introduced, and with this end in view, 10 off-road vehicles with upgraded technical parameters and video recorders were bought and given to field units.

In the framework of the program's implementation, the Police Headquarters bought 70,000 drug tests, which are used to detect psychoactive substances in the human organism. The tests were given to the field units. The provisions of the agreement between the Chairman of the Polish Motor Association, the Chief of Police, the Minister of National Education, and the Minister of Infrastructure that were implemented concerned organizing the All-Polish Safety in Road Traffic Tournament for primary and middle school students and the Automotive Youth Tournament for secondary school students. A yearly analysis of road accidents and their causes was prepared, and its objective was to develop the basic directions of actions associated with occurring dangers. The study was popularized in institutions and organizations responsible for undertakings in the field of safety in road traffic. Activities for safety on roads were also promoted, and their task was to raise the consciousness of road users. These activities were implemented in cooperation with the Ministry of National Education, the Ministry of Transport, the National Council for Road Safety, the General Directorate for National Roads and Motorways, the Military Police, the Polish Motor Association, insurance companies, foundations, and associations, but also commercial companies that take action for road security. The efforts were undertaken in order to check the condition of vehicles used in transport of persons and goods and also the working time of drivers in road transport (Policja 2008).

Relation to Criminal Justice System

In article 182 of the Constitution of the Republic of Poland of April 2, 1997, it states that participation of citizens in performing justice administration will be specified by the legal acts. When it comes to criminal cases, the Code of Criminal Procedure is such a legal act, and in article 3, it states that the criminal procedure is conducted with participation of a social factor only within the limits specified by the act. It can be conducted in three forms:

1. Participation of lay judges in deciding by sentence (they have the same rights as professional judges)
   - In felony cases (article 28, paragraph 2, of the Code of Criminal Procedure)
   - In crime cases with life imprisonment penalty (article 28, paragraph 3, and article 554, paragraph 2, of the Code of Criminal Procedure)

2. Participation of social organization's representative according to stipulations in article 90 of the Code of Criminal Procedure
3. Guaranteeing by social organization as a form of preventive measure according to article 271 of the Code of Criminal Procedure (Grzeszczyk 2007)

Effectiveness of Community Policing

Cooperation between the police and the society demands improving certain conditions. It is necessary to base them on certain assumptions:

1. The administrative reform made it possible to implement community policing. Without changes in police responsibilities, there were new formal and economical foundations laid. They concerned developing preventive actions for the local society's benefit.
2. The problem of eliminating the threats ceased to be confined only in the police domain. They became the subject of common interest of the public administration authorities and local councils. It led to new areas of cooperation with police.
3. The only restriction on the preventive actions is the diversity of tasks imposed on civil servants. For these people, the problem of public safety is often an additional problem and is also an extra task to be taken.
4. The basic requirement for cooperation to be successful is to select appropriate personnel to cooperate with nonpolice institutions. Police officers very often identify their actions only with crime detection, after the crime is already committed. For that very reason, all the initiative connected with improving preventive actions and cooperation with nonpolice institutions is not understood properly.
5. The basic requirement for success in this field is personnel stability. However police officers working in prevention units are promoted and moved to the criminal preventions department. Both lack of staff stability and expecting promotion are the main reasons for the negative attitude toward crime prevention as well as partners and problems as subjects of cooperation.
6. Lack of personnel stability in the field of cooperation with society a particularly constant changes in community officers' position prevent the establishment of proper conditions for integrating local authorities in partnerships dealing with public safety.
7. We need to face the problem of spending funds on prevention. It is not only society and police officers' will and enthusiasm that can help in preventive actions. For that very reason, it is important to rely on donations that can be spent on crime prevention. This problem is well understood by the police managerial staff, but it is somehow beyond nonpolice institutions' awareness.

All attempts to transform Polish society into civil society need to be appreciated. One may expect a lot from the initiative of the Ministry of Social Policy, that is, the project "Civic Society Operational Program—National Development Plan 2007–2013" (Pozytek). One of the program's aims, which is increasing the activity of local societies in local partnerships, is supposed to be achieved by projects, which include the following:

- Increasing the feeling of security and rootedness among the local community by creating counseling points and help lines and establishing direct connections with representatives of local services—district constable, education, trainings, and workshops that aim at danger prevention (Program Operacyjny Społeczeństwo Obywatelskie 2005)
- Increasing local trust by developing programs of neighborly cooperation for security (Program Operacyjny Społeczeństwo Obywatelskie 2005)

However, the essence of the issue is the necessity to balance the needs of the formal control system and the informal mechanisms in such a way that they lead to effective cooperation for public security. It seems reasonable to treat the system of security as a macro system coordinated by the president and the National Security Bureau, the Parliament, and the Cabinet. In this macro system, two subsystems must be separated: (1) external security, national defense, and (2) internal security, citizens' public safety, and anticrisis security.

References

Brand, P. and Jamróz, A. 1995. *Demokracja wczoraj i dziś (Democracy Yesterday and Today)*. Bialystok: Temida.

Caparini, M. and Marenin, O. (eds.) 2004. *Transforming Police in Central and Eastern Europe. Process and Progress*. Muenster: DCAF, LIT Verlag.

Grzeszczyk, W. 2007. *Kodeks postępowania karnego. Komentarz*, Warsaw: Lexis-Nexis, p. 18.

Hołyst, B. 1999. *Kryminologia*, Warsaw, p. 1054.

Laskowski, S. 2005. "Policja-samorząd. Współpraca i współodpowiedzialność za bezpieczeństwo." In A. Babiński and P. Bogdalski (eds.), *Policja w strukturach administracji publicznej, Seminar Materials*, Szczytno: Police Academy, pp. 88 ff.

Łojek, K. 2008. *Metodyka rozwiązywania problemow kryminalnych*, Szczytno, pp. 185 ff.

Misiuk, A. 1998. "Community policing in Poland in the 1990s." *The Police Journal*, LXXI(2): 152–153.

Pływaczewski, E. W. 2000. "The challenges of policing democracy in Poland." In D. K. Das and O. Marenin (eds.), *Challenges of Policing Democracies. A World Perspective*. Amsterdam: Gordon and Breach Publishers, pp. 148 ff.

Plywaczewski, E. W., and Walancik, P. 2004. "Challenges and changes to the police system in Poland." In M. Caparini and O. Marenin (eds.), *Transforming Police in Central and Eastern Europe*. Münster: Lit Verlag, pp. 93–113.

Policja. 2008. Available at http://www.policja.pl/portal/pol/137/7954/ZADANIA_ZREALIZOWANE_ PRZEZ_POLICJE_W_RAMACH_PROGRAMU_RZADOWEGO_RAZEM_BEZPIECZNIE .html, accessed August 5, 2008.

Pozytek. http://www.pozytek.gov.pl/files/pozytek/PO_Spol_Obywat/poso.pdf.

Program Operacyjny Społeczeństwo Obywatelskie Narodowy Plan Rozwoju 2007–2013, Warsaw 2005, pp. 59, 60.

Vogel, D. 1994. *Policing in Central and Eastern Europe. Report on a Study Tour*, HEUNI Publication Series No. 23, Helsinki, pp. 16 ff.

Serbia

33

ZVONIMIR IVANOVIĆ
SERGEJ ULJANOV

Contents

Geopolitical Characteristics

Serbia, officially constituted as the Republic of Serbia, is a landlocked country located at the crossroads of Central and Southeast Europe, covering the southern part of the Carpathian basin and spreading over the central part of the Balkan peninsula. Serbia borders Hungary to the north; Romania and Bulgaria to the east; the Former Yugoslav Republic of Macedonia to the south; Croatia to the northwest; Bosnia and Herzegovina to the west; and Montenegro to the southwest. Additionally, it borders Albania through Kosovo. Located at the crossroads between Central and Southern Europe, Serbia is found in the Balkan peninsula and the Pannonian Plain. Including Kosovo, it lies between latitudes 41° and 47° N, and longitudes 18° and 23° E. The province of Vojvodina covers the northern third of the country and is entirely located within the Central European Pannonian Plain. The Dinaric Alps, gradually rising toward the south, cover most of western and central Serbia. The easternmost tip of Serbia extends into the Wallachian Plain. The eastern border of the country intersects with the Carpathian Mountain ranges, which run through the whole of Central Europe. The capital of Serbia, Belgrade, is among the largest cities in Southeast Europe (populated by 1,731,425 enumerated persons [and 1,639,121 populated citizens] registered by the census) (Census of Population, Households and Dwellings 2011).*

After the arrival of the Serbs in the Balkans (as one of the Slavs tribes, they were a part of South wing, such as Croats or Bulgarians) in the seventh century, several medieval states were formed, which evolved into the Serbian Empire in the fourteenth century. By the sixteenth century, Serbia was conquered and occupied by the Ottoman Empire, at times interrupted by the Habsburgs. In the early nineteenth century, the Serbian revolution

---

* The difference in figures for populated back in 2002 could be determined if we acknowledge that the population back then was 1,576,124 people in this region of the capital city Belgrade.

reestablished the country as the constitutional monarchy, and royal family subsequently expanded its territory and pioneered the abolition of feudalism in the Balkans. The former Habsburg crown land of Vojvodina united with Serbia in 1918. Following World War I, Serbia formed Yugoslavia with other South Slavic people, and it existed in several forms up until 2006, when Serbia regained its independence. From 2003 to 2006, Serbia was part of the "State Union of Serbia and Montenegro." This union was the successor to the Federal Republic of Yugoslavia.* After 88 years in various federations, the parliament of Serbia announced a constitutional referendum that would replace the former Yugoslav-era constitution and created the new framework for the country by ratifying a new constitution. Kosovo has been governed since 1999 by United Nations Interim Administration Mission in Kosovo (UNMIK), a United Nations (UN) mission. In February 2008, the parliament of UNMIK-governed Kosovo, Serbia's southern province, unilaterally declared independence. In April 2008, Serbia was invited to join the intensified dialogue program with the North Atlantic Treaty Organization (NATO) despite the diplomatic rift with the alliance over Kosovo. Serbia officially applied for European Union (EU) membership on December 22, 2009. Serbia is a member of the UN, Council of Europe, Partnership for Peace (PfP), The Organization of the Black Sea Economic Cooperation (BSEC), and Central European Free Trade Agreement (CEFTA). It is also an EU membership applicant and a self-declared neutral country.

As of December 2012, Serbia (without Kosovo) has an estimated population of 7,120,666 (not including more than 200,000 internally displaced persons [IDPs] from Kosovo, who will be counted as a permanent population in the next census).

Ethnic Groups

Serbs are the largest ethnic group in Serbia, representing 83% of the total population, excluding Kosovo. With a population of 290,000, Hungarians are the second largest ethnic group in Serbia, representing 3.9% (and 14.3% of the population in Vojvodina). Other minority groups include[†] Bosniaks, Roma, Albanians, Croats, Bulgarians, Montenegrins, Macedonians, Slovaks, Vlachs, Romanians, and Chinese. According to UN estimates, around 500,000 Roma live in Serbia (Webrzs 2011). The German minority in the northern province of Vojvodina was more numerous in the past (336,430 in 1900, or 23.5% of Vojvodina's population), and this is due to World War II. Serbia has the largest refugee population in Europe. Refugees and IDPs in Serbia comprise between 7% and 7.5% of its population—about half a million refugees sought refuge in the country following the series of Yugoslav wars, mainly from Croatia and, to a lesser extent, from Bosnia and Herzegovina, and the IDPs from Kosovo, which are currently the most numerous at over 200,000.

---

* On May 21, 2006, Montenegro held a referendum to determine whether or not to end its union with Serbia, which then ended up giving Serbia its independence.
† In conclusion, the ethnic groups in Serbia (excluding Kosovo) in 2002 were Serbs, 82.86%; Hungarians, 3.91%; Bosniaks, 1.81%; Roma, 1.44%; Yugoslavs, 1.08%; Croats, 0.94%; Montenegrins, 0.92%; Albanians, 0.82%; Slovaks, 0.79%; Vlachs, 0.53%; Bulgarian, 0.28%; other, 4.90%.

Religious Groups

Among the Eastern Orthodox Churches, the Serbian Orthodox Church is the largest in the country. According to the 2002 census, 82% of the population of Serbia, excluding Kosovo, or 6.2 million people declared their nationality as Serbian, who are overwhelmingly adherents of the Serbian Orthodox Church. Other Orthodox Christian communities in Serbia include Romanians, Vlachs, Macedonians, and Bulgarians. Together they comprise about 84% of the entire population.

Catholicism is present mostly in Vojvodina, especially its northern part, which is home to minority ethnic groups such as Hungarians, Slovaks, Croats, Bunjevci, and Czechs. There are an estimated 388,000 baptized Catholics in Serbia, roughly 6.2% of the population, mostly in northern Serbia.

Protestantism accounts for about 1.1% of the country's population, chiefly among Reformist Hungarians and Slovaks in Vojvodina. Islam has a strong historic following in the southern regions of Serbia—southern Raška and Preševo Valley municipalities in the southeast. Bosniaks are the largest Muslim community in Serbia, with 140,000 followers or 2% of the total population, followed by Albanians, whereas some Roma are Muslim.

Police Organization and Education of Police Staff

Until the end of the nineteenth century, Serbia had no special institution for education of the Ministry of Interior's staff. The first gendarmerie school was founded in 1899 on Dorćol and operated for only a year, and the famous Gendarmerie School for Non-commissioned Officers in Sremska Kamenica was founded after World War I, on February 1, 1920. In the same year, the book *A Contribution toward the Reorganization of the Police* was published, written by Dr. Rodolphe Archibald Reiss (Simonović 2007), leading criminalistic expert and founder of the Institute of Police Science and Criminology in Lausanne, Switzerland. He would be of the greatest importance for Serbian police in the years to come. The Ministry of Interior (MOI) hired Reiss to refine and reform the police, and his *Contribution* advised establishing police schools in Belgrade and other towns in Serbia. Thanks to his effort, in the period between the two World Wars, Belgrade police gained professional staff and modern organization.

After World War II, the problem of leading staff education occurred again, and the School for Non-commissioned Officers of the People's Militia began working in 1947 in Vrbas. During that period, the School for People's Town Militia in Pančevo and the School for Station Commanders of People's Militia in Zemun were founded. By the decision of the Assembly of the Socialistic Republic of Serbia, the Police High School "Pane Đukić" in Sremska Kamenica began working on September 1, 1967 and became a main center for education and training of staff for the purpose of public security.

In 1972, the Law on the Advanced School of Internal Affairs in Zemun was enacted, and the school began working that same year. Two decades later, on June 30, 1993, with the enactment of the Law on the Police Academy, the first educational–scientific higher-education institution for police profession was established. In accordance with contemporary demands and needs of the profession, the Academy of Criminalistic and Police Studies (ACPS) was established on July 27, 2006 by the decision of the Government of the

Republic of Serbia. It is an independent higher-education institution that provides academic and professional study programs of all levels for the purpose of police education and police and security affairs. The ACPS came into being by the merging of the Advanced School of Internal Affairs and the Police Academy—the two most important institutions specialized for conducting educational and scientific activities for the purpose of police education—and the ACPS is their legal successor.

Reform of Police in Serbia

Political Reform

The reform started back in 2002, with normative aspects and depoliticization of the police as well as decentralization of police structure and management. At the top management positions, 400 new highly educated officers were appointed as successors of former politically oriented colleagues, who were retired or relocated. Later in time, the depoliticization and demilitarization went on with enacting the Police Law in 2005, when ranks at the police, mostly military oriented, were replaced with civil ranks managed by the law on public civil service officials, as a public service organization.

The reform and all of the processes of change were planned and enforced with Organization for Security and Co-operation in Europe (OSCE), and many new projects were started in consultation (and monitoring by) with international partners. In the first round, there were four international partners: OSCE and the governments of Great Britain Department for International Development (DFID), Switzerland, and Norway. The main goals of the reform were training of police personnel in order to apply new orientation mainly focused on proactive doing, prevention of crime and implementation of modern policing standards, cooperation with the citizens, and improvement of safety throughout the Republic of Serbia.

Structural Reform

In 2004 and 2005, there were a few pilot projects started in several cities of Serbia oriented in community policing and problem-oriented policing (POP). Those pilot projects were started in the Belgrade municipal community of Zvezdara, Novi Bečej, and also in Vrnjačka Banja, Kragujevac, Novi Sad, and municipalities in southern Serbia, mostly populated by ethnic Albanians: Bujanovac, Medveđa, and Preševo. Also, at every secretariat of the MOI, special anticorruption teams consisting of representatives of the public prosecutor's office and police were created. For the JUNO project, the government of Norway donated 750,000 EUR to the police of Bačka Palanka municipality in order to uphold the project of community policing in that town. That project and its effort were evaluated by all participants, and all evaluations were satisfactory. Because of these positive evaluation results, another project was started, called JUNO II. The government of Norway, together with OSCE, provided funds and intelligence to the Novi Sad (New Sad) project concerning policing matters. The government of Switzerland donated 500,000 CHF for the realization of a project in the city of Požega, called Citizens Police. All of those projects differed in methods and means for community policing due to their donors' views. A community policing seminar was organized in 2003 by the government

of Great Britain (DFID), OSCE, and MOI of Serbia. In order to facilitate better cooperation with the community, a constable officer would be appointed, who would be
a police officer locally stationed and possibly with his home in that locality, familiar
with local problems and issues of community matters. His (or her) main duties are to
maintain connections with the community, to patrol and observe security-related issues
(and therefore to act in prevention), to gather security-related information, and in some
cases, to act in a police repression manner, when necessary. Also, the police officials
must maintain connections with the community institutions and form security councils
with municipal officials. Those councils will have only consulting powers but should be a
place to exchange views and opinions. In the manner of preventive and proactive action,
school police officers (SPOs) were introduced in 250 elementary and high schools in
Serbia in coordination and cooperation with the Ministry of Education. The SPO model
is represented by a police officer in civilian suit, with main goals of enforcing the law in
the school, maintaining security of the teachers and pupils in the school, and preventing acts of violence and other acts of crime (drug trafficking, assault, kidnapping, etc.),
which could be disturbing the normal course of education. The main duties of an SPO
are maintaining presence in a school area at the start and end of teaching courses, shifts,
main breaks, and so forth; spotting and detecting actions and behavior with elements
of criminal acts and misdemeanor and initiating specific measures toward acting persons; acting in traffic safety of pupils; spotting nonschool member persons in the school
courtyard; spotting and dealing with actions aimed to disturb the course of teaching and
taking strong measures in eliminating such disturbances; and so forth.

Police officers of female gender, after the first contingent of the COPO course (The
Ministry of Interior Affairs Republic of Serbia 2011) in Sremska Kamenica, were fully
engaged in action in every type of police action and unit. Also, the constitution of multiethnic police was started in South Serbia due to apparent rising of ethnic intolerances.
Settlers in the area of all ethnic minorities, especially ethnic Albanians, were trainees and
were promised a secure job position after the course, with full and certain payment, without any discriminating element.

Mentioned pilot projects of community policing were evaluated, and it was concluded that the results were very good, so the MOI conducted project community policing for all of Serbia. It was done through establishing the draft strategy of community
policing, the education of certain police officers, and also enacting, monitoring, and
evaluation of further projects for community policing, strategically determined by
police authorities. The strategy of communication was also adopted by MOI, (Republic
of Serbia Ministry of Interior 2011a) in which it was stipulated how exchange of information with the general public should be facilitated.

Also, there were several police actions with further or closer relations to community
policing, such as Central action of focused traffic control of selective content–school, aimed
to increase control of traffic areas around school traffic passages, and also free or closely
focused actions, such as the School without Violence program, Safe Schools program,
SPOs, and other projects and actions with main goal of improving communication of the
children with the police and upholding trust in police. Currently, there are 311 engaged
police officers on duty in 568 schools: 129 SPOs in 188 schools in Belgrade, 15 SPOs in 26
schools in Novi Sad, 10 SPOs in 41 schools in Niš, and 12 SPOs in 25 schools in Kragujevac
(Republic of Serbia Ministry of Interior 2011b).

Communal Police

In further development of municipal and community relations with police in 2009, the Law on Communal Police (Official Messenger 2009) was enacted for the cities in Serbia and especially the city of Belgrade (the capital). The full implementation of the law was postponed until January 23, 2010. The main idea was to decentralize policing business and to transfer some of the police powers to a new agency—a state organ—the communal police, and, on the other hand, to bring better connections with the people in the community with this form of policing. This is done without breaking up or stopping all of the projects of community policing. Now, a few cities in Serbia have the communal police, and their relation and cooperation with the police are proscribed by the Law on Communal Police, memorandum of understanding, other regulations and general and statutory acts.

Communal police members perform tasks related to directing peace and order maintenance stipulated by municipal (statute) law and other (regional and state) law acts and those acts of importance for public utilities, in the course of maintaining order, preventing disorder, and establishing disturbed public order. Particular examples include the following:

- Preventing interference in municipal activities and protecting community (municipal) objects from dirt, damage, and destruction
- Preventing the illegal seizure and damage of areas for public purposes (through moving vehicles and other objects; putting up barriers for vehicles; setting up temporary prefabricated structures; etc.)
- Combating illegal sales and other illegal activities in areas of public use and other public places
- Preventing activities that could harm the general arrangement of the city (soiling and damaging outer regions of facilities and other buildings as well as monuments and sculptures, graffiti, putting up posters and advertising in public and other surfaces, dirt and damage to urban furniture, leaving construction debris and other types of waste in areas of public use, sewage spills and other debris in areas of public use, other activities that harm the neatness and cleanliness of the city) and executing prescribed duties in maintaining buildings and premises in a clean and orderly condition
- Control of snow and ice removal
- Prevention of begging, wandering, and use of flammable and explosive devices in public places (firecrackers and the like)
- Detection and, within the limits of authority, prevention of illegal construction of buildings and controlling the external security and proper marking of building sites
- Maintenance of control of public animal hygiene and ways of holding and conducting of pets
- Ensuring compliance with house rules in apartment buildings
- Maintaining order in the water area (water protection, the use of proper vessels, etc.) and river banks
- Securing and providing conditions for the implementation of measures for fire protection (free access to buildings, fire roads, stairs, etc.)
- Ensuring compliance with working hours of catering and other facilities whose operations may endanger the peace and public order of the citizens

- Operating surveillance in public, suburban, and other local traffic areas, in accordance with law and regulations of the city, with particular regard to public transport, taxis, parking and traffic control, environmental protection, protection of municipal areas and streets, protection of cultural property, preservation of city resources, responding to natural and other disasters, fire protection, and other protection in the jurisdiction of the city

The main activities of the communal police are conducted according to strategic and annual plans, which are adopted by the city council and authorized by the municipal assembly, assisted by MOI. Also, mutual relations and coordination and cooperation between police and communal police could be further regulated by a memorandum of understanding between the mayor and Minister of Interior for every city in Serbia; also, together they could form coordination bodies and engage in other acts of cooperation. Communal police members have the following powers: warnings or cautioning of an individual, issuing of a verbal order, identification (identity confirmation or checking), detention, stop and search power, temporary deprivation of belongings, closed-circuit television monitoring, and use of forceful means (physical force, baton, and handcuffs).

Conclusion

In the Serbian police, there have been many projects concerning community policing, most of which have been successful. Therefore, after a few years, in 2009, the MOI adopted a draft strategy of community policing in Serbia, which allowed for the establishment and development of communal police; the powers invested in this force are similar but different from those of the regular police.

To a large extent, community policing programs in Serbia resemble those commonly seen in the developed Western countries. But the history-related issues and some programs in the past are similar to these new proactive measures, such as the police constable, and there has been a discourse speculating that, in the past, Serbia had a community policing measure. This of course is not true due to different political perspectives and regime change, but positive things from the early history of Serbian policing can now be freely used.

References

Census of Population, Households and Dwellings. 2011. Available at http://webrzs.stat.gov.rs/WebSite/public/PublicationView.aspx?pKey=41&pLevel=1&pubType=2&pubKey=834, last accessed November 30, 2011.

Mellish, D., & Đurđević, Z. (2004). Rezultati evaluacije projekta policija u lokalnoj zajednici i bezbedna zajednica u Srbiji. *Nauka, bezbednost, policija*, 9(2–3), 215–234.

Official Messenger of Republic Serbia, nr. 51/09, 2009.

Plačkov, R. (2008). Problemi rada policije na lokalnom području. *Nauka, bezbednost, policija*, 13(3), 129–147.

Republic of Serbia Ministry of Interior. 2011a. Available at http://www.mup.rs/cms_cir/sadrzaj.nsf/informator.h, last accessed December 3, 2011.

Republic of Serbia Ministry of Interior. 2011b. Available at http://www.mup.rs/cms_cir/sadrzaj.nsf/informator.h, last accessed December 2, 2011.

Simonović, B. (2007). Rad policije u multietničkoj zajednici—pregled inostrane literature, moguća unapređenja u našim uslovima. *Revija za kriminologiju i krivično pravo*, 45(2), 75–97.

Simonović, B. (2010). Pojam i vrste policijske preventivne i represivne delatnosti. *Revija za kriminologiju i krivično pravo*, 48(3), 87–105.

Simonović, B. (2011). Istraživanje stavova pripadnika kriminalističke policije MUP-a Republike Srbije o strateškom pristupu suzbijanja kriminala. *Bezbednost, Beograd*, 53(1), 5–27.

The Ministry of Interior Affairs Republic of Serbia. 2011. Available at http://www.copo.edu.rs/Centar_Za_Osnovnu_Policijsku_Obuku-1-1, last accessed November 29, 2011.

Webrzs. 2011. Available at http://webrzs.stat.gov.rs/WebSite/repository/documents/00/00/22/37/G20114001.pdf, last accessed November 27, 2011.

Slovenia

34

MAJA JERE
GORAZD MEŠKO
ANDREJ SOTLAR

Contents

Background

Slovenia is a Central European country covering 20,237 km^2 and borders Italy to the west, Austria to its north, Hungary to its east, and Croatia to the south. On July 1, 2010, Slovenia had 2,049,261 inhabitants. According to the 2002 census, the ethnic composition of the population was as follows: Slovenians, 83.1%; Croats, 1.8%; Serbs, 2.0%; Muslims (including Bosniaks), 1.6%; Hungarians, 0.3%, Italians, 0.1%; others, 2.2%; and unknown, 8.9%. The official language is Slovenian, and in ethnically mixed areas where indigenous minorities live, the official languages are also Italian and Hungarian. The 2002 census revealed that 58% of inhabitants belong to the Roman Catholic religion. In Slovenia, there are 42 registered churches and other religious communities. The capital city is Ljubljana, which has about 300,000 inhabitants (Government of the Republic of Slovenia 2010).

Slovenes, just like many other Slavic nations, have experienced tumultuous changes in their history and, in most cases, did not depend only on themselves. For centuries, they were governed within multinational countries: up to 1918 within the Austro-Hungarian Empire and between 1918 and 1941 within the state of "Slovenes, Croats, and Serbs," or "The Kingdom of Yugoslavia." During the World War II (1941–1945), the territory of the present-day Slovenia was occupied by Germany, Italy, and Hungary. After the World War II, Slovenia joined the new Socialist Federal Republic of Yugoslavia, where it remained until it gained its independence on June 25, 1991. The declaration of independence was followed by a 10-day armed conflict (June–July 1991) between the combined Slovenian military and police forces on one hand and the Yugoslav armed forces on the other. This conflict led to the departure of the Yugoslav People's Army (YPA) from Slovenia in October 1991. At the end of that year, the Constitution of the Republic of Slovenia was adopted; in the following months, Slovenia experienced wide international recognition since it was recognized by the most important countries of the European Community, and later, also by the

United States, so that in May 1992, Slovenia became a member of the United Nations. In the next two decades, Slovenia became a member of other major global political, security, and economic organizations (European Union [EU], North Atlantic Treaty Organization [NATO], Council of Europe, Organization for Security and Co-operation in Europe [OSCE], Organisation for Economic Co-operation and Development [OECD], etc.) and even presided over some of them.

Concomitant with the reform events in Eastern Europe in the 1980s and the collapse of the Union of Soviet Socialist Republics (USSR), political and economic changes in Slovenia led to a multiparty parliamentary system of liberal democracy of a Western type and to the beginnings of the capitalist economy.

In the years after independence, Slovenia was considered a "success story," especially in comparison to other countries that emerged from the ruins of the former Yugoslavia, all of which were directly or indirectly involved in civil wars (e.g., Croatia, Bosnia and Herzegovina, Serbia, Montenegro, Kosovo, Macedonia). Gross domestic product (GDP) per capita increased from 8150 euros in 1995 to 18,437 euros in 2008, when Slovenia was at the peak of its GDP growth and before it was hit by the economic and financial crisis (http://pxweb.stat.si/pxweb/dialog/Saveshow.asp). Due to constant economic growth and the stable political situation, the year before (January 1, 2007), Slovenia joined the euro area and adopted the euro as its currency. The human development index for 2011 (prepared by the United Nations Development Programme) puts Slovenia in twenty-first place in the world (http://hdrstats.undp.org/en/countries/profiles/SVN.html), and according to the Gini coefficient of inequality (22.7), Slovenia is supposed to have the smallest social disparities in the EU (Hren 2011).

Police Organization

According to the General Police Directorate, in 2011, there were 7666 police officers in Slovenia (5945 uniformed police officers and 885 criminal investigators), or one police officer for 267 inhabitants (Policija 2011a). The Police Act (Zakon o Policiji 1998) states that the Slovenian police service is a body within the Ministry of the Interior and carries out tasks at three levels—national (General Police Directorate), regional (eight police directorates), and local (police stations).

Police stations are classified according to the tasks they perform: (general) police stations, traffic police stations, border police stations, maritime police stations, airport police stations, mounted police stations, service dog handler stations, and police stations for compensatory measures (Policija 2011b).

The police station area is divided into police districts, which comprise one or more municipalities or only a part of the municipality. A police district is intended to implement the social role of the police, and the community policing officer is responsible for preventative tasks within local communities. Where necessary, due to safety issues or distance from a police station, police offices may be established in facilities away from the police headquarters in order to provide a direct police presence.

The director general runs the police and is a public servant who, according to the proposal of the minister, can be appointed and dismissed by the government (Zakon o Policiji 1998). Article 21 of the Police Act provides that in the framework of their competence, the police collaborate with local authorities, organizations, and institutions in areas related to improving safety in local communities. In order to successfully cooperate, they mutually establish councils, advisory committees, commissions, or other forms of partnership, which represent a foundation for community policing.

Origin of Community Policing

In Slovenia, community policing was introduced as part of the democratization process and the process of transferring ideas about police work from the West (Meško 2009; Lobnikar and Meško 2010). After Slovenia gained its independence in 1991, the old practices of social supervision were abandoned, and various reforms were implemented that would introduce the Slovenian police to the Western ideas of police work. Like many other postcommunist countries, Slovenia at the declarative level followed the concept of community policing along the lines of the United States and Great Britain, but due to the haste and the lack of understanding of the underlying philosophy and basic requirements, in particular, legal regulations that do not give the police such wide discretion as in the countries of the origin of community policing, there were problems in implementation (Meško and Klemenčič 2007; Meško 2009).

In 1992, the police started to implement new foundations of police prevention and community policing with the project "Public Safety," which in 1995 became the "Police Project." One of the basic characteristics of the preventative police work should be constant active communication with the public with the goal of increasing public safety awareness and involving other public services and citizens in controlling disruptive and dangerous occurrences (Žaberl 2004). In the process of reorganizing the police at the local level, in 1992, from 635 safety districts, there emerged 318 newly created police districts (Meško and Lobnikar 2005; Žerak 2004).

Before being defined in the legislation, community policing was defined in some strategic and operational documents of the Ministry of the Interior and the police. The document entitled *Basic Guidelines for the Preparation of a Medium-Term Plan for Police Development and Work for the Period from 2003 to 2007* (*Temeljne usmeritve za pripravo srednjeročnega načrta razvoja in dela policije za obdobje od leta 2003 do 2007*) (Ministrstvo za notranje zadeve 2003) explicitly states that the guiding principle of the Slovenian police is to perform community policing, while its mission is to help people and take care of their safety and the safety of their property, and its vision is to provide a safe life for people through partnership with individuals and communities. In the *Annual Work Plan of the Police in 2003* (*Letni načrt dela policije za leto 2003*) (Ministrstvo za notranje zadeve 2003), the strategic goal is to develop partnerships with individuals and communities, while minor goals include the establishment and development of partnership relations between the police and citizens in all local communities, constant consideration of the direction of policing in communities, and directions for implementing preventative work and the development of prevention programs for community safety.

Current *Basic Guidelines for the Preparation of a Medium-Term Plan for Police Development and Work for the Period from 2008 to 2012* (*Temeljne usmeritve za pripravo srednjeročnega načrta razvoja in dela policije v obdobju 2008–2012*) (Ministrstvo za notranje zadeve 2008) emphasizes the creation and development of partnerships with the community, while the changed role of community policing officers and the increased presence of police officers in the streets are also mentioned. Among other things, the development of new methods of police work in local communities and the development of prevention programs are also expected. The current *Guidelines and Mandatory Instructions for the Preparation of the Annual Plan of the Police Work in 2011* (*Usmeritve in obvezna navodila za pripravo letnega načrta dela policije v letu 2011*) (Ministrstvo za notranje zadeve 2010b) dictates that the annual plan should reflect the priority of the strengthening of preventative activities and community policing. The task of the police in the current year is also to verify the adequacy of the existing territorial division of police districts, identify new forms of direct cooperation, and maintain contacts with the population in urban areas by the community policing officers and other police officers. Where necessary, the duties of community policing officers should be supplemented or redefined, so that they would become very familiar with the problems in the local environment and act primarily in a preventative way.

At the criminal policy level for the Republic of Slovenia, community policing is also mentioned in the *Resolution on the Prevention and Suppression of Crime* (*Resolucija o preprečevanju in zatiranju kriminalitete* 2006). Among other things, this document states that for crime at the local level, situational preventive tasks may be successfully accomplished by the police who, years ago, began implementing a strategy of community policing. The emphasis is on methods and forms of work, such as consultancy, working in consultative bodies, working in police offices, the education of children and adults, and the informal ways of socializing and connecting with people. The role of the community policing officer is especially important. To achieve a greater sense of security for citizens and demotivation of potential offenders, police officers should be physically present at the local level, integrated into the local environment (awareness of problems, personal contact with problematic people, particularly young people, verbal counseling, and warning), and a good example to others. The proposed *Resolution on the National Program of Prevention and Suppression of Crime for the Period 2012–2016* (*Resolucija o nacionalnem programu preprečevanja in zatiranja kriminalitete za obdobje 2012–2016*) (Ministrstvo za notranje zadeve 2011) states that community policing currently represents one of the central concepts in the (police) prevention of crime and reducing fear of crime.

On several occasions, the Director General of the Slovenian Police stressed the importance of openness and cooperation of the police with other institutions, communities, and individuals. At the round-table discussion on preparing the resolution on a national program of prevention and suppression of crime for the period 2012 to 2016, the director general of the police stressed the great importance of partnership with citizens and civil society for effective policing and justice, which requires a multidisciplinary approach to crime policy, providing for close interdepartmental cooperation on crime policy and involvement of various participants in the search for modern and efficient solutions for preventing and combating crime (Jere et al. 2011).

In the same period (early 2010), the Ministry of the Interior commissioned a study of Slovenian public views regarding the police (Černič et al. 2009), which showed that the population is satisfied with the way the police cooperate with the local environment. Their efforts to solve problems were rated the best, while their presence in the streets was rated the worst. Two-thirds of respondents believe that police officers are trying very hard or are at least trying to solve problems in the local environment, while cooperation between people and the community policing officers was assessed as satisfactory. More than half of the respondents believe that the community policing officer is good or very good at working with people in communities.

How Does Community Policing Work?

Article 21 of the Police Act (Zakon o Policiji 1998) provides that the police should collaborate with local authorities and other organizations and institutions in areas related to improving safety in local communities. The Act on Local Police (Zakon o občinskem redarstvu 2006) states that municipal councils should adopt a municipal security program, which, on the basis of assessed security conditions, defines the certain types and scope of tasks of the local police. Article 9 provides that municipal wardens, with regard to their tasks and powers, should collaborate with police officers.

The Local Self-Government Act (Zakon o lokalni samoupravi 2007) is also very important, since article 29 enables mayors to create consultative bodies regarding problems in the local community (municipality). For purposes of partnership collaboration in crime prevention and response to disorder in communities, councils, advisory committees, commissions, and other forms of collaboration may be established. Within several municipalities in Slovenia, there are 179 local safety councils. In most cases, mayors are the founders of local safety councils in which police officers, representatives of schools, social services, private security companies, associations, nongovernmental organizations (NGOs), and private companies also collaborate (Ministrstvo za notranje zadeve 2010a). Local safety councils are part of the strategy of community policing and represent an organized way of setting priorities for crime prevention and provision of safety at the local level (Meško 2004; Meško and Lobnikar 2005; Meško et al. 2006).

The local safety council should be a body that comprises the local community, the police, and other interest groups from the local environment. All these participants search for common solutions to improve safety at the local level. Similar practice with local safety councils in every local community existed in Slovenia, even before 1991, when crime prevention and public safety were promoted and implemented within the framework of social self-protection. In this sense, it is all about a reintroduction of the already-known strategies to ensure safety at the local level in the new sociopolitical environment. As to the operation of local safety councils and community policing in general, the Slovenian police have contributed a lot, but the main challenge remains how to attract local people to address common security issues (Meško 2006). Local safety councils deal with traffic safety, maintenance of public order and peace, and crime prevention. Their duties include the analysis of the security situation in the local community; the development of strategies in the field of safety; the implementation of projects; the acquisition of financial assets;* establishment of working groups at the neighborhood level, residential quarters, and local communities; issuing of preventative materials (leaflets, posters); organization of round tables and public forums; and informing the public on the work of local safety councils (Policija 2003).

The research from the year 2000 about differences between police officers and residents of Ljubljana and its surroundings, in relation to community policing and the willingness of citizens to participate in individual police tasks, showed that both police officers and residents are more inclined to community policing than to the traditional approach of implementing police activities. Another interesting finding was that citizens are willing

---

* Funding for the operation of local safety councils is not formally guaranteed, so individual councils obtain it in different ways—by drawing funds from the state budget, donations, and contributions from businesses, organizations, and individuals (Policija 2003).

to cooperate with the police to a much greater extent than perceived by the police (Pagon and Lobnikar 2001).

The results of the study on the professionalism of the Slovenian police (Meško 2006a) show that 61.2% of police officers in a sample of more than 900 police officers responded that community policing is useful for the police and people in the communities. The problems they mentioned were that there are few people willing to cooperate with the police in solving problems in the neighborhoods where they live (28%) and even less people willing to cooperate in providing information in the investigation of crime (21%), but in somewhat greater numbers, they are ready to call the police and inform them when they see something suspicious (35%). The problem reported by the community policing officers is the lack of police officers at police stations, which means that the community policing officers also perform other police functions and therefore have limited time for community policing. A community policing officer is a safety partner of the citizens, who can ask the officer for advice and help. Police officers with years of experience and communication skills usually become community policing officers. A police district is a basic geographic area where community policing officers perform their duties. The official site of the The official site of the Slovenian police (Police 2011) includes the names of all 317 community policing officers in Slovenia, basic information on their duties, instructions on when and where to call them, and an appeal to citizens to help create favorable and safe conditions in the community (Policija 2003; Lobnikar and Meško 2010).

Community policing is also a subject of police training in general and, later, of the training of community policing officers. The training for community policing is attended by the community policing officers as well as the commanders of police stations. The starting points for community police training are contributions of police officers and researchers (Meško 2001; Mikulan 1997). The results of research on the views of police station commanders of community policing, from 2004, show that police station commanders are relatively satisfied with the motivation of the community policing officers to work in communities and content with the community policing strategy and guidelines for carrying out prevention work, but they are significantly less satisfied with the instructions for keeping a record of prevention work. According to the police station commanders, the community policing officers either entirely or very well know the content of documents that define community policing, and they also believe that the community policing officers, to a lesser extent, perform repressive tasks. Commanders believe that the police have the necessary legal basis for work in consultative bodies, and commanders themselves are involved in their formation, but they feel the lack of sensitivity of local communities to work in consultative bodies (Kosmač and Gorenak 2004).

The community policing officer is the bearer of the community policing and is responsible for cooperation with other police officers, residents, representatives of local communities, associations, organizations, businesses, institutions, bodies, and other interest groups (Meško and Lobnikar 2005). In the context of their own actions, especially preventative ones, they also cooperate in preventing and detecting criminal offenses and offenders, identifying and monitoring crime hot spots, informing people of the manifestations of crime and violations, reminding and advising the people on the prevention of criminal offenses and misdemeanors, lecturing in schools and kindergartens, visiting injured parties and victims, returning found or seized items, and obtaining information from interviews (Policija 2011a). Duties of the community policing officers are defined in *Police Rules, Strategy of*

Community Policing, Guidelines for the Implementation of Preventative Work, Measures to Improve Community-Oriented Policing, and *Basic Guidelines for the Preparation of a Mid-term Plan for Police Development and Work for the Period 2003 to 2007* (Meško and Lobnikar 2005; Virtič and Lobnikar 2004).

Effectiveness of Community Policing

The implementation of community policing has not been completely satisfactory (Meško and Lobnikar 2005; Meško and Klemenčič 2007) and, the start especially, was marred by organizational, staffing, and content-related problems (Pečar 2002). The main obstacles to implementation were related to the poor adaptation of the imported model to a Slovenian legal and social context and the conceptual problems in the philosophy of community policing, but the issue of professional police work in general can be questioned as well (Meško and Klemenčič 2007).

Meško and Klemenčič (2007) note that despite numerous reforms introduced since 1991, there still are no key changes in the mindset of police officers, particularly in individuals who joined the police force before 1990, reflecting the well-known gap between the adopted strategies and their actual engagement in practice. It should be noted that in Slovenia, community policing existed even before 1991, but it was more ideologically oriented, in terms of the comprehensive social and political control of citizens. Thus, the experiences and memories of the communist regime can act positively on the public's willingness to participate, but they can also stop people from participating. Particular practices are reminiscent of total state control, while others are accepted as basic factors of community safety and the maintenance of public order (Meško and Klemenčič 2007; Meško 2009).

Establishing local partnerships through local safety councils is a step in the right direction, but, as can be seen, it has not yet brought the desired results. The primary responsibility for solving various problems is still in the hands of the police, which was noted also by Meško and Lobnikar (2005) in a study on local safety councils. According to the respondents, the ones responsible for solving security problems at the local level are mainly police officers, followed by social welfare entities, public prosecutors, courts, NGOs, and educational institutions. Respondents argue that the obstacles to solving security problems in local safety councils are primarily connected to unclearly defined roles of participants, different perceptions of security problems, misunderstanding of partnership relations, the lack of people's interest, and centralized organization. Meško and Lobnikar (2005) note that preventive activities at the local level have more impact on reducing the fear of crime and the feelings of threat, rather than the actual reduction of disorder in the community. In regard to the reduction of fear of crime by implementation of community policing, findings are mixed. While in some communities, police presence reduces fear of crime, in others, it triggers increased concern of local habitants about crime and disorder (Meško et al. 2007).

The proposals of citizens for more effective community policing refer primarily to police patrols in the local environment, the presence and accessibility of police officers in the streets, improvement of communication and cooperation between police officers and the local population, development of communication and interpersonal skills, and the improvement of the skills of police officers in cultural diversity. In a study of the views of members of the local safety councils, on various aspects of cooperation between the local community, police, and local police, which was conducted in 2010 under the auspices of the Ministry of the Interior (Ministrstvo za notranje zadeve 2010a), respondents reported that members of the local safety councils usually meet once or three times a year and that safety in the municipalities primarily concerns the police, followed by the local police and private security companies.

An example of a recent project in community policing is "Back to the People" (Ivančič 2011). The *Guidelines and Mandatory Instructions for Preparation of the Annual Policing Plan in 2011 (Usmeritve in obvezna navodila za pripravo letnega načrta dela policije v letu 2011)* (Ministrstvo za notranje zadeve 2010b) defines the project as an example of good practice to strengthen community policing. In 2009, the management of the Police Directorate of Murska Sobota decided to start with intensive activities for guiding the work of community policing officers, police stations, and the police directorate in the local community, that is, toward the people. The basic tasks that were planned in the project included the improvement of safety in local communities by implementing certain police measures and accepting the help of the local population. Besides that, measures were determined in cooperation with the people, and the processes of analyzing problems, coordinating joint actions, and performance monitoring at the end of the year were established. Within this project, in March 2011, the Police Directorate of Murska Sobota organized a round-table entitled "The Cooperation of Local Communities and the Police," which was, in addition to the professional public, director general of the police, directors of police directorates, and other members of the police, attended also by mayors from the Pomurje region. After 2 years of implementation, Ivančič (2011) decided to interview the representatives of municipalities and the police in order to determine how well they knew the project "Back to the People" and whether the project contributed to better cooperation and the improved security situation at a local level. Among respondents,* 55% were satisfied and 20% were very satisfied with the current security situation in the Pomurje region, while in identifying problems, planning actions, implementing tasks, and measuring the effects of those tasks, the police are still leading the way regarding the level of involvement. The most successful cooperation between the police and local community can be seen in public events, while violence against older people, peer violence, the problems of multiethnic communities, and drugs are not yet solved successfully.

As community policing is a priority for the police in Slovenia, the Ministry of the Interior funded a project entitled "Feelings of Threat and Ensuring Safety in Local Communities," which was conducted by the Faculty of Criminal Justice and Security (2010–2012). The project objectives are to identify the level of police involvement in certain local communities, analyze partnerships between the police and local communities, and analyze the current forms of community policing and the functioning of local safety councils in municipalities. The project includes interviewing police officers and people in communities across Slovenia, and focused group interviews with police chiefs, representatives of municipalities, and civil society, about the importance and role of community policing (Svetek 2011).

---

* The study involved police officers and representatives of local communities of the Pomurje region in the eastern part of Slovenia.

Conclusion

Community policing within democratic policing is not yet fully established, since it was newly introduced into Slovenia only about a decade ago. Nevertheless, progress has been made, and it seems that the Slovenian police overcame the problems that occurred at the beginning of implementing new supervisory strategies and philosophies.

The successful development of community policing can be attributed to the planned work of the Slovenian police, as community policing is one of their main priorities. In practice, this is reflected in the fact that community policing is an integral part of basic training for new police officers and a part of the specialized training for police chiefs and the community policing officers. In terms of the development of police science, a very important fact is that the Slovenian police fund the research of policing, and community policing has been shown to have a clear advantage over all other forms of policing. This can be seen in studies performed from the mid-1990s to the present day. Studies have shown a variety of problems, which were dealt with by the police together with representatives of municipalities. Community policing in Slovenia is intended for all inhabitants, not only citizens and indigenous people. Community policing has proved to be quite effective and successful in creating a feeling of safety and commonly addressing security problems in the community. The success of solving security problems in community policing has proved effective to varying degrees, since expectations that community policing can take care of all security problems sometimes did not come true.

As elsewhere, Slovenian police, in the early stages of community policing development, were faced with staffing problems, lack of knowledge, and lack of skills to work with people in accordance with the principles of community policing. In terms of understanding the concept and philosophy of community policing, there were some problems since some police chiefs interpreted this work only as a form of repressive police work in problem communities. These problems have been resolved, but occasionally, there are problems caused by the lack of police officers, and therefore, the community policing officers have to perform other police duties, which may be in conflict with community policing (Meško 2006).

In terms of organizational culture in the police, community policing is appreciated among police officers more and more because many police officers have the opinion that such police work contributes to the social capital in Slovenian society and that it is an important part of the overall police activities.

Despite the fact that an in-depth evaluation of community policing in Slovenia has not yet been done, it can be observed that the willingness of people to cooperate with the police has increased (Ivančič 2011). Despite significant progress, in practice, there is still a fairly large difference between the prescribed philosophy of community policing (Trojanowicz and Bucqueroux 1990) and its implementation, viewed in the past context of the Slovenian practice of controlling society (Meško 2006). Recent findings suggest that for effective community policing, it is necessary to ensure a high degree of integrity on both sides, the police and representatives of local communities, and especially mayors and directors of municipal administrations.

Further Information

The Association of Municipalities of Slovenia: http://www.zdruzenjeobcin.si/index.php?lang=en
Faculty of Criminal Justice and Security web site: http://www.fvv.uni-mb.si/en/

Slovene Police web site: http://www.policija.si/eng/index.php
The Slovene Police, book: http://www.policija.si/eng/images/stories/Publications/book_slovene-police.

Further Reading

Gorazd Meško and Bojan Dobovšek (Eds.) (2007). *Policing in Emerging Democracies: Critical Reflections*. Ljubljana: University of Maribor, Faculty of Criminal Justice and Security.
Gorazd Meško and Chuck Fields (Eds.) (2009). Policing in Central and Eastern Europe, and beyond—Contemporary issues in social control. *Policing: An International Journal of Police Strategies and Management, 32*(3).
Gorazd Meško and Helmut Kury (Eds.) (2009). *Crime Policy, Crime Control and Crime Prevention—Slovenian Perspectives*. Ljubljana: University of Maribor, Faculty of Criminal Justice and Security.

References

Černič, M., Makarovič, M., and Macur, M. (2009). *Javnomnenjska raziskava o ocenah in stališčih prebivalcev Republike Slovenije o delu policije*: 2009 [Public opinion on the police work in the Republic of Slovenia]. Nova Gorica: Fakulteta za uporabne družbene študije v Novi Gorici.
Government of the Republic of Slovenia (2010). *O Sloveniji*. Retrieved December 17, 2011, from http://www.vlada.si/si/o_sloveniji/.
Hren, B. (2011). Slovenija po dohodkovni (ne)enakosti še v socializmu [Slovenia regarding the income (in)equality still in the socialism]. *Dnevnik*, March 12, 2011. Retrieved December 17, 2011, from http://dnevnik.si/objektiv/vec_vsebin/1042430243.
Ivančič, D. (2011). *Sodelovanje lokalne skupnosti in policije v Pomurju [Cooperation of Local Community and Police in the Pomurje Region]*. Magistrsko delo. Fakulteta za varnostne vede Univerze v Mariboru.
Jere, M., Eman, K., and Bučar-Ručman, A. (2011). Priprava nove resolucije o preprečevanju in zatiranju kriminalitete—poročilo o okrogli mizi [Drafting of the new resolution on crime prevention—round table report]. *Revija za kriminalistiko in kriminologijo, 62*(2), 217–220.
Kosmač, F. and Gorenak, V. (2004). Stališča komandirjev policijskih postaj do policijskega dela v skupnosti [Police station chiefs' attitudes towards community policing]. In B. Lobnikar (Ed.), *5. Slovenski dnevi varstvoslovja* (pp. 714–726). Ljubljana: Fakulteta za policijsko-varnostne vede.
Lobnikar, B. and Meško, G. (2010). Responses of police and local authorities to security issues in Ljubljana, the capital of Slovenia. In M. Cools et al. (Eds.), *Police, Policing, Policy and the City in Europe* (pp. 175–195). The Hague: Eleven International Publishing.
Meško, G. (2001). V skupnost usmerjeno policijsko delo—izziv za slovensko policijo? [Community policing—challenge for the Slovene police?]. *Teorija in praksa, 38*(2), 272–289.
Meško, G. (2004). Partnersko zagotavljanje varnosti v lokalni skupnosti—želje, ideali in ovire [Partnership in local community safety provision—wishes, ideals and obstacles]. *Revija za kriminalistiko in kriminologijo, 55*(3), 258–265.
Meško, G. (2006). Perceptions of security: Local safety councils in Slovenia. In U. Gori and I. Paparela (Eds.), *Invisible Threats: Financial and Information Technology Crimes and National Security* (pp. 69–89). Amsterdam: IOS Press.
Meško, G. (2006a). Policing in a post-socialist country: Critical reflections. In *Understanding Crime: Structural and Developmental Dimensions, and Their Implications for Policy*. (Plenary address at the annual conference of the ESC). Tübingen: Institut für Kriminologie der Universität Tübingen.
Meško, G. (2009). Transfer of crime control ideas—Introductory reflections. In G. Meško and H. Kury (Eds.), *Crime Policy, Crime Control and Crime Prevention—Slovenian Perspectives* (pp. 5–19). Ljubljana: Tipografija.

Meško, G. and Klemenčič, G. (2007). Rebuilding legitimacy and police professionalism in an emerging democracy: The Slovenian experience. In T. R. Tyler (Ed.), *Legitimacy and Criminal Justice* (pp. 84–115). New York: Russell Sage Foundation.

Meško, G. and Lobnikar, B. (2005). The contribution of local safety councils to local responsibility in crime prevention and provision of safety. *Policing: An International Journal of Police Strategies and Management, 28*(2), 353–373.

Meško, G., Fallshore, M., Rep, M., and Huisman, A. (2007). Police efforts in the reduction of fear of crime in local communities: Big expectations and questionable effects. *Sociologija, Mintis ir veiksmas, 2*(20), 70–91.

Meško, G., Nalla, M., and Sotlar, A. (2006). Cooperation on police and private security officers in crime prevention in Slovenia. In E. Marks, A. Meyer, and R. Linssen (Eds.), *Quality in Crime Prevention* (pp. 133–143). Norderstedt: Books on Demand.

Mikulan, M. (1997). *Preprečujmo kriminal skupaj [Let us Prevent Crime Together]*. Ljubljana: Mihelač.

Ministrstvo za notranje zadeve [Ministry of the Interior] (2003). *Letni načrtu dela policije za leto 2003 [Annual Work Plan of the Police in 2003]*.

Ministrstvo za notranje zadeve [Ministry of the Interior] (2008). *Temeljne usmeritve za pripravo srednjeročnega načrta razvoja in dela policije v obdobju 2008-2012 [Basic Guidelines for the Preparation of a Medium-Term Plan for Police Development and Work for the Period from 2003 to 2007]*.

Ministrstvo za notranje zadeve [Ministry of the Interior] (2010a). *Poročilo o raziskavi stanja na področju v skupnost usmerjenega policijskega dela—stališča občinskih varnostnih sosvetov [Report on Current State of Community Policing Survey—Local Safety Councils' Perspectives]*.

Ministrstvo za notranje zadeve [Ministry of the Interior] (2010b). *Usmeritve in obvezna navodila za pripravo letnega načrta dela policije v letu 2011 [Guidelines and Obligatory Instructions for the Preparation of Annual Work Plan of the Police]*.

Ministrstvo za notranje zadeve [Ministry of the Interior]. (2011). *Predlog Resolucije o nacionalnem programu preprečevanja in zatiranja kriminalitete za obdobje 2012-2016 [Draft of the Resolution on National Plan on the Prevention and Combating of Crime for the Period 2012-2016]*.

Pagon, M. and Lobnikar, B. (2001). *V skupnost usmerjeno policijsko delo v mestu Ljubljana: ugotavljanje potreb za ustanovitev mestne policije ali redefiniranja dela državne policije: končno poročilo s popravki [Community Policing in Ljubljana: Identifying the Needs for the Establishment of Local Police or Redefinition of State Police Work: Final Report with Corrections]*. Ljubljana: Visoka policijsko-varnostna šola.

Pečar, J. (2002). Preprečevanje kriminalitete in policija [Crime prevention and the police]. In M. Pagon (Ed.), 3. *Slovenski dnevi varstvoslovja* (12 p.). Ljubljana: Visoka policijsko-varnostna šola.

Policija (2003). *Slovenska policija [The Slovene Police]*. Ljubljana: Ministrstvo za notranje zadeve, Policija, Generalna policijska uprava.

Police (2011). Ministry of the Interior. Police. Retrieved December 16, 2011, from http://www.policija.si/eng/.

Policija (2011a). *About the Police*. Retrieved December 17, 2011, from http://www.policija.si/eng/index.php/aboutthepolice.

Policija (2011b). *About Police Stations*. Retrieved December 17, 2011, from http://www.policija.si/eng/index.php/aboutthepolice/organization/69.

Policija (2011c). *Vodje policijskih okolišev po policijskih upravah [Community Policing Officers in Police Directorates]*. Retrieved October 17, 2011, from http://www.policija.si/index.php/dravljani-in-policija/vodje-policijskih-okoliev.

Resolucija o preprečevanju in zatiranju kriminalitete [Resolution on the Prevention and Combating of Crime] (2006). *Uradni list Republike Slovenije*, 43.

Svetek, S. (2011). Občutek ogroženosti in vloga policije pri zagotavljanju varnosti na lokalni ravni [Fear of crime and police role in local safety provision]. In P. Umek (Ed.), *12. Slovenski dnevi varstvoslovja*. Ljubljana: Fakulteta za varnostne vede.

Trojanowicz, R. and Bucqueroux, B. (1990). *Community Policing: A Contemporary Perspective.* Cincinnati: Anderson Publishing Co.

Virtič, F., and Lobnikar, B. (2004). Implementacija policijskega dela v skupnosti v slovenski policiji [Implementation of community policing in Slovenia]. In B. Lobnikar (Ed.), 5. *slovenski dnevi varstvoslovja* (pp. 745–750). Ljubljana: Fakulteta za policijsko-varnostne vede.

Zakon o lokalni samoupravi [Local Self-Government Act] (2007). *Uradni list Republike Slovenije*, 94.

Zakon o občinskem redarstvu [Act on Local Police]. (2006). *Uradni list Republike Slovenije*, 106.

Zakon o Policiji [Police Act]. (1998). *Uradni list Republike Slovenije*, 49.

Žaberl, M. (2004). Vodja policijskega okoliša—slovenski policist za preventivo [Community policing officer—Slovene police officer for prevention]. In G. Meško (Ed.), *Preprečevanje kriminalitete— teorija, praksa in dileme [Crime Prevention—Theory, Practice and Dilemmas]* (pp. 271–285). Ljubljana: Inštitut za kriminologijo pri Pravni fakulteti.

Žerak, A. (2004). V skupnost usmerjeno policijsko delo v severno primorski regiji: primerjava mnenja policistov in prebivalcev [Community policing in northern Primorska region: A comparison of police officers' and citizens' opinion]. In B. Lobnikar (Ed.), 5. *Slovenski dnevi varstvoslovja* (pp. 751–760). Ljubljana: Visoka policijsko-varnostna šola.

Spain

35

JUAN JOSE MEDINA ARIZA
ESTER BLAY

Contents

Sociopolitical Context

After 40 years of dictatorship, Spain is now a democracy organized in the form of a parliamentary government under a constitutional monarchy. The Constitution of 1978 provided Spain with an open quasifederal structure around 17 self-governing "autonomous communities." Autonomous communities have their own parliaments and are responsible for some public services including, in some places, policing. This arrangement is, however, perceived by some in the regions with a stronger national identity (e.g., Catalonia, Basque Country, etc.) as insufficient. The peaceful democratic transition was a remarkable achievement, although concerns continue about the poor development of civil society, the hijacking of decision making by elites, lack of transparency, low standard of corporate governance, and corruption (Heywood 2005).

Spain is a developed country, with the twelfth largest economy in the world and very high living standards (twentieth highest Human Development Index in 2010). After almost 15 years of above-average gross domestic product (GDP) growth, the Spanish economy began to slow down in late 2007 and entered into a recession in 2008. The unemployment rate rose to more than 20% in August 2010. Even before the recession, poverty* and inequality[†] were high by comparison with other countries of similar living standards. The economy also suffers from a highly segregated job market and other structural problems, such as a comparatively large shadow economy (Schneider 2006), the limited productivity of its workforce, or poor investment in research and development. The prospects for the economy are still uncertain; recovery is expected to be rather slow and traumatic, particularly for the so-called lost generation of young people entering into the labor market for the first time (CIA 2009).

---

* 14.2% of the population living below 50% of median income (Human Development Report 2009).
† Gini index of 34.7 and a proportion of 10.3 of the richest 10% to the poorest 10% (Human Development Report 2009).

In 1981, only about 0.5% of the Spanish population were foreign nationals, a percentage that slowly grew to reach 1.6% of the population by 1998. Since then, Spain has experienced a rather dramatic change that led to one of the largest immigration rates across the world. This trend of rapid expansion has stabilized more recently. By 2010, about 12.2% of the registered Spanish population were foreign nationals. The largest immigrant contingents are made up of Moroccans, Romanians, Ecuadorians, British, and Colombians.

From a criminological point of view, Spain is a safe country. In 2005, Spain had the lowest overall victimization rate in the European Union (Van Dijk et al. 2008),* and these rates have not changed much (García España et al. 2010). However, Spaniards manifest comparatively high levels of fear of crime (Van Dijk et al. 2008) and suffer from one of the most punitive regimes in Europe (16,542 inmates per 100,000 inhabitants in August 2010 according to the online statistics of the Ministry of Interior).

The main features of the police organization in Spain were developed in a 1986 law that aimed to provide the basic principles of policing within the new democratic regime. The organization is closely bounded to the territorial political organization described above. There are two main armed police forces, *Policia Nacional* (a civil force) and *Guardia Civil* (a paramilitary force), which respectively have, traditionally and broadly speaking, been the police forces of the urban and the rural areas. Coexisting with these two national forces, most municipalities (>5000 inhabitants) are entitled to have their own municipal armed police forces for purposes of traffic control, administrative regulatory enforcement, and minor community concerns. Through the decentralization process described above, a small number of regional governments have acquired the political power to create their own armed police forces. In those towns where there is no municipal police, its functions are undertaken by the national or regional police forces, if there is one. In practice, this means that most of the population gets police services from municipal police, sometimes regional and national police. Coordination and clear demarcation of responsibilities among the different forces are a continuous source of conflict and political debate. Some research suggests that municipal police is the one with most frequent contacts with the public and that the public often asks of it to deal with situations (e.g., dealing with crime) for which it has no legal authority (García 2006). Indeed, there have been calls in the past to increase the mandate of municipal police. It is very important to highlight that police scholarship in Spain remains an almost nonexisting academic specialism, and there are very few empirical studies on policing in Spain.

Origins of Community Policing in Spain

Brogden and Nihjar (2005) consider community policing an Anglo-American invention sold in the global market of ideas as *the way* of doing policing. Community policing is certainly not an original feature of the Spanish policing history. The 2/1986 Law of the Security Forces of the State attributes to the police the exclusive responsibility for policing and leaves little room for citizen participation or community engagement. Indeed, most of the debates about policing philosophies or "waves" of policing reform, including

---

* These surveys, however, do not capture the much higher victimization rates of the millions of tourists that visit Spain every year.

community policing, have been largely absent in the Spanish context.* There has been a lot of debate about the "police model," in the sense of an organizational model corresponding to the new semifederal political structure, but very little debate about a police model in the sense of thinking about the police function, strategies and tactics, and ways of engaging with the community and other public bodies (Torrente 1997). The priorities for democratic police reform, particularly during the first decades of the democratic regime, were also eschewed by the heavy emphasis on addressing the terrorist violence of separatists from the Basque Country.

Yet, as in most of Europe, the official discourse is supportive of community policing,[†] even if practical implementation has been traditionally hampered by the centralist tradition of the national police forces (Brogden and Nihjar 2005). Rabot (2004), in fact, has remarked that the community policing discourse in Spain acquired even more messianic, ideological, and mythical connotations than in English-speaking countries, since it was constructed as a solution to the democratic deficit inherited from Francoism. Criticisms of this ideal were considered reactionary and antidemocratic. In this way, in Spain, like previously in France, we witnessed the adaptation of "proximity police."[‡] By 1987, the Ministry of Interior had a training manual for neighborhood police that emphasized crime prevention and the permanent assignation of officers to specific areas (Recassens 2007). During the 1990s, the Ministry of Interior pushed forward these ideas, such as in the *Plan Belloch* (Medina 2012). But it was the Plan Police 2000 that, in a more explicit fashion, developed the ideas of community policing within the context of the *Policía Nacional*. This plan also incorporated some notions from new public managerialism (defining citizens as clients, governance by performance indicators, etc.) and COMPSTAT (crime mapping, responsibilization for crime levels, etc.). Subsequent plans of the Ministry of Interior have continued this official support for the ideas of community policing.

Regional police forces have assumed the community policing discourse even more so, since their political construction presents them as closer to the "national" communities (i.e., Basque, Catalan, etc.) to be policed. But, it is not clear whether they have been more successful developing an articulated model or in implementing it (Recassens 2007; Rabot 2004). However, it is true that some aims of community policing are increasingly present in the organization and in some of the governing documents of some regional police forces. In Catalonia, for example, the General Security Plan (*Plan de Seguridad de Catalunya 2008–2011*) presents as core elements citizen participation and civil society collaboration. Moreover, the law regulating the security system of Catalonia (4/2003) encourages civil society to participate directly in the decision-making process around public security, at

---

* Publications in Spanish about community policing, quality-of-life or order-maintenance policing, problem-order policing, and many other ways of thinking about the police function and strategies are few and far between and, for the most part, tend to be reflections about trends outside Spain. This is not to say that the concerns and issues addressed or encompassed by these waves of policing have been absent in the Spanish landscape or that the Spanish police forces have remained absolutely hermetic to those "waves," but knowledge of these models among practitioners, academics, and policy makers in Spain remains limited and difficult to measure.

† Nonetheless, the recent National Strategy for National Police and Guardia Civil 2009–2012 did not mention even once this idea (Velazquez 2009).

‡ Although it should be highlighted that this is the official, rather hidden from the public, bureaucratic discourse, there is little use of the notion of "proximity" policing in the same open public relations way employed in English-speaking countries. It is fair to argue that the Spanish public feels little excitement about this concept.

least in a consulting fashion (Ayguasenosa 2009). Finally, the idea of proximity policing has been particularly important for (and developed by) municipal police agencies (Recassens 2007; Rabot 2004), albeit in many different ways and to very different degrees, since the return to democracy. The opinion prevails that it is at the municipal level where these initiatives may work better, given its local character and the general perception of municipal police as arbiters for minor community concerns and incivilities (Medina 2012), while the other forces deal with "real crime."

How Community Policing Works in Spain

As the Spanish literature on community policing is very scarce and often more normative than evaluative (Coll and Martínez 2010; Carrasco 2008), and police forces have not formalized and published their proximity model, we interviewed a small sample of heads of municipal police and local community police officers and commanders from the Catalan regional police.* The description given, therefore, is that of community policing in the Catalan region.

The first manifestation of proximity policing in Spain during the 1980s was foot patrols by officers, who were assigned to particular neighborhoods for long spells. This has changed in time. Today, the translation of a proximity model in police structures and working practices is very diverse, reflecting the local police chief's autonomy to shape his or her force and varied leadership styles (Alvarez 2009), uneven understanding of and commitment to the idea, as well as diverse local government priorities and availability of resources. Some towns have all but eliminated foot patrol, substituting physical presence in large and lowly occupied public spaces with constant availability through the telephone and Internet (e.g., Sant Quirze). In other more densely populated cities with a greater conflicting use of public space, foot patrol is still a feature of proximity policing.

Not all municipal police forces have specialist community policing officers or units. Local resources and priorities are particularly relevant here, and forces with a low police-per-citizen ratio tend to assign community relations to regular officers. However, in many municipal police forces and in the regional police, specific community policing officers are separated from other tasks so they may focus exclusively on proximity work. The Catalan regional police has a Community Relations Office in every police area.† These specialist officers deal with community members and associations through regular meetings and exchanges and through the delivery in schools, businesses, or public halls of centrally scripted lectures on issues such as business safety, safe Internet use for youngsters, or preventing youth violence.

The job stability and training of specialist officers are varied. Moreover, proximity is not always a favored destination despite some perks (such as office working hours: not working night or weekend shifts), perhaps because the work involved does not always fit officers' expectations of "real policing." Specific training available on community relations

* Ten in-depth interviews have been held with heads of municipal police and community police officers from the municipal police of El Prat, Figueres, Girona, Santa Coloma, and Sant Quirze; interviews have been held with two commanders from the Mossos d'Esquadra.
† Service delivery is organized in 59 basic police areas, covering all Catalonia. In less populated zones, an area may comprise various towns and may have only a police station; in larger cities or more populated areas, basic areas may comprise of only a town or even a part of it and have more than one police station.

through the police academies serving regional and municipal forces consists of a 1-week noncompulsory course (even for "proximity officers"). Although some municipal police heads require community officers to undergo training in alternative conflict resolution or community relations or even encourage them to undertake university degrees, there is considerable room for improvement in training for community policing (Carrasco 2005: 30).

Partnership work plays an important role in the official discourse (Carrasco 2008; Coll and Martínez 2010). This importance has been stressed in interviews by both regional and local police officers, but it seems to be especially strong in cities where there is a sustained commitment by local authorities to addressing social problems through the interrelated work of various local and civic agencies, a commitment particularly linked with progressive local governments (e.g., El Prat, Santa Coloma). Partnerships are particularly active in addressing security issues and conflicts in schools (absenteeism, fighting, or drug use), and officers from municipal and regional police forces actively participate in them, alongside school administrators, parents' associations, youth justice officials, and mediators, in order to detect and address these conflicts. Officers' roles are varied: they participate in meetings, and their presence is often required in or around schools as an element of coercion or prevention. There are frequent visits at schools to deliver lectures about road safety, safe Internet, gangs, violence toward girls, or binge drinking. Similar partnership work has also developed to address issues linked to the very active and alcohol-fuelled nighttime economy, particularly in areas having large concentrations of youth or tourists.

Another area in which partnership work is common is intimate partner violence—a key focus of policy action in Spain over the last decade. In police forces, this policy focus has led to the creation of specialist units and the development of a common protocol involving health professionals and social and support services alongside criminal justice agencies. A similar initiative involves the development of partnerships of regional police officers with Senegalese and Gambian Women's associations and public prosecutors to develop a working protocol for the prevention of female circumcision. Although there is constant interaction between the various agencies involved in providing victims services, paradoxically, many of the interviewees did not regard this as part of the community relations work. This underscores the narrow construction of the model and the limited understanding of community policing as a core philosophy by some police practitioners. The accounts of partnerships gathered through interviews are overwhelmingly positive. But more research is needed to ascertain working practices, the distribution of power, roles and tasks, as well as the benefits of partnership work.

Besides partnerships with other public services, the initiative for the establishment of working relationships (information exchanges, demands, etc.) with community members usually lies with police officers, not with civic associations. These contacts are made by regional police community officers with a "set list" of associations (neighborhood associations, shopkeepers associations, immigrant associations), which are granted status as "representatives" both by themselves and by the police. Due to changes, diversity and conflict within communities, and the existence of very difficult-to-reach groups, the question of how representative these associations are is unclear and likely to be limited. However, current practice does not seem to identify this as a concern requiring active solutions. In some municipalities, community members are recruited in a very informal and casual manner, particularly from communities with which it is difficult to establish communication channels (e.g., Chinese immigrant workers). Some communities remain aloof, and some officers acknowledge that they have not been able to cooperate with particular groups (e.g., gypsies, in Sant Cosme, El Prat).

Information from citizens and groups about their security concerns is regularly gathered in meetings and patrol visits to local associations and also from other bodies (such as consulates for some large migrant groups). In forces with sufficient resources, police officers set temporary weekly hours in a nonpolice setting (e.g., a local council building) for receiving citizen inputs, requests, and complaints (e.g., Girona), and there is an incipient albeit increasing police presence in virtual social nets (Facebook and Twitter), which provides police information and also citizen feedback.

Although community policing historically developed in some countries as a way of responding to the difficult or nonexistent relations between the police and ethnic minority communities, this remains also an area relatively unexplored in Spain; however, recent changes in immigration mean police forces have to develop more inclusionary and tolerant practices. Although there are good examples of sophisticated police attitudes toward this issue (see, e.g., Paradell et al. 2004), the historical record is poor, and there are serious concerns about institutional racism within Spanish police. For example, with the exception of the regional police of Catalonia, we are unaware of any specific plans to attract and recruit officers from ethnic minorities (Blay 2008).

Greater police responsiveness to citizens' calls and demands is one of the promises of community policing (Mastrofski 2006). Responding to calls for service promptly, professionally, and respectfully is part of the public compromise acquired by the regional police in its Services Charter and is stressed, as well, by all interviewed heads of municipal police. This emphasis on police responsiveness has led to an extension of the police mandate (Skogan 2006) to encompass conflicts arising from urban life, increasing social diversity, and sharing of public spaces (Coll and Martínez 2010). Some municipal police heads acknowledge that the overwhelming majority of cases they deal with are not related to crime but with quality of life and disorder, and that the police often receives the demand but refers it to other public agencies for a more appropriate response.

Public disorder has been a source of great concern in many cities, which have responded by enacting Civic Orders and carrying on stricter enforcement practices regarding alcohol consumption, prostitution, and other signs of disorder (Larrauri 2007; Coll and Martínez 2010). Disorder is now perceived as a police concern (Coll and Martínez 2010), and police response to conflicting demands on the use of public space in increasingly diverse areas depends very much on the attitude of local authorities. Thus, where there has been a great concern to address these conflicts as manifestations of social problems, the police has participated in partnership with other local agencies, social services, and civic associations, often using conflict resolution and mediation. However, other perspectives have led to stricter law enforcement practices.

It is difficult to assess how embedded proximity policing is in the various communities. Since the political transition, some Spanish municipalities have combined more traditional and common territorial consultative councils for general local government matters and the expansion of mechanisms to address citizens' concerns (residents charter of rights, local residents' ombudsman) with different, and more involved, mechanisms of direct democracy (participatory budgets, citizen juries, deliberative surveys, etc.). But use of these mechanisms is uneven and limited (Navarro et al. 2009), and there are few well-documented experiences of their use in public security matters (for an exception, see Galdos 2009). Our interviews in Catalonia reflect this well. With the exception of cities with a greater tradition of participation, encouraged by local authorities (i.e., El Prat, L'Hospitalet), direct involvement and participation in security issues, as in the delivery of other public goods, are rather low. This is so despite high citizen concern about security at times. Perhaps as a legacy of the 40-year dictatorship, there is a limited tradition of citizen participation in public governance (Subirats 1999; Aranguren Gonzalo 2004). There is a shared political culture whereby citizens expect public institutions to deliver services to address their needs and tend to regard security as a right or good to be delivered by a public body, not something they have to be actively working for (Coll and Martínez 2010).

Moreover, although research is limited, the role of civic associations in institutions specifically set for citizen participation in defining security concerns and policies (local security boards, consultative council) has been described as "symbolic," with these institutions being primarily a setting for local politicians to publicize their policies and gather information from police heads. Our interviews suggest that police practitioners believe that it is basically through police response to citizens' requests and demands that citizens end up shaping what police do. However, what and how the police responds are regarded as a technical professional matter, and civilian or nonpolice intervention is not particularly welcomed in police forces. Perhaps the recent establishment in some municipal police forces of "civic officers" charged with preventive tasks regarding disorder in public spaces (e.g., in Girona) could be seen as a sign of change. However, these are full-time local authority employees, not volunteers, and the emphasis is not on civic participation but on effectively addressing disorder while saving public resources. Thus, it is doubtful that the Spanish proximity models of community policing involve changing decision-making processes in police departments.

Effectiveness

Spain has a very limited public policy evaluation culture; this is also the case in policing matters. Although there is ongoing research on community policing (e.g., Requena, at the University of Barcelona), most recent works have not been evaluative but, rather, descriptive and sometimes prescriptive (Coll and Martínez 2010; Carrasco 2008). Thus, we do not know much about the effectiveness of Spanish proximity policing. As hinted above, we do not even know much about how the model is being translated into working practices, changes in police departments and culture, and effective citizen participation in decision making. There is no research on citizens' and civic associations' participation in security-related councils and other institutions, and to what extent and with which consequences citizens engage in security matters in neighborhoods together with police officers.

Conclusion

In order to work, community or proximity models require active citizen participation. Although with some exceptions, the dominant political culture in Spanish society militates against citizen involvement in public concerns and thus against an easy implementation of some of the more participative forms of community policing. Besides citizen attitudes, some features of police services, particularly at a national and regional level, may be hampering the effective development of community policing. To move beyond discourse, practices and structures need to change, which requires not only transformative leadership but also changes in the rank-and-file professional culture. Most examples of best practices remain at the local level. These practices have been particularly identified in cities where there has been a strong commitment to inclusive social policies, partnership, and the promotion of civic associations and citizen participation in local affairs, with security being part of this commitment. The municipal level is also the natural space for proximity, and local police services offer the flexibility and decentralization needed for implementing community policing. The trend among police officers described by Rabot in 2004, voicing their desire to divide police functions between the different police services, with local police being responsible for community work, is underlined today with the added argument of the current need to rationalize public expenditure and redefine public services.

Acknowledgments

The authors are very thankful to Gonzalo Escobar, Joan Miquel Capell, and Juan Carlos Jerez for their help and advice, and to all the interviewed police officers, who have been extremely generous, both in time and ideas. This chapter was written with the support of the following research projects: *Género y marginación: victimización y delincuencia* (DER2009-083444), from the Spanish Ministry of Science and Innovation, and *Criminología aplicada a la penología* (2009SGR-01117), from the Catalan Government (AGAUR).

References

Ayguasenosa, N. 2009. "La gestión alternativa de conflictos (GAC) aplicada al campo de la seguridad." *Revista Catalana de Seguretat Pública*, 2:125–141.
Aranguren Gonzalo, L. A. 2004. *Educar en el Sujeto Solidario*. Bilbao: Bakeaz.
Alvarez, J. O. 2009. "Estilos de liderazgo en la policía local de la Comunidad valenciana." Unpublished PhD dissertation.
Blay, E. 2008. "Incorporación de minorías étnicas a la policía." *Revista Electrónica de Ciencia Penal y Criminología*, 10-4:1–25.
Brogden, M. and Nihjar, P. 2005. *Community Policing*. Cullompton: Willan.
Carrasco, T. 2005. "Policía local: proximidad y convivencia." In L. Paradell, R. Negre, T. Carrasco (eds.), *Inmigración y Seguridad: Una Visión desde la Policía*. Barcelona: CIDOB, pp. 25–31.
Carrasco, T. 2008. "De l ordre públic a la seguretat pública des de la proximitat." In *Mirades 2: Seguretat*. Barcelona: ICV-EuiA-EPM, pp. 69–85.
CIA. 2009. *The World Factbook*. US Government.
Coll, J. and Martínez, E. 2010. "Estratègia i gestió de l'espai públic. Intervenció policial." *Apunts de Seguretat*, 7:71–103.
Galdos, L. 2009. *Deliberación y Preferencias Ciudadanas*. Madrid: CIS.
Garcia, J. 2006. "La percepción ciudadana de la policía local." *Boletín Criminológico*, 91:1–4.
Garcìa España, E., Diez Ripollés, J. L., Pérez Jiménez, F., Benítez Jiménez, M. J., and Cerezo Domínguez, A. I. 2010. "Evolución de la delincuencia en España: análisis longitudinal con encuestas de victimación." [Trends on criminal victimization in Spain: an analysis of victim survey data.] *Revista Española de Investigación Criminológica*.
Heywood, P. M. 2005. "Corruption, democracy and governance in contemporary Spain." In S. Balfour (ed.), *The Politics of Contemporary Spain*. London: Routledge.
Larrauri, E. 2007. "2 Ayuntamientos de izquierdas y control del delito." *Indret*, 3:1–23.
Mastrofski, S. 2006. "Community policing: a skeptical view." In D. Weisburd, A. Braga (eds.), *Police Innovation. Contrasting Perspectives*. Cambridge: Cambridge University Press, pp. 44–73.

Medina, J. 2012. *Políticas y Estrategias de Prevención de la Delincuencia y Seguridad Ciudadana.* Barcelona: BdeF.

Navarro, C., Cuesta, M. and Font, J. 2009. *Municipios Participativos?* Madrid: CIS.

Paradell, L., Negre, R. and Carrasco, T. 2004. *Inmigración y Seguridad: Una Visión desde la Policía.* Barcelona: CIDOB.

Rabot, A. 2004. "The implementation and evaluation of community policing in Spain: results and future prospects." *European Journal of Crime, Criminal Law and Criminal Justice* 12(3): 212–231.

Recassens, A. 2007. *La Seguridad y Sus Políticas.* Barcelona: Atelier.

Schneider, F. 2006. "Shadow economies and corruption all over the world: What do we really know?" *IZA Discussion Paper,* No. 2315.

Skogan, W. 2006. "The promise of community policing." In D. Weisburd, A. Braga (eds.) *Police Innovation. Contrasting Perspectives.* Cambridge: Cambridge University Press, pp. 27–43.

Subirats, J. (ed.) 1999. *Existe Sociedad Civil en España? Responsabilidades Públicas y Valores Colectivos.* Madrid: Ediciones Fundación Encuentro.

Tilley, N. 2008. "Modern approaches to policing: community, problem-oriented and intelligence-led." In T. Newburn (ed.), *Handbook of Policing.* 2nd edition. Collumpton: Willan Publishing, pp. 373–403.

Torrente, D. 1997. *La Sociedad Policial.* Barcelona: Universidad de Barcelona.

Van Dijk, J., van Kesteren, J. and Smit, P. 2008. *Criminal Victimisation in International Perspective. Key Findings from the 2004–2005 ICVS and EU ICS.* WODC: The Hague.

Velazquez, J. M. 2009. "Plan Estratégico 2009–2012 de la Dirección General de la Policía Nacional y la Guardia Civil." *Seguridad y Ciudadanía: Revista del Ministerio de Interior,* 1:31–50.

Turkey

36

KAAN BOKE

Contents

Background

Turkey is a democratic, secular, unitary, constitutional republic, with an ancient cultural heritage. It is situated in between two continents (Asia and Europe) and has an area of 783,562 km². Turkey also has a total coastline of 8333 km, which covers the borders of the Black Sea, the Aegean, the Marmara Sea, and the Mediterranean. It is surrounded by Bulgaria, Greece, Georgia, Armenia, Azerbaijan, Iran, Iraq, and Syria.

Historically, "protect and serve" was the primary principle of the Turkish police organization, and centralization of power has been a traditional feature of the general political administrative structure (Aydın 2006). The Turkish National Police (TNP) has newly started a community policing area and has made significant changes in the traditional style of policing.

The professional police force was first founded in 1845. Before 1845, military forces (Janissaries) carried out public order, and policing functions were accepted in the military duties. After the destruction of Janissaries, police were placed under the new police directorate, Zaptiye Mushiriyeti, and gradually turned into a separate police ministry (Swanson 1972). Upon the foundation of the new Turkish Republic, the name of the police organization was changed to General Directorate of Security and totally separated from the military and attached to the ministry of interior. Because of the highly centralized management style of the new Turkish Republic, the new police force has gradually turned into a highly centralized paramilitary police force, and centralization became a new crucial component of new policing (Sullivan 2005).

The TNP is responsible for policing in municipal boundaries of cities and towns. It takes its authorization from direct legislative authority and has a police regulation act as well as procedural guidelines. There are almost 145 different auxiliary acts, which are directly or indirectly connected with police service. The three forces have separate arrangements for finance, central headquarters in the capital, provincial units, training schools, and communication systems. The highest officials of the organizations are attached to the Minister of Interior in regard to their law enforcement functions. The local units are under the control of the highest local authority; however, they are attached to the Public Prosecutor in terms of their judicial functions (Aydın 2006).

Turkish Ministry of Interior has the authority to control and fund the police. Turkish National Police has a centralized structure and each city has its own police department under the command of headquarters, which is located in Ankara. Depending on the size and the population of the cities, the extent of the police departments varies. In city districts, city police also work under the authority of the city governor. Salary is tied to rank and length of service, and normal employee length is 20 years for women and 25 years for men (Boke 2009).

The police system in Turkey is highly centralized, and the police force is designed as the national base, which has almost 175,000 police officers and almost 5000 supervisors. The police ranks starting from line officer/patrol officer through middle managers (sergeant, lieutenant, captain) and top command (from major through commander and deputy chief of police). The chief of police commands each of the 81 city police directorates.

Origins of Community Policing in Turkey

Over the last couple of years, TNP top officials have been interested in the process of changing the old style of policing and starting to implement community policing/community-oriented policing.

TNP command has also started to use the term "community policing–community-oriented policing." In 2005, the TNP started a European Union (EU) Twinning Project with Spain, and one of the components of the project was "community policing." During that time, EU and TNP experts reviewed both TNP and EU Member States' policing styles, and then 200 TNP personnel received a "Community Policing" course. After finishing that project, TNP experts, based on previous project findings and detailed area analysis, developed "TNP Community Policing Service Standards," which reflected the TNP's practice and Turkish culture. TNP Community Policing Service Standards aim to strengthen police efforts on the issue of fighting crime by developing Turkish community involvement and support for security services. After developing the aforementioned standards and giving related in-service training, in 2006, the TNP started to implement pilot Community Policing implementations in 20 police centers, which are located in 10 different cities.

After getting a lot of interest from the public and increasing community satisfaction from the police service and positive feedback, the TNP generalized community policing implementations to whole police districts in Turkey in April 2009.

Community policing has two different formations: one in the TNP headquarters (HQ) and the other one in the city districts. In TNP HQ, the Community Policing Center Implementation and Evaluation Committee, consisting of 11 members, follows and develops community policing services and solves problems. In city districts, community policing services are coordinated by community policing divisions.

How Does Community Policing Work in Turkey?

Turkey's traditional cultural values are shared by most of the people. For that reason, TNP community policing also shares these values and reflects them in practice. The following are good examples of how community policing works in Turkey.

Responsibility Area Peace Meetings

Based on community policing officers' responsibility areas, police, community members, and local store owners meet and discuss the issues related to security services and bring new suggestions on how to develop or how to improve security services. Participation in these meetings is voluntary, and people can share their opinion freely. In 2011, more than 300,000 people were involved in those meetings from all police district areas in Turkey.

Briefing Meetings

From the community policing services perspective, increased awareness of the public about general security and individual security issues is crucial and has a special position in TNP community policing implementation. In addition to one-to-one interaction with people, briefing meetings help TNP community policing officers to inform more people on policing and security service issues. The main target groups for briefing meetings are students, shop owners, citizens, public officials, private security officers, and nongovernmental organizations (NGOs). In 2011, more than 1.5 million people participated in those meetings from all police districts in Turkey.

General Security Awareness

To create a safer and more secure society and increase total quality of life, officers inform people on the different security topics (such as how to prevent theft from home or car, etc.). In 2011, more than 4 million brochures, about 100,000 booklets, and numerous other materials were published and shared with the community.

Individual Contacts

Community policing officers in their districts make frequent contact with people. And officers try to take into consideration their concerns.

Problem Solver

When people get used to their community policing officers, they start to talk, discuss, and inform them about different unsolved problems related to various services. And community policing officers share these problems with responsible authorities. Each solved case increases peoples' trust in community policing officers.

School–Family Meetings

In each school, there are parent–teacher associations, and they try to create a better school environment for good-quality education. Community policing officers regularly inform them about security issues and kindly ask for their support to eliminate problems and crime.

Social Events

Community policing officers try to coordinate social events and voluntarily get involved in peoples' social events, like weddings, new openings, etc.

Social Help

Community policing officers also provide special care to elderly people, children, and disabled people. Officers talk with responsible authorities to quickly and effectively solve their problems.

Effectiveness of Community Policing

Over the last couple of years, TNP top officials have been interested in the process of changing the old style of policing and starting to implement community policing/community-oriented policing.

Even though TNP has not done a comprehensive evaluation on community policing issues, TNP officials, based on their internal evaluations and real-life feedback from the citizens, believe that the following results have been achieved by implementation of community policing:

- Through community policing implementation, citizens' awareness level is increased.
- Police–citizen partnership has developed and started to create two-way communication channels.
- Information coming from citizens is increased.
- Police's effectiveness on the issue of fighting crime is strengthened.
- In the context of defining and solving the community's problems, police interaction with other public officials is increased.
- Police officers have created new ways to help elderly people, children, disabled people, and previously victimized people.

Since traditional policing in Turkey is perceived as a part of political function and its first priority is to serve the government, the citizen is one of the most neglected subjects in police work. After starting community policing implementation, officers no longer see the police job as just dealing with crime and begin to see it as a way of serving the public.

Community policing also acts as a means of police–citizen feedback and helps top police managers to modify new strategies to increase quality of life in the society.

Throughout Turkish history, law enforcement duty has been more reactive (incident/ call driven) than proactive (information driven). And most of the time, what citizens think about the police service and how they help the police to prevent and solve crime have been ignored, and the public has been perceived as a passive agent of police work. This gap between the police and the society leads to isolation of the police from the society so that the police are solely focused on the law-and-order issues. After starting community policing implementations, officers have begun to accept that the public's possession of information and resources may help the police to perform their duties more effectively.

Conclusion

In recent years, the TNP has started to understand side effects of traditional policing. Top TNP command has begun to make changes in policing style. The TNP has undertaken the mission of implementing an extensive program of police reform with the aim of changing old traditional policing into community-oriented policing. Top TNP officials' new emphasis on the service role of the police and the importance of developing positive relationships with citizens shows important signs of changes in the context of policing style. Top officials demand movement beyond incident-driven policing and get the community involved in policing.

Due to the fact that the main characteristics of community policing (such as decentralized structure, autonomy for line officers, etc.) are considered to be significant departures from the TNP's policing style, the TNP has undertaken the important mission of changing its policing style.

Further Information

Boke, K. (2009). Police Culture in Turkey and U.S. Saarbrucken, Deutschland: VDM Verlag Publication.

References

Aydın, A. H. (2006). Turkey. In D. K. Das (Ed.). *World Police Encyclopedia* (pp. 855–861). New York, NY: Routledge.
Boke, K. (2009). *Police Culture in Turkey and the United States* Saarbrucken, Deutschland: VDM Verlag Publication.
Sullivan, L. E. (2005). *Encyclopedia of Law Enforcement*. Thousand Oaks, CA: Sage Publication.
Swanson, G. W. (1972). The Ottoman Police. *Journal of Contemporary History*, 7 (1/2), 243–260.
Turkish National Police Web Site. www.egm.gov.tr.

Index

Page numbers followed by n indicate notes.

0 1341 1661300 8

DATE DUE	RETURNED